standard catalog of®

JEEP

1940-2003

PATRICK FOSTER

Published by

700 East State Street • Iola, WI 54990-0001
715-445-2214 • 888-457-2873
www.krause.com

Please call or write for our free catalog of publications. Our toll-free
number to place an order or obtain a free catalog is (800) 258-0929.

Library of Congress Catalog Number: 2003105289
ISBN: 0-87349-522-5

Edited by: Brian Earnest
Designed by: Jamie Griffin
Front Cover Photography by: Ken Brubaker

*I'd like to dedicate this book to my fans and readers,
the loyal friends who make it possible for me to pursue
my dream. I owe you my grateful thanks and offer you
these simple words of advice, which I hope you'll always
keep in your heart:*

*Live in peace
Love one another
And remember the poor.*

Foreword

In the nearly 65 years since its inception, Jeep has evolved in many ways, in the process becoming a legendary machine with an almost mystical aura surrounding it. Over time Jeep has grown to become a symbol of all the things that are great and good in America, because at its very essence Jeep embodies the American character, the American spirit. It has been stamped with greatness.

For many years now it has been my great privilege and pleasure to write about Jeep, to pass on to readers some words that try to explain the heritage behind this great vehicle and how it came to be. If you love Jeep vehicles, don't be afraid to admit it. They are worth loving.

Contents

The Jeeps that Started the Legend
1940-1944

America was still at peace in 1940. Although war gripped Europe in an embrace of suffering and pain, many Americans considered it a far-off conflict of little importance in their daily lives. In the Pacific region, aggressive actions by the empire of Japan occupied the thoughts of defense strategists, but held scant interest for Main Street America. Luckily, the U.S. military realized the likelihood that America would get drawn into the conflict that was spreading across the globe like a flame. They began to prepare.

The stunning advance of the German Blitzkrieg across Europe convinced them that this new war would be characterized by rapid movements made possible only by a highly mechanized army. The day of the romantic cavalry charge, drawn sabers gleaming in the sun, belonged to the ancient past. In its place would be the roar of engines, the grinding of gears, and the chatter of automatic weapons fire.

Another view of the Bantam prototype. The metal badge seen on the firewall reads "American Bantam Special."

The first Jeep, the Bantam prototype, undergoing preliminary testing at Camp Holabird in Maryland.

Even the heavy military trucks already in use wouldn't be enough. What was needed, the U.S. Army realized, was a light vehicle capable of carrying two or more men plus a heavy machine gun and communications equipment; a sturdy machine that could ford streams, climb hills, and not bog down even in the muddiest terrain. A light reconnaissance car was the way some envisioned it. A mobile gun platform or light assault vehicle was how others saw it. What everyone knew, though, without doubt, was that it had to be powerful, fast, and tough. And it was needed right away.

Motorcycles were tried because they were lightweight and very inexpensive. But the bikes proved unusable in sand and mud conditions, and lacked the

**Here's the original Willys prototype, the Willys Quad.
Its powerful engine was the major factor in its terrific showing in tests.**

necessary carrying capacity. Attempts were made to use modified Ford Model T touring cars stripped down to bare essentials. In tests these machines did quite well, but problems developed when the Army added needed equipment and additional features. The Fords soon became too heavy for off-road use. The Army then tested a handful of small roadsters produced by American Bantam Company. The performance demonstrated by these vehicles seemed closest to what was desired.

Finally, a committee of military engineers drew up specifications for a vehicle that would encompass all their various requirements. Soon after, an invitation was made via letters mailed to 135 manufacturers to

This MK II series vehicle is one the later Bantams. Note the squared-off front fenders. The door openings and headlight grilles are also different from the prototype.

After Willys redesigned its prototype, the new version was dubbed the Willys MA.

Actors and celebrities loved to have their pictures taken in Jeep vehicles. Here the great actor Wallace Beery poses in a Willys MA at Camp Ord, California, while on location for scenes in the movie *Doan of the USA*.

The Army tested the new Jeeps under rigorous conditions. This Willys is literally flying over the crest of a hill.

compete for a contract to build a prototype of the new vehicle. It was the largest number of manufacturers the military had ever contacted in connection with a motor vehicle contract.

Only two firms bothered to submit proposals. The time frame was too tight for most of the companies, and the specifications were too difficult to meet. Additionally, the contract itself wasn't big enough to interest most large corporations—there wasn't enough money involved to make it worth the extra effort. However, the deal was just big enough for one tiny Butler, Pennsylvania, company. American Bantam desperately needed the business. Its line of tiny four-cylinder passenger cars had failed, the firm was near bankruptcy, and the only life preserver in sight was the military contract open for bidding. Bantam hoped the Army would buy large numbers of slightly modified Bantam roadsters like the ones they had already tested.

Unfortunately, when the bid specifications were released, Bantam realized that the specs called for a machine that simply couldn't be built with the technology at hand in the time allotted. The Army wanted the thing to have four-wheel-drive, which few companies had any experience with, plus a four-cylinder engine. It had to be able to hold four men plus equipment, weigh no more than 1,300 lbs., be able to carry a 600-lb. payload—and the Army wanted it built and

ready to roll in 49 days. After that, the winning company would have just 26 days to build 70 additional pilot models. Oh yes, and whatever firm felt it could produce such a miracle also had to be the low bidder. Only a desperate company would bother trying to meet such impossible specifications—a company like Bantam.

Or Willys-Overland. Although Willys wasn't in quite as bad a shape as Bantam, the company was none too robust. Willys was producing a line of four-cylinder family cars priced to undercut both Ford and Chevrolet. Even though the Willys was a larger car than the miniscule Bantam, it was still considered a small car, and Americans weren't really interested in such

DaimlerChrysler photo

The civilian CJ-2A debuted in 1945 with a suggested retail price of $1,090.

basic machines. Sales were sluggish. The chance to produce military trucks seemed like a good way for Willys to supplement its core business. The added volume would certainly help the bottom line. Delmar "Barney" Roos, Willys' vice president of engineering, decided he would take a crack at it.

Meanwhile, back in Butler, Pennsylvania, Bantam hired Karl Probst, an independent engineer who had formerly worked for several U.S. automobile manufacturers and had a reputation for brilliance. Probst realized instantly that Bantam would be unable to meet the Army's 1300-lb. weight bogey, but he was not especially worried about it. After all, he noted, the other companies wouldn't be able to meet that specification either. Probst sat down at a drafting board in the nearly deserted Bantam headquarters and got to work. In three long, heroic days he worked his magic, sketching out complete design drawings and spec sheets for a new vehicle unlike anything the world had ever seen before.

In Toledo, Willys didn't put in nearly as much effort. Its hastily assembled bid lacked detailed drawings or lists of components, consisting mainly of time and cost numbers. Still, it was more than most companies had done.

On the appointed day the bids were opened. Although Willys actually underbid Bantam, the company felt it would need more than 49 days to build the prototype. A per-day penalty fine was added to Willys'

bid, resulting in Bantam's bid being lower. American Bantam was awarded the contract.

The rush was now on for Bantam to actually produce the vehicle it had designed. In the weeks that followed, Bantam employees, working night and day, managed to put together a prototype vehicle. The Bantam engine couldn't produce the 40 hp specified, so a Continental engine was substituted. More troublesome was that there were no suitable axles in production. In Toledo, the Spicer company frantically tried to adapt an existing design used in the Studebaker Champion, but ran into problems. Perhaps divine intervention finally cleared the

Here's a neat action shot of a Willys MA. Note the soldier is wearing a World War I-type helmet, which was used for a short time early in World War II.

A 1944 MB owned by Steve Lash of Santa Rosa, California.

logjam, because mere days before the contract deadline the axle problem was finally sorted out.

On Sunday, September 22, 1940, the prototype was ready for its first test drive. Someone poured gasoline in the tank, Karl Probst climbed in and turned the key. The little Bantam's engine fired right up; Probst put it in gear and roared off. Spotting a steep off-road hill, Probst engaged four-wheel-drive and climbed up with ease. "Whatever it is," he said, "it's a performer."

What it was, in fact, was the very first Jeep.

The next morning the prototype was driven across the vast span of Pennsylvania to Camp Holabird in Maryland. Proving how close the timing was, Probst pulled into the Army camp just 30 minutes before the contract deadline. Major Lawes, the officer in charge of purchasing and contracts, promptly climbed in behind the wheel and took the little machine through the Army's punishing test route, pounding it over ruts and stones, flying over bumps, all at a frantic pace that probably would have destroyed an ordinary vehicle. Upon his return, Lawes faced the waiting men, summing up his first impressions in a simple pronouncement that remains one of the most prophetic in history. "I have driven every unit the services have purchased for the last 20 years," he said, "I can judge them in 15 minutes. This vehicle is going to be outstanding. I believe this unit

The venerable 1941 Willys MA.

will make history."

One core problem still needed to be resolved—the vehicle's weight. When asked, Probst explained that the Bantam weighed 1,840 lbs., some 540 lbs. over the contract specification. As a circle of military men stood pondering that news, a Cavalry general stepped up to settle the matter. "If two men can take it out of a ditch," he said, "we need it." The general was a big man, standing 6-foot-3, and weighing in at about 250 lbs. He

Willys built 1,555 MA vehicles during World War II. This survivor is owned by Chet Krause of Iola, Wisconsin.

The Willys MB proved itself immediately as a worthy do-everything vehicle.

DaimlerChrysler photo

stepped to the rear of the Bantam, grabbed it, and with a grunt lifted the back end off the ground. He turned to the other officers and nodded his approval. The matter was settled; the Army would get the new machine.

But the military feared that Bantam wouldn't be able to build the new reconnaissance cars in large enough volume. Everyone knew the company was cash-starved and the feeling developed that Bantam might prove to be an unreliable supplier. That, the Army felt, would be an intolerable situation. Better to have two or three companies building the new vehicles.

In Toledo, Willys-Overland continued to work on a prototype. Ford Motor Company also was invited to submit an entry and bid on the contract for production

vehicles. Ford's immense assembly capacity made it very attractive, and some military men would have preferred Ford be the exclusive supplier. Representatives from Ford and Willys were allowed to look over the Bantam's design, and they made detailed sketches of the layout.

Bantam, meanwhile, got to work building the additional 70 pilot models specified in the contract. They incorporated many improvements brought about from the Army's aggressive trial runs with the original prototype.

Testing of the Willys-Overland prototype, which was called the Willys Quad, began on November 13th, 1940. During its 5,000 miles of testing, it greatly impressed the soldiers. With its powerful Go-Devil engine, 63 hp versus

**This Bantam Jeep is towing a cannon, all wheels in the air. Speed and
stamina were crucial features of the military Jeep.**

This 1942 Willys MB owned by Ralph Daubeck is still ready to roll.

the Bantam's 46 hp, the Willys was a veritable hot rod. The Willys engine was sturdy, too, although it dated back to the 1920s. In its early days it had developed a reputation for being unreliable, but during the late 1930s Willys Chief Engineer Barney Roos and assistant Floyd Kishline went through the engine with an eye on improving durability and smoothness. Much of the basic engine was redesigned. The cylinder block was reworked to extend the water jackets down the full length of the cylinder barrels, aluminum pistons and a counterweighted crankshaft were fitted, the cylinder head featured a new combustion chamber design with a higher compression ratio, the camshaft had increased valve lift, a new timing chain with friction damping was provided, larger intake valves were utilized, and improved material was specified for the exhaust valves. Because of this extensive re-engineering, the Willys motor was by all accounts the best four-cylinder engine in America by 1940.

Meanwhile, Ford Motor Company came up with a reconnaissance vehicle, though obviously following the design theme set down by Bantam. Ford had ceased using four-cylinder engines in passenger cars some years before, but had a sturdy if unremarkable four in its line of farm tractors. This motor was fitted to the Ford prototype, which was dubbed the Pygmy.

Just as Karl Probst had predicted, none of the companies could meet the weight goal. The Army set a

new weight limit of 2,160 lbs. The three prototypes from Willys, Bantam, and Ford were deemed acceptable, though Willys was some 260 lbs. over the limit. Each of the three companies was given an order for an additional 1,500 vehicles, which the Army would test under real world conditions. The only problem in all this surfaced when the Army informed Willys that its vehicle would have to meet the weight standard. On that point no excuses would be accepted.

How does one reduce hundreds of pounds on a vehicle that's already stripped to the bone? That's the question Barney Roos faced, and he answered it with a quiet determination. He ordered his staff to go through the entire design nut by bolt, reducing an ounce here, a pound there until they reached the goal. Bolts were reduced in length, cotter pins reduced in size, the frame and some body panels were redone in lighter weight, higher-strength steel. Even the paint was scrutinized; Roos would allow only one coat of paint, because a second coat could put the vehicle over the target weight.

According to reports, in the end the weight target was met with but 7 ounces to spare. One Army colonel commented that the Willys, "…was so closely within the limit that if a little dust and dirt got on it that was enough to put it over the line."

The initial Willys production unit was dubbed the MA, the Ford unit was known as the GP, and the Bantam was the Model 40 BRC. Tests by various Army units and the Infantry Board determined that the Willys was the best performer by far. Its powerful engine gave it a tremendous edge over the other two vehicles. Somewhat surprisingly, Bantam was rated second overall. Although less powerful, the Bantam's lower weight proved a great asset off-road.

In July 1941, the Quartermaster General called for production of 16,000 units of a standardized design. The Army knew that a standardized design was the best route to go—it made no sense to produce three distinct vehicles. A standard design would make it easier for technicians to service the vehicles and also make the stocking of replacement parts less complicated. All three companies would be allowed to bid on the big new contract. In fact, other companies were also allowed to bid, including Checker Motors Company of Kalamazoo, Michigan.

Checker Motors submitted the lowest bid of all, but the offer was not accepted because the firm could not commence delivery in a short enough time. Of the remaining hopefuls, Bantam bid $788.32 per vehicle; Ford's bid was $782.59. Willys undercut everyone with a bid of just $748.74 per unit. Surprisingly, some Army men asked that the bids be ignored and the contract awarded to Ford. Their reasoning was that Ford alone would be able to produce the vehicles in the numbers that would soon be needed. In the end, however, the

contract for 16,000 machines (later increased to 18,600) was awarded to Willys. Deliveries were scheduled to begin in November, 1941.

Having decided to settle on only one design, the Army determined that "the standard vehicle should be based on the Willys chassis," but incorporating the best features of the other two vehicles. The standard Jeep design would be called the MB. Although Willys' engineer Barney Roos was proud of his accomplishment, he was realistic in his assessment of the vehicle he created. "It is purely a combat vehicle," he said, "designed with

President Franklin D. Roosevelt doffs his hat in salute as he reviews troops from the front seat of a Jeep. The flat hood and stamped steel grille became the standard "look" for Jeeps fairly early in production.

This 1943 Army MB was assigned to a four-star general. It has been restored by Bob Crossman of Vero Beach, Florida.

simplicity to do a specific job. It makes no concessions to art and damned little to comfort."

The Army called its new vehicle a "General Purpose truck, 1/4 ton, 4x4." Soldiers already had a better name for it—they called it a "jeep." The jeep nickname had already been bestowed on other military vehicles over the years, including a tractor used to haul heavy guns, an airplane, an autogyro, and some heavy trucks.

But an incident occurred that caused the other uses of the jeep label to quickly fade away. It seems some reporters were observing a demonstration of the remarkable new military car. Watching it climb a long set of stairs in front of a building, one reporter was especially impressed. "What is it?" she asked. "A jeep" was the reply. Soon afterwards there appeared a newspaper story describing the amazing roadster and referring to it as a jeep. Forever after, that is what it has been called. From that point onwards people understood that the word jeep referred to the gutsy little fighter from Willys. Later on, songs such as "Jeep Jockey Jump," "Little Bo Peep has Lost Her Jeep," and "Six Jerks in a Jeep" would further popularize the name, as would a movie, *Four Jills in a Jeep*. Willys later copyrighted the name, and since then the Jeep name has been capitalized.

Although the Willys design was the standard, everyone preferred the frontal appearance of the Ford GP, with its flat hood and fenders, so that was adopted. Heavy grille bars were also copied from the GP, but before long a stamped steel grill replaced the bars. To ensure sufficient manufacturing capacity, Ford was invited in November 1941 to produce Jeeps in its own factories. At the Army's insistence the Ford-built Jeeps would have to be built to the standard Willys design, and were called GPW's—meaning General Purpose Willys." It was a very lucky thing the Army had moved so swiftly to bring about the new Jeep. The following month, on December 7, 1941, Japan launched a sneak attack on the America naval base at Pearl Harbor in Hawaii. Suddenly, the nation was at war.

There were calls almost immediately to increase Jeep production, and soon the assembly lines were humming. America's ability to place its factories and economy on a war footing in a short time amazed its allies and enemies alike. Before long, U.S. manufacturers were busy turning out huge amounts of war materiel. In Russia, England, and elsewhere, these tools of war helped turn the tide.

It was within that terrible cauldron of war that the Jeep's mighty legend was forged. The vehicle surprised

A well-preserved 1942 GPW owned by Hank Snow of Tulsa, Oklahoma.

This 1941 bare-bones Ford-built GP is owned by Neil Freeman of New London, Wisconsin.

even its greatest admirers with its versatility. It was more than the sum of its parts, and it inspired entirely new methods of warfare. Because Jeeps were not confined to roads, they could travel just about anywhere and were much speedier than other military vehicles. A Jeep carrying two or three soldiers and mounting a heavy machine gun proved a formidable weapon. Mountains, streams, and jungles couldn't stop it. Columns of Jeeps could travel many miles of desert overnight, gain position behind enemy lines, and swoop down on unsuspecting foes. Men and equipment could be moved faster than ever before. GIs used them to evacuate the wounded, and to bring ammunition, food, and medical supplies to the front. Engineers fitted homemade plow blades and used Jeeps to clear runways and dig ditches for laying telephone wire. Chaplains were given Jeeps equipped with portable altars so they could bring holy services right to the front lines. In areas where the locomotive trains had been lost to bombing, soldiers fitted steel wheels to Jeeps and put them to work as freight engines.

A soldier in the Pacific theater related this story. During an attack his buddy was seriously wounded. They were stranded deep in the jungle and the wounded man was losing blood fast. Suddenly, in the midst of the carnage, the men heard the roar of a Jeep being driven hell-for-leather through thick undergrowth and bomb-blasted shell holes, its driver grimly determined to reach them. He did; the wounded man was evacuated, and his life was saved.

Jeeps went out reconnoitering ahead of troops, helped generals stay in closer contact with units under their command, and even served as mobile control towers at makeshift runways. Enterprising soldiers rigged belts to the wheels so the Jeeps could provide power for sawmills. Jeep was a staff car, a command car, a mobile power plant, and a field ambulance. President Franklin Roosevelt reviewed the troops in a Jeep; so did Winston Churchill. Jeeps parachuted into action in Europe and Africa, opened up the Burma Road, and ran through hellish gauntlets on the beaches at Guadalcanal, Iwo Jima, and Omaha. "Good Lord, I don't think we could continue without the Jeep," said beloved war correspondent Ernie Pyle. General George C. Marshall, U.S. Army Chief of Staff, called it "America's greatest contribution to modern warfare."

The numbers of military vehicles produced was staggering. By war's end nearly 650,000 Jeeps had been manufactured. Willys built more than 360,000 MBs, along with 1,555 of its MA, and two quad prototypes. Ford Motor Company built 277,896 GPWs, 4,458 of its own GP (Pygmy) design, and the two original Pygmy prototypes. For the most part Bantam was left out of the action, producing only 2,675 vehicles in all. During much of the war, Bantam was reduced to building aircraft landing gear and Jeep trailers.

Long before hostilities ceased, Jeep had become a hero, maybe the most beloved vehicle in the world. After the war, many Jeeps returned home and the Army even

15

donated a special one to the Smithsonian Institute—the oldest survivor of the original group of machines built by Bantam. The soldiers called it "Gramps."

The U.S. Marine Corps seemed to have felt a special empathy with the rugged Jeep. When the fighting was over it awarded one Willys Jeep the Purple Heart for wounds received in action—two shrapnel holes in its windshield. A veteran of the bitter fighting on Guadalcanal, this Willys, dubbed "Old Faithful," was enshrined at the Marine Corps Museum at Quantico, Virginia.

A good and noble record of wartime service was thus recognized by a grateful military. But what is there for a soldier to do when the fighting is over? Jeep, like thousands of other veterans, now had to find a place in the postwar economy.

Production Totals—Wartime Jeeps
American Bantam—all (including 1 prototype): 2,675.
Ford Motor Co.—all (including 2 prototypes): 281,448.
Willys-Overland—all (including 2 prototypes): 362,531.
Total WWII military models: 646,841.

A powerful Jeep roars over a hilltop in a cloud of dust.

This 1942 GPW built by Ford was one of more than 277,000 such vehicles built during World War II.

Jeep Enters the Civilian Market
1945-1949

The last Jeep produced for World War II was built in Toledo on August 20, 1945. Willys-Overland was soon faced with the problem of reestablishing itself in the civilian marketplace.

The overriding question was what to build in the postwar era. Past conflicts provided little to go on. During World War I, the trucks the Army used as tactical vehicles were ordinary commercial units adapted to military needs, including the beloved Nash Quad. When that war ended the companies that built Army trucks simply got back into the commercial truck business, building essentially the same vehicles. The types of machines they produced for the Army were the same ones truck buyers always needed, so they simply continued building and selling the same products.

The situation with Jeep was different—Jeep was designed from the ground up as a military vehicle, not as a commercial work truck. It had no history of commercial service, and the people who operated truck fleets were unfamiliar with it. Nor did Willys-Overland have a strong image as a truck builder. Willys sold relatively few trucks prior to the war and based its prewar business on small and economical family cars. From the mid-1930s on it was a meager existence.

Because there was no Jeep prior to the war, there wasn't a large body of loyal owners ready to buy another one. Jeep would have to build a client base one sale at a time.

Fortunately, the Willys name was synonymous with Jeep, so when (and if) people began to think of buying a Jeep they naturally thought of Willys-Overland. Before long many people were anxious to own their own copy of the vehicle that helped win the war. With the strong Jeep brand name, unequaled public reverence, and a record of outstanding ruggedness and durability, the military Jeep assembly lines were just waiting to be switched over to civilian production. Luckily, Willys was unrivalled in the four-wheel-drive market. Ford wouldn't build a competitor until it could develop one on its own, and that would take many years.

However, in order to be profitable, Willys needed to sell a lot of vehicles. Useful as the little Jeep was, its sales potential was completely unknown. Even its marketing niche was uncharted territory. There was no off-road market whatsoever; it hadn't been invented yet. The term "sport utility" had yet to be used. Jeep would have to be sold to people who ordinarily bought cars and pickup trucks, and they would somehow have to be convinced that a Jeep was the best vehicle for their needs.

But what could the Jeep be used for? Although it was an extraordinary military vehicle, it wasn't very comfortable. The fabric top was drafty and on cold days the interior was chilly, so few shoppers were likely to buy one for daily transportation. It might be sold as a work truck, but the Jeep's cargo area was tiny, so no one was going to buy it for delivery use. It offered only the 134.2-cid Go-Devil four-cylinder engine, which couldn't pull big trailers down the highway. The main problem for Willys was finding commercial uses for the Jeep.

Willys-Overland engineers and marketing people mulled over the limitations of the basic Jeep and soon developed a plan. In the immediate postwar era, the Jeep would be aimed primarily at farmers and their families. It made good sense; farm work involves much off-road driving, where Jeep's four-wheel-drive would be an asset. Wartime experience had shown how adaptable the Jeep could be for a variety of jobs. G.I.s routinely ran drive belts off the Jeep's wheels to provide power for well pumps, saw mills, laundry tubs, electric generators, grist mills—the list was nearly endless. Jeep could do the same for America's noble farmers.

The first suggested use for a peacetime Jeep was as a farm tractor. Prototypes were produced in 1944 of a civilian Jeep that was referred to as an Agrijeep. In July 1945, at a research farm in New Hudson, Michigan, a small number of early civilian-type Jeeps were hooked up to a variety of agricultural implements including plows, mowers, disk and harrow, seed planters, and more. The machines demonstrated an amazing ability to handle a wide variety of farm chores. Using power

This vintage vehicle is the one that launched Jeep in the civilian market—the CJ-2A, the civilian version of the WWII Jeep MB.

takeoffs, the Jeeps powered saws and pumps, threshed wheat, and filled a silo. Just as in war, the Jeep seemed able to do any job it was given. One farm manager said that for belt work the Jeep was superior to any other device he'd ever used. Tests showed the Jeep was a pretty good farm tractor and, of course, it had the advantage of being a very capable car as well. A farmer could work the Jeep all day, plowing fields, hauling grain, or digging wells, then use it to drive into town for dinner and a movie. Jeep could do it all.

Before very long, Jeep vehicles could be seen in Florida, where their small size and narrow width made them ideal for use in orange and grapefruit groves. In the Midwest and Southeast, Jeeps pulled cultivators and harvesters, ran threshers, and powered well pumps that brought water to parched fields. Arkansas rice paddies were a natural for the Jeep's rugged four-wheel-drive. In the "snow belt," Jeeps were used for plowing roads and rescuing stuck cars. Jeeps were even seen at fashionable Long Island golf courses pulling gang mowers to keep the fairways neat and trim. And the Jeep was a vital emergency/rescue vehicle in extreme weather conditions or for off-road duties.

A big problem remained for Willys-Overland. Although the firm would be successful in marketing the wartime Jeep to civilians, the company still needed additional products to sell. While it was true that the little Jeep was a profitable line of vehicles, it couldn't hope to generate enough profits to carry the entire company. A full line of vehicles appealing to a broad range of customers was needed. There were two schools of thought about exactly what those additional vehicles should be. Ward Canaday, a former advertising executive and now the power behind Willys, wanted the company to return to producing automobiles, as it had before the war. Canaday knew, as everyone did, that pent-up demand for cars would trigger a postwar sellers' market that could be extremely profitable for anyone in the car-building business. But Willy's President Charles Sorensen believed that it wouldn't be possible for Willys to produce automobiles. Sorensen realized that demand for new cars would create shortages, but he reasoned that the few remaining independent body manufacturers, the ones who ordinarily produced car bodies for small companies like Willys, would be swamped with business from the "Big Three" automakers and therefore wouldn't be interested in Willys' relatively small volume of production. Without bodies, of course, Willys could not produce cars. Furthermore, Sorensen knew he wouldn't even be able to buy tooling to build his own bodies because the big firms would snap up every machine tool available. He was convinced that Willys would not be able to return to the passenger car business for several years, if ever. That point is where company management began to battle with one another.

In the end, Sorensen's logic won out. Luckily, he was able to buy a factory that produced sheet metal panels for household appliances. Sorensen instructed independent designer Brooks Stevens to design a range of vehicles for which the body panels could be stamped out in the appliance factory. He called for products that would build on Jeep's reputation. Due to the limitations of the metal forming equipment, the sheet metal would have to be relatively flat and couldn't include curved fenders or complex shapes. Stevens came up with a line of vehicles that included a pick-up, box truck, station wagon, delivery sedan, and a sporty ragtop. The design work was remarkable. The new vehicles looked like Jeeps, but were larger and more useful. Willys got them into production as quickly as possible, though the first would not be introduced until mid-1946, with others coming in 1947-49.

The first civilian Jeep was a prototype called the CJ-1A, though it's sometimes also referred to as the CJ-1. According to Jeep, 22 CJ-1A prototypes were built for testing in 1944. Sometime later Willys built a small number, apparently less than 50, of an improved civilian prototype model, dubbed the CJ-2 and also referred to as the Agrijeep. These incorporated several engineering changes that would be included in the civilian Jeeps being readied for volume production. The Agrijeep name was a marketing idea meant to convey the concept that the Jeep was an agricultural machine. Wiser heads soon realized such a designation would pigeonhole the Jeep into a narrow marketing niche, so the name was changed to connote a more universal usefulness when production of the first true civilian Jeep began. Officially dubbed the Universal Jeep CJ-2A, in advertisements the vehicle was referred to it as simply the Universal Jeep.

Assembly of the Jeep CJ-2A began in the Jeep plant at Toledo, Ohio, on July 17, 1945. The CJ-2A carried a suggested retail price of $1,090 and came in brown, light tan, gray, and light blue. At first, olive drab wasn't offered on the civilian Jeeps, probably because returning GIs were sick of seeing it! However, olive drab eventually did make it onto the list of available colors.

To produce the civilian Jeep, many revisions were needed in the basic design. Although not a complete redesign, the sum of the changes made Jeep a better vehicle for its new intended uses. Larger headlights were set into a grille that had seven slots rather than the nine previously used. A larger clutch was fitted to handle increased starting loads, different gear ratios for improved low-speed pulling power, and a fan shroud for better low-speed cooling. The Jeep's gearshift was moved to the column initially, but mid-year it reverted back to the floor. The rear of the vehicle now featured a handy tailgate for easier loading. The Jeep's ride was a bit more comfortable, and the seats had more padding. The famous Willys Go-Devil 134.2-cid four-cylinder engine was rated at 63 hp. The fuel filler was moved to the outside of the vehicle, rather than under the seat.

Probably the most important alteration, as far as suitability for work was concerned, was the addition of optional power take-offs for the front, rear, or center so that the Jeep could provide power for a range of farm duties. With a power take-off, Jeep owners wouldn't need to hook up a belt to a drive wheel to power a sawmill—a trick invented by GIs. Many other pieces of work equipment were made available, including a drawbar, portable welding equipment, and power generators.

The new civilian Jeep was warmly received by a public eager to own a legend. In the last part of 1945, some 1,824 CJ-2As were built.

NOTABLE FOR 1945: The workhorse 1/4-ton Jeep CJ-2A utility vehicle was offered as a civilian model in 1945. The civilian Jeep (CJ) had the same engine as its military counterpart, but the gear ratios in the transmission and axle were changed. A significant improvement was an available power take-off. Geared to the Jeep's transmission, it could drive farm equipment, shred corn, fill a silo, operate a winch, etc. There were also better shock absorbers and springs. Other refinements were made in combustion chamber design and in the radiator shroud. Standard equipment included a remote gas filler (military models were filled by first lifting the driver's seat), seven-inch headlights, an automatic windshield wiper, and rear tailgate.

I.D. DATA: Serial number located on plate at left side of driver's seat on floor riser in Jeep. Starting: 10001. Ending: 11824. Military Jeeps were produced from 1941-1944. No numbers were released for the civilian market in these years. Engine numbers located on right side of cylinder block; stamped on water pump boss on front of cylinder block. On most Jeep models the engine and serial numbers were the same.

Model	Body Type	Price	Weight
Willys Jeep — 1/4-Ton — Four-cyl. — 4x4			
CJ-2A	Universal	$1,090	2,037 lbs.

PRODUCTION: Calendar year 1945 production: 1,824 civilian Jeep vehicles.

ENGINE: Inline. L-head. Four-cylinder. Cast-iron block. Bore & stroke: 3 1/8 x 4 3/8 in. Displacement: 134.2 cid. Compression ratio: 6.5:1. Brake hp: 60 at 4000 rpm. Net hp: 15.63 (NACC). Torque: 105 lbs.-ft. at 2000 rpm. Three main bearings. Solid valve lifters. Carburetor: Carter model WA-1 (613S).

CHASSIS: (Jeep CJ-2A): Wheelbase: 80 1/6 in. Length: 129 7/8 in. Height: 67 1/4 in. Front and rear tread: 48 7/16 in. Tires: 6.00 x 16 four-ply.

TECHNICAL: Synchromesh transmission. Speeds: 3F/1R. Transfer case: two-speeds. Column-mounted gearshift lever on initial models, floor shift on later. Single-plate, dry-disc with torsional dampening clutch. Hypoid axles: full-floating front, semi-floating rear. Bendix hydraulic brakes. Five disc-type five-stud wheels, size 4.50 x 16 in.

OPTIONS: Power take-off ($96.25). Pulley drive ($57.40). Motor governor ($28.65). Special wheels and 7-in. tires ($40). Front canvas top ($57.80). Hydraulic lift ($225).

The original 1946 Jeep wagons were painted Luzon Red, like this example
owned by James Dinehart of Elkhart, Indiana.

In January 1946, former GM executive James D. Mooney became president of Willys-Overland, replacing Charles Sorensen. Mooney also took over the title of chairman of the board of directors from Ward Canaday, who was a very large stockholder and the real power behind Willys management. The company was already building civilian Jeep vehicles, having begun production of a civilian model the previous summer.

The new civilian Jeep CJ-2A proved to be a hit in its first full year of production with 71,554 produced in 1946. Willys was fortunate to have such a high production rate, because for much of that period the CJ-2A would be the only vehicle it had to offer. But on July 11, 1946, a new Jeep went into production. The Model 463 was a rugged and stylish station wagon built on a 104-in. wheelbase. This was the first of the all-new vehicles designed by Brooks Stevens to provide Willys with a full product line. It was a marvel of ingenuity. Stevens, working within the severe limitations of the sheet metal plant, styled the wagon with slab sides, a gently rounded roof, and flat fenders. Although it shared no sheet metal parts with the CJ-2A, the station wagon clearly was styled to show a family resemblance with wartime Jeeps and no one could have any doubt about its ancestry.

The new Jeep wagon was a seven-passenger vehicle and featured all-steel construction — the first regular-production passenger station wagon to do so. To make it more stylish Stevens came up with a unique paint scheme in which the doors and side panels were painted to resemble the very expensive wood-bodied station wagons that were offered by other automakers. Initially, all Jeep wagons were painted a deep maroon called Luzon Red. Fitted with the Willys four-cylinder engine and a three-speed transmission, the Jeep wagon was not especially quick, but power was adequate for most uses and it could reach a top speed of about 65 mph. Even though the new Jeep wagon was offered only in a two-wheel-drive model, it was popular with farm families because of its rugged construction and terrific carrying capacity.

Buyers assumed the Jeep wagons would be as durable as the wartime Jeep and they weren't disappointed. The newest Jeeps proved their usefulness to families and small businesses across the country. Sales got off to a slow start, though, with just 6,534 built the first year.

All in all, 1946 was a decent year for Willys-Overland. The immense costs of conversion to peacetime, plus the expense of tooling up the new station wagon, were offset by strong Jeep sales, so the company was able to report a profit of $402,900 for the year. Not a lot of money, but a profit nonetheless in spite of extreme conditions. With more new products coming, 1947 was bound to be a better year.

NOTABLE FOR 1946: The 1946 Jeep CJ-2A was part of the same series that first hit the market in 1945. There were no significant changes. By the end of 1946, over 71,000 examples were built for the civilian market. The new Willys station wagon debuted.

I.D. DATA — CJ: Serial number located on plate at left side of driver's seat on floor riser in 1946-1948 model CJ-2A. Starting: 11,825. Ending: 83,379. Engine numbers located on right side of cylinder block; stamped on water pump boss on front of cylinder block. On most Jeep models the engine and serial numbers were the same.

I.D DATA: Vehicle identification number is the same as the serial number. VIN locations: on a plate at the left of the driver's seat on the floor riser; on left door sill; on frame front cross member ahead of front spring hanger; on front frame cross member at center; on right side of cowl below hood; and on inside of frame on left. Serial numbers for 1946 were 10001 to 16534. The engine number was the same as the serial number and was located on the top of the water pump boss, at the right front upper corner of the engine block.

Model	Body Type	Price	Weight
Willys Jeep — 1/4-Ton —Four-cyl —			
CJ-2A	Jeep Universal	$1,146	2,074 lbs.
Willys Jeep Station Wagon — Four-cyl — 2x4			
463	2d Sta Wag-5P	$1,495	—

NOTE: Wagon price increased to $1,549 late in 1946.

PRODUCTION: Calendar Year 1946 Production 78,808 civilian Jeep vehicles (Estimate).

ENGINE: Inline. L-head. Four-cylinder. Cast-iron block. Bore & stroke: 3 1/8 in. x 4 3/8 in. Displacement: 134.2 cid. Compression ratio: 6.5:1. Brake hp: 60 at 4000 rpm. Net hp: 15.63 (NACC) Max. Torque: 105 lbs.-ft. at 2000 rpm. Three main bearings. Solid valve lifters. Carburetor: Carter model WA-1 (613S).

CHASSIS

CJ-2: Wheelbase: 80 in. Length: 129 7/8 in. Height: 67 1/4 in. Front tread: 55 1/4

(DaimlerChrysler photo)

The 1946 Willys Jeep station wagon was the first all-steel station wagon developed for the passenger car market, and the forerunner of today's modern SUV.

in. Rear tread: 57 in. Tires: 6.00 x 15 four-ply.

STATION WAGON: Wheelbase: 104 in. Overall length: 174 in. Tires: 6.00 x 15 tube-type.

TECHNICAL: Synchromesh transmission. Speeds: 3F/1R. Two-speed transfer case. Single-plate, dry-disc clutch. Hypoid rear axle. Bendix hydraulic brakes. Disc wheels. Three-speed manual transmission with overdrive was standard on wagons.

OPTIONS

Power take-off ($96.25). Pulley drive ($57.40). Motor governor ($28.65). Special wheels and 7-in. tires ($40). Front canvas top ($57.80). Hydraulic lift ($225). Metal top (price varied according to style and manufacturer).

STATION WAGON OPTIONS: Wheel trim rings. Front bumper guards. Rear bumper guards. Spotlight. Fog lamps. Heavy-duty air cleaner.

(DaimlerChrysler photo)

The 1946 Panel Delivery used the same body as the station wagon, but with a flat metal panel instead of side windows.

The CJ-2A remained the stalwart of the Jeep line in 1947. This fine example
belongs to Duane Demars of Billings, Montana.

For 1947, CJ-2A's popularity continued to grow. Color choices were expanded, apparently beginning midway through the 1946 model year. Yellow, black, and red were new options. There was great demand for the Jeeps. Since no new trucks were built during the war, America's fleet of service trucks was just about worn out. Additionally, American farmers required many more work vehicles to serve their expanding needs. Willys was quick to capitalize on the increased demand.

The biggest product news this year was the introduction of the Jeep truck, the second model of the line of Brooks Stevens-designed Jeeps. The Jeep truck was a surprisingly attractive pick-up. Riding a 118-in. wheelbase, it was offered with a step-side box or stake bed, or could be ordered as a cab and chassis unit, or as a chassis only. Jeep truck offered a choice of two- or four-wheel drive. Powered by the Go-Devil four, it wasn't all that fast, but it was rugged and could be had in 1/2-ton and 1-ton configurations.

During the year, 2,642 two-wheel-drive and 2,346 four-wheel-drive Jeep trucks were produced. A companion panel delivery truck was also introduced. It used the same body as the station wagon, but with a flat metal panel where the rear side windows usually were. Additionally, panel deliveries didn't get the "wood-sided" paint treatment seen on the station wagons.

Willys had a great year in 1947. Total sales of $138.1 million were recorded, with 113,628 vehicles produced. The company claimed its profit of $3.3 million was the best peacetime profit since the glory days of 1928. Willys reopened its West Coast plant in Los Angeles.

NOTABLE FOR 1947: New this year was a line of Jeep trucks, a pickup and a panel delivery. The panel delivery used the basic station wagon body but without rear side windows. Pick-ups had an all-steel cab and split windshield. Chrome bumpers were available front and rear. Chrome hubcaps were also available. Front end styling use the same theme as the Universal Jeep, though no parts were interchangable. The CJ-2A was basically identical to the previous year's model.

I.D. DATA: Serial number located on plate at left side of driver's seat on floor riser in 1946-1948 model CJ-2A; on left side of dash under hood in 4x2 and 4x4 models; and on left floor riser in back of seat in 1947-1949 models 463. Serial numbers: (Jeep) 83381 to 148459; (Panel) 16535 to H4044; (Trucks) 10001 to 12346. Engine numbers located on right side of cylinder block; stamped on water pump boss on front of cylinder block. On most Jeep models the engine and serial numbers were the same. Station wagon serial numbers for 1947 were 16535 to 44045. The engine number was the same as the serial number and was located on the top of the water pump boss, at the right front upper corner of the engine block.

Model	Body Type	Price	Weight
Willys Jeep — 1/4-Ton — Four-cyl — 4x4			
CJ-2A	Jeep Universal	$1,241	2,074 lbs.
Willys Truck — 1/2-Ton — Four-cyl — 4x4			
463	Panel	$1,358	2,587 lbs.
Willys Truck — 1-Ton — Four-cyl — 4x4			
4x4	Chassis	$1,175	1,974 lbs.
4x4	Chassis & Cab	$1,529	2,809 lbs.
4x4	Pickup	$1,620	3,129 lbs.
4x4	Platform Stake	$1,685	3,431 lbs.
Willys Station Wagon — Four-cyl — 2x4			
463	2-dr Sta Wag	$1,616	—

PRODUCTION: Fiscal-year 1947 (October 1, 1946-September 1947) production — 113,602.

ENGINES: Inline. L-head. Four-cylinder. Cast-iron block. Bore & stroke: 3 1/8 x 4 3/8 in. Displacement: 134.2 cid. Compression ratio: 6.5:1. Brake hp: 60 at 4000 rpm. Net hp: 15.63 (NACC) Max. Torque: 105 lbs.-ft. at 2000 rpm. Three main bearings. Solid valve lifters. Carburetor: Carter type WA-1 model 613S.

CHASSIS

(JEEP CJ-2A): Wheelbase: 80 in. Tires: 6.00 x 15 in.

(MODEL 463): Wheelbase: 104 in. Front tread: 55 1/4 in. Rear tread:

The 1947 Jeep Station Wagon changed little from the previous year. The handsome wood-look paint treatment was attractive and very popular.

57 in. Tires: 6.50 x 15 in.

(PICKUP): Wheelbase: 118 in. Front tread: 55 1/4 in. Rear tread: 57 in. Tires: (4x2) 6.5 x 16 in.; (4x4) 7.00 x 16 in.

TECHNICAL: Synchromesh transmission. Speeds: 3F/1R. Floor-mounted gearshift. Single-plate, dry-disc clutch. Hypoid rear axle. Bendix hydraulic brakes. Disc wheels. Three-speed manual transmission with overdrive was standard on station wagons.

OPTIONS

Power take-off*. Pulley drive*. Motor governor. Special wheels and tires. Front canvas top. Hydraulic lift. Metal top.

NOTE: (*) Applicable to both CJ-2A and Model 473 four-wheel-drive trucks. All others applicable to CJ-2A only.

STATION WAGON OPTIONS: Wheel trim rings. Front bumper guards. Rear bumper guards. Spotlight. Fog lamps. Heavy-duty air cleaner.

The 1947 Willys Pickup was offered in two- and four-wheel drive and could be ordered in several configurations.

The 1948 Jeepster was Willys' effort to sell in the conventional passenger car market.
This particular car has non-stock tires and wheel.

Denise Coulson photo

1948

It was still a postwar sellers' market this year, but that was plainly nearing an end. The Willys line was mostly carry-over with few substantial changes. There was a new station wagon model aimed at family wagon buyers. Called the Station Sedan, it was designed to appeal to the ladies and featured basket weave decals on the exterior side panels, a chrome T-shaped grille overlay, and upgraded interior trim. Equipped with a new six-cylinder engine and designated as Model 663, some reports claim it was added in January 1948. Other sources claim the 663 actually debuted at the end of the 1947 model year, though only about 50 were produced before the changeover to 1948 models. The new six, called the Lightning, was a small engine, only 148 cid,

and produced just 72 hp. It certainly wasn't everything the market wanted, but it was much smoother than the Go-Devil four and allowed a higher cruising speed.

On May 3, 1948, Willys introduced a model that was as close to a family-type car as the company had been able to get since before the war. At first glance, the Willys Jeepster seemed a queer duck. It looked a lot like a Jeep (albeit the nicest Jeep anyone had ever seen), but it didn't have four-wheel drive. It was a phaeton—the last true phaeton produced by a major car producer. But the reason other automobile companies had ceased building phaetons was the lack of demand for that type of open body. Willys-Overland expected young couples and families to buy the new sportster, but the Jeepster's soft top and plastic side curtains weren't very good for keeping the interior warm and draft-free. And Jeepster offered only a four-cylinder engine, though the company wisely included overdrive as standard equipment so buyers would be able to cruise the highway at a decent speed.

However, probably the biggest detriment to sales was the Jeepster's $1,765 price. By comparison, a Ford Super Deluxe Club Convertible priced at $1,740 had fancier styling, roll-down windows and a V-8 engine. For what Willys was asking for a Jeepster, you could buy a new Mercury sedan and get some change back. A basic Chevrolet two-door sedan cost hundreds less.

The Jeepster was designed by Brooks Stevens. He envisioned a sports car for returning GIs, or anyone who loved a rakish, open, sporty automobile. Jeepster was the final body style in the series Stevens had been commissioned by Charles Sorensen to design during the waning days of WWII. It was Stevens' first passenger car and remained one of his favorites—he reportedly bought the first Jeepster off the line for his personal use. Based upon the 104-in. wheelbase Willy's chassis, the first-year Jeepster was designated the Model VJ-2. Sales proved underwhelming as only 10,326 VJ-2 Jeepster's were produced.

In late 1948, Willys began producing an improved version of its basic civilian Universal Jeep. Called the CJ-3A, it boasted several enhancements. A taller, one-piece windshield was fitted, and wipers were now mounted at the base rather than the top of the windshield. Ventilation was improved, and front-seat passengers got a little bit more legroom. The Universal Jeep CJ-2A continued in production as assembly of the CJ-3A ramped up.

Willys had an extraordinarily good year in 1948, with 135,528 vehicles produced and a profit of over $6.5 million. The company noted it was now ranked fifth in export sales, a considerable achievement for such a small firm.

NOTABLE FOR 1948: The CJ-2A Universal Jeep was again carried over. There were no significant changes. The 1-ton 4x4 Jeep truck line included a pickup and platform stake truck. The Jeepster debuted.

I.D. DATA: Serial number located on plate at left side of driver's seat on floor riser in 1946-1948 model CJ-2A; on left side of dash under hood in 1948-1951 models 4x2 and 4x4; on left floor riser in back of seat in 1947-1949 models 463. Serial numbers: (CJ-2A) 148,459 to 219,588; (463) 44,045-79,715; (4x2) 12,643-21,010, and (4x4) 12,347-30,575. Engine numbers located on right side of cylinder block; stamped on water pump boss on front of cylinder block. On most Jeep models, the engine and serial numbers were the same. Station wagon VIN locations: on a plate at the left of the driver's seat on the floor riser; on left door sill; on frame front cross member

ahead of front spring hanger; on front frame cross member at center; on right side of cowl below hood; and on inside of frame on left. Serial numbers for early-series 1948 models were: Series 463 station wagon: 44046 to 79715; Series 663 station sedan: 10001 to 13118. Series VJ2 Jeepster: 65199 to 79715. The engine number was the same as the serial number and was located on the top of the water pump boss, at the right front upper corner of the engine block.

Model	Body Type	Price	Weight
Willys Jeep— 1/4-Ton — Four-cyl — 4x4			
CJ-2A	Jeep Universal	$1,262	2,037 lbs.
Willys Truck — 1/2-Ton — Four-cyl — 4x2			
463	Panel	$1,477	2,587 lbs.
Willys Truck — 1-Ton — Four-cyl — 4x2			
—	4x2 Chassis & Cab	$1,334	2,677 lbs.
—	4x2 Pickup	$1,427	2,995 lbs.
—	4x2 Platform	$1,493	3,299 lbs.
Willys Truck — 1-Ton — Four-cyl. — 4x4			
—	4x4 Chassis & Cab	$1,652	2,809 lbs.
—	4x4 Pickup	$1,743	3,129 lbs.
—	4x4 Platform	$1,807	3,431 lbs.
Willys Jeepster			
VJ2	2-d Phae-4P	$1,765	—
Willys Station Wagon			
463	2-d Sta Wag-5P	$1,645	2,895 lbs.
663	2-d Sta Wag-5P	$1,890	2,900 lbs.

PRODUCTION: Fiscal Year 1948 (October 1 1947-Sept. 1948) production — 135,528 vehicles.

ENGINES

(CJ-2A): Inline. L-head. Four-cylinder. Cast-iron block. Bore & stroke: 3 1/8 in. x 4 3/8 in. Displacement: 134.2 cid. Compression ratio: 6.5:1. Brake hp: 60 at 4000 rpm. Net hp: 15.63 (NACC) Max. Torque: 105 lbs.-ft. at 2000 rpm. Three main bearings. Solid valve lifters. Carburetor: Carter model WA-1 (613S).

(463/VJ2/TRUCK) Inline. L-head. Four-cylinder. Cast-iron block. Bore & stroke: 3 1/8 in. x 4 3/8 in. Displacement: 134.2 cid. Compression ratio: 6.48:1. Brake hp: 63 at 4000 rpm. Net hp: 15.63 (NACC). Torque: 105 lbs.-ft. at 2000 rpm. Three main bearings. Solid valve lifters. Carburetor: Carter WA-1 model 613S.

(MODEL 663): Inline. L-head. Six-cylinder Cast-iron block. Displacement: 148.5 cid. Bore and stroke: 3.00 x 3.50 in. Compression ratio: 6.42:1. Brake hp: 72 at 4000 rpm. Carburetor: Carter WA1-645S single-barrel. Four main bearings. Solid valve lifters.

CHASSIS

(JEEP CJ-2A): Wheelbase: 80 in. Front tread: 55 1/4 in. Rear tread: 57 in. Tires: 6.00 x 15 in.

(MODEL 463/VJ2): Wheelbase: 104 in. Front tread: 55 1/4 in. Rear tread: 57 in. Tires: 6.00 x 15 in.

The 1948 Jeepster shown in this factory press release photo has correct hubcaps and wide whitewall tires. Note the chrome side steps and continental spare tire.

(TRUCKS): Wheelbase:118 in. Front tread: 55 1/4 in. Rear tread: 57 in. Tires: (4x2) 6.5 x 16 in.; (4x4) 7.00 x 16 in.

TECHNICAL: Synchromesh transmission. Speeds: 3F/1R. Two-speed 4x4 transfer case. Floor-mounted gearshift. Single-plate, dry-disc clutch. Hypoid rear axle. Hydraulic brakes. Disc wheels. Three-speed transmission with overdrive was standard on station wagons and Jeepster.

OPTIONS

(CJ): Power take-off*. Pulley drive*. Motor governor. Front canvas top. Hydraulic lift. Metal top.

NOTE: * Applicable to both CJ-2A and Model 473 four-wheel-drive trucks. All others applicable to CJ-2A only.

(463/663/VJ2): Front bumper guards. Rear bumper guards. Front grille guard. Wheel trim rings. Full wheel discs. Radio and antenna. License plate frames. White sidewall tires. High-compression 7.0:1 cylinder head. Heavy-duty air cleaner.

The 1949 Jeep CJ-3A was an improved version of the CJ-2A, and featured a one-piece windshield and an air vent in the lower part of the windshield frame. This vehicle is owned by Gary Keating.

Production of the Universal Jeep CJ-3A continued to grow this year as it gradually superceded the CJ-2A, though both models were sold side by side for many months. The truck line saw no substantial changes. A historic vehicle debuted this year when Willys announced a four-wheel-drive version of its station wagon. Dubbed the Model 4x463, the four-wheel-drive Willys wagon was in fact the world's first sport utility wagon, because it wasn't a commercial truck, but rather a family wagon marketed to families, and its four-wheel-drive was factory installed, not an aftermarket conversion. The only engine offered was the Willys Go-Devil four. The four-wheel-drive wagon had come about as a result of a request from the federal government in 1948 for such a vehicle. After assembling the requested machine, the company realized it had a new product that could potentially become a very profitable seller. It promised to schedule "an appropriate number" for production.

By mid-season it was obvious that the Jeepster wasn't selling well, so a de-contented version designated the Model VJ-3 was introduced with a suggested price of just $1,495. Formerly standard equipment such as whitewall tires, wheel discs, overdrive, and the fancy chromed T-shaped grill overlay were now optionally available—at extra cost, of course. The 72-hp Lightening six-cylinder engine was available in a new Jeepster model VJ3-6 that arrived late in the model year. Of the 1949 Jeepster's, 2,697 four-cylinder models were built and 653 six-cylinder models.

Other than noting that its California assembly plant produced 5,295 Jeep vehicles, Willys didn't announce Jeep production figures in its annual report. That's probably because total vehicle production fell dramatically to approximately 83,250 units as the postwar sellers' market came to an end and the other automakers put renewed emphasis on truck sales. Sales fell to $142 million and profits of $3.4 million were less than half the 1948 amount. However, the company was in good shape, with cash on hand, inventories under control, and no bank debt. Willys-Overland looked to the future with optimism. The decade that was destined to become known as one of the greatest of all time — the Fifties!

NOTABLE FOR 1949: There were no major changes in the 1949 Jeep line. Some trucks formerly available only as 4x4s could now be had as 4x2s.

I.D. DATA: Serial number located on right side of dash

The 1949 CJ-2A could be had new for $1,270. This machine belongs to John Lee of Tunkhannock, Pennsylvania.

under hood in 1949-1954 models CJ-2A and CJ-3A/CJ-3B; on left side of dash under hood in 1948-1951 models 4x2 and 4x4; on left floor riser in back of seat in 4-63. Serial numbers: (CJ-2A) 219,589-224,764; (CJ-3A) 10,001 to 35,688; (463) 79,716-106,503; (4x2) 21,011-26,562 and (4x4) 30,576-43,586. Engine numbers located on right side of cylinder block; stamped on water pump boss on front of cylinder block. Station wagon ID number is the same as the serial number. VIN locations: on a plate at the left of the driver's seat on the floor riser; on left door sill; on frame front cross member ahead of front spring hanger; on front frame cross member at center; on right side of cowl below hood; and on inside of frame on left. Serial numbers for the cars in the late-1948/early-1949 styles were: (463 Station Wagon) 79716 to 106504; (663 Station Sedan) 13119 to 22769; (463 Jeepster) 79716 to 106504. Serial numbers for the vehicles introduced in July 1949 were: (four-cylinder wagon) 10001 to 13186; (four-cylinder Jeepster) 10001 to 12698; (six-cylinder Jeepster) 10001 to 10654. The engine number was the same as the serial number and was located on the top of the water pump boss, at the right front upper corner of the engine block.

Model	Body Type	Price	Weight
Willys Jeep — 1/4-Ton — Four-cyl — 4x4			
CJ-2A	Jeep Universal	$1,270	2,037 lbs.
CJ-3A	Jeep Universal	$1,270	2,110 lbs.
Willys Truck — 1/2-Ton — Four-cyl — 4x4			
463	Panel	$1,375	2,587 lbs.
Willys Truck — 1/2-Ton — Four-cyl — 4x2			
—	4x2 Chassis & Cab	$1,282	2,677 lbs.
—	4x2 Pickup	$1,375	2,995 lbs.
—	4x2 Platform	$1,442	3,299 lbs.
Willys Truck — 1-Ton — Four-cyl — 4x4			
—	4x4 Chassis & Cab	$1,700	2,809 lbs.
—	4x4 Pickup	$1,792	3,129 lbs.
—	4x4 Platform Stake	$1,856	3,431 lbs.
Willys Station Wagon — Four-cyl — 2x4			
463	2-dr Sta Wag-5P	$1,595	2,895 lbs.

The big news for the Jeepster in 1949 was the addition of a new six-cylinder engine. This example is owned by David Bennett of Monroe, Georgia.

Willys Station Wagon — Four-cyl — 4x4			
4x463	2-dr 4WD Wag-5P	$1,895	3,136 lbs.
Willys Station Wagon — Six-cyl — 2x4			
633	2-dr Sta Wag-5P	$1,695	2,890 lbs.
633	2-dr Sta Sed-5P	$1,745	2,890 lbs.
Willys Jeepster — Six-cyl			
VJ3	2-dr Jeepster-4P	$1,495	2,468 lbs.
Willys Jeepster — Six-cyl			
VJ3-6	2-dr Jeepster-4P	$1,530	2,392 lbs.

PRODUCTION: Fiscal-year 1949 (October 1 1948-September 1949) production — 83,250 Jeep vehicles (estimate).

ENGINES

(CJ-2A/CJ-3A FOUR): Inline. L-head. Four-cylinder. Cast-iron block. Bore & stroke: 3 1/8 in. x 4 3/8 in. Displacement: 134.2 cid. Compression ratio: 6.5:1. Brake hp: 60 at 4000 rpm. Net hp: 15.63 (NACC). Torque: 105 lbs.-ft. at 2000 rpm. Three main bearings. Solid valve lifters. Carburetor: (CJ models) Carter type WA-1 model 613S.

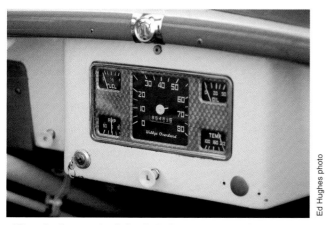

Ed Hughes photo

The dash panel of the '49 Jeepster was located to the driver's right and was fairly basic.

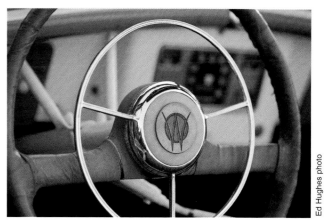

Ed Hughes photo

The steering wheel for the 1949 Jeepster was large and featured a substantial inside ring.

Ed Hughes photo

The 1949 Jeepster has remained a popular collector car.

Ed Hughes photo

This 1949 Jeepster is in almost-new condition.

Ed Hughes photo

The spare tire on the 1949 Jeepster was located in a familiar spot above the rear bumper.

(MODEL 463): Inline. L-head. Four-cylinder. Cast-iron block. Bore & stroke: 3 1/8 in. x 4 3/8 in. Displacement: 134.2 cid. Compression ratio: 6.48:1. Brake hp: 63 at 4000 rpm. Torque: 105 lbs.-ft. at 2000 rpm. Three main bearings. Solid valve lifters. Carburetor: (2x2) Carter type WA-1 model 613S; (4x4) Carter type WO models 596S or 636S.

(MODEL 663/VJ3-6): Inline. L-head. Six-cylinder. Cast-iron block. Displacement: 148.5 cid. Bore and stroke: 3.00 x 3.50 in. Compression ratio: 6.42:1. Brake hp: 72 at 4000 rpm. Carburetor: Carter WA1-645S single-barrel. Four main bearings. Solid valve lifters.

CHASSIS

(JEEP): Wheelbase: 80 in. Front tread: 55 1/4 in. Rear tread: 57 in. Tires: 6.00 x 15.

(MODEL 463): Wheelbase: 104 in. Front tread: 55 1/4 in. Rear tread: 57 in. Tires: 6.50 x 16.

(TRUCKS): Wheelbase: 118 in. Front tread: 55 1/4 in. Rear tread: 57 in. Tires: (4x2) 6.50 x 16 in.; (4x4) 7.00 x 16.

TECHNICAL: Synchromesh transmission. Speeds: 3F/1R (4x4s have two-speed transfer case). Floor-mounted gearshift lever. Single-plate, dry-disc clutch. Hypoid rear axle. Four-wheel hydraulic brakes. Disc wheels.

OPTIONS

(CJ): Power-take-off.* Pulley drive.* Motor governor. Soft top. Hydraulic lift. Metal top.

NOTE: *Applicable to CJ-2A, CJ-3A, and Model 463 four-wheel-drive trucks.

(463/663/JEEPSTER): Front bumper guards. Rear bumper guards. Front grille guard. License plate frames. Large wheel discs. White sidewall tires. Wheel trim rings. Radio and antenna. Oversize tires. Special paint. Spotlights. Fog lights. Heater and defroster. Four-cylinder 134.2 cid, 7.0:1 compression engine (no cost). Heavy-duty air cleaner was optional at extra cost.

"THAT'S THE SIGN TO LOOK FOR!"

Drive in with confidence wherever you see this sign. It identifies Willys-Overland Dealers from coast to coast and tells where to get Factory-Authorized Willys-Overland Service, using factory-approved methods and genuine Willys-Overland replacement parts. It's the one way to protect your investment and be sure of the highest performance at the lowest operating cost.

"That's the Sign to Look For" when your Jeepster needs service, according to this 1949 vintage Willys picture.

EXPANDING THE JEEP LINEUP
1950-1959

The story of Jeep during the 1950s is a chronicle of perseverance as Willys-Overland tried to find its way in the civilian market. The decade started off well enough, but by the mid-1950s orders from farmers declined when farm implement manufacturers brought new agricultural equipment to market. Additionally, the rapidly growing trend towards fewer, larger farms worked against Jeep, because on big farms a large purpose-built tractor could do the job better and more efficiently than a CJ.

The automobile market compounded Willys' problems during 1950-1954 by doing a complete about-face and becoming a buyers' market. Raw materials were no longer being rationed so automobile manufacturers could build as many cars as they wanted to. And build them they did. Faced with a broader range of choices and more availability, buyers who might have bought a Jeep vehicle often ended up buying a "Big Three" product. Hand in hand with the increased automotive production came hefty marketing efforts and considerable price discounting—all of which cut into Jeep's business.

Early in the decade Ward Canaday was finally able to fulfill his dream of getting Willys back into the passenger car business, and he did it with a car that, although completely new, was a spiritual descendent of the prewar Willys. However, Canaday had seriously miscalculated the intensity of the competition among automakers, and in the end his dream car would not find success.

A new war flared up in Korea in the middle of the decade and Willys introduced a new military Jeep vehicle just in time for it to take part in that sometimes frustrating struggle.

Willys-Overland also celebrated its 50th anniversary early in the decade and as a way of marking its birthday decided that the stylized "W" which traditionally adorned Willys products would be gold colored for that one year.

But during the same year Willys-Overland was celebrating its 50th birthday, the company was sold to Kaiser Industries, a conglomerate run by the fabulously successful Henry J. Kaiser, a living legend who won the world's undying gratitude when his shipyards built hundreds of Liberty ships during World War II. The Kaiser acquisition would alter the course that Willys was following. Kaiser was an international-minded firm and quickly stepped up efforts to expand Jeep sales around the world. One of the first steps Kaiser would take was to change the name of its new automotive subsidiary.

While Jeep's reputation as a revolutionary tool of war was forged during the 1940s, during the 1950s Jeep established a new reputation as a rugged tool for a wide variety of business uses. It almost seemed as if the biblical prediction of Isaiah—*"they shall beat their swords into plowshares, and their spears into pruning hooks"*—was coming true. As the decade drew to a close Jeep would introduce some fascinating new products and demonstrate an ability to continually find new uses for its products.

**1950 Jeepster buyers had a choice of four- or six-cylinder models.
This four-cylinder show winner is owned by Dan Chiles of Yorba Linda, California.**

On March 3, 1950, Willys-Overland hosted a large gathering of its dealers in Toledo, Ohio, to announce its newest models. However, despite the fanfare, the Jeep lineup consisted mostly of carry-over products, albeit featuring mechanical improvements, upgraded power trains and styling refinements. Willys-Overland proudly boasted that 1950 marked the company's "10th year of progress in the manufacture of the world's most useful vehicles."

With a conflict breaking out in Korea, the U.S. Army realized it needed some new wheels. After all, many of the MBs in its fleet were almost 10 years old, the rest were not much newer, and the vehicles were getting tired. Willys developed a new military Jeep called the M38 (or MC). The M38 resembled the civilian Universal Jeep CJ-3A and had a one-piece windshield, 24-volt electrical system, and higher ground clearance than the MB. Improvements included a stronger frame, transmission, transfer case, and springs. Electric wipers and 7-inch headlights were fitted. By the end of the year the company had an order backlog for these vehicle totaling approximately $110 million.

On the civilian side, Willys introduced a new Jeep four-cylinder engine named the Hurricane and also an improved Lightning six. The Hurricane was based on the Willys Go-Devil, but featured a novel F-head. With the F-head, the exhaust valves remained mounted in the block, but the intake valves were placed in the head. This allowed larger intake valves to be fitted, which greatly improved breathing characteristics and provided more power. The Hurricane four produced 72 hp at 4000 rpm, which was a great improvement over the Go-Devil.

The Lightning inline six-cylinder engine got an increase in displacement to 161 cid. It retained its

**The Jeepster line got improvements
in 1950 with revised front-end
styling and more powerful engines.**

The military M38 first saw action in the Korean War. This vehicle is owned by Gary Keating of Connecticut.

flathead design but, thanks to the increase in cubic inches, now produced 75 hp at 4000 rpm.

Jeep station wagons, panel delivery wagons and trucks got new frontal styling, including rounder, more graceful fenders with a handsome peak on the front edge, a V-shaped grille with five chrome bars, and a redesigned instrument panel. Since these new models arrived midway through the model year, there were two series of 1950 Jeep products. The first series looked the same as before and used the older style engines, while the second series got the newer engines and improved styling. The Station Sedan model was dropped. The Jeep wagon was the most popular station wagon on the market.

Jeepsters also received the updated styling and more powerful engines. Jeepsters carrying the new four-cylinder engine and revamped styling were designated VJ-473, while six-cylinder models were dubbed VJ-673. Because the new models arrived mid-year, there were two series of 1950 Jeepsters. The earlier, first-series fours were designated VJ-3 463, while the first-series sixes were VJ-3 663.

The Universal Jeep CJ-2A was no longer being produced, leaving CJ-3A as the only CJ model available.

Willys-Overland also completed an intensive program to concentrate all body-building operations in Toledo. Substantial savings in freight, manufacturing,

and administrative expenses resulted, along with lower costs for the finished bodies, and improved quality. The ability to manufacture all its own bodies in-house was strong evidence that the company was growing.

Willys' gross sales volume fell to $107,886,248, from $142,362,944 in 1949. The 250,000th civilian Jeep CJ was produced during the year.

NOTABLE FOR 1950: There was a lot that was new this year. The CJ-3A replaced the CJ-2A as the basic Universal Jeep. Trucks and station wagons got new front-

1950s-vintage Jeep four-wheel-drive trucks pretty much owned the market for light-duty 4x4 pickups.

33

end styling. Front fenders now had a peaked front edge. The new grille consisted of five horizontal bright metal moldings running across nine vertical moldings. There was a chrome ornament on the tip of the hood. Two engines, the "Hurricane" four and the "Lightning" six, were offered in wagons, but not trucks. There was a new 1/2-ton 4x2 truck

I.D. DATA: Serial number located on right side of dash under hood in 1949-1954 models CJ-2A and CJ-3A/CJ-3B; on left side of dash under hood in 1948-1951 models 4x2 and 4x4. Serial numbers: (CJ-3A) 35,689-63,784; (463) 106,504-112,402; (1/2-ton) 26,563-27,787 and (1-ton) 43,587-47,709. Engine numbers located on right side of cylinder block; stamped on water pump boss on front of cylinder block. On most Jeep models the engine and serial numbers were the same. Station wagon and Jeepster ID locations: on a plate at the left of the driver's seat on the floor riser; on left door sill; on frame front cross member ahead of front spring hanger; on front frame cross member at center; on right side of cowl below hood; and on inside of frame on left. Series 463 station wagon serial numbers began at 106504 and went up to 112425; 4x463 station wagons began at 13186 and went up 17167; the VJ3-four Jeepsters began at 12698 and went up to 13190; the VJ3-six Jeepsters began at 10654 and went up to 11001; the 663-six station sedans began at 22769 and went up to 27786; and the 473-four station wagons and Jeepsters and the four-cylinder 4x473 four-wheel-drive station wagons began at 10001 and went up to 12045 in mixed production. 673-six station wagons and Jeepsters began at 10001 and went up to 17456 in mixed production. The engine number was the same as the serial number and was located on the top of the water pump boss, at the right front upper corner of the engine block.

Model	Body Type	Price	Weight
Willys Jeep — 1/4-Ton — Four-cyl — 4x4			
CJ-3A	Jeep Universal	$1,270	2,110 lbs.
Willys Truck — 1/2-Ton — Four-cyl — 4x2			
463	1/2-Ton Panel	$1,374	2,587 lbs.
Willys Truck — 1/2-Ton — Four-cyl — 4x4			
4x4	Chassis & Cab	$1,282	2,677 lbs.
4x4	Pickup	$1,375	2,995 lbs.
4x4	Platform Stake	$1,441	3,299 lbs.
Willys Truck — 1-Ton — Four-cyl — 4x4			
4x4	Chassis & Cab	$1,700	2,809 lbs.
4x4	Pickup	$,1792	3,129 lbs.
4x4	Platform Stake	$1,856	3,431 lbs.
Willys Truck — 1/2-Ton — Four-cyl — 4x2			
—	4x2 Chassis & Cab	$1,282	2,677 lbs.
—	4x2 Pickup	$1,375	2,995 lbs.
—	4x2 Platform	$1,442	3,299 lbs.
Willys Station Wagon — Four-cyl — First Series			
463	2d Sta Wag-6P	$1,595	2,895 lbs.
463x4	2d 4WD Sta Wag-6P	$1,895	—
Willys Station Wagon — Four-cyl — Second Series			
473SW	2d Sta Wag-6P	$1,495	2,818 lbs.
473x4	2d 4WD Sta Wag-6P	$1,990	—
Willys Station Wagon — Six-cyl — First Series			
663	2d Sta Wag-6P	$1,695	—
Willys Station Wagon — Six-cyl — Second Series			
673SW	2d Sta Wag-6P	$1,575	2,831 lbs.
Willys Jeepster — Four-cyl — First Series			
VJ3	2d Jeepster-5P	$1,495	2,468 lbs.
Willys Jeepster — Four-cyl — Second Series			
473 VJ	2d Jeepster-5P	$1,390	2,459 lbs.
Willys Jeepster — Six-cyl — First Series			
VJ3-6	2d Jeepster-5P	$1,530	—
Willys Jeepster — Six-cyl — Second Series			
673 VJ	2d Jeepster-5P	$1,490	2,485 lbs.

M&M Photography

F-head four-cylinder 1950s are scarce today, but could be had new for less than $1,500. This mint-condition model belongs to James Sommer of Pittsburgh.

PRODUCTION: 90,424 Jeep vehicles (estimate).

ENGINES

(CJ-3A FOUR): Inline. L-head. Cast-iron block. Bore & stroke: 3 1/8 x 4 3/8 in. Displacement: 134.2 cid. Compression ratio: 6.5:1. Brake hp: 60 at 4000 rpm. Torque: 105 lbs.-ft. at 2000 rpm. Three main bearings. Solid valve lifters. Carburetor: (4x2) Carter-type WA-1 model 613S; (4x4) Carter-type WO models 596S or 636S.

(FIRST SERIES 463/463x4/VJ-3 FOUR): Inline. L-head. Cast-iron block. Displacement: 134.2 cid. Bore and stroke: 3.13 x 4.38 in. Compression ratio: 6.48:1. Brake hp: 63 at 4000 rpm. Carburetor: Carter WA1-613S single-barrel. Three main bearings. Solid valve lifters.

(FIRST SERIES 663/VJ-3 SIX): Inline. L-head. Cast-iron block. Displacement: 148.5 cid. Bore and stroke: 3.0 x 3.5 in. Compression ratio: 6.42:1. Brake hp: 72 at 4000 rpm. Carburetor: Carter WA1-645S single-barrel. Four main bearings. Solid valve lifters.

(SECOND SERIES 473/473X4 FOUR): Inline. F-head. Cast-iron block. Exhaust valves in engine block and intake valves in the cylinder head. Displacement: 134.2 cid. Bore and stroke: 3.13 x 4.38 in. Compression ratio: 7.4:1. Brake hp: 72 at 4000 rpm. Carburetor: Carter WA1-613S single-barrel. Three main bearings. Solid valve lifters.

(SECOND SERIES 673 SIX): Inline. L-head. Cast-iron block. Displacement: 161 cid. Bore and stroke: 3 1/8 x 3 1/2 in. Compression ratio: 6.9:1. Brake hp: 75 at 4000 rpm. Carburetor: Carter WA1-645S single-barrel. Four main bearings. Solid valve lifters.

CHASSIS

(JEEP): Wheelbase: 80 in. Front tread: 55 1/4 in. Rear tread: 57 in. Tires: 6.00 x 15 in.

(MODEL 463): Wheelbase: 104 in. Front tread: 55 1/4 in. Rear tread: 57 in. Tires: 6.50 x 16 in.

(MODEL 473): Wheelbase: 118 in. Front tread: 55 1/4 in. Rear tread: 57 in. Tires: (4x2) 6.50 x 16 in.; (4x4) 7.00 x 16 in.

TECHNICAL

Synchromesh transmission. Speeds: 3F/1R (4x4s have two-speed transfer case). Floor-mounted gearshift lever. Single-plate, dry-disc clutch. Hypoid front axle with 4x4. Hypoid rear axle. Four-wheel hydraulic brakes. Disc wheels.

OPTIONS

(CJ SERIES): Power take-off*. Pulley drive*. Motor governor*. Soft top. Hydraulic lift. Metal top.

NOTE: *Also applicable also to Model 473 four-wheel drive trucks.

(OTHER MODELS): Front bumper guards. Rear bumper guards. Front grille guard. License plate frames. Large wheel discs. Wheel trim rings. White sidewall tires. Dual wipers on fours. Cigar lighter in fours. Special paint. Radio and antenna. Overdrive in Jeepster. Inside rearview mirror. Outside rearview mirror. Four-cylinder 134.2-cid, 7.8:1 high-compression engine (no cost). Heavy-duty air cleaner was optional at extra cost.

James Dinehart photo

Jeepster was the last phaeton from a major manufacturer.
Jeepsters like this one that had the new styling and six-cylinder engine were named VJ-673s.

**The 1951 Jeepsters were actually leftover 1950 models.
Lew Retzer of Kampsville, Illinois, is the owner of this example.**

Lew Retzer photo

In December of 1950, Willys engineers began working on yet another improved military Jeep. Earlier they had produced a civilian prototype dubbed the CJ-4, which combined the Hurricane F-head engine with a modified chassis and a CJ-3A body tub. The CJ-4 had a taller cowl and hood that was necessary to provide clearance for the tall F-head engine. The CJ-4 was a great improvement over prior Jeeps because of its powerful engine. In the end, however, Willys management chose not to put it into production. But the lessons learned in developing it were utilized when developing a more modern Army Jeep. Designated the M38-A1, (also known as the MD), the new military Jeep used a waterproofed version of the Hurricane engine, 24-volt electrical system, 81-inch wheelbase, and curved front fenders. Interior room was greatly improved.

The Army paid the development cost for this vehicle, and when Willys later expressed the hope of producing a civilian version of it, it was flatly turned down by the military. The Army was right. After all, the development costs were substantial and had been paid for with taxpayer dollars. The Army owned the tooling and didn't want to share it.

The problem was that Willys really needed a newer, more powerful civilian CJ series, and it had been counting on using the M38-A1 as the basis for a planned Jeep replacement. Without the Army's OK, Willys was stuck without a new civilian product. The only other solution would be to modify the CJ-3A to accept the more powerful Hurricane engine. Willys' engineers stepped up to the challenge of redesigning the CJ-3A on a shoestring budget. The engine's height was the big problem—it was much taller than the old flathead mill. After some trial and error the engineers came up with a low-cost compromise that worked surprisingly well. The new vehicle debuted the following year.

The civilian Jeeps were mostly carryover for 1951, understandable considering the cost of the substantial (by Willys standards) revamping seen mid-year in 1950.

The Panel Delivery wagon was renamed the Sedan Delivery (Model 473-SD) this year. Two new Universal models were offered. The Farm Jeep featured six forward speeds, hydraulic lift, drawbar, heavier springs, and a reinforced frame, making it ideal for farm work. Power takeoff (PTO) was available as optional equipment. The Jeep Tractor was likewise derived from the Universal Jeep. It included a hydraulic lift as standard equipment and offered a range of optional farm implements. Essentially no Jeepsters were produced, although there was a 1951 Jeepster model in the showrooms. These were leftover 1950s that were re-titled as 1951s. One report claims a small batch of 1951 Jeepsters—less than 20—were produced, but no corroborating evidence was offered.

Willys sales were up 104 percent for the year, to $219,861,553, which marked a new high point. That dollar volume was 3 percent higher than the old record of $212,458,489 set in 1944. Willys reported production of 119,189 units, 21 percent of which were military Jeeps. The company reported net profits of $4,585,566. All in all, it was a very good year.

NOTABLE FOR 1951: Willys continued to offer the 80-in. wheelbase Universal Jeep CJ-3A. The CJ-3A was available in standard utility for and also as a stripped chassis. For agricultural markets there was a new model called the Farm Jeep with a power take-off (PTO) attachment. According to one source, only three stripped chassis and 62 Farm Jeeps were built. Jeep trucks retained the grille design introduced in 1950. All were built on a 118-in. wheelbase, except the sedan delivery, which had a 104-in. wheelbase. The Sedan Delivery came only as a 4x2 model. Other truck offerings included a stripped chassis, chassis & cab, pickup and platform stake truck models. The Sedan Delivery had a 4,000-lb. GVW rating. All other 4x2 trucks had a 4,250-lb. GVW and the 4x4s were rated for 5,300 lbs. (CJ-3A had a 3500 lb. GVW rating). Power for the trucks was provided by the F-head four-cylinder. The 4x4 trucks had "4-Wheel-Drive" insignia on the side of the hood.

I.D. DATA: Serial number located on plate on right side of dash under hood on CJ-3A; on left side of dash under hood in 1948-1951 models 4x2 and 4x4. Serial numbers: (FJ) 451-GC1 — 10,001-10,062; (CJ-3(S)) 451-GA1 — 10,001-10,003; (CJ-3(O)) 451-GB1 — 10,001-54,158; (473 chassis) CA-1 10,001-15,440; (473 Chassis & Cab) DB1 — 10,001-10,530; (473 pickup) DC1 — 10,001-13,016; (473 stake) DD1 — 10,001 to ending; (473E Chassis & Cab) — EB1 — 10,001-11,894; (473E pickup) — EC1 — 10,001-26,029; (473E Stake) — ED1 — 10,001-10,420. Engine numbers located on right side of cylinder block; and stamped on water pump boss on front of cylinder block. Beginning around 1951 and continuing through at least 1953, each model had a specific serial number prefix, such as 451-4GC. The first number indicated the number of cylinders. The second and third numbers indicated model year. The first letter indicated basic chassis and body type. The second letter indicated model. The fourth number indicated series in

any one model year. On most Jeep models the engine and serial numbers were the same. **Model 473 and Jeepster** VIN locations: on a plate at the left of the driver's seat on the floor riser; on left door sill; on frame front cross member ahead of front spring hanger; and on front frame cross member at center; on right side of cowl below hood; on inside of frame on left. Serial numbers took the format 473-SW-451-AA1-10001. First symbol indicates type of engine: 4=four-cylinder; 6=six-cylinder, except four-wheel-drive models have the prefix 4x to indicate 4x4 system (i.e.: 4x473). Next two symbols (73) indicate series. Next two symbols indicate body type: SW=station wagon; VJ=Jeepster. Next symbol indicates engine type again, followed by a pair of symbols indicating model year: 51=1951. Next group of symbols is an alpha-numerical code: AA1=4x2 station wagon; FA1=4x4 station wagon; BA1=4x2 Jeepster. Beginning and ending serial numbers according to model were: (473-SW) 451-AA1-10001 to 451-AA1-25906; (4x473-SW) 451-FA1-10001 to 451-FA1-21854; (473-VJ) 451-BA1-10001 to 451-BA1-14086; (673-SW) 651-AA1-10001 to 651-AA1-18470; (673-VJ) 651-BA1-10001 to 651-BA1-11779. The engine number was the same as the serial number and was located on the top of the water pump boss, at the right front upper corner of the engine block.

Model	Body Type	Price	Weight
Willys Jeep — 1/4-Ton — Four-cyl — 4x4			
FJ	Farm Jeep	$1,550	2,280 lbs.
CJ-3A	Chassis	$1,055	1,692 lbs.
CJ-3A	Jeep Universal	$1,290	2,110 lbs.
Jeep Trucks — 1/2-Ton — Four-cyl — 4x2			
473-SD	Sedan Delivery	$1,469	2,406 lbs.
Jeep Trucks — 1-Ton — Four-cyl — 4x2			
473-D	Chassis	$865	1,716 lbs.
473-D	Chassis & Cab	$1,220	2,406 lbs.
473-D	Pickup	$1,295	2,722 lbs.
473-D	Platform Stake	$1,365	2,963 lbs.
Jeep Trucks — 1-Ton — Four-cyl — 4x4			
473-E	Chassis	$1,205	2,109 lbs.
473-E	Chassis & Cab	$1,595	2,799 lbs.
473-E	Pickup	$1,678	3,115 lbs.
473-E	Platform Stake	$1,736	3,356 lbs.
Willys Station Wagon — Four-cyl			
473SW	2d Sta Wag-6P	$1,758	2,818 lbs.
4X473	2d 2wd Wag-6P	$2,180	3,174 lbs.
Willys Station Wagon — Six-cyl			
673SW	2d Sta Wag-6P	$1,841	2,831 lbs.
Willys Jeepster — Four-cyl			
473VJ	2d Jeepster-5P	$1,426	2,459 lbs.
Willys Jeepster — Six-cyl			
673VJ	2d Jeepster-5P	$1,529	2,485 lbs.

PRODUCTION: 119,189 Jeep vehicles.

ENGINES

(CJ-2A FOUR): Inline. L-head. Cast-iron block. Bore & stroke: 3 1/8 in. x 4 3/8 in. Displacement: 134.2 cid. Compression ratio: 6.5:1. Brake hp: 60 at 4000 rpm. Torque: 105 lbs.-ft. at 2000 rpm. Three main bearings.

Solid valve lifters. Carburetor: Carter-type YF models 832S or 832SA.

(473/JEEPSTER FOUR): Inline. L-head. Cast-iron block. Bore & stroke: 3 1/8 in. x 4 3/8 in. Displacement: 134.2 cid. Compression ratio: 7.4:1. Brake hp: 72 at 4000 rpm. Torque: 114 lbs.-ft. at 2000 rpm. Three main bearings. Solid valve lifters. Carburetor: Carter type YF model 832S/832SA one-barrel.

(673/JEEPSTER SIX): Inline. L-head. Cast-iron block. Displacement: 161.1 cid. Bore and stroke: 3.13 x 3.50 in. Compression ratio: 6.9:1. Brake hp: 75 @ 4000 rpm. Carburetor: Zenith 39 one-barrel. Four main bearings. Solid valve lifters.

CHASSIS

(FJ/CJ-3A): Wheelbase: 80 1/16 in. Length: 129 7/8 in. Height: 67 1/4 in. (top up). Front and rear tread: 48 7/16 in. Tires: 6.00 x 16 in.

(473 SEDAN DELIVERY): Wheelbase: 104.5 in. Length: 176.25 in. Height: 73.62 in. Front and rear tread: 57 in. Tires: (4x2) 6.70 x 15 in.

(473 TRUCK): Wheelbase: 118 in. Length: 183.7 in. Height: 74.3 in. Front and rear tread: 57 in. Tires: (4x2) 6.70 x 15 in.; (4x4) 7.00 x 15 in.

(STATION WAGON/JEEPSTER): Wheelbase: (four-wheel-drive models) 104.5 in.; (4x2 models) 104 in. Overall length: (station wagon) 176.25 in.; (Jeepster) 176.25 in.; (four-wheel-drive) 175.8 in. Front tread: (all) 55 in. Rear tread: (all) 57 in. Tires: (Jeepsters) 6.40 x 15 in.; (4x2 station wagons) 6.70 x 15 in.; (4x4 station wagon) 7.00 x 15 in.

Carl Carvell photo

Engineers began redesign work on the CJ-3A in 1951, but the new model didn't appear until the following year. This 1951 belongs to Carl Carvell of Glastonbury, Connecticut.

The 1-ton, 4x4, long-wheelbase pickups were the big rigs of the 1951 Jeep line. This restored 1951 workhorse belongs to Howard Thompson of N. Canton, Ohio.

TECHNICAL

Synchromesh transmission. Speeds: 3F/1R. Floor-mounted gearshift. Single-plate clutch. Hypoid rear axle. Overall ratio: 5.38:1. Four-wheel hydraulic brakes. Disc wheels. 4x4 models had a full-floating hyboid axle in front; semi-floating rear, and two-speed transfer case. Axle capacity (CJ-3A) 2,000 lbs. front; 2,500 lbs. rear.

OPTIONS

(CJ/TRUCK): Power take-off. Pulley drive. Motor governor. Soft top. Hydraulic lift. Metal top. Options available for Jeep trucks included: Chrome front bumper. Chrome rear bumper. Rearview mirrors. Chrome wheel discs. Bumper guards. Clearance lights.

STATION WAGON/JEEPSTER: Front bumper guards. Rear bumper guards. Front grille guard. License frames. Large wheel discs. Wheel trim rings. White sidewall tires. Dual wipers on four-cylinders. Cigar lighter on four-cylinders. Special paint. Radio and antenna. Overdrive in Jeepster. Inside rearview mirror. Outside rearview mirror. Four-cylinder 134.2-cid, 7.8:1 high-compression engine (no cost). Heavy-duty air cleaner was optional at extra cost.

John L. Russell photo

**M-38 owner George Gregory of Traverse City, Michigan,
celebrated the 50th birthday of his 1952 Army Jeep with a cake.**

In January 1952, Willys Overland introduced its newest product and, for the first time in 10 years, it wasn't a new Jeep vehicle. The Aero Willys was something new; a smaller, full-size family car on a short 108-inch wheelbase. It should be considered the first intermediate car because it was one size below traditional big cars, yet one size larger than compacts. However, since the Aero Willys was not a Jeep vehicle, a detailed discussion of the car is not included in this book.

An immediate result of the Aero Willys introduction was the dropping of the Jeepster line. Jeepster had been Willys' first attempt to break into the postwar passenger car market and it was wholly unsuccessful—just over 19,000 Jeepsters were produced in all.

The combination of the huge expense of introducing the new passenger car and some very considerable military orders meant that Willy's civilian Jeep vehicles were again mainly carryover. The 161-cid six got an F-head this year, boosting output to 90 hp. The new version was dubbed the Hurricane Six. The two-wheel-

drive Jeep pickup truck was discontinued at the end of the 1951 model run. Although small numbers were reportedly produced in later years for special orders, no two-wheel-drive Jeep pickups would be available as a regular offering until the 1963 models were introduced.

Willys reported that unfilled orders totaled $225 million by the end of the fiscal year, noting that its present contracts would keep military Jeep production going thru mid-1954. Willys proudly noted that it had risen from ninth place in 1950 to fifth place in U.S. vehicle production by 1952. In March, the 1 millionth Jeep was produced.

Willys was clearly on a roll. The company set another sales record in 1952, with sales volume of $301,695,020—up a whopping 37 percent over 1951, which was Willys' previous best year. Total vehicle production (including cars) was up 24.4 percent and totaled 148,216 units, of which 32 percent were military Jeeps. A profit of just over $6 million was reported.

NOTABLE FOR 1952: Willys production lines were

This 1952 Willys M38 was equipped with a fording kit.

running all-out to fill military orders for Korean War Jeeps. Civilian models also sold well. All trucks were 4x4 models, except for the Sedan Delivery, were offered as a conventional 4x2.

I.D. DATA: Serial number located on right side of dash under hood in CJ-3A, on left side of dash under hood in models 473. Starting: (CJ-3A) 452-GA1-10,001 to 10,013; (CJ-3A open) 452-GB1-10,001 to 39,652; (473-SD) 452-GA1-10,001 to 12,091; (473 chassis) 452-FA1-10,001 & up; (473 chassis & cab) 452-EB1-10,001 to 11,085; (473 pickup) 452-EC1-10,001 to 23,183; (473 stake) 452-ED1-10,001 to 10,358. Engine numbers located on right side of cylinder block; stamped on water pump boss on front of cylinder block. Beginning around 1951 and continuing through at least 1953, each model had a specific serial number prefix, such as 451-4GC. The first number indicated the number of cylinders. The second and third numbers indicated model year. The first letter indicated the basic chassis and body type. The second letter indicated model. The fourth number indicated series in any one model year. On most Jeep models the engine and serial numbers were the same.

Model	BodyType	Price	Weight
Willys Jeep — 1/4-Ton — Four-cyl — 4x4			
CJ-3A	Chassis	$1,224	1,692 lbs.
CJ-3A	Jeep Universal	$1,352	2,108 lbs.
Jeep Trucks — 1/2-Ton — Four-cyl — 4x2			
473-SD	Sedan Delivery	$1,469	2,406 lbs.
Jeep Trucks — 1-Ton — Four-cyl — 4x4			
473	Chassis Stripped	$1,296	2,109 lbs.
473	Chassis & Cab	$1,712	2,799 lbs.
473	Pickup	$1,805	3,115 lbs.
473	Platform Stake	$1,870	3,356 lbs.

Willys Station Wagon — Four-cyl			
475SW	2d Sta Wag-6P	$1,705	2,818 lbs.
4X475	2d 4x4 Sta Wag	$2,134	3,174 lbs.
Willys Station Wagon — Six-cyl			
685	2d Sta Wag-6P	$1,786	2,850 lbs.

PRODUCTION: Total 1952 Willys production for the fiscal year October 1 1951-September 30, 1952, including passenger cars, was 148,216 vehicles. Of this, military Jeep vehicles accounted for approximagely 47,500 vehicles. An estimated 57,879 civilian Jeep vehicles were produced.

ENGINES

(CJ-3A FOUR): Inline. L-head. Cast-iron block. Bore & stroke: 3 1/8 in. x 4 3/8 in. Displacement: 134.2 cid. Compression ratio: 6.5:1. Brake hp: 60 at 4000 rpm. Max. Torque: 105 lbs.-ft. at 2000 rpm. Three main bearings. Solid valve lifters. Carburetor: Carter type YF model 938S or 938SA.

(473 TRUCK/475 STATION WAGON FOUR): Inline. F-head. Cast-iron block. Bore & stroke: 3 1/8 in. x 4 3/8 in. Displacement: 134.2 cid. Compression ratio: 7.4:1. Brake hp: 72 at 4000 rpm. Torque: 114 lbs.-ft. at 2000 rpm. Three main bearings. Solid valve lifters. Carburetor: Carter type YF model 951S.

(685 STATION WAGON SIX): Inline. F-head. Cast-iron block. Exhaust valves in the engine block and intake valves in the cylinder head. Displacement: 161.1 cid. Bore and stroke: 3.13 x 3.50 in. Compression ratio: 7.6:1. Brake hp: 90 at 4200 rpm. Carburetor: Carter YS-

This 1952 Willys 1-ton utility tow truck is still on the road. It belongs to Don Dugal of Woonsocket, Rhode Island.

Don Dugal photo

Delmar Haynes photo

Not all Jeeps were created equal. This 1952 model belonging to Delmar Haynes of Knoxville, Tennessee, is equipped for amphibious duty and sports a .30-caliber machine gun.

924S single-barrel. Four main bearings. Solid valve lifters.

CHASSIS

(CJ-3A): Wheelbase: 80 1/16 in. Length: 129 7/8 in. Height: 67 1/4 in. (top up). Front and rear tread: 48 7/16 in. Tires: 6.00 x 16.

(SEDAN DELIVERY): Wheelbase: 104 in. Length: 176 1/4 in. Height: 73.62 in. Front and rear tread: 57 in. Tires: (4x2) 6.70 x 15.

(STATION WAGONS) Wheelbase: 104 in. (two-wheel-drive); 104.5 in. (4x473/4x475 wagons). Overall length: 176.3 in.; (4x473/4x475 station wagons) 178 in. Tires: (4x2) 6.70 x 15 tube-type blackwall; (4x4) 7.00 x 15.

(TRUCK): Wheelbase: 118 in. Length: 183.7 in. Height: 74.3 in. Front and rear tread: 57 in. Tires: (4x4) 7.00 x 15.

TECHNICAL: Synchromesh transmission. Speeds: 3F/1R Floor-mounted gearshift. Single-plate clutch. Hypoid rear axle. Overall ratio: 5.38:1. Four-wheel hydraulic brakes. Disc wheels. The 4x2 models had a 2,000 lbs. capacity front I-beam axle. The 4x4 models

had a 2,000-lb. capacity, full-floating type hypoid front axle, and two-speed transfer case. A 2,500-lb. capacity, semi-floating hypoid rear axle was used on both 4x2 and 4x4 models.

OPTIONS

(CJ): Power take-off. Pulley drive. Motor governor. Soft top. Hydraulic lift. Metal top.

(4x4 TRUCKS): Power take-off. Pulley drive. Motor governor. Rearview mirror. Side-mount spare on pickups/stakes. Chrome bumper. License frame.

(SEDAN DELIVERY): Chrome front bumper. Chrome rear bumper. License frame. Chrome wheel disc. Bumperettes. Bumper guards. Wheel trim rings. Whitewall tires. Rearview mirror. Radio and antenna.

(STATION WAGON): Front bumper guards. Rear bumper guards. Front grille guard. License plate frames. Large wheel discs. Wheel trim rings. White sidewall tires. Dual wipers on fours. Cigar lighter in fours. Special paint. Radio and antenna. Inside rearview mirror. Outside rearview mirror. Four-cylinder 134.2 cid, 7.8:1 high-compression engine (no cost). Heavy-duty air cleaner was optional at extra cost.

**Paul Denski was issued this Army Jeep in March of 1953, during the Korean War.
Thankfully, Jeep and driver were reunited in the U.S.**

Willys-Overland celebrated its 50th anniversary in 1953. On April 28, 1953, Kaiser Motors Corporation, with the financial help of the Henry J. Kaiser Company, bought Willys-Overland Motors Inc. for just over $60.8 million. Edgar Kaiser, son of the legendary Henry J. Kaiser, was named president of the combined firms, while his father held the title of chairman of the board. One of the first steps taken by the new owners was to change the corporate title. The venerable Overland name was dropped and the organization was renamed Willys Motors Inc. The company became a division of Kaiser Motors Inc. Willy's Toledo plant underwent many

changes as Kaiser automobile production equipment was transferred from Kaiser's Willow Run plant in Michigan to the 5,200,000-sq. ft. Willys plant in Toledo. The Willow Run plant was sold to GM for $26 million.

The Sedan Delivery (panel delivery) wagon line added a four-wheel-drive model in response to requests from firms whose worksites were often far off road.

The most important Jeep vehicle this year was introduced on January 28, 1953. This was the more powerful CJ that Jeep engineers had been laboring on, the new Universal Jeep CJ-3B. The goal had been to fit the potent F-head four-cylinder engine from the larger Jeep products under the hood of the littlest Jeep, and that was accomplished. To save money, the engineers retained the CJ-3A's body tub, but fitted it with a new cowl and much taller hood. The overall look was somewhat awkward and a bit ungainly, but it provided the necessary clearance and the Universal Jeep CJ now offered 70hp—and that extra power is what consumers were hollering for. The Willys name was stamped on the grille and sides of the hood, not that anyone was likely to confuse the CJ-3B with a vehicle from any other company. Also this year, renewed marketing efforts were put into promoting the Farm Jeep.

The corporation reported that it had developed a new lightweight military product, the 1,400-lb. Aero Jeep, for use in airborne military operations. In addition, the company received contracts to develop a 700-lb. mechanized infantry weapons carrier. Other commercial products included new specialized mail delivery vehicles, and front line ambulance models based on a lengthened Jeep chassis that could carry three litter patients. There were two mail carriers being tested, one built on a Utility wagon chassis, the other on a Universal Jeep chassis fitted with a specially built all-steel cab.

The Kaiser affiliation dragged down the earnings of the corporation for the year. Kaiser Motors Corp. and its subsidiaries (including Willys Motors) lost a staggering $27 million during 1953. Willys Vice President of Engineering Delmar Barney Roos resigned before the year was out. Late in the year, Willys reached an agreement with Mitsubishi of Japan granting them the rights to manufacture Jeep CJ-3Bs in that country. Few would have guessed at that time that Mitsubishi would end up producing Jeep vehicles for more than 40 years.

NOTABLE FOR 1953: The CJ-3B bowed as an additional civilian model for 1953. It was similar to the CJ-3A, but had a raised hood and grille to fit the 70-hp "Hurricane" four F-head

engine. Willys lettering appeared on the front and sides of the hood.

I.D. DATA: Serial number located on plate at left side of driver's seat on floor riser on right side of dash under hood in CJ-3A/CJ-3B; on left side of dash under hood on Model 473 trucks. Serial numbers: (CJ-3B open) 453-GB2-10,001 to 37,550; (CJ-3B Farm) 453-GC2-10,001 & up; (CJ-3A) 453-GB1-10,001 & up; (4x2 Sedan Delivery) 453-CA2-10,001 to 12,347; (4x4 Sedan Delivery) 453-RA2-10,001 to 10,992; (4x4 chassis) 453-EB2-10,001 to 11,516; (4x4 pickup) 453-EC2-10,001 to 24,128 and (4x4 stake) 453-ED2-10,001 to 10,694. Engine numbers located on right side of cylinder block; stamped on water pump boss on front of cylinder block. Beginning around 1951 and continuing through at least 1953, each model had a specific serial number prefix such as 451-4GC. The first number indicated the number of cylinders. The second and third numbers indicated model year. Letters indicated the model code. The fourth number indicated series in any one model year. On most Jeep models the engine and serial numbers were the same. **Station wagon I.D. number locations:** on a plate at the left of the driver's seat on the floor riser; on left door sill; on frame front cross member ahead of front spring hanger; on front frame cross member at center; on right side of cowl below hood; on inside of frame on left. Serial numbers took the format 453-AA2-10001. First symbol indicates type of engine: 4=four-cylinder; 6=six-cylinder. Second and third symbols indicate model year: 53=1953. Next group of symbols is a series code: FA2=second series 4x4 station wagon. Model 475 station wagon models began at 453-AA2-10001 and went up to 453-AA2-14747. Model 4X475 station wagons began at 453-FA2-10001 and went up to 453-FA2-20631. Model 685 Deluxe station wagons began at 685-AA2-10001 and went up to 685-AA2-17548. The engine number was the same as the serial number and was located on the top of the water pump boss, at the right front upper corner of the engine block.

The CJ-3B replaced the CJ-3A in 1953.

Model	Body Type	Price	Weight
Willys Jeep — 1/4-Ton — Four-cyl — 4x4			
CJ-3A	Jeep Universal	$1,352	2,108 lbs.
CJ-3B	Jeep Universal	$1,377	2,134 lbs.
CJ-3B	Farm Jeep	$1,439	2,134 lbs.
Jeep Sedan Delivery — 1/2-Ton — Four-cyl — 4x2			
475	Sedan Delivery	$1,469	2,620 lbs.
Jeep Sedan Delivery — 1/2-Ton — Four-cyl — 4x4			
475SD	Sedan Delivery	$1,920	2,976 lbs.
Jeep Trucks — 1-Ton — Four-cyl — 4x4			
475	Chassis & Cab	$1,712	2,799 lbs.
475	Pickup	$1,805	3,115 lbs.
475	Platform Stake	$1,870	3,356 lbs.
Willys Jeep Station Wagon — Four-cyl			
475SW	2d Sta Wag-6	$1,750	2,818 lbs.
4x475	2d 4x4 Sta Wag-6	$2,134	3,174 lbs.
Willys Jeep Station Wagon — Six-cyl			
685	2d Sta Wag-6P	$1,786	2,850 lbs.

This famous picture shows four military Jeep vehicles. Left to right they are: the Willys Quad prototype, Jeep MB, Jeep MC (M38), and Jeep MD (M38-A1).

PRODUCTION: Kaiser Motors fiscal year was the same as the calendar year, ending December 31, 1953. For the year production totaled 75,759 Jeep vehicles (estimated).

ENGINES

(CJ-3A FOUR): Inline. L-head. Cast-iron block. Bore & stroke: 3 1/8 in. x 4 3/8 in. Displacement: 134.2 cid. Compression ratio: 6.48:1. Brake hp: 60 at 4000 rpm. Net hp: 15.63 (NACC). Torque: 105 lbs.-ft. at 2000 rpm. Three main bearings. Solid valve lifters. Carburetor: Carter-type model YF models 938S; 938SA.

(CJ-3B FOUR): Inline. F-head. Cast-iron block. Bore & stroke: 3 1/8 in. x 4 3/8 in. Displacement: 134.2 cid. Compression ratio: 6.90:1. Brake hp: 70 at 4000 rpm. Net hp: 15.63 (NACC). Torque: 114 lbs.-ft. at 2000 rpm. Three main bearings. Solid valve lifters. Carburetor: Carter-type YF model 951S.

(475 FOUR): Inline. F-head. Cast-iron block. Bore & stroke: 3 1/8 in. x 4 3/8 in. Displacement: 134.2 cid. Compression ratio: 7.40:1. Brake hp: 72 at 4000 rpm. Net hp: 15.63. Torque: 114 lbs.-ft. at 2000 rpm. Three main bearings. Solid valve lifters. Carburetor: Carter-type YF model 951S.

(685 STATION WAGON SIX): Inline. F-head. Cast-iron block. Exhaust valves in the engine block and intake valves in the cylinder head. Displacement: 161.1 cid. Bore and stroke: 3.13 x 3.50 in. Compression ratio: 7.6:1. Brake hp: 90 at 4400 rpm. Carburetor: Carter YS-924S single-barrel. Four main bearings. Solid valve lifters.

CHASSIS

(CJ-3A/CJ-3B): Wheelbase: 80 1/16 in. Length: 129-7/8 in. Height: 67 1/4 in. Front and rear tread: 48 7/16 in. Tires: 6.00 x 16.

(SEDAN DELIVERY 4x2): Wheelbase: 104 in. Length: 176 1/4 in. Height: 73.62 in. Front and rear tread: 57 in. Tires: (4x2) 6.70 x 15.

(SEDAN DELIVERY 4x4): Wheelbase: 104 1/2 in. Length: 176 1/4 in. Height: 73.62 in. Front and rear tread: 57 in. Tires: (4x4) 7.00 x 15

(TRUCKS 4x4): Wheelbase: 118 in. Length: 183.7 in. Height: 74.3 in. Front and rear.

(STATION WAGON): Wheelbase: (4x475 station wagons) 104.5 in.; (other models) 104 in. Overall length: (wagons) 176.25 in.; (other models) 180 7/8 inches. Tires: (4x475 station wagons) 7.00 x 15 in.; (4x2 station wagons).

TECHNICAL

Synchromesh transmission. Speeds: 3F/1R Floor-mounted gearshift. Single-plate clutch. Hypoid rear axle. Overall ratio: 5.38:1. Four-wheel hydraulic brakes. Disc wheels. 4x2 models have I-beam front axle. 4x4 models have full-floating hypoid front axle. All models have semi-floating hypoid rear axle.

OPTIONS

(CJ): Power take-off. Pulley drive. Motor governor. Soft top. Hydraulic lift. Metal top.

(4x4 TRUCKS): Power take-off. Pulley drive. Motor governor. Rearview mirror. Side-mount spare on pickups/stakes. Chrome bumper. License frame.

(SEDAN DELIVERY): Chrome front bumper. Chrome rear bumper. License frame. Chrome wheel disc. Bumperettes. Bumper guards. Wheel trim rings. Whitewall tires. Rearview mirror. Radio and antenna.

(STATION WAGON): Front bumper guards. Rear bumper guards. Front grille guard. License plate frames. Large wheel discs. Wheel trim rings. White sidewall tires. Dual wipers on four-cylinders. Cigar lighter in four-cylinders. Special paint. Radio and antenna. Inside rearview mirror. Outside rearview mirror.

**The M170 was considered a "front-line" ambulance; it was small and highly maneuverable.
This vehicle is owned by Gary Keating.**

The Universal Jeep CJ-3A went out of production. However, the new CJ-3B was not destined to be the sole Universal-type offering for very long, because in September Willys Motors unveiled an all-new and greatly improved civilian Jeep. This was designated as the Universal Jeep CJ-5 and it would go on to become one of the most legendary Jeep vehicles of all time.

The new CJ-5 was better than previous small Jeeps in just about every way. It utilized the same 70-hp Hurricane Four as the CJ-3B, but featured a longer 81-in. wheelbase, cleaner styling, larger and more comfortable interior, and better riding qualities. Based on the military M38-A1, the CJ-5 retained the cowl-mounted battery box and even used the military style hood, though a sheet metal cover was placed over the slot where the deep-fording kit's air snorkel would go.

This year Willys was also able to upgrade the engine power on the Jeep four-wheel-drive wagons and four-wheel-drive pick-ups. People were complaining that the old 161-cid/90-hp Hurricane Six wasn't powerful enough,

so it was replaced in the four-wheel-drive wagons and trucks by a new six dubbed the Super Hurricane. The Super Hurricane was the same 226-cid six-cylinder used in Kaiser automobiles. With 115 hp, it provided the extra grunt consumers were looking for.

**The CJ-3B was an improvement over the CJ-3A, with
more power than before.**

The Jeep pickups and station wagon models also saw minor changes in the grille. The grilles now had three horizontal grille bars instead of five. New two-tone color treatments were introduced.

There was a bit of change in nomenclature this year. The Jeep station wagon was now referred to as the Utility Wagon, the delivery wagon became the Utility Delivery and the Jeep truck became the Utility Truck.

Realizing that the fate of the automotive division rested on the success of its commercial lines, the company launched a major effort to train the sales force on how to operate and sell the many work implements offered for Jeep vehicles. The company recognized that knowledge of the many commercial uses for Jeep

With its tall hood and flat front fenders, the CJ-3B is easy to identify.

vehicles would lead to greater Jeep sales. This training helped many of the Kaiser dealers to become successful Jeep dealers.

Willys-Overland do Brasil was established in Sao Paulo during the year. This operation would eventually grow to become the largest overseas Jeep affiliate, with production sometimes rivaling that of the home plant. Continuing its efforts to sell its products globally via local assembly affiliates, Willys set up Industrias Kaiser Argentina during 1955 to produce a full line of Jeep vehicles, plus Kaiser passenger cars.

The company suffered another big financial hit this year, losing $35 million on total sales of $213 million. However, integration of the Kaiser and Willys operations was beginning to yield important benefits and management estimated that business for the first quarter of 1955 would be profitable.

NOTABLE FOR 1954: The three Universal Jeeps offered this season were CJ-3B models. The engine was the F-head four-cylinder. On truck and wagon models the grille had only three bright metal moldings, running horizontally across the top, middle, and bottom. All pickup trucks were 4x4s. There were new six-cylinder truck models powered by a 115-hp L-head engine dubbed the "Super Hurricane Six."

I.D. DATA: Serial number located on right side of dash under hood; on front frame cross-member; on left floor riser in back of driver's seat. Serial numbers: (CJ-5 chassis) 54-10,001 to 12,600 and 454-GA2-10,601 up;

The rugged 1954 1-ton four-wheel-drive Willys Pickup could be purchased new for less than $2,000.

(CJ-3B-OB) 54-10,001 to 12,600 and 454-GB2-12,001 up; (454-GC2) 10,001 to 10,012; (454-FA2) 10,001 to 13,528; (454-EC2) 10,001 to 13,606; (454-ED2) 10,001 to 10,185; (454-EB2) 10,001 to 10,681; (654-CA2) 10,001 to 10,308; (654-EC2) 10,001 to 14,927; (654-EB2) 10,001 to 10,439; (654-RA2) 10,001 to 10,243 and (654-FA2) 10,001 to 13,528. Engine numbers located on right side of cylinder block and stamped on water pump boss on front of cylinder block. On most Jeep models, the engine and serial numbers are the same. Station Wagon I.D. numbers: on a plate at the left of the driver's seat on the floor riser; on left door sill; on frame front cross-member ahead of front spring hanger; on front frame cross-member at center; on right side of cowl below hood; on inside of frame on left. Serial numbers took the format 454-FA2-10001. First symbol indicates type of engine: 4=four-cylinder; 6=six-cylinder. Second and third symbols indicate model year: 54=1954. Next group of symbols is a series code: FA2=4x2 station wagon; AA2=4x4 station wagon. Beginning and ending serial numbers according to model were: (four-cylinder 4x2 station wagon) 454-FA2-10001 to 454-FA2-5047; (4x2 station wagon with Willys six-cylinder) AA2-10001 to AA2-10945; (4x2 station wagon with Kaiser six-cylinder) 6-226-FA2-10001 to 6-226-FA2-12645. The engine number was the same as the serial number and was located on the top of the water pump boss, at the right front upper corner of the engine block.

The greatly improved Jeep CJ-5 debuted in the fall of 1954, and remained in production into the 1980s.

Model	Body Type	Price	Weight
Willys Jeep — 1/4-Ton — Four-cyl — 4x4			
CJ-3B	Chassis	$1,145	1,718 lbs.
CJ-3B	Jeep Universal	$1,377	2,306 lbs.
CJ-3B	Farm Jeep	$1,439	2,184 lbs.
CJ-5	Jeep	$1,476	2,164 lbs.
Jeep Sedan Delivery — 1/2-Ton — Four-cyl — 4x4			
454-CA2	Sedan Delivery	$1,520	2,711 lbs.
Jeep Trucks — 1-Ton — Four-cyl — 4x2			
454-EB2	Chassis & Cab	$1,712	2,774 lbs.
454-EC2	Pickup	$1,805	3,135 lbs.
454-ED2	Platform Stake	$1,870	3,356 lbs.

A fine 1954 M38-A1 owned by Eric Tedeschi.

Jeep Sedan Delivery — 1/2-Ton — Six-cyl — 4x4

654-RA2	Sedan Delivery	$2,009	3,055 lbs.

Jeep Trucks — 1-Ton — 6-cyl — 4x4

654-EB2	Chassis & Cab	$1,802	2,850 lbs.
654-EC2	Pickup	$1,895	3,141 lbs.
654-ED2	Platform Stake	$1,960	3,362 lbs.

Jeep Station Wagons

454	2d Sta Wag-6P	$2,134	3,115 lbs.
654	2d Sta Wag-6P	$1,808	2,381 lbs.
6-226	2d Del 4x4 Sta Wag	$2,223	3,278 lbs.

PRODUCTION: Kaiser Motors fiscal year was the same as the calendar year, ending December 31, 1954. For the year, production totaled 46,002 Jeep vehicles (estimated).

ENGINES

(CJ-3B FOUR): Inline. F-head. Cast-iron block. Bore & stroke: 3 1/8 in. x 4 3/8 in. Displacement: 134.2 cid. Compression ratio: 6.90:1. Brake hp: 70 at 4000 rpm. Torque: 114 lbs.-ft. at 2000 rpm. Three main bearings. Solid valve lifters. Carburetor: Carter YF model 938S or 938SA one-barrel.

(454 SEDAN DELIVERY/TRUCK FOUR): Inline. F-head. Cast-iron block. Bore & stroke: 3 1/8 in. x 4 3/8 in. Displacement: 134.2 cid. Compression ratio: 7.40:1. Brake hp: 72 at 4000 rpm. Net hp: 15.63. Torque: 114 lbs.-ft. at 2000 rpm. Three main bearings. Solid valve lifters. Carburetor: Carter YF model 951S one-barrel.

(654 SEDAN DELIVERY/STATION WAGON-/TRUCK SIX): Inline. F-head. Cast-iron block. Bore & stroke: 3 1/8 in. x 3 1/2 in. Displacement: 161.5 cid. Compression ratio: 7.6:1. Brake hp: 90 at 4200 rpm. Net hp: 23.44. Max. Torque: 135 lbs.-ft. at 2000 rpm. Four main bearings. Solid valve lifters. Carburetor: Carter YF model 924S or 2071S one-barrel.

(6-226 STATION WAGON SIX): Inline. L-head. Cast-iron block. Bore & stroke: 3 5/16 in. x 4 3/8 in. Displacement: 226.2 cid. Compression ratio: 6.86:1. Brake hp: 115 at 3650 rpm. Net hp: 26.3. Torque: 190 lbs.-ft. at 1800 rpm. Four main bearings. Solid valve lifters. Carburetor: Carter WDG model 2052S or 2052SA one-barrel.

CHASSIS

(CJ-3B): Wheelbase: 80 1/16 in. Length: 129 7/8 in. Height: 67 1/4 in. Front and rear tread: 48 7/16 in. Tires: 6.00 x 16.

(SEDAN DELIVERY 4x2): Wheelbase: 104 in. Length: 176 1/4 in. Height: 73.62 in. Front and rear tread: 57 in. Tires: 6.70 x 15.

(SEDAN DELIVERY 4x4): Wheelbase: 104 1/2 in. Length: 176 1/4 in. Height: 73.62 in. Front and rear tread: 57 in. Tires: 7.00 x 15.

The CJ-5 had some major improvements and changes from its debut the previous year.

(TRUCKS 4x4): Wheelbase: 118 in. Length: 183.7 in. Height: 74.3 in. Front and rear tread: 57 in. Tires: 7.00 x 15 in.

(STATION WAGON): Wheelbase: (654 four-wheel-drive station wagon) 104.5 in.; (other models) 104 in. Overall length: (654 four-wheel-drive station wagon) 176.25 in.; (other models) 176.25 in. Tires: (four-wheel-drive station wagons) 7.00 x 15 in.; (other models) 6.70 x 15 tube-type blackwall.

TECHNICAL

Synchromesh transmission. Speeds: 3F/1R. Floor-mounted gearshift. Single-plate clutch. Overall ratio: 5.38:1. Four-wheel hydraulic brakes. Disc wheels. 4x2 models had I-beam front axle. 4x4 models have full-floating hypoid front axle and two-speed transfer case All models have semi-floating hypoid rear axle.

OPTIONS

(CJ): Power take-off. Pulley drive. Motor governor. Soft top. Hydraulic lift . Metal top. **(4x4 TRUCKS):** Power take-off. Pulley drive. Motor governor. Rearview mirror. Sidemount spare on pickups/stakes. Chrome bumper. License frame.

(SEDAN DELIVERY): Chrome front bumper. Chrome rear bumper. License frame. Chrome wheel disc. Bumperettes. Bumper guards. Wheel trim rings. Whitewall tires. Rearview mirror. Radio and antenna.

(STATION WAGON): Front bumper guards. Rear bumper guards. Front grille guard. License plate frames. Large wheel discs. Wheel trim rings. White sidewall tires. Special paint. Radio and antenna. Inside rearview mirror. Outside rearview mirror.

In 1955, as today, red was a very popular color for Jeeps. This is a CJ-5.

Willys' big news this year was the new Universal Jeep CJ-5 announced during the previous fall season. CJ-5's better styling looked especially appealing when showcased next to a CJ-3B. Beyond looks, however, the CJ-5 was simply a more capable vehicle. Willys Motors placed extra emphasis on offering a broad line of work equipment for the CJ-5. Included were: a forklift hydraulic loader, post hole digger, trench digger, arc welding equipment, snow plows, and a vast array of farm implements.

Willys engineers searched constantly for new uses for Jeep vehicles, then quickly brought specialized Jeep variations to market. By 1955 the lineup of specialized Jeep vehicles was extensive, and included a four-wheel-drive utility ambulance built on the Sedan Delivery body, and a bigger ambulance on the longer 118-in. wheelbase truck chassis fitted with a much larger, specially built body. Also on the 118-in. wheelbase was an open-top cargo/personnel carrier. Jeep CJ-5 was offered in a special "crash wagon" version for airports and oil refineries. It was fitted with a 40-gallon foam-type

fire extinguisher, 50-foot hose, handheld extinguishers, and other fire suppression equipment. A CJ fire engine was also offered, as well as a larger "Commando" four-wheel-drive fire truck based on the Willys truck chassis. Winches were available on all Jeep four-wheel-drive models, and Jeep CJs could be fitted with steel half cabs or full cabs. There was even a bed extension offered for CJs with an extra 6 sq. ft. of floor space.

Total Willys sales volume for the year was $160 million. In 1955, Willys ceased production of passenger cars. The division's future rested solely on the success of Jeep.

NOTABLE FOR 1955: The civilian CJ-5 introduced in September 1954 was a greatly improved vehicle. The entirely new body and chassis featured lower door openings, recessed headlights, and an 81-in. wheelbase. Front fenders had curved front edges. Trucks used the same grille that debuted in 1954. Willys Motors stopped production of conventional passenger cars (Willys Aero). The company was intent on building its image as a truck maker.

I.D. DATA: Serial number located on right side of dash under hood; on front frame cross-member; on left floor riser in back of driver's seat. Serial numbers began with "55" (1955) or "54" (1954 carryover), followed by three digits designating a specific model. Next came a hyphen and four or five digits indicating production sequence. Starting: (all) 5001. Ending: numbers are not available. A typical serial number looked like this: 55268-5001. The 55268 designated the model number (see chart below) and the 5001 was the beginning sequential number. Engine numbers located on right side of cylinder block; stamped on water pump boss on front of cylinder block. On most Jeep models the engine and serial numbers are the same.

Model	Body Type	Price	Weight
Willys Jeep — 1/4-Ton — Four-cyl — 4x4			
CJ-3B	Jeep	$1,411	2,134 lbs.
Willys Jeep — 1/4-Ton — Four-cyl — 4x4			
CJ-5	Jeep	$1,476	2,164 lbs.
Sedan Delivery — 1/2-Ton — Four-cyl — 4x2			
475	Sedan Delivery	$1,494	2,786 lbs.
Utility Wagon — 1/2-Ton — Four-cyl — 4x2			
475	Utility Wagon	$1,748	3,009 lbs.
Sedan Delivery — 1/2-Ton — Six-cyl — 4x2			
685	Sedan Delivery	$1,545	2,633 lbs.
Sedan Delivery — 1/2-Ton — Six-cyl — 4x4			
6-226	Sedan Delivery	$2,036	3,055 lbs.
Trucks — 1-Ton — Six-cyl — 4x2			
6-226	Chassis & Cab	$1,833	2,782 lbs.
6-226	Pickup	$1,927	3,141 lbs.
6-226	Platform Stake	$1,992	3,355 lbs.
Sedan Delivery — Six-cyl — 4x2			
6-226	Sedan Delivery	$1,584	2,890 lbs.
Utility Wagon — 1/2-Ton — Six-cyl — 4x2			
6-226	Utility Wagon	$1,837	3,113 lbs.

PRODUCTION: Kaiser Motors fiscal year was the same as the calendar year, ending December 31, 1955. For the year, production totaled 64,166 Jeep vehicles (estimated).

ENGINES

(CJ-3B/CJ-5 FOUR): Inline. F-head. Cast-iron block. Bore & stroke: 3 1/8 in. x 4 3/8 in. Displacement: 134.2 cid. Compression ratio: 6.9:1. Brake hp: 70 at 4000 rpm. Torque: 114 lbs.-ft. at 2000 rpm. Three main bearings. Solid valve lifters. Carburetor: Carter YF model 938S or 938SA one-barrel.

(475 SEDAN DELIVERY/UTILITY WAGON FOUR): Inline. F-head. Four-cylinder. Cast-iron block. Bore & stroke: 3 1/8 in. x 4 3/8 in. Displacement: 134.2 cid. Compression ratio: 7.4:1. Brake hp: 72 at 4000 rpm. Torque: 114 lbs.-ft. at 2000 rpm. Three main bearings. Solid valve lifters. Carburetor: Carter YF model 951S one-barrel.

(685 SEDAN DELIVERY SIX): Inline. F-head. Six-cylinder. Cast-iron block. Bore & stroke: 3 1/8 in. x 3 1/2 in. Displacement: 161.5 cid. Compression ratio: 7.6:1. Brake hp: 90 at 4200 rpm. Torque: 135 lbs.-ft. at 2000 rpm. Four main bearings. Solid valve lifters. Carburetor: Carter YF model 924S or 2071S one-barrel.

(6-226 SEDAN DELIVERY/TRUCK/UTILITY WAGON SIX): Inline. Six-cylinder. Cast-iron block. Bore & stroke: 3 5/16 in. x 4 3/8 in. Displacement: 226.2 cid. Compression ratio: 6.86:1. Brake hp: 115 at 3650 rpm. Torque: 190 lbs.-ft. at 1800 rpm. Four main bearings. Solid valve lifters. Carburetor: Carter WDG model 2052S or 2052SA one-barrel.

CHASSIS

(CJ-5): Wheelbase: 81 in. Length: 135 1/2 in. Height: 69 1/2 in. Front and rear tread: 48 7/16 in. Tires: 6.00 x 16.

(CJ-3B): Wheelbase: 80 1/16 in. Length: 129 7/8 in. Height: 67 1/4 in. Front and rear tread: 48 7/16 in. Tires: 6.00 x 16.

(SEDAN DELIVERY 4x2): Wheelbase: 104 in. Length: 176 1/4 in. Height: 73.62 in. Front and rear tread: 57 in. Tires: 6.70 x 15.

(SEDAN DELIVERY 4x4): Wheelbase: 104 1/2 in. Length: 176 1/4 in. Height: 73.62 in. Front and rear tread: 57 in. Tires: 7.00 x 15.

(TRUCKS 4x4): Wheelbase: 118 in. Length: 183.7 in. Height: 74.3 in. Front and rear tread: 57 in. Tires: 7.00 x 15.

(STATION WAGON): Wheelbase: (6-226 utility wagons) 104.5 in.; (685 models) 104 in. Overall length: 176.3 in. Tires: (6-226 utility wagons) 6.40 x 15 tube-type blackwall; (other models) 6.70 x 15 tube-type blackwall.

TECHNICAL

(CJ-5): Synchromesh transmission. Speeds: 3F/1R Floor-mounted gearshift. Single-plate clutch with torsional dampening, 72 sq. in. area. Full-floating hypoid front axle. Semi-floating hypoid rear axle. Overall ratio: 5.38:1. Two-speed transfer case. Bendix hydraulic 9-in. drum brakes. Five 4.50 x 16 five-stud disc wheels.

(OTHER MODELS): Synchromesh transmission. Speeds: 3F/1R. Floor-mounted gearshift. Single-plate clutch. Overall ratio: 5.38:1. Four-wheel hydraulic brakes. 4x2 models had I-beam front axle. 4x4 models have full-floating hypoid front axle and two-speed transfer case. All models have semi-floating hypoid rear axle.

OPTIONS

(CJ-3B): Power take-off. Pulley drive. Motor governor. Soft top. Hydraulic lift. Metal top.

(4x4 TRUCKS): Power take-off. Pulley drive. Motor governor. Rearview mirror. Sidemount spare on pickups/stakes. Chrome bumper. License frame.

(SEDAN DELIVERY): Chrome front bumper. Chrome rear bumper. License frame. Chrome wheel disc. Bumperettes. Bumper guards. Wheel trim rings. Whitewall tires. Rearview mirror. Radio and antenna.

(CJ-5): Five metal and fabric-top options. Ventilating windshield. Power take-off. Eight body color choices. Approved snow plow. Winch. 36 x 39 1/4 in. steel cargo box.

(UTILITY WAGON): Front bumper guards. Rear bumper guards. Front grille guard. License plate frames. Large wheel discs. Wheel trim rings. White sidewall tires. Dual wipers on fours. Cigar lighter in fours. Special paint. Radio and antenna. Inside rearview mirror. Outside rearview mirror.

In the 1955 calender year, Willys built 12,265 Station Wagons.

The middle grille bar on senior Jeeps was moved closer to the top of the grille for 1956.

Not surprisingly, no military Jeeps were produced during 1956. The world was enjoying a relatively peaceful year, so military orders were almost non-existent. However, Willys received contracts to produce 1,450 of its new "Mechanical Mule" mechanized Infantry Weapons Carrier vehicles. Production was scheduled to begin in 1957.

Willys Motors unveiled several new civilian models this year. Notable was the new CJ-6, based on the CJ-5 but sporting a longer 101-inch wheelbase for greater load-carrying ability. With two sideways-facing rear benches, the CJ-6 could carry up to eight people.

Also new were three two-wheel-drive models in the new Dispatcher (DJ) series. These vehicles were essentially two-wheel-drive versions of the former CJ-3A model and utilized an I-beam front axle and the old Go-Devil flathead four-cylinder engine. The DJ-3A basic model was an open roadster priced at just $1,205. The same vehicle with a soft top was priced at $1,261, and a hardtop version was priced at $1,397, making them America's lowest-priced delivery vehicles.

Grille bars on wagons and trucks were slightly different this year. The center horizontal bar moved up closer to the top bar. This year an I-beam axle became standard equipment on the senior Jeep two-wheel-drive models, and the old Willys Planadyne suspension was finally dropped.

There were big changes in the corporate structure during 1956. On March 13, the stockholders of Kaiser Motors Corporation approved a major restructuring of the company. The company name was changed to Kaiser Industries Corporation. The company then purchased the assets of the Henry J. Kaiser Company, along with its many subsidiaries, including Kaiser Sand & Gravel, Kaiser Engineers, Kaiser Steel Corp., Kaiser Aluminum, Kaiser Metals, and more. It brought under one umbrella all of these various Kaiser-related businesses, reducing in importance the role of Willys Motors. For the year, a profit of just under $15 million was reported for the entire corporation, of which $3,593,000 came from Willys Motors. Willys' sales volume for the year was $140 million.

NOTABLE FOR 1956: New from Willys this season was the Jeep CJ-6 4x4 and a new line of 4x2 models named Dispatchers. The CJ-6 was a stretched version of the CJ-5, with a 20-in.-longer wheelbase. The rear of the body was lengthened to add twin benches with room for up to eight people. The new Dispatcher DJ-3A models had old-style flat fenders. The front axle was a solid I-beam. Also new for 1955 was the addition of Sedan Delivery, Utility Wagon and Pickup models with four-cylinder engines and four-wheel-drive. Trucks with 4x4 running gear had "4-Wheel-Drive" identification on both sides of the hood. Four different engines were standard in specific models.

I.D. DATA: Serial number located on right side of dash under hood; on front frame cross-member; on left floor riser in back of driver's seat. Engine numbers located on right side of cylinder block; stamped on water pump boss on front of cylinder block. On most Jeep models the engine and serial numbers are the same.

Model	Body Type	Price	Weight
Willys Jeep — 1/4-Ton — Four-cyl — 4x4 — 80-in. w.b.			
CJ-3B	Jeep Universal	$1,503	2,134 lbs.
Willys Jeep — 1/4-Ton — Four-cyl — 4x4 — 81-in. w.b.			
CJ-5	Jeep Universal	$1,577	2,164 lbs.
Willys Jeep — 1/2-Ton — Four-cyl — 4x4 — 101-in. w.b.			
CJ-6	Jeep Universal	$1,731	2,305 lbs.
Dispatcher — 1/4-Ton — Four-cyl — 4x2 — 80-in. w.b.			
DJ-3A	Basic	$1,205	1,968 lbs.
DJ-3A	Canvas Top	$1,261	2,016 lbs.
DJ-3A	Hardtop	$1,397	2,205 lbs.
Jeep Trucks — 1/2-Ton — Four-cyl — 4x2 — 104.5-in. w.b.			
475	Utility Wagon	$2,012	2,944 lbs.
475	Sedan Delivery	$1,700	2,746 lbs.
Jeep Trucks — 1/2-Ton — Six-cyl — 4x2 — 104.5-in. w.b.			
L6-226	Utility Wagon	$2,118	3,057 lbs.
L6-226	Sedan Delivery	$2,311	2,859 lbs.
Jeep Trucks — 1/2-Ton — Four-cyl — 4x4 — 104.5-in. w.b.			
475	Sedan Delivery	$2,114	2,951 lbs.
475	Station Wagon	$2,287	3,174 lbs.
475	Pickup	$1,997	3,065 lbs.
Jeep Trucks — 1/2-Ton — Six-cyl — 4x4 — 104.5-in. w.b.			
L6-226	Sedan Delivery	$2,176	3,055 lbs.
L6-226	Station Wagon	$2,250	3,278 lbs.
Jeep Trucks — 1-Ton — Six-cyl — 4x4 — 118-in. w.b.			
L6-226	Pickup	$2,187	3,176 lbs.
L6-226	Stake	$2,118	3,341 lbs.

PRODUCTION: Kaiser Motors fiscal year was the same as the calendar year, ending December, 31, 1956. For the year production totaled 64,600 Jeep vehicles (estimated).

ENGINES

(CJ-3B/CJ-5 FOUR): Inline. F-head. Four-cylinder. Cast-iron block. Bore & stroke: 3 1/8 in. x 4 3/8 in. Displacement: 134.2 cid. Compression ratio: 6.9:1. Brake hp: 70 at 4000 rpm. Max. Torque: 114 lbs.-ft. at 2000 rpm. Three main bearings. Solid valve lifters. Carburetor: Carter YF models 938S or 938SA one-barrel.

(CJ-6/475 FOUR): Inline. F-head. Four-cylinder. Cast-iron block. Bore & stroke: 3 1/8 in. x 4 3/8 in. Displacement: 134.2 cid. Compression ratio: 7.4:1. Brake hp: 72 at 4,000 rpm. Torque: 114 lbs.-ft. at 2000 rpm. Three main bearings. Solid valve lifters. Carburetor: Carter YF models 938S or 938SA one-barrel.

(DJ-3 FOUR): Inline. L-head. Four-cylinder. Cast-iron block. Bore & stroke: 3 1/8 in. x 4 3/8 in. Displacement: 134 cid. Compression ratio: 7.4:1. Brake hp: 60 at 4000 rpm.

(6-226 SIX): Inline. L-head. Six-cylinder. Cast-iron block. Bore & stroke: 3 5/16 in. x 4 3/8 in. Displacement: 226.2 cid. Compression ratio: 6.86:1. Brake hp: 115 at 3650 rpm. Torque: 190 lbs.-ft. at 1800 rpm. Four main bearings. Solid valve lifters. Carburetor: Carter WDG

model 2052S or 2052SA one-barrel; Carter WCD model 2204S two-barrel.

CHASSIS

(CJ-3B): Wheelbase: 80 1/16 in. Length: 129 7/8 in. Height: 67 1/4 in. Front and rear tread: 48 7/16 in. Tires: 6.00 x 16.

(CJ-5): Wheelbase: 81 in. Length: 135 1/2 in. Height: 69 1/2 in. Front and rear tread: 48 7/16 in. Tires: 6.00 x 16.

(CJ-6): Wheelbase: 101 in. Length: 155 1/2 in. Height: 68 1/4 in. Front & rear tread: 48 7/16 in. Tires: 6.00 x 16.

(DJ-3): Wheelbase: 80.09 in. Length: 125 1/2 in. Height: 62 3/4 in. (windshield raised). Front and rear tread: 48.25 in. Tires: 6.50 x 15 four-ply tubeless.

(SEDAN DELIVERY 4x2): Wheelbase: 104 in. Length: 176 1/4 in. Height: 73 5/8 in. Front and rear tread: 57 in. Tires: 6.70 x 15.

(SEDAN DELIVERY 4x4): Wheelbase: 104 1/2 in. Length: 176 1/4 in. Height: 73 5/8 in. Front and rear tread: 57 in. Tires: 7.00 x 15.

(TRUCKS 4x4): Wheelbase: 118 in. Length: 183 3/4 in. Height: 74 1/3 in. Front and rear tread: 57 in. Tires: 7.00 x 15.

TECHNICAL

(ALL MODELS): Synchromesh transmission. Speeds: 3F/1R. Floor-mounted gearshift lever. Single-plate clutch. Hypoid semi-floating rear axle. Overall ratio: 3.54:1, 4.56:1 or 5.38:1. Four-wheel hydraulic brakes. Disc wheels. 4x2 models have I-beam type front axle. 4x4 models have full-floating hypoid front axle.

OPTIONS

(CJ): (CJs) Power take-off. Pulley drive. Motor governor. Soft top. Hydraulic lift. Metal top. (CJ-5): Five metal and fabric-top options. Ventilating windshield. Power take-off. Eight body color choices. Approved snow plow. Winch. All-steel cargo box (36 x 39 1/4 in.). (CJ-6): All-weather canvas tops. Oversize tires.

(DISPATCHER): (DJ-3A) Convertible top. 40 cu. ft. hardtop with 36 in. wide rear opening. Whitewall tires. Chrome wheel discs. Chrome front bumper. Chrome rear bumper. Eight standard body colors. "Law Enforcement" package.

(TRUCKS): (4x4 trucks) Power take-off. Pulley drive. Motor governor. Rearview mirror. Sidemount spare on pickups/stakes. Chrome bumper. License frame. (Sedan Delivery): Chrome front bumper. Chrome rear bumper. License frame. Chrome wheel discs. Bumperettes. Bumper guards. Wheel trim rings. Whitewall tires. Rearview mirror. Radio and antenna.

The 1957 FC-170 came in pickup, stake, and cab-and-chassis configurations.

In December of 1956, Willys Motors unveiled a line of excitingly new and dramatically different 1957 Jeep models. These were the uniquely styled Forward Control pickup trucks, a new range of commercial truck models. The first of the new trucks was the FC-150, on a short 81-in. wheelbase, with a 5,000-lb. GVW rating. In May this was joined by the FC-170, a 7,000-lb. GVW truck on a longer 103.5-in. wheelbase. Some automotive writers of the era said the FC trucks' unique styling looked very much like a miniature version of a highway tractor/trailer. One writer dubbed the styling the "helicopter look." However, Willys' advertisements referred to it as "up-front" styling.

Regardless how they were described, they were unusual looking. Rugged as anvils, the heavy-duty rigs were the first all-new Jeep pickups since the originals that debuted just after the war. Each series, FC-150 and FC-170, offered three models: pickup, stake, and cab & chassis. Available deluxe cab trim included: dual sun visors, dual arm rests, acoustical trim on the doors and headliner, foam rubber seats, cigarette lighter, and neat-looking rear quarter windows.

In an effort to dress up some of its other vehicles an optional one-piece windshield and lower roof panel became available for the line of Jeep station wagons. Other than that there were few changes to the old Jeep stand-bys. In September, production of the first Mechanical Mules (the M-274 model) began. Powered by a four-cylinder engine, the Mules were about 100 inches long, 46 in. wide, and weighed some 750 lbs. In all, 4,618 would be built from 1957-1965.

The division's sales were flat again this year, stalled at $140 million. Willys Motors' profit for the year, however, was up a bit, to $5 million. Output of 60,500 vehicles was down 5 percent from the previous year.

NOTABLE FOR 1957: The major innovation of 1957 was the Forward Control (FC) cab-over-engine pickup truck. Universal Jeeps available this year included the CJ-3B/CJ-5/CJ-6. None had significant changes. There were three Dispatchers. New truck models included 4x4 trucks in chassis-with-windshield and chassis-with-flat face-cowl configurations.

I.D. DATA: Serial number located on right side of dash under hood; on front frame cross-member; on left floor riser in back of driver's seat. Engine numbers located on right side of cylinder block; stamped on water pump boss on front of cylinder block. On most Jeep models the engine and serial numbers are the same.

Model	Body Type	Price	Weight
Willys Jeep — 1/4-Ton — Four-cyl — 4x4 — 80-in. w.b.			
CJ-3B	Jeep Universal	$1,799	2,132 lbs.
Willys Jeep — 1/4-Ton — Four-cyl — 4x4 — 81-in. w.b.			
CJ-5	Jeep Universal	$1,886	2,163 lbs.
Willys Jeep — 1/2-Ton — Four-cyl — 4x4 — 101-in. w.b.			
CJ-6	Jeep Universal	$2,068	2,225 lbs.
Dispatcher — 1/4-Ton — Four-cyl — 4x2 — 80-in. w.b.			
DJ-3A	Basic	$1,303	1,709 lbs.
DJ-3A	Soft Top	$1,363	1,769 lbs.
DJ-3A	Hardtop	$1,511	2,004 lbs.
Jeep Trucks — 1/2-Ton — Four-cyl — 4x2 — 104.5-in. w.b.			
F4-134	Delivery	$1,843	2,746 lbs.
F4-134	Utility Wagon	$2,152	2,944 lbs.
Jeep Trucks — 1-Ton — Four-cyl — 4x4 — 104.5-in. w.b.			
F4-134	Delivery	$2,391	2,895 lbs.
F4-134	Pickup	$2,256	3,065 lbs.
FC-150 — 1/2-Ton — Four-cyl — 4x4 — 81-in. w.b.			
FC-150	Chassis & Cab	$2,217	2,764 lbs.
FC-150	Pickup	$2,320	3,020 lbs.
FC-150	Stake	$2,410	3,187 lbs.
Jeep Trucks — 1/2-Ton — Six-cyl — 4x4 — 104.5-in. w.b.			
L6-226	Chassis	$1,822	1,963 lbs.
L6-226	Chassis & Cowl	$2,122	2,140 lbs.
L6-226	Delivery	$2,505	3,008 lbs.
L6-226	Utility Wagon	$2,265	3,057 lbs.
Jeep Trucks — 1/2-Ton — Six-cyl — 4x2 — 104.5-in. w.b.			
L6-226	Delivery	$1,958	2,859 lbs.
L6-226	Utility Wagon	$2,764	3,206 lbs.
Jeep Trucks — 1-Ton — Six-cyl — 4x4 — 118 in w.b.			
L6-226	Chassis	$1,824	2,127 lbs.
L6-226	Chassis & Cowl	$2124	2,237 lbs.
L6-226	Chassis & Windshield	$2,150	2,256 lbs.
L6-226	Chassis & Cab	$2,251	2,817 lbs.
L6-226	Pickup	$2,370	3,176 lbs.
L6-226	Stake	$2,453	3,341 lbs.
FC-170 — 1-Ton — Six-cyl — 4x4 — 103.5-in. w.b.			
FC-170	Chassis & Cab	$2,593	2,901 lbs.
FC-170	Pickup	$2,713	3,331 lbs.
FC-170	Stake	$2,896	3,564 lbs.

PRODUCTION: Kaiser Motors' fiscal year was the same as the calendar year, ending Dec 31st, 1957. For the year, the company reported production of 60,500 Jeep vehicles.

ENGINES

(CJ-3B/CJ-5 FOUR): Inline. F-head. Cast-iron block. Bore & stroke: 3 1/8 in. x 4 3/8 in. Displacement: 134.2 cid. Compression ratio: 6.9:1. Brake hp: 70 at 4000 rpm. Net hp: 15.63. Torque: 114 lbs.-ft. at 2000 rpm. Three main bearings. Solid valve lifters. Carburetor: Carter YF model 938S or 938SA.

(CJ6/F4-134 FOUR): Inline. F-head. Cast-iron block. Bore & stroke: 3 1/8 in. x 4 3/8 in. Displacement: 134.2 cid. Compression ratio: 7.4:1. Brake hp: 72 at 4000 rpm. Net hp: 15.63. Torque: 114 lbs.-ft. at 2000 rpm. Three main bearings. Solid valve lifters. Carburetor: Carter YF models 938S or 938SA one-barrel.

(DJ-3 FOUR): Inline. L-head. Cast-iron block. Bore & stroke: 3 1/8 in. x 4 3/8 in. Displacement: 134 cid. Compression ratio: 7.4:1. Brake hp: 60 hp

(FC-150 FOUR): Inline. L-head. Cast-iron block. Bore & stroke: 3 1/8 in. x 4 3/8 in. Displacement: 134.2 cid. Compression ratio: 7.40:1. Brake hp: 72 at 4000 rpm. Net hp: 15.63. Torque: 114 lbs.-ft. at 2000 rpm. Three main bearings. Solid valve lifters. Carburetor: Carter YF model 2392S one-barrel.

(6-226/FC-170 SIX): Inline. L-head. Six-cylinder. Cast-iron block. Bore & stroke: 3 5/16 in. x 4 3/8 in. Displacement: 226.2 cid. Compression ratio: 6.86:1. Brake hp: 115 at 3650 rpm. Net hp: 26.3. Torque: 190 lbs.-ft. at 1800 rpm. Four main bearings. Solid valve lifters. Carburetor: Carter WDG model 2052S or 2052SA one-barrel; Carter WC model 2204S two-barrel.

CHASSIS

(CJ-3B): Wheelbase: 80 1/16 in. Length: 129 7/8 in. Height: 67 1/4 in. Front and rear tread: 48 7/16 in. Tires: 6.00 x 16.

(CJ-5): Wheelbase: 81 in. Length: 135 1/2 in. Height: 69 1/2 in. Front and rear tread: 48 7/16 in. Tires: 6.00 x 16.

(CJ-6): Wheelbase: 101 in. Length: 155 1/2 in. Height: 68 1/4 in. Front and rear tread: 48 7/16 in. Tires: 6.00 x 16 in. all-service type.

(DJ-3): Wheelbase: 80.09 in. Length: 125.45 in. Height: 62.74 in. (windshield raised). Front and rear tread: 48.25 in. Tires: 6.50 x 15 four-ply tubeless.

(SEDAN DELIVERY 4x2): Wheelbase: 104 in. Length: 176 1/4 in. Height: 73 5/8 in. Front and rear tread: 57 in. Tires: 6.70 x 15.

(SEDAN DELIVERY 4x4): Wheelbase: 104 1/2 in. Length: 176 1/4 in. Height: 73 5/8 in. Front and rear tread: 57 in. Tires: 7.00 x 15.

(TRUCKS 4x4): Wheelbase: 118 in. Length: 183 3/4 in. Height: 74 1/3 in. Front and rear tread: 57 in. Tires: 7.00 x 15.

(FC-150): Wheelbase: 81 in. Length: 147 1/2 in. Height: 77 3/8 in. Front tread: 48 1/4 in. Rear tread: 48 1/4 in. Tires: 7.00 x 15 four-ply All-Service.

(FC-170): Wheelbase: 103 5/8 in. Length: 203 in. Height: 79 1/8 in. Front tread: 63 1/2 in. Rear tread: 63 1/2 in. Tires: 7.00 x 16 six-ply.

TECHNICAL

(ALL EXCEPT FC): Synchromesh transmission. Speeds: 3F/1R. Floor-mounted gearshift. Single-plate clutch. Hypoid semi-floating rear axle. Overall ratio: 3.54:1, 4.56:1, or 5.38:1. Four-wheel hydraulic brakes. Disc wheels. 4x2 models have I-beam type front axle. 4x4 models have full-floating hypoid front axle and two-speed transfer case.

(FC): Synchromesh transmission. Speeds: 3F/1R (four-speed optional). Floor-mounted gearshift. Single-plate, dry-disc clutch (heavy-duty on FC-170). Rear axle: (FC-150) semi-floating hypoid; (FC-170) full-floating hypoid rear axle. Overall axle ratio: (FC-150) 5.38:1; (FC-170) 4.89:1. Four-wheel hydraulic brakes (heavy-duty on FC-170). Disc wheels (dual rear available on FC-170).

OPTIONS

(CJ-5): Five metal and fabric-top options. Ventilating windshield. Power take-off. Eight body color choices. Approved snowplow. Winch. 36 x 39 1/4-in. steel cargo box.

(CJs): Power take-off. Pulley drive. Motor governor. Soft top. Hydraulic lift. Metal top.

(4x4 TRUCKS): Power take-off. Pulley drive. Motor governor. Rearview mirror. Side-mount spare on pickups/stakes. Chrome bumper. License frame.

(SEDAN DELIVERY): Chrome front bumper. Chrome rear bumper. License frame. Chrome wheel disc. Bumperettes. Bumper guards. Wheel trim rings. Whitewall tires. Rearview mirror. Radio and antenna.

(CJ-6): All-weather soft tops. Oversize tires.

DISPATCHER: (DJ-3A) Convertible top. Hardtop with 36-in.-wide gate opening. Whitewall tires. Chrome wheel discs. Chrome front bumper. Chrome rear bumper. Eight standard body colors. "Law Enforcement" package.

FC-150/170: Fresh air heater. Radio. Tu-tone paint. Front bumper guards. Direction signals. E-Z-Eye glass. Windshield washer. Front air vent. Double passenger seat. Oil bath air cleaner. Oil filter. High-altitude cylinder head (no charge). Four-speed transmission. Power-Lok differential. Heavy-duty rear axle. Heavy-duty springs and shocks. Transmission brake. Hot climate radiator. Power take-off (center and rear). Governor. Various size/type tires. Draw-bar. Stabilizer bar. Rear bumperettes. Selective drive hubs. Bed and/or front-mount winch. Snow plow. Dozer blade. Wrecker equipment. Jeep-A-Trench. Service bodies.

Roy Rogers and Dale Evans were Jeep fans and owned a Jeep they named Nelly Belle.

There were not very many changes to the Jeep line this year. By 1958, 12-volt electrical systems had become standard equipment in Jeep vehicles.

Jeep was still almost by itself in the marketplace, with no real domestic competitor in four-wheel-drive wagons and not very much in the four-wheel-drive truck segment. The CJ (or Universal, as the company preferred to call it) was utterly unique—no one else had anything like it. So, despite the fact that the trucks and wagons were getting a bit long in the tooth, Jeep's competitive situation was still acceptable. Total unit sales over the

59

previous two years were not all that good, but in retrospect a great deal of that probably had to do with the fewer number of dealers Jeep had, and buyers' concern caused by the cessation of Willys and Kaiser car production.

However, as a result of efforts to strengthen and improve its dealer organization, Jeep sales increased sharply in the latter half of 1958. Unit sales were at the highest level since 1955. Kaiser Industries reported that Willys Motors Inc. was the third-largest producer of commercial vehicles in the United States in 1958. In addition, the division retained its title as the world's largest producer of four-wheel-drive vehicles.

One competitive disadvantage Jeep faced was that it continued to lag behind consumers' desire for more power. The F-head four was certainly an improvement over the old Go-Devil, but it didn't provide as much guts as many people wanted. The situation was similar with the six-cylinder trucks and wagons. The improved output from the 226 engine was nice, but the hot item in the 1950s was the V-8 engine, and no one got excited about a six no matter how much power it had. Jeep could get by for the time being with what it had, but a day would come when it would have to face the problem.

At times during 1958, Willys Motors actually seemed to be more active overseas than in the U.S. In February, the company announced a $3 million Jeep order for India, and in March a new Australian affiliate produced its first Jeep vehicles. Willys-Overland do Brazil announced a $22 million expansion project in July, which by 1960 would boost annual output to 60,000 units—close to what the Toledo operation was producing and a remarkable level for an affiliate.

For the year Willys Motors sales volume was $136.6 million, and profits rose to $6.8 million.

NOTABLE FOR 1958: This year saw only minor refinements. The chassis/cab models were no longer cataloged, except in the L-226 1-ton truck and the FC Series.

I.D. DATA: Serial number located on right side of dash under hood; on front frame cross-member; on left floor riser in back of driver's seat. Engine numbers located on right side of cylinder block; stamped on water pump boss on front of cylinder block. On most Jeep models the engine and serial numbers are the same.

Model	Body Type	Price	Weight
Willys Jeep — 1/4-Ton — Four-cyl — 4x4 — 80-in. w.b.			
CJ-3B	Jeep Universal	$1,888	2,132 lbs.
Willys Jeep — 1/4-Ton — Four-cyl — 4x4 — 81-in. w.b.			
CJ-5	Jeep Universal	$1,979	2,163 lbs.
Willys Jeep — 1/2-Ton — Four-cyl — 4x4 — 101-in. w.b.			
CJ-6	Jeep Universal	$2,171	2,225 lbs.
Dispatcher — 1/4-Ton — Four-cyl — 4x2 — 80-in. w.b.			
DJ-3A	Basic	$1,367	1,709 lbs.
DJ-3A	Soft Top	$1,430	1,769 lbs.
DJ-3A	Hardtop	$1,586	2,004 lbs.

Jeep Trucks — 1/2-Ton — Four-cyl — 4x2 — 104.5-in. w.b.			
FA-134	Delivery	$1,934	2,746 lbs.
FA-134	Utility Wagon	$2,152	2,944 lbs.
Jeep Trucks — 1/2-Ton — Four-cyl — 4x4 — 104.5-in. w.b.			
4F-134	Delivery	$2,510	2,893 lbs.
4F-134	Utility Wagon	$2,654	3,093 lbs.
Jeep Trucks — 1-Ton — Four-cyl — 4x4 — 118-in. w.b.			
4F-134	Pickup	$2,367	3,065 lbs.
FC Forward Control — 1/2-Ton — Four-cyl — 4x4 — 81-in. w.b.			
FC-150	Chassis	$2,327	2,764 lbs.
FC-150	Pickup	$2,444	3,020 lbs.
FC-150	Stake	$2,545	3,187 lbs.
Jeep Trucks — 1/2-Ton — Six-cyl — 4x2 — 104.5-in. w.b.			
L6-226	Delivery	$2,055	2,859 lbs.
L6-226	Utility Wagon	$2,265	3,057 lbs.
Jeep Trucks — 1/2-Ton — Six-cyl — 4x4 — 104.5-in. w.b.			
L6-226	Delivery	$2,630	3,008 lbs.
L6-226	Utility Wagon	$2,764	3,206 lbs.
Jeep Trucks — 1-Ton — Six-cyl — 4x2 — 118-in. w.b.			
L6-226	Chassis & Cab	$2,363	2,817 lbs.
L6-226	Pickup	$2,488	3,176 lbs.
L6-226	Stake	$2,575	3,341 lbs.
Forward Control — 1-Ton — Six-cyl — 4x4 — 103.5-in. w.b.			
FC-170	Chassis & Cab	$2,722	2,901 lbs.
FC-170	Pickup	$2,858	3,331 lbs.
FC-170	Stake	$3,065	3,200 lbs.

PRODUCTION: Jeep didn't disclose production for the year, but it has been estimated that 43,303 civilian Jeeps were produced in the U.S.

ENGINES

(CJ-3B/CJ-5 FOUR): Inline. F-head. Cast-iron block. Bore & stroke: 3 1/8 in. x 4 3/8 in. Displacement: 134.2 cid. Compression ratio: 6.9:1. Brake hp: 70 at 4000 rpm. Torque: 114 lbs. ft. at 2000 rpm. Three main bearings. Solid valve lifters. Carburetor: Carter YF models 938S or 938SA.

(CJ6/F4-134 FOUR): Inline. F-head. Cast-iron block. Bore & stroke: 3 1/8 in. x 4 3/8 in. Displacement: 134.2 cid. Compression ratio: 7.4:1. Brake hp: 72 at 4000 rpm. Torque: 114 lbs. ft. at 2000 rpm. Three main bearings. Solid valve lifters. Carburetor: Carter YF models 938S or 938SA one-barrel.

(DJ-3 FOUR): Inline. L-head. Cast-iron block. Bore & stroke: 3 1/8 in. x 4 3/8 in. Displacement: 134 cid. Compression ratio: 7.4:1. Brake hp: 60.

(FC-150 FOUR): Inline. L-head. Cast-iron block. Bore & stroke: 3 1/8 in. x 4 3/8 in. Displacement: 134.2 cid. Compression ratio: 7.40:1. Brake hp: 72 at 4000 rpm. Torque: 114 lbs.-ft. at 2000 rpm. Three main bearings. Solid valve lifters. Carburetor: Carter YF model 2392S one-barrel.

(6-226/FC-170 SIX): Inline. L-head. Six-cylinder. Cast-iron block. Bore & stroke: 3 5/16 in. x 4 3/8 in. Displacement: 226.2 cid. Compression ratio: 6.86:1. Brake hp: 115 at 3650 rpm. Torque: 190 lbs.-ft. at 1800 rpm. Four main bearings. Solid valve lifters. Carburetor: Carter WDG model 2052S or 2052SA one-barrel; Carter WC model 2204S two-barrel.

CHASSIS

(CJs): Wheelbase: (CJ3B) 80 in.; (CJ5) 81 in.; (CJ6) 101 in. Length: (CJ3B) 129 7/8 in.; (CJ5) 135 1/2 in.; (CJ6) 155 1/2 in. Height: (CJ3B) 67 1/4 in.; (CJ5) 69 1/2 in.; (CJ6) 68 1/4 in. Front tread: (All) 48 7/16 in. Rear tread: (All) 48 7/16 in. Tires: 6.00 x 16 in. four-ply.

(DISPATCHER): Wheelbase: 80.09 in. Length: 125.45 in. Height: 62.74 in. Front tread: 55 1/4 in. Rear tread: 57 in. Tires: 6.40 x 15.

(TRUCKS): Wheelbase: (SWB) 104 1/2 in.; (LWB) 118 in. Length: (SWB) 176.2 in.; (LWB) 183.7 in. Height: (SWB) 72.1 in.; (LWB) 74.3 in. Front tread: (SWB) 57 in.; (LWB) 57 in. (except 1-ton). Rear tread: (SWB) 57 in.; (LWB) 63.5 in. (except 1-ton). Tires: 6.70 x 15; 7.00 x 15; 7.00 x 16 (4x4). (SWB=short wheelbase; LWB=long wheelbase.)

(FC-150): Wheelbase: 81 in. Length: 147.3 in. Height: 78 in. Front tread: 57 in. Rear tread: 57 in. Tires: 7.00 x 15.

(FC-170): Wheelbase: 103 1/2 in. Length: 181.4 in. Height: 79.4 in. Front tread: 63.4 in. Rear tread: 63.8 in. Tires: 7.00 x 16.

TECHNICAL

(ALL EXCEPT FC): Three-speed synchromesh transmission. Floor-mounted gearshift. Single-plate clutch. Hypoid semi-floating rear axle. Overall ratio: 3.54:1, 4.56:1, or 5.38:1. Four-wheel hydraulic brakes. Disc wheels. 4x4 models have two-speed transfer case and full-floating hypoid front axle. 4x2 models have I-beam type front axle.

(FC): Synchromesh transmission. Speeds: 3F/1R (four-speed optional). Floor-mounted gearshift. Single-plate clutch (heavy-duty on FC-170). Rear axle: (FC-150) Semi-floating hypoid; (FC-170) full-floating hypoid rear axle. Overall axle ratio: (FC-150) 5.38:1; (FC-170) 4.89:1. Four-wheel hydraulic brakes (heavy-duty on FC-170). Disc wheels. Dual rear wheels available on FC-170.

OPTIONS

(CJ): Power take-off. Motor governor. Soft top. Hydraulic lift. Metal top. (CJ-5): Five metal and fabric-top options. Ventilating windshield. Power take-off. Eight body color choices. Snowplow. Winch. 36 x 39 1/4 in. cargo box.

(CJ-6): All-weather canvas tops. Oversize tires.

(DJ-3A): Convertible top. 40-cu. ft. hardtop with rippled fiberglass roof and 36-in.-wide gate opening. Whitewall tires. Chrome wheel discs. Chrome front bumper. Chrome rear bumper. Eight standard body colors. "Law Enforcement" package.

(4x4 TRUCKS): Power take-off. Pulley drive. Motor governor. Rearview mirror. Side-mount spare on pickups/stakes. Chrome bumper. License frame.

(SEDAN DELIVERY): Chrome front bumper. Chrome rear bumper. License frame. Chrome wheel disc. Bumperettes. Bumper guards. Wheel trim rings. Whitewall tires. Rearview mirror. Radio and antenna.

(FC-150/FC-170): Fresh air heater. Radio. Tu-tone paint. Front bumper guards. Direction signals. E-Z-Eye glass. Windshield washer. Front air vent. Double passenger seat. Oil bath air cleaner. Oil filter. High-altitude cylinder head (no charge). Four-speed transmission. Power-Lok differential. Heavy-duty rear axle. Heavy-duty springs and shocks. Transmission brake. Hot climate radiator. Power take-off (center and rear). Governor. Various size/type tires. Draw-bar. Stabilizer bar. Rear bumperettes. Selective-drive hubs. Bed and/or front-mount winch. Snow plow. Dozer blade. Wrecker equipment. Jeep-A-Trench. Service bodies.

**Talk about confusion! The Jeep Gala was later renamed the Surrey, and Jeep often referred to it as the Surrey-Gala. It was offered only as a smartly trimmed two-wheel-drive roadster.
Standard equipment included a surrey top with fringe.**

Probably the most memorable (and collectible) new Jeep vehicle this year was the Jeep Gala. Based on the two-wheel-drive Dispatcher, the Gala featured a striped surrey-style top with fringe, matching spare tire cover, striped seats and optional whitewall tires and full wheel discs. Three colors were offered: blue, green and pink. The famed Las Brisas resort hotel in Acapulco, Mexico, purchased a fleet of Galas for use by its guests. The balance of the Dispatcher line continued mostly unchanged and included hardtop and soft-top models.

Extra emphasis was placed on Jeep wagons this year, with much advertising going to the Jeep Maverick, a two-toned, dressed-up and specially priced two-wheel-drive Jeep station wagon aimed at families. Jeep stylists also created a special show car this year—the Jeep Harlequin. It was a stylishly trimmed version of the Jeep station wagon.

Willys Motors produced a total of 114,881 vehicles in 1959. Although Kaiser Industries liked to view itself as a broadly diversified organization, the importance of its Willys Motors operation can be seen very clearly in the company annual report for 1959. Of the corporation's

total profit of $15,740,000 that year, more than $10.6 million was generated by Willys Motors. Willys sales volume for the year was $153.8 million, up from $136.6 million the prior year.

As the decade came to a close it was easy to see that Willys had prospered despite being a small producer in an industry where size matters greatly. The company had managed to transition itself from producing mainly a line of agricultural vehicles to a point where it now was a leader in station wagons, offered a full line of inexpensive light-duty delivery vehicles, and produced trucks used in mining, industrial and service applications, as well as fire trucks and airport rescue vehicles. In the decade to come, the company's continued success would rest upon its ability to find new niches where Jeep vehicles could be useful. Ultimately, the Jeep line would need the emergence of a whole new market.

NOTABLE FOR 1959: New this season was a fringe-top version of the Dispatcher named the Gala. Features included a fringed-and-striped surrey top, chrome bumpers, wheel discs and bright trim. The striped top came in pink, green, or blue contrasted with white. Jeep stylists also turned out the Harlequin, an all-steel wagon with special trim, including Kaiser's three-diamond logo on the doors.

I.D. DATA: Serial number located on right side of dash under hood; on front frame cross-member; on left floor riser in back of driver's seat. Engine numbers located on right side of cylinder block; stamped on water pump boss on front of cylinder block. On most Jeep models the engine and serial numbers are the same.

Model	Body Type	Price	Weight
Jeep — 1/4-Ton — Four-cyl — 4x4 — 80-in. w.b.			
CJ-3B	Jeep Universal	$1,888	2,132 lbs.
Jeep — 1/4-Ton — Four-cyl — 4x4 — 81-in. w.b.			
CJ-5	Jeep Universal	$1,976	2,163 lbs.
Jeep — 1/2-Ton — Four-cyl — 4x4 — 101-in. w.b.			
CJ-6	Jeep Universal	$2,171	2,225 lbs.
Dispatcher — 1/4-Ton — Four-cyl — 4x2 — 80-in. w.b.			
DJ-3A	Basic	N/A	1,709 lbs.
DJ-3A	Soft Top	$1,430	1,769 lbs.
DJ-3A	Hardtop	$1,586	2,004 lbs.
DJ-3A	Gala/Surrey	N/A	N/A
Jeep Trucks — 1/2-Ton — Four-cyl — 4x2 — 104.5-in. w.b.			
F4-134	Chassis	$1,582	1,855 lbs.
F4-134	Delivery	$1,934	2,746 lbs.
Jeep Trucks — 1-Ton — Four-cyl — 4x4 — 118-in. w.b.			
F4-134	Chassis	$2,510	2,893 lbs.
F4-134	Pickup	$2,368	3,065 lbs.
Forward Control — 1/2-Ton — Four-cyl — 4x4 — 81-in. w.b.			
FC-150	Chassis & Cab	$2,416	2,764 lbs.
FC-150	Pickup	$2,533	3,024 lbs.
FC-150	Stake	$2,634	3,187 lbs.
Jeep Trucks — 1/2-Ton — Six-cyl — 4x2 — 104.5-in. w.b.			
L6-226	Delivery	$2,055	2,859 lbs.
L6-226	Wagon	$2,378	3,057 lbs.
Jeep Trucks — 1/2-Ton — Six-cyl — 4x4 — 104.5-in. w.b.			
L6-226	Delivery	$2,630	3,008 lbs.
L6-226	Wagon	$2,901	3,206 lbs.
Jeep Trucks — 1-Ton — Six-cyl — 4x4 — 118-in. w.b.			
L6-226	Chassis & Cab	$2,363	2,817 lbs.
L6-226	Pickup	$2,488	3,176 lbs.
L6-226	Stake	$2,575	3,341 lbs.
Forward Control — 1-Ton — Six-cyl — 4x4 — 103.5-in. w.b.			
FC-170	Chassis & Cab	$2,722	2,901 lbs.
FC-170	Pickup	$2,858	3,331 lbs.
FC-170	Stake	$3,065	3,564 lbs.

PRODUCTION: For the calendar year ending December 31, 1959, the company reported production of 114,881 Jeep vehicles.

ENGINES

(CJ-3B/CJ-5 FOUR): Inline. F-head. Cast-iron block. Bore & stroke: 3 1/8 in. x 4 3/8 in. Displacement: 134.2 cid. Compression ratio: 6.9:1. Brake hp: 70 at 4000 rpm. Torque: 114 lbs.-ft. at 2000 rpm. Three main bearings. Solid valve lifters. Carburetor: Carter YF model 938S or 938SA.

(CJ6/F4-134 FOUR): Inline. F-head. Cast-iron block. Bore & stroke: 3 1/8 x 4 3/8 in. Displacement: 134.2 cid. Compression ratio: 7.4:1. Brake hp: 72 at 4000 rpm. Torque: 114 lbs.-ft. at 2000 rpm. Three main bearings. Solid valve lifters. Carburetor: Carter YF model 938S or 938SA one-barrel.

(DJ-3 FOUR): Inline. L-head. Cast-iron block. Bore & stroke: 3 1/8 x 4 3/8 in. Displacement: 134 cid. Compression ratio: 7.4:1. Brake hp: 60.

(FC-150 FOUR): Inline. L-head. Cast-iron block. Bore & stroke: 3 1/8 x 4 3/8 in. Displacement: 134.2 cid. Compression ratio: 7.40:1. Brake hp: 72 at 4000 rpm. Torque: 114 lbs.-ft. at 2000 rpm. Three main bearings. Solid valve lifters. Carburetor: Carter YF model 2392S one-barrel.

(6-226/FC-170 SIX): Inline. L-head. Cast-iron block. Bore & stroke: 3 5/16 x 4 3/8 in. Displacement: 226.2 cid. Compression ratio: 6.86:1. Brake hp: 115 at 3650 rpm. Torque: 190 lbs.-ft. at 1800 rpm. Four main bearings. Solid valve lifters. Carburetor: Carter WDG model 2052S or 2052SA one-barrel; Carter WC model 2204S two-barrel.

CHASSIS

(CJ): Wheelbase: (CJ-3B) 80 in.; (CJ-5) 81 in.; (CJ-6) 101 in. Length: (CJ-3B) 129 7/8 in.; (CJ-5) 135 1/2 in.; (CJ-6) 155 1/2 in. Height: (CJ-3B) 67 1/4 in.; (CJ-5) 69 1/2 in.; (CJ-6) 68 1/4 in. Front tread: (All) 48 7/16 in. Rear tread: (All) 48 7/16 in. Tires: 6.00 x 16.

(DJ): Wheelbase: 80.09 in. Length: 125.45 in. Height: 62.74 in. Front tread: 55 1/4 in. Rear tread: 57 in. Tires: 6.40 x 15.

(TRUCKS): Wheelbase: (SWB) 104.5 in.; (LWB) 118 in. Length: (SWB) 176.2 in.; (LWB) 183.7 in. Height: (SWB) 72.1 in.; (LWB) 74.3 in. Front tread: (SWB) 57 in.; (LWB) 57 in. Rear tread: (SWB) 57 in.; (LWB) 63.5 in. (except 1-tons). (SWB=short wheelbase; LWB=long wheelbase.)

(FC-150): Wheelbase: 81 in. Length: 147.3 in. Height: 78 in. Front tread: 57 in. Rear tread: 57 in. Tires: 7.00 x 15

(FC-170): Wheelbase: 103 1/2 in. Length: 181.4 in. Height: 79.4 in. Front tread: 63.4 in. Rear tread: 63.8 in. Tires: 7.00 x 16 in. (Dual rear wheels available on heavy-duty models.)

TECHNICAL

(ALL EXCEPT FC): Three speed synchromesh transmission. Floor-mounted gearshift. Single-plate clutch. Hypoid semi-floating rear axle. Overall ratio: 3.54:1, 4.56:1 or 5.38:1. Four-wheel hydraulic brakes. Disc wheels. 4x4 models have two-speed transfer case and full-floating hypoid front axle. 4x2 models have I-beam type front axle.

(FC-150/FC-170): Synchromesh transmission. Speeds: 3F/1R (four-speed optional). Floor-mounted gearshift lever. Single plate clutch (heavy-duty on FC-170). Rear axle: (FC-150) Semi-floating hypoid; (FC-170) full-floating hypoid rear axle. Overall ratio: (FC-150) 5.38:1; (FC-170) 4.89:1. Four-wheel hydraulic brakes (heavy-duty on FC-170). Disc wheels (dual rear on heavy-duty FC-170).

OPTIONS

(CJs): Chrome front bumper. Chrome rear bumper. Chrome bumperettes. Chrome wheel discs. Power take-off. Pulley drive. Motor governor. Soft top. Hydraulic lift. Metal top. **(CJ-5):** Five metal and fabric-top options. Ventilating windshield. Power take-off. Snow plow. Winch. Cargo box (36 x 39 1/4 in.). **(CJ-6):** Soft top. Oversize tires.

(DJ): Soft top. Hardtop. Whitewall tires. Chrome wheel discs. Chrome front bumper. Chrome rear bumper. Eight standard body colors. "Law Enforcement" package. Three different color striped tops for Surrey/Gala.

(4x4 TRUCKS): Standard and deluxe cab trim. Power take-off. Pulley drive. Motor governor. Rearview mirror. Side-mount spare on pickups/stakes. Chrome bumper. License frame.

(SEDAN DELIVERY): Chrome front bumper. Chrome rear bumper. License frame. Chrome wheel disc. Bumperettes. Bumper guards. Wheel trim rings. Whitewall tires. Rearview mirror. Radio and antenna. Two-tone paint.

(FC-150/FC-170): Heater. Radio. Tu-tone paint. Front bumper guards. Direction signals. E-Z-Eye glass. Windshield washer. Front air vent. Double passenger seat. Oil bath air cleaner. Oil filter. High-altitude cylinder head (no charge). Four-speed transmission. Powr-Lok differential. Heavy-duty rear axle. Heavy-duty springs and shocks. Transmission brake. Hot climate radiator. Power take-off (center and rear). Governor. Various size/type tires. Draw-bar. Stabilizer bar. Rear bumperettes. Free-wheeling hubs. Bed or front mount winch. Snow plow. Dozer blade. Wrecker body. Jeep-A-Trench. Service bodies.

This would make a nice collectible today—the 1959 Jeep Maverick, a two-wheel-drive station wagon aimed at the family car market.

FROM WILLYS MOTORS TO KAISER JEEP
1960-1969

During this turbulent decade the Willys name disappeared from the American scene and a new brand name, Kaiser Jeep, emerged. The 1960s would see the unveiling of two entirely new lines of Jeep vehicles, a tremendous expansion of military vehicle output, and continued growth in overseas markets. In addition, a new market for sport utility vehicles would begin to take shape. By the end of the decade, however, Jeep's future would become hazy as it prepared for another change of ownership.

Two-wheel-drive Jeep Dispatchers are not often seen today, but they make a good, inexpensive old car for the hobbyist mainly looking for fun. They're simple in design and easy to repair.

The first year of the new decade proved to be another successful year for Willys Motors. There wasn't much in the way of product news to talk about in 1960, but sales of Jeep vehicles continued to grow. A new "Economy Delivery" model was added to the line of two-wheel-drive wagons, while the carry-over wagons got new side trim and paint treatments.

The decade began with the Kaiser family firmly in control at Kaiser Industries. Henry J. Kaiser continued as chairman of the board of directors, Edgar Kaiser as a director and company president, and Henry J. Kaiser Jr. as director and vice president.

Company profits fell by more than half in 1960, but the blame was mostly in Kaiser's engineering and construction businesses. Willys Motors earned $9.2 million for the year; down from $11.6 million because increased material and labor costs were not offset by price increases until late in the year. Jeep commercial sales set a new record for 1960. Sales volume was $157,142,000 for the year. Sales of Jeeps in overseas markets amounted to 28,600 units and domestic retail sales of 31,100 units were reported. The company had 1,425 U.S. dealers at the time. Retail sales of more than 10,000 units for the final quarter of 1960 were the highest for any quarter. It was noted that the sales organization had improved much over the years. The company stated that an important trend was "the increasing sales of Jeep commercial vehicles by dealers in large cities. While ... Jeep vehicles have a worldwide reputation for 'off-the-road' usage, industrial and other business usage is growing rapidly."

Iran purchased 3,586 Jeeps in 1960; Denmark bought 500 military Jeeps, and another 1,492 Jeeps went to The Netherlands. Assembly plants were opened in Nigeria and South Africa. Vietnam also bought a number of Jeeps.

The two biggest overseas affiliates, Willys Motors Brazil (WOB) and Industrias Kaiser Argentina (IKA), had grown dramatically. In 1960, IKA sold 32,900 Jeep commercial vehicles and passenger cars, and WOB sold 38,500.

According to the company annual report that year, the Government Sales Division had a $17 million backlog of orders for Jeep vehicles and parts for the military and civil agencies of the U.S. government.

The company included a very interesting paragraph in its annual report. It reveals a lot about how the basic business was conducted:

"The vehicle models currently manufactured at the Willys plant in Toledo, Ohio are the Jeep Universal, Jeep Dispatcher, Jeep Station Wagon, Jeep Panel Delivery, Jeep Pickup Truck and Forward Control Jeep Trucks. While large quantities of standard production line vehicles are sold, a significant part of the Willys business consists of the modification or adaptation of vehicles for special uses. A railroad company recently purchased a fleet of Jeep forward control trucks equipped for operation either on or off rails and also equipped with snowplows."

The problem was that a significant part of Willys sales were specially modified vehicles. The firm wasn't selling as many standard model Jeep vehicles to retail buyers, especially families, as it should have. In the public's mind—and maybe in the company's as well—Jeeps were still viewed primarily as work vehicles. Apparently, the idea of vast numbers of people buying a Jeep as an alternative to the family car hadn't occurred to anyone.

NOTABLE FOR 1960: New body trim, similar to the 1959 Jeep Maverick, was now available on all Jeep trucks except Foward Control models. FC models had their own standard and deluxe treatments for exteriors and interiors. A new "economy" delivery wagon made its appearance in the two-wheel-drive 1/2-ton truck lineup. Jeep referred to its specially trimmed DJ-3A Surrey as the Surrey, Gala, and Surrey Gala. Take your pick.

I.D. DATA: Serial number located on right side of dash under hood; on front frame cross-member; on left floor riser in back of driver's seat. Engine numbers located on right side of cylinder block; stamped on water pump boss on front of cylinder block. On most Jeep models, the engine and serial numbers are the same.

The Surrey represented a definite change in style for Jeep. This pristine 1960 DJ-3A belongs to Ron Szymanski of Toledo, Ohio.

Model	Body Type	Price	Weight
Jeep — 1/4-Ton — Four-cyl — 4x4 — 80-in. w.b.			
CJ-3B	Jeep Universal	$1,888	2,132 lbs.
Jeep — 1/4-Ton — Four-cyl — 4x4 — 81-in. w.b.			
CJ-5	Jeep Universal	$1,979	2,163 lbs.
Jeep — 1/2-Ton — Four-cyl — 4x4 — 101-in. w.b.			
CJ-6	Jeep Universal	$2,171	2,225 lbs.
Dispatcher — 1/4-Ton — Four-cyl — 4x2 — 80-in. w.b.			
DJ-3A	Soft Top	$1,430	1,769 lbs.
DJ-3A	Hardtop	$1,586	2,004 lbs.
DJ-3A	Surrey	$1,650	1,819 lbs.
Jeep Trucks — 1/2-Ton — Four-cyl — 4x2 — 104.5-in. w.b.			
FA-134	Economy Delivery	$1,582	1,855 lbs.
FA-134	Station Wagon	$1,995	2,858 lbs.
FA-134	Utility Wagon	$2,258	2,944 lbs.
FA-134	Utility Delivery	$1,934	2,746 lbs.
Jeep Trucks — 1/2-Ton — Four-cyl — 4x4 — 104.5-in. w.b.			
FA-134	Utility Wagon	$2,782	3,093 lbs.
FA-134	Utility Delivery	$2,510	2,895 lbs.
Jeep Trucks — 1-Ton — Four-cyl — 4x4 — 118-in. w.b.			
FA-134	Pickup	$2,368	3,065 lbs.
FA-134	Stake	$2,455	3,230 lbs.
Jeep FC-150 — 1/2-Ton — Four-cyl — 4x4 — 81-in. w.b.			
FC-150	Chassis & Cab	$2,416	2,896 lbs.
FC-150	Pickup	$2,533	3,152 lbs.
FC-150	Stake	$2,634	3,319 lbs.
Jeep Trucks — 1/2-Ton — Six-cyl — 4x2 — 104.5-in. w.b.			
L6-226	Station Wagon	$2,258	2,971 lbs.
L6-226	Utility Wagon	$2,378	3,057 lbs.
L6-226	Utility Delivery	$2,055	2,859 lbs.
Jeep Trucks — 1/2-Ton — Six-cyl — 4x4 — 104.5-in. w.b.			
L6-226	Utility Wagon	$2,901	3,206 lbs.
L6-226	Utility Delivery	$2,630	3,008 lbs.
Jeep Trucks — 1-Ton — Six-cyl — 4x4 — 118-in. w.b.			
L6-226	Chassis & Cab	$2,363	2,817 lbs.
L6-226	Pickup	$2,488	3,176 lbs.
L6-226	Stake	$2,575	3,341 lbs.
FC-170 — 1-Ton — Six-cyl — 4x4 — 103.5-in. w.b.			
FC-170	Chassis & Cab	$2,722	2,901 lbs.
FC-170	Pickup	$2,858	3,331 lbs.
FC-170	Stake	$3,065	3,564 lbs.

PRODUCTION: The company did not report a consolidated production total but noted that domestic sales during the calendar year totaled 31,940 units (31,100 retail deliveries), and export sales totaled 28,600 units.

ENGINES

(CJ-3B/CJ-5 FOUR): Inline. F-head. Cast-iron block. Bore & stroke: 3 1/8 x 4 3/8 in. Displacement: 134.2 cid. Compression ratio: 6.9:1. Brake hp: 70 at 4000 rpm. Torque: 114 lbs.-ft. at 2000 rpm. Three main bearings. Solid valve lifters. Carburetor: Carter YF model 938S or 938SA.

(CJ6/F4-134 FOUR): Inline. F-head. Four-cylinder. Cast-iron block. Bore & stroke: 3 1/8 x 4 3/8 in. Displacement: 134.2 cid. Compression ratio: 7.4:1. Brake hp: 72 at 4000 rpm. Torque: 114 lbs.-ft. at 2000 rpm. Three main bearings. Solid valve lifters. Carburetor: Carter YF model 938S or 938SA one-barrel.

(DJ-3 FOUR): Inline. L-head. Four-cylinder. Cast-iron block. Bore & stroke: 3 1/8 x 4 3/8 in. Displacement: 134 cid. Compression ratio: 7.4:1. Brake hp: 60 hp.

The sturdy 1960 4x4 Jeep Station Wagon. This one has aftermarket wheels and tires.

(FC-150 FOUR): Inline. L-head. Four-cylinder. Cast-iron block. Bore & stroke: 3 1/8 x 4 3/8 in. Displacement: 134.2 cid. Compression ratio: 7.40:1. Brake hp: 72 at 4000 rpm. Torque: 114 lbs.-ft. at 2000 rpm. Three main bearings. Solid valve lifters. Carburetor: Carter YF model 2392S one-barrel.

(6-226/FC-170 SIX): Inline. L-head. Cast-iron block. Bore & stroke: 3 5/16 in. x 4 3/8 in. Displacement 226.2 cid. Compression ratio: 6.86:1. Brake hp: 115 at 3650 rpm. Torque: 190 lbs.-ft. at 1800 rpm. Four main bearings. Solid valve lifters. Carburetor: Carter WDG model 2052S or 2052SA one-barrel; Carter WC model 2204S two-barrel.

CHASSIS

(CJ-3-B): Wheelbase: 80 in. Length: 129 7/8 in. Height: 67 1/4 in. Front tread: 48 7/16. Rear tread: 48 7/16 in. Tires: 6.00 x 16.

(CJ-5): Wheelbase: 81.09 in. Length: 135.50 in. Height: 69.50 in. Front tread: 48 7/16 in. Rear tread: 48 7/16 in. Tires: 6.00 x 16.

(CJ-6): Wheelbase: 101 in. Length: 155 1/2 in. Height: 68 1/4 in. Front tread: 48 7/16 in. Rear tread: 48 7/16 in. Tires: 6.00 x 16.

(DJ-3): Wheelbase: 80.1 in. Length: 125.4 in. Height: 59.8 in. Front tread: 48.2 in. Rear tread: 48.5 in. Tires: 6.50 x 15.

(SHORT-WHEELBASE TRUCKS): Wheelbase: 104.5 in. Length: 176.2 in. Height: 72.1 in. Front tread: 57 in. Rear tread: 57 in. Tires: 7.00 x 15 in. (6.70 x 15 on Station Wagon).

(LONG-WHEELBASE TRUCKS): Wheelbase: 118 in. Length: 183.7 in. Height: 74.3 in. Front tread: 57 in. Rear tread: 63.5 in. Tires: 7.00 x 16.

(FC-150): Wheelbase: 81 in. Tires: 7.00 x 15.

(FC-170): Wheelbase: 103 1/2 in. Tires: 7.00 x 16.

TECHNICAL

(ALL EXCEPT FC): Synchromesh transmission. Speeds: 3F/1R. Floor-mounted gearshift lever. Single-plate clutch. Hypoid semi-floating rear axle. Overall ratio: 3.54:1, 4.56:1, or 5.38:1. Four-wheel hydraulic brakes. Disc wheels. 4x2 models have I-beam type front axle. 4x4 models have full-floating hypoid front axle and two-speed transfer case.

(FC-150/FC-170): Synchromesh transmission. Speeds: 3F/1R (four-speed optional). Floor-mounted gearshift lever. Single-plate, dry-disc clutch (heavy-duty on FC-170). Rear axle: (FC-150) Semi-floating hypoid; (FC-170) full-floating hypoid rear axle. Overall ratio: (FC-150) 5.38:1; (FC-170) 4.89:1. Four-wheel hydraulic (heavy-duty on FC-170) brakes. Disc wheels (dual rear on FC-170 heavy-duty model).

OPTIONS

(CJ): Chrome front bumper. Chrome rear bumper. Chrome bumperettes. Wheel discs. Power take-off. Pulley drive. Motor governor. Soft top. Hydraulic lift. Metal top. (CJ-6): Soft top. Oversize tires. (CJ-5): Five metal and fabric-top options. Ventilating windshield. Power take-off. Eight body color choices. Snowplow. Winch. Steel cargo box.

(DJ): Soft top. Hardtop. Whitewall tires. Chrome wheel discs. Chrome front bumper. Chrome rear bumper. Eight standard body colors. "Law Enforcement" package. Three different color striped tops for Surrey/Gala.

(4x4 TRUCKS): Standard and deluxe cab trim. Power take-off. Pulley drive. Motor governor. Rearview mirror. Side-mount spare on pickups/stakes. Chrome bumper. License frame.

(SEDAN DELIVERY): Chrome front bumper. Chrome rear bumper. License frame. Chrome wheel disc. Bumperettes. Bumper guards. Wheel trim rings. Whitewall tires. Rearview mirror. Radio and antenna. Two-tone paint.

(FC): Fresh air heater. Radio. Two-tone paint. Front bumper guards. Direction signals. E-Z-Eye glass. Windshield washer. Front air vent. Double passenger seat. Oil bath air cleaner. Oil filter. High-altitude cylinder head (no charge). Four-speed transmission. Powr-Lok differential. Heavy-duty rear axle. Heavy-duty springs and shocks. Transmission brake. Hot climate radiator. Power take-off (center and rear). Governor. Draw-bar. Stabilizer bar. Rear bumperettes. Selective drive hubs. Bed and/or front mount winch. Snowplow. Dozer blade. Wrecker equipment. Jeep-A-Trench. Service bodies.

HISTORICAL: Barney Roos, sometimes called "The Father of the Willys Jeep," died of a heart attack in New York City in 1960.

One of the rarest Jeep vehicles is the FJ-3A Fleetvan. Longer than the FJ-3 purchased by the U.S. Postal Service, the FJ-3A was not a particularly good seller when new.

Another new year and another new Jeep vehicle. This Jeep, however, was destined to be almost completely forgotten before the decade was out. The vehicle was the new two-wheel-drive Jeep FJ-3 Fleetvan, a stand-and-drive, multi-stop, light-duty mail delivery van. It was Willys' latest effort to win some business from the U.S. Post Office Department, owner of the largest non-military vehicle fleet in America. A Jeep four-cylinder engine powered the Fleetvan. The 80-in.-wheelbase chassis were assembled in Toledo, then shipped out to a subcontractor for installation of the van body. By that fall, Willys introduced a regular commercial version of the Fleetvan, designated the FJ-3A, which would be sold to small businesses through its dealers. Built on an 81-in. wheelbase, the commercial FJ-3A used a longer body than the FJ-3 postal unit, providing 170 cu. ft. of cargo capacity. With a curb weight of 3,000 lbs., the Fleetvan could haul 1,000 lbs. of payload.

In the Forward Control line, three new 1-ton dual-rear wheel FC-170 models—pickup, stake and cab & chassis—were available for heavy-duty usage.

Willys commenced a major new product development program. Three all-new products were

planned: a new station wagon, new pick-up truck, and a new engine. They would all go into production before the end of 1962.

During the year, the company completed production of 4,000 CJ-3B Jeeps for use by the Turkish Army. The vehicles were shipped to Turkey in component form to be assembled at the Turk Willys-Overland plant. Also completed was a Post Office Department order for 6,025 Jeep Fleetvans, and an order for the first front line ambulances requisitioned by the military since 1955.

The four-wheel-drive Jeep Universal models remained very popular. According to Jeep, of the CJ-type vehicles produced in 1961, 17,918 were CJ-3Bs, 15,269 were CJ-5s, and 1,991 were CJ-6s. A Perkins four-cylinder diesel engine was introduced as an option on Jeep Universal. It's unknown exactly how many were produced, but it's likely that most of them were sold overseas.

Profits of Willys Motors were off a bit, to $7.2 million for the year, from $9.2 million the prior year. This reflected an overall slowdown in the auto industry for 1961, though Willys fared better than the average company. By the fourth quarter the market was back on track, and Jeep sales and earnings were the highest for any quarter in the company's history. For the year, sales to the government market were the highest since 1955, registering a whopping 69-percent increase over 1960.

NOTABLE FOR 1961: The big news for Willys was the new Fleetvan. Intended for multi-stop delivery work, it featured a stand or sit driving position and was equipped with the four-cylinder F-head engine. The 1-ton 4x4 stake truck with four-cylinder engine was dropped.

I.D. DATA: Serial number located on right side of dash under hood; on front frame cross-member; on left floor riser in back of driver's seat. Engine numbers located on right side of cylinder block; stamped on water pump boss on front of cylinder block. On most Jeep models the engine and serial numbers are the same.

Model	Body Type	Price	Weight
Jeep — 1/4-Ton — Four-cyl — 4x4 — 80-in. w.b.			
CJ-3B	Jeep Universal	$1,890	2,220 lbs.
Jeep — 1/4-Ton — Four-cyl — 4x4 — 81-in. w.b.			
CJ-5	Jeep Universal	$1,980	2,251 lbs.
Jeep — 1/2-Ton — Four-cyl — 4x4 — 101-in. w.b.			
CJ-6	Jeep Universal	$2,170	2,313 lbs.
Dispatcher — 1/4-Ton — Four-cyl — 4x4 — 80-in. w.b.			
DJ-3A	Basic	$1,365	2,797 lbs.
DJ-3A	Soft Top	$1,430	1,857 lbs.
DJ-3A	Hardtop	$1,585	2,092 lbs.
Fleetvan — 1/2-Ton — Four-cyl — 4x2 — Delivery Van			
FJ-3	Fleetvan (postal)	—	—
FJ-3A	Fleetvan (commercial)	—	3,045 lbs.
Jeep Trucks — 1/2-Ton — Four-cyl — 4x2 — 104.5-in. w.b.			
F4-134	Economy Delivery	$1,580	1,987 lbs.
F4-134	Station Wagon	$1,995	2,990 lbs.
F4-134	Utility Wagon	$2,260	3,076 lbs.
F4-134	Utility Delivery	$1,935	2,878 lbs.
Jeep Trucks — 1/2-Ton — Four-cyl — 4x4 — 104.5-in. w.b.			
F4-134	Utility Wagon	$2,780	3,225 lbs.
F4-134	Utility Delivery	$2,510	3,025 lbs.
Jeep Trucks — 1-Ton — Four-cyl — 4x4 — 118-in. w.b.			
F4-134	Pickup	$2,365	3,197 lbs.
FC-150 — 1/2-Ton — Four-cyl — 4x4 — 81-in. w.b.			
FC-150	Chassis & Cab	$2,415	2,884 lbs.
FC-150	Pickup	$2,535	3,140 lbs.
FC-150	Platform Stake	$2,635	3,307 lbs.
Jeep Truck — 1/2-Ton — Six-cyl — 4x2 — 104.5-in. w.b.			
L6-226	Utility Wagon	$2,380	3,172 lbs.
L6-226	Utility Delivery	$2,055	2,974 lbs.
L6-226	Station Wagon	$2,260	3,103 lbs.
Jeep Truck — 1/2-Ton — Six-cyl — 4x4 — 104.5-in. w.b.			
L6-226	Utility Wagon	$2,900	3,321 lbs.
L6-226	Utility Delivery	$2,630	3,123 lbs.
Jeep Truck — 1-Ton — Six-cyl — 4x4 — 118-in. w.b.			
L6-226	Pickup	$2,490	3,291 lbs.
L6-226	Platform Stake	$2,575	3,456 lbs.
L6-226	Chassis & Cab	$2,365	2,932 lbs.
FC-170 — 1-Ton — Six-cyl — 4x4 — 103.5-in. w.b.			
FC-170	Chassis & Cab	$2,720	3,056 lbs.
FC-170	Pickup	$2,855	3,486 lbs.
FC-170	Platform Stake	$3,065	3,719 lbs.
FC-170 (Dual Rear) 1-Ton — Six-cyl — 4x4 — 103.5-in. w.b.			
FC-170	Chassis & Cab	$3,395	3,726 lbs.
FC-170	Pickup	$3,531	4,156 lbs.
FC-170	Platform Stake	$3,835	4,505 lbs.

PRODUCTION/SALES: The company did not report total production, but it is estimated that 49,073 civilian Jeeps were produced for the U.S. market.

ENGINES

(CJ-3B/CJ-5 FOUR): Inline. F-head. Cast-iron block. Bore & stroke: 3 1/8 in. x 4 3/8 in. Displacement: 134.2 cid. Compression ratio: 6.9:1. Brake hp: 70 at 4000 rpm. Torque: 114 lbs.-ft. at 2000 rpm. Three main bearings. Solid valve lifters. Carburetor: Carter YF model 938S or 938SA.

(CJ6/F4-134 FOUR): Inline. F-head. Cast-iron block. Bore & stroke: 3 1/8 in. x 4 3/8 in. Displacement: 134.2 cid. Compression ratio: 7.4:1. Brake hp: 72 at 4000 rpm. Torque: 114 lbs.-ft. at 2000 rpm. Three main bearings. Solid valve lifters. Carburetor: Carter YF model 938S or 938SA one-barrel.

(DJ-3 FOUR): Inline. L-head. Cast-iron block. Bore & stroke: 3 1/8 in. x 4 3/8 in. Displacement: 134 cid. Compression ratio: 7.4:1. Brake hp: 60 hp.

(FLEETVAN FOUR): Inline. F-head. Cast-iron block. Bore & stroke: 3 1/8 in. x 4 3/8 in. Displacement: 134.2 cid. Compression ratio: 7.4:1. Brake hp: 75 at 4000 rpm. Torque: 115 lbs.-ft. at 2000 rpm. Three main bearings. Solid valve lifters. Carburetor: Carter model YF.

(FC-150 FOUR): Inline. L-head. Cast-iron block. Bore & stroke: 3 1/8 in. x 4 3/8 in. Displacement: 134.2 cid. Compression ratio: 7.40:1. Brake hp: 72 at 4000 rpm. Torque: 114 lbs.-ft. at 2000 rpm. Three main bearings. Solid valve lifters. Carburetor: Carter YF model 2392S one-barrel.

(6-226/FC-170 SIX): Inline. L-head. Cast-iron block. Bore & stroke: 3 5/16 in. x 4 3/8 in. Displacement: 226.2 cid. Compression ratio: 6.86:1. Brake hp: 115 at 3650 rpm. Torque: 190 lbs.-ft. at 1800 rpm. Four main bearings. Solid valve lifters. Carburetor: Carter WDG model 2052S or 2052SA one-barrel; Carter WC model 2204S two-barrel.

CHASSIS

(CJ-3-B): Wheelbase: 80 in. Length: 129 7/8 in. Height: 67 1/4 in. Front tread: 48 7/16. Rear tread: 48 7/16 in. Tires: 6.00 x 16.

(CJ-5): Wheelbase: 81.09 in. Length: 135.50 in. Height: 69.50 in. Front tread: 48 7/16 in. Rear tread: 48 7/16 in. Tires: 6.00 x 16.

(CJ-6): Wheelbase: 101 in. Length: 155 1/2 in. Height: 68 1/4 in. Front tread: 48 7/16 in. Rear tread: 48 7/16 in. Tires: 6.00 x 16.

71

(DJ-3): Wheelbase: 80.1 in. Length: 125.4 in. Height: 59.8 in. Front tread: 48.2 in. Rear tread: 48.5 in. Tires: 6.50 x 15.

(FJ-3A FLEETVAN): Wheelbase: 81 in. Length: 154 in. Height: 90.12 in. Front tread: 48 9/16 in. Rear tread: 48 9/16 in. Tires: 6.70 x 15 four-ply tubeless.

(SHORT-WHEELBASE TRUCKS): Wheelbase: 104.5 in. Length: 176.2 in. Height: 72.1 in. Front tread: 57 in. Rear tread: 57 in. Tires: 7.00 x 15 in. (6.70 x 15 on Station Wagon).

(LONG-WHEELBASE TRUCKS): Wheelbase: 118 in. Length: 183.7 in. Height: 74.3 in. Front tread: 57 in. Rear tread: 63.5 in. Tires: 7.00 x 16.

(FC-150): Wheelbase: 81 in. Tires: 7.00 x 15.

(FC-170): Wheelbase: 103 1/2 in. Tires: 7.00 x 16.

TECHNICAL

(FC-150/FC-170): Synchromesh transmission. Speeds: 3F/1R (four-speed optional). Floor-mounted gearshift lever. Single-plate, dry-disc clutch (heavy-duty on FC-170). Rear axle: (FC-150) Semi-floating hypoid; (FC-170) Full-floating hypoid rear axle. Overall ratio: (FC-150) 5.38:1; (FC-170) 4.89:1. Four-wheel hydraulic brakes (heavy-duty on FC-170). Disc wheels (dual rear on FC-170 heavy-duty models).

(FLEETVAN): Synchromesh transmission. Speeds: 3F/1R. Floor-mounted gearshift lever. Single-plate, dry-disc clutch, 72 sq. in. frictional area. I-beam front axle. Hypoid semi-floating rear axle. Overall ratio: 4.56:1. Hydraulic 9 in. drum brakes. Four 15 x 5.00 five-bolt disc wheels.

(ALL OTHER MODELS): Three-speed synchromesh transmission. Floor-mounted gearshift. Single-plate clutch. Hypoid semi-floating rear axle. Overall ratio: 3.54:1, 4.56:1, or 5.38:1. Four-wheel hydraulic brakes. Disc wheels. 4x4 models have two-speed transfer case and full-floating hypoid front axle. 4x2 models have I-beam type front axle.

OPTIONS

(CJ): Chrome front bumper. Chrome rear bumper. Chrome bumperettes. Chrome wheel discs. Power take-off. Pulley drive. Motor governor. Soft top. Hydraulic lift. Metal top. (CJ-5): Five metal and fabric-top options. Ventilating windshield. Power take-off. Snow plow. Winch. Steel cargo box. (CJ-6): All-weather canvas tops. Oversize tires.

(DJ): Soft top. Hardtop with 36-in.-wide rear opening. Whitewall tires. Chrome wheel discs. Chrome front bumper. Chrome rear bumper. Eight standard body colors. Law Enforcement package. Three different color striped tops for Surrey.

(FLEETVAN): Two-tone paint. Ladder racks. Heater.

(4x4 TRUCKS): Standard and deluxe cab trim. Power-take-off. Pulley drive. Motor governor. Rearview mirror. Sidemount spare on pickups/stakes. Chrome bumper. License frame.

(SEDAN DELIVERY): Chrome front bumper. Chrome rear bumper. License frame. Chrome wheel disc. Bumperettes. Bumper guards. Wheel trim rings. Whitewall tires. Rearview mirror. Radio and antenna. New two-tone paint combinations.

(FC): Fresh air heater. Radio. Two-tone paint. Front bumper guards. Direction signals. E-Z-Eye glass. Windshield washer. Front air vent. Double passenger seat. Oil bath air cleaner. Oil filter. High-altitude cylinder head (no charge). Four-speed transmission. Powr-Lok differential. Heavy-duty rear axle. Heavy-duty springs and shocks. Transmission brake. Hot climate radiator. Power take-off (center and rear). Governor. Various size/type tires. Draw-bar. Stabilizer bar. Rear bumperettes. Selective drive hubs. Bed and/or front mount winch. Snowplow. Dozer blade. Wrecker equipment. Jeep-A-Trench. Service bodies.

The Jeep Station Wagons of 1962 were often very colorful, but after 17 years on the market they were hardly exciting.

Willys renamed its station wagon models this year and now called them Jeep Travelers. New color schemes debuted in an effort to make the aging products look more up to date. In May, a new engine appeared for the wagons and trucks. This was a really different sort of power plant for Willys: an overhead-cam (OHC), 230-cid, six-cylinder engine that Willys named the Tornado OHC. Producing 140 hp and 210 lbs.-ft. of torque, the Tornado was the only OHC engine being produced by an American company at that time. The automotive press loved the new mill, with one writer calling it a "140-hp bomb!"

In Toledo, Willys Motors was assembling a new 1/4-ton military vehicle, but it wasn't one of Willys' own designs. The M151 looked a lot like a Jeep, but it used a unitized chassis. It had previously been built by Ford, and the design was owned by the U.S. government. Willys Motors was the lowest bidder on a new contract to assemble 18,625 the M151 models, so a production line was set up at the Toledo plant and the company had another new product. The company also booked an order for 1,321 Fleetvan trucks. Overseas license agreements were signed for assembly of Jeep vehicles in Morocco, Italy, Northern Rhodesia, and Venezuela. Willys Overland Brazil had its most successful year yet, with 48,362 vehicles sold. In Argentina, IKA sold 42,948 units total, including several models of Rambler cars, which were now being built and marketed by IKA under license from American Motors.

The company reported record sales volume during the fall, when it launched all new lines of Jeep wagons and trucks. However, the expense of developing and tooling for the new Jeep vehicles caused the division to report a loss for the year of $469,000, versus a profit the year before of $7.2 million. This was quite a reversal of fortunes and it might have been avoided except that the company's Argentinean and Brazilian affiliates suffered reversals caused by economic problems in South America. However, the losses illustrated one inescapable fact: Tooling for new vehicles was (and is) very expensive. In fact, the cost of retooling had been the single greatest factor in the demise of many of the other independent automakers. Because Jeep vehicles didn't require redesign as often as conventional cars, the expense hadn't dragged Willys Motors under. But it was always a concern.

Willys Motors ended the year with 1,600 U.S. dealers, which was the highest level in many years. The company reported a government order backlog of approximately $80 million.

NOTABLE FOR 1962: Station wagons were now referred to as Jeep Traveler models. They could be had in solid colors or in one of several two-tone treatments. One style featured a solid body color with the roof in a contrasting white. The second treatment is usually described as "Rocket" style trim. With this, a contrasting panel (generally white) shaped somewhat like a missile

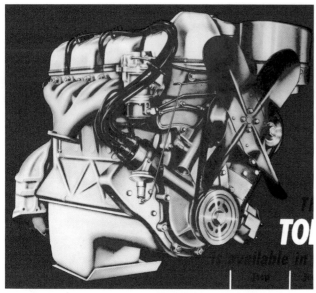

The all-new Tornado OHC (overhead-cam) six-cylinder engine was much more powerful than previous Jeep sixes. Debuting in 1962, it was the only overhead-cam six produced by an American company at that time.

ran the full length of the body side. The roof was painted to match it. A new overhead cam six-cylinder engine was available in the Jeep Utility Wagons, Station Wagons, Pickups, and Panel Delivery trucks.

I.D. DATA: Serial number located on right side of dash under hood; on front frame cross-member; on left floor riser in back of driver's seat. Engine numbers located on right side of cylinder block; stamped on water pump boss on front of cylinder block. On most Jeep models the engine and serial numbers are the same.

Model	Body Type	Price	Weight
Jeep — 1/4-Ton — Four-cyl — 4x4 — 80-in. w.b.			
CJ-3B	Jeep Universal	$1,960	2,220 lbs.
Jeep — 1/4-Ton — Four-cyl — 4x4 — 81-in. w.b.			
CJ-5	Jeep Universal	$2,055	2,251 lbs.
Jeep — 1/2-Ton — Four-cyl — 4x4 — 101-in. w.b.			
CJ-6	Jeep Universal	$2,150	2,313 lbs.
Dispatcher — 1/4-Ton — 4x2 — Four-cyl — 80-in. w.b.			
DJ-3A	Basic	$1,435	1,797 lbs.
DJ-3A	Soft Top	$1,505	1,857 lbs.
DJ-3A	Hardtop	$1,665	2,092 lbs.
DJ-3A	Surrey	$1,775	2,007 lbs.
Fleetvan — 1/2-Ton — Four-cyl — 4x2 — Delivery Van			
FJ-3	Fleetvan (postal)	—	—
FJ-3A	Fleetvan (commercial)	—	3,045 lbs.
Jeep Trucks — 1/2-Ton — Four-cyl — 4x2 — 104.5-in. w.b.			
F4-134	Economy Delivery	$1,695	1,987 lbs.
F4-134	Station Wagon	$2,095	2,990 lbs.
F4-134	Utility Wagon	—	3,076 lbs.
F4-134	Utility Delivery	$2,005	2,878 lbs.
Jeep Trucks — 1/2-Ton — Four-cyl — 4x4 — 104.5-in. w.b.			
F4-134	Utility Wagon	$2,885	3,225 lbs.
F4-134	Utility Delivery	$2,605	3,025 lbs.
Jeep Truck — 1-Ton — Four-cyl — 4x4 — 118-in. w.b.			
F4-134	Pickup	$2,370	3,197 lbs.

FC-150-1/2-Ton — Four-cyl — 4x4 — 81-in. w.b.			
FC-150	Chassis & Cab	$2,505	2,884 lbs.
FC-150	Pickup	$2,625	3,140 lbs.
FC-150	Platform Stake	$2,725	3,307 lbs.
Jeep Trucks — 1/2-Ton — Six-cyl — 4x2 — 104.5-in. w.b.			
L6-226	Utility Wagon	$2,345	3,172 lbs.
L6-226	Utility Delivery	$2,130	2,974 lbs.
L6-226	Station Wagon	$2,345	3,103 lbs.
Jeep Trucks — 1/2-Ton — Six-cyl — 4x4 — 104.5-in. w.b.			
L6-226	Utility Wagon	$3,010	3,321 lbs.
L6-226	Utility Delivery	$2,730	3,123 lbs.
Jeep Trucks — 1-Ton — Six-cyl — 4x4 — 118-in. w.b.			
L6-226	Pickup	$2,490	3,291 lbs.
L6-226	Platform Stake	$2,575	3,456 lbs.
L6-226	Chassis & Cab	$2,365	2,932 lbs.
FC-170 — 1-Ton — Six-cyl — 4x4 — 103.5-in. w.b. (Single rear wheels)			
FC-170	Chassis & Cab	$2,825	3,056 lbs.
FC-170	Pickup	$2,960	3,486 lbs.
FC-170	Platform Stake	$3,165	3,719 lbs.
(Dual rear wheels/8,000 lbs. GVW)			
FC-170	Chassis & Cab	$3,315	3,726 lbs.
(Dual rear wheels/9,000 lbs. GVW)			
FC-170	Chassis & Cab	$3,525	3,726 lbs.

PRODUCTION: The company did not report total production, but it is estimated that 85,457 Jeeps were produced.

ENGINES

(CJ-3B/CJ-5 FOUR): Inline. F-head. Cast-iron block. Bore & stroke: 3 1/8 x 4 3/8 in. Displacement: 134.2 cid. Compression ratio: 6.9:1. Brake hp: 70 at 4000 rpm. Torque: 114 lbs.-ft. at 2000 rpm. Three main bearings. Solid valve lifters. Carburetor: Carter YF model 938S or 938SA.

(CJ6/F4-134 FOUR): Inline. F-head. Cast-iron block. Bore & stroke: 3 1/8 x 4 3/8 in. Displacement: 134.2 cid. Compression ratio: 7.4:1. Brake hp: 72 at 4000 rpm. Torque: 114 lbs.-ft. at 2000 rpm. Three main bearings. Solid valve lifters. Carburetor: Carter YF model 938S/938SA one-barrel.

(DJ-3 FOUR): Inline. L-head. Cast-iron block. Bore & stroke: 3 1/8 x 4 3/8 in. Displacement: 134 cid. Compression ratio: 7.4:1. Brake hp: 60 hp.

(FLEETVAN FOUR): Inline. F-head. Cast-iron block. Bore & stroke: 3 1/8 x 4 3/8 in. Displacement: 134.2 cid. Compression ratio: 7.4:1. Brake hp: 75 at 4000 rpm. Torque: 115 lbs.-ft. at 2000 rpm. Three main bearings. Solid valve lifters. Carburetor: Carter model YF.

(FC-150 FOUR): Inline. L-head. Cast-iron block. Bore & stroke: 3 1/8 x 4 3/8 in. Displacement: 134.2 cid. Compression ratio: 7.40:1. Brake hp: 72 at 4000 rpm. Torque: 114 lbs.-ft. at 2000 rpm. Three main bearings. Solid valve lifters. Carburetor: Carter YF model 2392S one-barrel.

(**6-226/FC-170 SIX**): Inline. L-head.. Cast-iron block. Bore & stroke: 3 5/16 in. x 4 3/8 in. Displacement: 226.2 cid. Compression ratio: 6.86:1. Brake hp: 115 at 3650 rpm. Torque: 190 lbs.-ft. at 1800 rpm. Four main bearings. Solid valve lifters. Carburetor: Carter WDG model 2052S or 2052SA one-barrel; Carter WC model 2204S two-barrel.

(**TORNADO 230 SIX**): Inline. Overhead valve/overhead cam. Cast-iron with extensive use of aluminum components. Bore & stroke: 3.34 x 4.38 in. Displacement: 230 cid. Compression ratio: 8.5:1. Brake hp: 140 at 4000 rpm. Torque: 210 lbs.-ft. @ 1750 rpm. Overhead valve lifters.

CHASSIS

(**CJ-3B**): Wheelbase: 80 in. Length: 129 7/8 in. Height: 67 1/4 in. Front tread: 48 7/16. Rear tread: 48 7/16 in. Tires: 6.00 x 16 in.

(**CJ-5**): Wheelbase: 81.09 in. Length: 135.50 in. Height: 69.50 in. Front tread: 48 7/16 in. Rear tread: 48 7/16 in. Tires: 6.00 x 16 in.

(**CJ-6**): Wheelbase: 101 in. Length: 155 1/2 in. Height: 68 1/4 in. Front tread: 48 7/16 in. Rear tread: 48 7/16 in. Tires: 6.00 x 16 in.

(**DJ-3**): Wheelbase: 80.1 in. Length: 125.4 in. Height: 59.8 in. Front tread: 48.2 in. Rear tread: 48.5 in. Tires: 6.50 x 15 in.

(**FLEETVAN FJ-3A**): Wheelbase: 81 in. Length: 154 in. Height: 90.12 in. Front tread: 48 9/16 in. Rear tread: 48 9/16 in. Tires: 6.70 x 15 in. four-ply tubeless.

(**SHORT-WHEELBASE TRUCKS**): Wheelbase: 104.5 in. Length: 176.2 in. Height: 72.1 in. Front tread: 57 in. Rear tread: 57 in. Tires: 7.00 x 15 in. (6.70 x 15 on Traveler).

(**LONG-WHEELBASE TRUCKS**): Wheelbase: 118 in. Length: 183.7 in. Height: 74.3 in. Front tread: 57 in. Rear tread: 63.5 in. Tires: 7.00 x 16 in.

(**FC-150**): Wheelbase: 81 in. Tires: 7.00 x 15 in.

(**FC-170**): Wheelbase: 103 1/2 in. Tires: 7.00 x 16 in.

TECHNICAL

(**FC-150/FC-170**): Three-speed synchromesh transmission (four-speed optional). Floor-mounted gearshift. Single-plate clutch (heavy-duty on FC-170). Rear axle: (FC-150) Semi-floating hypoid; (FC-170) full-floating hypoid rear axle. Overall ratios: (FC-150) 5.38:1; (FC-170) 4.89:1. Four-wheel hydraulic brakes (heavy-duty on FC-170). Disc wheels (dual rear on FC-170 Heavy-Duty model).

(**FLEETVAN**): Three-speed synchromesh transmission. Floor-mounted gearshift. Single-plate clutch, 72-sq. in. frictional area. I-beam front axle. Hypoid semi-floating rear axle. Overall ratio: 4.56:1. Hydraulic 9-in. drum brakes. Four 15 x 5.00 five-bolt disc wheels.

(**ALL OTHER MODELS**): Three-speed synchromesh transmission. Floor-mounted gearshift. Single-plate clutch. Hypoid semi-floating rear axle. Overall ratio: 3.54:1, 4.56:1, or 5.38:1. Four-wheel hydraulic brakes. Disc wheels. 4x4 models have two-speed transfer case and full-floating hypoid front axle. 4x2 models have I-beam type front axle.

OPTIONS

(**CJ**): Chrome front bumper. Chrome rear bumper. Chrome bumperettes. Chrome wheel discs. Power take-off. Pulley drive. Motor governor. Soft top. Hydraulic lift. Metal top. (CJ-5): Five metal and fabric-top options. Ventilating windshield. Power take-off. Snowplow. Winch. Add-on cargo box. (CJ-6): All-weather canvas tops. Oversize tires.

(**DJ-3A**): Soft top. Hardtop. Whitewall tires. Chrome wheel discs. Chrome front bumper. Chrome rear bumper. Eight standard body colors. "Law Enforcement" package. Three different color striped tops for Surrey.

(**FJ**): (Fleetvan): Two-tone paint. Ladder racks. Heater.

(**TRUCKS 4x4**): Standard and deluxe cab trim. Power take-off. Pulley drive. Motor governor. Rearview mirror. Sidemount spare on pickups/stakes. Chrome bumper. License frame.

(**SEDAN DELIVERY**): Chrome front bumper. Chrome rear bumper. License frame. Chrome wheel disc. Bumperettes. Bumper guards. Wheel trim rings. Whitewall tires. Rearview mirror. Radio and antenna. Two-tone paint combinations.

(**FC**): Fresh air heater. Radio. Two-tone paint. Front bumper guards. Direction signals. E-Z-Eye glass. Windshield washer. Front air vent. Double passenger seat. Oil bath air cleaner. Oil filter. High-altitude cylinder head (no charge). Four-speed transmission. Powr-Lok differential. Heavy-duty rear axle. Heavy-duty springs and shocks. Transmission brake. Hot climate radiator. Power take-off (center and rear). Governor. Various size/type tires. Draw-bar. Stabilizer bar. Rear bumperettes. Selective drive hubs. Bed- and/or front-mount winch. Snowplow. Dozer blade. Wrecker equipment. Jeep-A-Trench. Service bodies.

The all-new Jeep Gladiator pickup for 1963. Some Jeep enthusiasts have questioned details of this factory photograph, because the circular trim pieces flanking the grille are painted rather than bright metal. However, sales literature indicates the painted pieces were standard, with the bright metal items installed if the chrome grille was ordered—as it usually was. This is a very plain model. Note the painted bumper and grille.

1963

In October of 1962, Willys Motors introduced two entirely new lines of Jeep vehicles—and they were sensational! New Jeep station wagons were built on a 110-in. wheelbase and were longer than the old Jeep wagons for improved ride and passenger room, yet shorter and more compact than the giant work wagons offered by some competitors. Dubbed the Jeep Wagoneer, the new wagons were available in both two- and four-door versions, and in a choice of two-wheel or four-wheel drive. Because the four-wheel-drive models were the first station wagons to be designed from the ground up for four-wheel drive, the chassis integrated all the various mechanical elements neatly, providing low step-in height while still retaining good ground clearance. Increased width meant the Wagoneers could carry six big people comfortably. Cargo space was

likewise improved. The only engine offered was the 140-hp Tornado OHC six introduced earlier in 1962. The Wagoneer introduced several new features to the market, the most important of which was the optional automatic transmission. Never before had a four-wheel-drive wagon offered the option of automatic shifting, and it instantly put Jeep Wagoneer within reach of thousands of new prospective buyers. Although manual transmissions were still very common in 1963, the market trend was clearly heading to automatic transmissions and it was fortunate that Jeep realized it. Wagoneer was also the first four-wheel-drive wagon to offer an optional independent front suspension.

Jeep Wagoneer offered two trim levels—plain or Deluxe. Deluxe models came with floor carpeting, nicer upholstery, fancier trim. The regular Wagoneers came with rubber floor covering and plain, serviceable upholstery. Sometime mid-year the Deluxe was renamed the Custom. All Wagoneer models came with a column-shifted three-speed manual transmission. Besides the optional automatic box, two-wheel-drive Wagoneers could also be ordered with overdrive at slight extra cost.

The two-door Wagoneer tended to be favored by businesses looking for a rugged work truck or a low-priced delivery wagon that could also serve as a passenger car. Families overwhelmingly favored the four-door models. A panel truck version of the two-door was offered in the commercial line, and these are particularly rare today. One important feature of the panel truck was the outward opening dual rear doors, which deliverymen found especially handy.

In that exciting year, Willys also introduced all-new trucks based on the new Jeep chassis. It was an extensive line of truck models, offered in 1/2-ton, 3/4-ton and 1-ton ratings. Called the Gladiators, they offered the same fine styling of the Wagoneers, and many of the new features. Offered in two- or four-wheel-drive models, the Gladiator J-200 series rode a 120-in. wheelbase, while the heavier duty J-300 rode a 126-in. chassis. Three models were offered—the stake-bed truck and two pick-ups. Of these, the Thriftside included an old-style stepside pickup bed with big rear fenders, while the Townside used a more modern-looking flat-sided box with the fender wells inside.

Gladiator's debut marked Jeep's return to the two-wheel-drive pickup market. The company hadn't offered a regular production two-wheel-drive pickup in the U.S. for about five years. The reason was the old Jeep truck's narrow body and old-fashion styling weren't competitive against the more modern entries from GM, Ford, International, Dodge, and even Studebaker. Since the mid-1950s, Jeep's four-wheel-drive truck expertise had been just about the only advantage it offered. With the all-new and very handsome truck, Jeep could once again compete with the best. As in the Wagoneer, the Gladiator's integrated four-wheel-drive design allowed for a lower body and reduced step-in height, and yet it still provided excellent ground clearance. Jeep boasted that the cargo loading height was more than 7 in. lower than some competitive trucks.

Collectively, the Wagoneers and Gladiators are called the J Series or, less commonly, the SJ (Senior Jeep) line.

With the old-style Jeep trucks and the Traveler station wagons, plus the CJ-3B, CJ-5, DJ-3

Dispatcher, Gala, FC trucks, and the Fleetvans, Willys Motors had the largest product lineup in its history. When all the variations and specialty versions were included, it was an almost bewilderingly complex product line.

Midway through the model year came some stunning news. In March 1963, Kaiser Industries Vice President Steve Girard announced that the company had changed the name of its vehicle division to Kaiser Jeep Corporation. The reason given was a desire "to properly identify the Toledo company as one of the growing Kaiser family of industries." Although the old name would continue in some overseas markets, the Willys brand would no longer be used in America.

Kaiser Jeep Corporation reported that retail deliveries of new Jeeps were up 55 percent for the year, and dollar volume increased by 42 percent over 1962. The company reported an operating profit of $9.3 million.

NOTABLE FOR 1963: There were three Jeep Universal models. The CJ-3B was characterized by its raised hood and flat fenders. Power came from a 72-hp Hurricane four-cylinder engine. CJ-5 had curved fenders. The base engine was a 75-hp version of the Hurricane. The CJ-6 was a stretched version of the CJ-5 with the CJ-3B engine under its hood. The three 4x2 Dispatcher models featured an I-beam front axle and the 60-hp "Lightning" L-head four. There were three series of the old-style Jeep wagons, pickups and panels available in 1963. All models were basically carryover. Pickups and Panel Deliveries were on a longer 118-in. wheelbase and rated for 1-ton payloads. Station Wagons were offered in standard or custom trim levels. There now was a circular badge with Kaiser corporate logo above the center of the grille. Forward Control Jeeps were also mostly carryover. FC-150 standard equipment included: dual wipers, key locks on both doors, dispatch

The all-new Jeep Wagoneer, which debuted as a 1963 model, was a revolutionary design and set the standard for years to come.

DaimlerChrysler photo

The 1963 Gladiator Townside Pickup

box, color-toned interiors, Plasti-Strand upholstery, ashtray, left-hand sun visor, dome light, rearview mirror and adjustable driver's seat. Deluxe equipment added dual sun visors, armrests, rear quarter windows, acoustical trim, vinyl windshield trim, chrome safety handrail, foam rubber seats, cigarette lighter, and front panel kick pads. The 1-ton FC-170 came with the 226-cid "Hurricane" L-head six. Also available were two FC-170 heavy-duty chassis configurations with dual rear wheels. Customers could have platform, stake, or special bodies mounted on this rugged chassis. Standard equipment included a Safety-View cab, acoustical trim panels on doors, engine cover insulation, vinyl covered dash, safety door latches, foam rubber seats, suspended pedals, and a single-control transfer case lever.

There was a completely new range of Jeep Wagoneers. New Gladiator trucks came in chassis-&-cab, pickup, and platform stake models. Pickups were offered in Thriftside (flared fender) and Townside (slab fender) models. Automatic transmission was available for the first time with a four-wheel-drive chassis. Two-wheel-drive Wagoneers and Gladiators were also offered. In all there were nine basic series on three wheelbases: 110, 120, and 126 inches. 1/2-ton, 3/4-ton, and 1-ton models were offered. Four 1/2-ton series had GVW ratings of 4,200-4,500, 4,000, 5,600, and 5,000 lbs. Three 3/4-ton series had GVWs of 6,000, 6,600, or 7,600 lbs. Both 1-ton series had GVWs of 8,600 lbs. The 230-cid overhead-cam six-cylinder engine was standard in all.

I.D. DATA: (CJ) Serial number located on floor riser. Starting numbers were distinct for each model: (CJ-3B) 57348-59127 and up; (CJ-5) 57548-90027 and up; (CJ-6) 57748-18221 and up; (DJ-3A) 56337-15704 and up. Ending numbers not available. (F-134/L6-226/ 6-230) Serial number located on door hinge pillar post. Each

model had a distinct starting number for 37 variations. The first five digits of the serial numbers identified the model. These were followed by a dash and the sequential number. (FC): Serial number located on door hinge pillar. Unlike other Jeeps, the FC-150 was numbered by series with 65548-20683 the starting number for all models. The FC-170 starting number was 61568-15897. However, the heavy-duty chassis each had distinct starting numbers, 61368-13-10001 for the chassis with windshield and 61568-13-10479 for the chassis and cab. (J Series): Serial number located on left-hand door hinge pillar. The first four digits indicated the truck line. The fifth symbol was a letter, followed by the sequential number. Starting number for each series was 10001 up. (All series): Engine numbers located on right-hand corner of block.

Model	Body Type	Price	Weight
CJ-3B — 1/4-Ton — 4x4 — 80-in. w.b.			
CJ-3B	Jeep Universal	$2,015	2,132 lbs.
CJ-5 — 1/4-Ton — 4x4 — 81-in. w.b.			
CJ-5	Jeep Universal	$2,109	2,163 lbs.
CJ-6 — 1/2-Ton — 4x4 — 101-in. w.b.			
CJ-6	Jeep Universal	$2,204	2,225 lbs.
DJ-3A — 1/4-Ton — 4x2 — 80-in. w.b.			
DJ-3A	Jeep	$1,492	1,709 lbs.
DJ-3A	Hardtop	$1,723	2,004 lbs.
DJ-3A	Soft Top	$1,559	1,769 lbs.
Fleetvan — 1/2-Ton — Four-cyl — 4x2 — Delivery Van			
FJ-3	Fleetvan (postal)	—	—
FJ-3A	Fleetvan (commercial)	—	—
Series F-134 — 1/2-Ton — 104.5-in. w.b.			
58147	Station Wagon (4x2)	$2,095	2,858 lbs.
54347	Traveler (4x2)	$2,561	3,077 lbs.
54147	Utility Wagon (4x2)	$2,258	2,944 lbs.
54148	Utility Wagon (4x4)	$2,887	3,093 lbs.
54247	Panel Delivery (4x2)	$2,007	2,746 lbs.
54248	Panel Delivery (4x4)	$2,605	2,893 lbs.

Series F-134 — 1-Ton — 118-in. w.b.

55248	Pickup (4x4)	$2,369	3,065 lbs.

Series L6-226 — 1/2-Ton — 104.5-in. w.b.

58167	Station Wagon (4x2)	$2,344	2,971 lbs.
54167	Utility Wagon (4x2)	$2,738	3,057 lbs.
54367	Traveler (4x2)	$2,378	2,939 lbs.
54168	Utility Wagon (4x4)	$3,010	3,206 lbs.
54467	Utility Chassis (4x2)	$1,814	1,968 lbs.
54267	Panel Delivery (4x2)	$2,132	2,859 lbs.
55468	Chassis (4x4)	$2,232	2,281 lbs.
54268	Panel Delivery (4x4)	$2,728	3,008 lbs.
54468	Utility Chassis (4x4)	$2,311	2,228 lbs.

Series L6-226 — 1-Ton — 118-in. w.b.

55168	Chassis & Cab (4x4)	$2,365	2,817 lbs.
55268	Pickup (4x4)	$2,490	3,176 lbs.
55368	Platform Stake (4x4)	$2,577	3,341 lbs.

Series 6-230 — 1/2-Ton — 104.5-in. w.b.

58177	Station Wagon (4x2)	$2,450	3,047 lbs.
54377	Traveler (4x2)	$2,792	3,240 lbs.
54178	Utility Wagon (4x4)	$3,117	3,307 lbs.
54378	Traveler (4x4)	$3,389	3,410 lbs.
54278*	Panel Delivery (4x4)	$2,835	3,561 lbs.
54277	Panel Delivery (4x2)	—	3,147 lbs.

Series 6-230 — 1-Ton — 118-in. w.b.

55178	Chassis & Cab (4x4)	$2,472	2,872 lbs.
55278	Pickup (4x4)	$2,597	3,238 lbs.
55378	Stake (4x4)	$2,684	3,373 lbs.

*Starting serial number for 1964 is identical, suggesting no 1963s were made.

Series FC-150 — 1/2-Ton — 4x4 — 81-in. w.b.

65548	Chassis & Cab	$2,507	2,764 lbs.
65548	Pickup	$2,624	3,020 lbs.
65548	Platform Stake	$2,725	3,187 lbs.

Series FC-170 — 1-Ton — 4x4 — 103.5-in. w.b.

61568	Chassis & Cab	$2,824	2,901 lbs.
61568	Pickup	$2,960	3,331 lbs.
61568	Platform Stake	$3,167	3,564 lbs.

Series FC-170HD — 1-Ton — 6x6 — 103.5-in. w.b.

61368	Chassis & Windshield	$3,144	3,028 lbs.
61568	Chassis & Cab	$3,315	3,561 lbs.

Series J-100 — 1/2-Ton — 4x2 — 110-in. w.b.

1314	4d Wagoneer	$2,589	3,480 lbs.
1312	2d Wagoneer	$2,546	3,453 lbs.
1314C	4d Custom Wagoneer	$2,783	3,515 lbs.
1312C	2d Custom Wagoneer	$2,738	3,488 lbs.
1313	Panel Delivery	$2,438	3,253 lbs.

Series J-100 — 1/2-Ton — 4x4 — 110-in. w.b.

1414	4d Wagoneer	$3,332	3,623 lbs.
1412	2d Wagoneer	$3,278	3,596 lbs.
1414C	4d Custom Wagoneer	$3,526	3,658 lbs.
1412C	2d Custom Wagoneer	$3,472	3,631 lbs.
1413	Panel Delivery	$2,996	3,396 lbs.

Series J-200 — 1/2-Ton — 4x2 — 120-in. w.b.

2306F	Chassis & Cab	$1,913	2,901 lbs.
2306F	Thriftside Pickup	$2,014	3,196 lbs.
2306F	Townside Pickup	$2,041	3,304 lbs.

Series J-200 — 1/2-Ton — 4x4 — 120-in. w.b.

2406F	Chassis & Cab	$2,596	3,061 lbs.
2406F	Thriftside Pickup	$2,696	3,361 lbs.
2406F	Townside Pickup	$2,722	3,461 lbs.

Series J-210 — 1/2-Ton — 4x2 — 120-in. w.b.

2306A	Chassis & Cab	$1,977	2,941 lbs.
2306A	Thriftside Pickup	$2,078	3,236 lbs.
2306A	Townside Pickup	$2,105	3,344 lbs.

Series J-210 — 1/2-Ton — 4x4 — 120-in. w.b.

2406A	Chassis & Cab	$2,653	3,096 lbs.

2406A	Thriftside Pickup	$2,734	3,396 lbs.
2406A	Townside Pickup	$2,781	3,496 lbs.

Series J-300 — 1/2-Ton — 4x2 — 126-in. w.b.

3306E	Chassis & Cab	$2,017	2,943 lbs.
3306E	Thriftside Pickup	$2,133	3,263 lbs.
3306E	Townside Pickup	$2,160	3,371 lbs.

Series J-300 — 1/2-Ton — 4x4 — 126-in. w.b.

3406E	Chassis & Cab	$2,654	3,091 lbs.
3406E	Thriftside Pickup	$2,769	3,441 lbs.
3406E	Townside Pickup	$2,796	3,541 lbs.

Series J-220 — 3/4-Ton — 4x2 — 120-in. w.b.

2306B	Chassis & Cab	$2,062	3,024 lbs.
2306B	Thriftside Pickup	$2,163	3,319 lbs.
2306B	Townside Pickup	$2,189	3,427 lbs.
2306B	Platform Stake	$2,368	3,680 lbs.

Series J-220 — 3/4-Ton — 4x4 — 120-in. w.b.

2406B	Chassis & Cab	$2,753	3,214 lbs.
2406B	Thriftside Pickup	$2,854	3,514 lbs.
2406B	Townside Pickup	$2,881	3,614 lbs.
2406B	Platform Stake	$3,060	3,894 lbs.

Series J-310 — 3/4-Ton — 4x2 — 126-in. w.b.

3306B	Chassis & Cab	$2,128	3,067 lbs.
3306B	Thriftside Pickup	$2,243	3,387 lbs.
3306B	Townside Pickup	$2,270	3,495 lbs.
3306B	Platform Stake	$2,468	3,771 lbs.

Series J-310 — 3/4-Ton — 4x4 — 126-in. w.b.

3406B	Chassis & Cab	$2,771	3,239 lbs.
3406B	Thriftside Pickup	$2,886	3,589 lbs.
3406B	Townside Pickup	$2,913	3,689 lbs.
3406B	Platform Stake	$3,111	3,979 lbs.

Series J-320 — 3/4-Ton — 4x2 — 126-in. w.b.

3306C	Chassis & Cab	$2,283	3,168 lbs.
3306C	Thriftside Pickup	$2,398	3,488 lbs.
3306C	Townside Pickup	$2,425	3,596 lbs.
3306C	Platform Stake	$2,623	3,872 lbs.

Series J-320 — 3/4-Ton — 4x4 — 126-in. w.b.

3406C	Chassis & Cab	$2,931	3,377 lbs.
3406C	Thriftside Pickup	$3,046	3,727 lbs.
3406C	Townside Pickup	$3,073	3,827 lbs.
3406C	Platform Stake	$3,271	4,117 lbs.

Series J-230 — 1-Ton — 4x2 — 120-in. w.b.

2406D	Chassis & Cab	$3,578	3,874 lbs.
2406D	Platform Stake	$3,970	4,714 lbs.

Series J-330 — 1-Ton — 4x2 — 126-in. w.b.

3406D	Chassis & Cab	$3,597	3,899 lbs.
3406D	Platform Stake	$4,011	4,799 lbs.

NOTE: Explanation of J-Series model number suffixes: A=5,600-lb. GVW; B=6,600-lb. GVW; C=7,600-lb. GVW; D=8,600-lb. GVW; E=5,000-lb. GVW; F=4,000-lb. GVW.

**The 1963 Wagoneer, seen at
an auto show in Europe.**

PRODUCTION: The company did not report total production, but it is estimated that 110,549 Jeeps were produced.

ENGINES

(CJ-3B/CJ-6/F-134 FOUR): Inline. F-head. Cast-iron block. Bore & stroke: 3 1/8 in. x 4 3/8 in. Displacement: 134.2 cid. Compression ratio: 6.9:1. Brake hp: 72 at 4000 rpm. Torque: 114 lbs.-ft. at 2000 rpm. Solid valve lifters. Carburetor: Carter.

(CJ-5/FC-150 FOUR): Inline. F-head. Cast-iron block. Bore & stroke: 3 1/8 in. x 4 3/8 in. Displacement: 134.2 cid. Compression ratio: 7.4:1. Brake hp: 75 at 4000 rpm. Torque: 114 lbs.-ft. at 2000 rpm. Solid valve lifters. Carburetor: Carter.

(DJ-3A FOUR): Inline. L-head. Cast-iron block. Bore & stroke: 3 1/8 in. x 4 3/8 in. Displacement: 134.2 cid. Compression ratio: 7.00:1. Brake hp: 60 at 4000 rpm. Torque: 114 lbs.-ft. at 2000 rpm. Solid valve lifters. Carburetor: Carter.

(L6-226/FC-170 SIX): Inline. L-head. Cast-iron block. Bore & stroke: 3 5/16 in. x 4 3/8 in. Displacement: 226.2 cid. Compression ratio: 6.86:1 (7.3:1 optional). Brake hp: 105 at 3600 rpm. Torque: 190 lbs.-ft. at 1400 rpm. Solid valve lifters. Carburetor: Carter.

(6-230/J-SERIES SIX): Overhead Cam. Inline. Cast-iron block. Bore & stroke: 3.34 in. x 4.38 in. Displacement: 230 cid. Compression ratio: 8.5:1. Brake hp: 140 at 4000 rpm. Torque: 210 lbs.-ft. at 1750 rpm. Solid valve lifters. Carburetor: Carter two-barrel.

CHASSIS

See model charts above for wheelbases. Overall length: (CJ-3B) 129.9 in.; (CJ-5) 135.5. in.; (CJ-6) 155.5 in.; (DJ-3A) 125.4 in.; (F-134/L6-226/6-230) 1/2-ton 176.2 in.; 1-ton 183.7 in.; (FC-150) 147.3 in.; (FC-170) 181.4 in.; (J-100) 183.66 in. Front tread: (CJ-3B) 48.4 in.; (CJ-5) 48.4 in.; (CJ-6) 48.4 in.; (DJ-3A) 48.2 in.; (F-134, L6-226, 6-230) 1/2-ton: 57 in.; 1-ton: 57 in.; (FC-150) 57 in.; (FC-170) 63.4 in.; (J-100) 57 in. Rear tread: (CJ-3B) 48.4 in.; (CJ-5) 48.4 in.; (CJ-6) 48.4 in.; (DJ-3A) 48.5 in.; (F-134/L6-226/6-230) 1/2-ton: 57 in.; 1-ton: 63.5 in.; (FC-150) 57 in.; (FC-170) 63.8 in.; (J-100) 57 in. Tires: (CJ-all models) 6.00 x 16 in.; (DJ-3A) 6.50 x 15 in.; (F-134/L6-226/6-230) 1/2-ton 4x2: 6.70 x 15 in.; 1/2-ton 4x4: 7.00 x 15 in; 1-ton 7.00 x 16 in.; (FC-150) 7.00 x 15 in.; (FC-170) 7.00 x 16

in.; (J-100, J-200) 6.70 x 15 in.; (J-210) 7.60 x 15 in.; (J-300) 7.10 x 15 in.; (J-320) 7.50 x 16 in.; (other models) 7.00 x 16 in.

TECHNICAL

Three-speed synchromesh transmission. Single-plate clutch. Semi-floating rear axle. Four-wheel hydraulic brakes. Steel disc wheels. 4x2 models have I-beam front axle. 4x4 models have hypoid, semi-floating front axle and two-speed transfer case.

OPTIONS

(CJ/DJ): Soft top. Fiberglass cab top. Metal cab top. Four-speed transmission.

(ALL MODELS): Rearview mirror. Radio w/antenna. Ramsey or Koenig winches for front, rear or bed mount. Warn or Cutlass free-wheeling hubs. Canfield wrecker for Universals, 4x4 pickup, or Forward Control models. Meyer angle dozers. Jeep-A-Trench. Tailgate loader for 600 lb. or 1,000 lb. rated models. Deluxe cab on Forward Control models. Fresh air heater. Two-tone paint. Front bumper guards. Directional signals. E-Z-Eye glass. Windshield washer. FC-150 front air vent. FC-150 double passenger seat. Oil bath air cleaner. Oil filter. High-altitude cylinder head (no charge). Powr-Lok rear differential. Heavy-duty rear axle. Heavy-duty springs and shock absorbers. Transmission brake. Hot-climate radiator. Variable and constant-speed governors. Various size and type tires including whitewalls in available sizes. Draw-bar. Stabilizer bar. Rear bumperettes. Automatic transmission in Wagoneers and Gladiators. Full wheel discs.

Jeep's Tornado OHC six, which debuted in 1962, was the only engine offered on the 1963 Wagoneer and Gladiator.

Gladiator was mostly unchanged for 1964. This optional fabric camper top has unusual side windows.

One year after the introduction of the new Wagoneer and Gladiator models it was the Jeep Universal's turn for some product news. Two new models, the CJ-5A Tuxedo Park and CJ-6A Tuxedo Park, were aimed at retail buyers looking for a fun vehicle. Jeep even referred to its Tuxedo Parks as sports cars. The new Jeeps featured upscale interior trim that included wheelhouse pads, floor mats, better seat upholstery, plus chrome-plated hood hold-downs, windshield hinges, bumpers, passenger grab handle, and mirrors. Color-coordinated soft tops and full wheel covers were also part of the Tuxedo Park look.

In other news, this year the FC-170 dual-rear-wheel truck was available only as a cab-&-chassis model. The rest of the FC truck line was still available.

Responding to concerns about engine pinging, the Jeep Wagoneer now offered an optional lower-compression 133-hp version of the OHC six-cylinder engine for folks living in high-altitude areas. New this year, and highly unusual for a four-wheel-drive vehicle, was optional air conditioning. With other options that included power brakes, power steering, and an electrically operated rear window, Jeep Wagoneer was fast becoming the vehicle that defined luxury in four-wheel-drive machines.

Early in the year the company purchased a modern 1 million-sq.-ft. plant in South Bend, Indiana, from Studebaker Corp., which was consolidating its automobile production by transferring it to Canada, and at the same time exiting the truck business. Along with the factory, Kaiser acquired an Army contract for production of 8,634 5-ton military trucks. This marked a new era for Jeep's involvement in tactical trucks, and would be the largest military vehicle the company had yet produced. This move, along with a surge in military orders for Jeep's other products, helped create a huge backlog of orders that was calculated at an incredible $272,873,000 by year's end. The Postal Service also placed a new order for 3,868 Fleetvans.

Overseas, Mahindra & Mahindra, licensees in India, reported production of its 50,000th Jeep vehicle, while in Mexico VAM introduced the new J Series Wagoneer and Gladiator, and began operation of a new engine plant.

The Jeep dealer network in the U.S. continued to grow and the company reported it had 2,150 dealers at year's end. The Kaiser Jeep division turned in a good fiscal performance for 1964 with a profit of $11.1 million on record sales of $255.5 million.

NOTABLE FOR 1964: Introduced as "the new idea in sports cars," the new CJ-5A and CJ-6A Tuxedo Park packages were upscale versions of the two base models. Everything else was much the same as 1963. The 75 hp four-cylinder Hurricane engine was used in CJs, while

Dispatchers had the 60-hp Lightning L-head four as base equipment. Jeep wagons, pickups and panel trucks continued to be offered in 1964. Several models in the L6-226 series were cut, leaving only the standard wheelbase 4x2 Station Wagon, 4x4 Utility Wagon and long-wheelbase 1-ton Pickup. Forward Control 1/2-ton and 1-ton models were carried over for 1964 with one minor model change. The FC-170 heavy-duty configuration, with dual rear wheels, was available now in chassis-and-cab form only. Returning this season was the Jeep Fleetvan in FJ-3 and FJ-3A models, designed for light-duty, multi-stop operation. The boxy little trucks could carry payloads up to 1,000 lbs. Kaiser advertised that "five Fleetvans take up less garage space than four nationally advertised competitive vehicles."

Kaiser's Jeep Wagoneer for 1964 came in two- or four-door wagons and looked the same as the 1963 models. New options included the lower-compression 133-hp version of the OHC six-cylinder engine, and air conditioning. The standard drive train was the 140-hp six linked to a three-speed manual transmission with gearshift lever on the steering column. Optional overdrive or an automatic transmission could be ordered on 4x2 Wagoneers, while only the automatic was optional on 4x4s. A choice of suspension systems was offered on both 4x2 and 4x4 models. Independent front suspension with torsion bars and rear leaf springs was one option. The other was leaf springs all around. Other extras included: deluxe trim, power take-off, power steering, power brakes, and a series of dash-mounted lights to indicate whether the Wagoneer was in 4x4 or 4x2 models. A floor-mounted lever engaged the 4x4 system. Gladiator trucks came in 1/2-ton, 3/4-ton and 1-ton configurations. The 1-tons were 4x4s only, while the others were available with 4x2 or 4x4 running gear. Wheelbases of 120 or 126 in. were available in all lines.

I.D. DATA: (All) VINs located right side of dash under hood; left side of dash under hood; left floor riser in back of driver's seat; or on left door post. Except for the J Series, early 1964 models used the 1963 numbering system, with the first five digits indicating series and model and the five digits after the dash representing the sequential number. On late-1964-and-up J Series models, there were four digits ahead of the dash. The four digit numbers are used in the charts below. For early 1964 models see 1963 codes. Engine numbers located on right-hand front of block.

Sales of military Jeeps began to rise in the 1960s as the war in Vietnam heated up.

Model	Body Type	Price	Weight
CJ-3B — 1/4-Ton — 4x4 — 80-in. w.b.			
CJ-3B	Jeep Universal	$2,117	2,132 lbs.
CJ-5 — 1/4-Ton — 4x4 — 81-in. w.b.			
CJ-5	Jeep Universal	$2,211	2,163 lbs.
CJ-5A	Jeep Universal Tuxedo Park	$2,306	2,163 lbs.
CJ-6 — 1/2-Ton — 4x4 — 101-in. w.b.			
CJ-6	Jeep Universal	$2,306	2,225 lbs.
CJ-6A	Jeep Universal Tuxedo Park	$2,401	2,225 lbs.
DJ-3A — 1/4-Ton — 4x2 — 80-in. w.b.			
DJ-3A	Jeep Universal	$1,518	1,709 lbs.
DJ-3A	Jeep Hardtop	$1,747	2,004 lbs.
DJ-3A	Jeep Soft Top	$1,660	1,769 lbs.
DJ-3A	Jeep Surrey	—	1,819 lbs.
Series FJ-3 Fleetvan — 1/2-Ton — 80-in. w.b.			
62847	Step-in Delivery	$2,360	2,900 lbs.
Series FJ-3A Fleetvan — 1/2-Ton — 81-in. w.b.			
62147	Step-in Delivery	$2,380	2,910 lbs.
Series F-134 — 1/2-Ton — 104.5-in. w.b.			
4112	Station Wagon (4x2)	$2,357	2,858 lbs.
54147	Utility Wagon (4x2)	$2,258	2,944 lbs.
4212	Utility Wagon (4x4)	$3,030	3,093 lbs.
4215	Traveler (4x4)	$3,302	3,077 lbs.
4113	Panel Delivery (4x2)	$2,143	2,746 lbs.
4213	Panel Delivery (4x4)	$2,741	2,893 lbs.
Series F-134 — 1-Ton — 118-in. w.b.			
4307	Pickup (4x4)	$2,514	3,065 lbs.
Series L6-226 — 1/2-Ton — 104.5-in. w.b.			
58167	Station Wagon (4x2)	$2,344	2,971 lbs.
54168	Utility Wagon (4x4)	$3,010	3,206 lbs.
4113	Panel Delivery (4x2)	$2,143	2,746 lbs.
4213	Panel Delivery (4x4)	$2,741	2,893 lbs.
Series L6-226 — 1-Ton — 118-in. w.b.			
4307	Pickup (4x4)	$2,514	3,065 lbs.
Series 6-230 — 1/2-Ton — 104.5-in. w.b.			
6412	Station Wagon (4x2)	$2,596	2,858 lbs.
6415	Utility Traveler (4x2)	$2,938	3,240 lbs.
6512	Utility Wagon (4x4)	$3,263	3,307 lbs.
6515	Utility Traveler (4x4)	$3,534	3,410 lbs.
6513	Panel Delivery (4x4)	$2,973	3,028 lbs.
6413	Panel Delivery (4x2)	$2,377	3,147 lbs.
Series 6-230 — 1-Ton — 4x4 — 118-in. w.b.			
6606	Chassis & Cab	$2,619	2,872 lbs.
6607	Pickup	$2,744	3,238 lbs.
6608	Stake	$2,831	3,873 lbs.
Series FC-150 — 1/2-Ton — 4x4 — 81-in. w.b.			
9209	Chassis & Cab	$2,735	2,764 lbs.
9209	Pickup	$2,853	3,020 lbs.
9209	Platform Stake	$2,954	3,187 lbs.
Series FC-170 — 1-Ton — 4x4 — 103.5-in. w.b.			
9309	Chassis & Cab	$3,056	2,901 lbs.
9309	Pickup	$3,192	3,331 lbs.
9309	Platform Stake	$3,399	3,564 lbs.
Series FC-170HD — 1-Ton — 6x6 — 103.5-in. w.b.			
9325	Chassis & Cab	$3,547	3,561 lbs.
Series J-100 — 1/2-Ton — 4x2 — 110-in. w.b.			
1314	4d Wagoneer	$2,673	3,480 lbs.
1312	2d Wagoneer	$2,629	3,453 lbs.
1314C	4d Custom Wagoneer	$2,871	3,515 lbs.
1312C	2d Custom Wagoneer	$2,827	3,488 lbs.
1313	Panel Delivery	$2,511	3,253 lbs.
Series J-100 — 1/2-Ton — 4x4 — 110-in. w.b.			
1414	4d Wagoneer	$3,434	3,623 lbs.
1412	2d Wagoneer	$3,379	3,596 lbs.
1414C	4d Custom Wagoneer	$3,633	3,658 lbs.
1412C	2d Custom Wagoneer	$3,578	3,631 lbs.
1413	Panel Delivery	$3,082	3,396 lbs.

Model	Body Type	Price	Weight
Series J-200 — 1/2-Ton — 4x2 — 120-in. w.b.			
2306F	Chassis & Cab	$1,980	2,901 lbs.
2306F	Thriftside Pickup	$2,081	3,196 lbs.
2306F	Townside Pickup	$2,108	3,304 lbs.
Series J-200 — 1/2-Ton — 4x4 — 120-in. w.b.			
2406F	Chassis & Cab	$2,679	3,061 lbs.
2406F	Thriftside Pickup	$2,779	3,361 lbs.
2406F	Townside Pickup	$2,806	3,461 lbs.
Series J-210 — 1/2-Ton — 4x2 — 120-in. w.b.			
2306A	Chassis & Cab	$2,046	2,941 lbs.
2306A	Thriftside Pickup	$2,147	3,236 lbs.
2306A	Townside Pickup	$2,173	3,344 lbs.
Series J-210 — 1/2-Ton — 4x4 — 120-in. w.b.			
2406A	Chassis & Cab	$2,738	3,096 lbs.
2406A	Thriftside Pickup	$2,839	3,396 lbs.
2406A	Townside Pickup	$2,866	3,496 lbs.
Series J-300 — 1/2-Ton — 4x2 — 126-in. w.b.			
3306E	Chassis & Cab	$2,087	2,943 lbs.
3306E	Thriftside Pickup	$2,202	3,263 lbs.
3306E	Townside Pickup	$2,229	3,371 lbs.
Series J-300 — 1/2-Ton — 4x4 — 126-in. w.b.			
3406E	Chassis & Cab	$2,739	3,091 lbs.
3406E	Thriftside Pickup	$2,854	3,441 lbs.
3406E	Townside Pickup	$2,881	3,541 lbs.
Series J-220 — 3/4-Ton — 4x2 — 120-in. w.b.			
2306B	Chassis & Cab	$2,132	3,024 lbs.
2306B	Thriftside Pickup	$2,233	3,319 lbs.
2306B	Townside Pickup	$2,260	3,427 lbs.
2306B	Platform Stake	$2,439	3,680 lbs.
Series J-220 — 3/4-Ton — 4x4 — 120-in. w.b.			
2406B	Chassis & Cab	$2,841	3,214 lbs.
2406B	Thriftside Pickup	$2,942	3,514 lbs.
2406B	Townside Pickup	$2,969	3,614 lbs.
2406B	Platform Stake	$3,148	3,894 lbs.
Series J-310 — 3/4-Ton — 4x2 — 126-in. w.b.			
3306B	Chassis & Cab	$2,201	3,067 lbs.
3306B	Thriftside Pickup	$2,316	3,387 lbs.
3306B	Townside Pickup	$2,343	3,495 lbs.
3306B	Platform Stake	$2,541	3,771 lbs.
Series J-310 — 3/4-Ton — 4x4 — 126-in. w.b.			
3406B	Chassis & Cab	$2,860	3,239 lbs.
3406B	Thriftside Pickup	$2,975	3,589 lbs.
3406B	Townside Pickup	$3,002	3,689 lbs.
3406B	Platform Stake	$3,200	3,979 lbs.
Series J-320 — 3/4-Ton — 4x2 — 126-in. w.b.			
3306C	Chassis & Cab	$2,359	3,168 lbs.
3306C	Thriftside Pickup	$2,474	3,488 lbs.
3306C	Townside Pickup	$2,501	3,596 lbs.
3306C	Platform Stake	$2,699	3,872 lbs.
Series J-320 — 3/4-Ton — 4x4 — 126-in. w.b.			
3406C	Chassis & Cab	$3,024	3,377 lbs.
3406C	Thriftside Pickup	$3,139	3,727 lbs.
3406C	Townside Pickup	$3,166	3,827 lbs.
3406C	Platform Stake	$3,364	4,117 lbs.
Series J-230 — 1-Ton — 4x4 — 120-in. w.b.			
2406D	Chassis & Cab	$3,687	3,874 lbs.
2406D	Platform Stake	$4,079	4,714 lbs.
Series J-330 — 1-Ton — 4x4 — 126-in. w.b.			
3406D	Chassis & Cab	$3,706	3,899 lbs.
3406D	Platform Stake	$4,120	4,790 lbs.

NOTE: Explanation of "J" series model number suffixes: A=5,600-lb. GVW; B=6,600-lb. GVW; C=7,600-lb. GVW; D=8,600-lb. GVW; E=5,000-lb. GVW; F=4,000-lb. GVW.

PRODUCTION: The company did not report total production, but it is estimated that 120,868 Jeeps were produced.

ENGINE

(CJ-3B/CJ-6/F-134 FOUR): Inline. F-head. Cast-iron block. Bore & stroke: 3 1/8 in. x 4 3/8 in. Displacement: 134.2 cid. Compression ratio: 6.9:1. Brake hp: 72 at 4000 rpm. Torque: 114 lbs.-ft. at 2000 rpm. Solid valve lifters. Carburetor: Carter.

(CJ-5/FC-150/FJ-3A FOUR): Inline. F-head. Cast-iron block. Bore & stroke: 3 1/8 in. x 4 3/8 in. Displacement: 134.2 cid. Compression ratio: 7.4:1. Brake hp: 75 at 4000 rpm. Torque: 114 lbs.-ft. at 2000 rpm. Solid valve lifters. Carburetor: Carter.

(DJ-3A FOUR): Inline. L-head. Cast-iron block. Bore & stroke: 3 1/8 in. x 4 3/8 in Displacement: 134.2 cid. Compression ratio: 7.00:1. Brake hp: 60 at 4000 rpm. Torque: 114 lbs.-ft. at 2000 rpm. Solid valve lifters. Carburetor: Carter.

(L6-226/FC-170 SIX): Inline. L-head. Cast-iron block. Bore & stroke: 3 5/16 in. x 4 3/8 in. Displacement: 226.2 cid. Compression ratio: 6.86:1 (7.3:1 optional). Brake hp: 105 at 3600 rpm. Torque: 190 lbs.-ft. at 1400 rpm. Solid valve lifters. Carburetor: Carter.

(6-230/J-SERIES SIX): Overhead cam. Inline. Cast-iron block. Bore & stroke: 3.34 in. x 4.38 in. Displacement: 230 cid. Compression ratio: 8.5:1. Brake hp: 140 at 4000 rpm. Torque: 210 lbs.-ft. at 1750 rpm. Solid valve lifters. Carburetor: Carter model two-barrel.

(6-230/J-SERIES ECONOMY OPTION SIX): Inline. Overhead camshaft. Cast-iron block. Bore & stroke: 3.344 in. x 4.375 in. Displacement: 230.5 cid. Compression ratio: 7.5:1. Brake hp: 133 at 4000 rpm. Torque: 199 lbs.-ft. at 2400 rpm. Solid valve lifters. Carburetor: Carter model two-barrel.

CHASSIS

For wheelbase see chart above. Overall length: (CJ-3B) 129.9 in.; (CJ-5) 135.5 in.; (CJ-6) 155.5 in.; (DJ-3A) 125.4 in.; (F-134/L6-226/6-230) 1/2-ton 176.2 in.; 1-ton 183.7 in.; (FC-150) 147.3 in.; (FC-170) 181.4 in.; (J-100) 183.66 in.; (Fleetvan) 154 in. Front tread: (CJ-3B) 48.4 in.; (CJ-5) 48.4 in.; (CJ-6) 48.4 in.; (DJ-3A) 48.2 in.; (F-134, L6-226, 6-230) 1/2-ton: 57 in.; 1-ton: 57 in.; (FC-150) 57 in.; (FC-170) 63.4 in.; (J-100) 57 in.; (Fleetvan) 48 9/15 in. Rear tread: (CJ-3B) 48.4 in.; (CJ-5) 48.4 in.; (CJ-6) 48.4 in.; (DJ-3A) 48.5 in.; (F-134/L6-226/6-230) 1/2-Ton: 57 in.; 1-ton: 63.5 in.; (FC-150) 57 in.; (FC-170) 63.8 in.; (J-100) 57 in.; (Fleetvan) 48-9/16 in. Tires: (CJ-all models) 6.00 x 16 in.; (DJ-3A) 6.50 x 15 in.; (Fleetvan) 6.70 x 15 in.; (F-134/L6-226/6-230) 1/2-ton 4x2: 6.70 x 15 in.; 1/2-ton 4x4: 7.00 x 15 in; 1-ton 7.00 x 16 in.; (FC-150) 7.00 x 15 in.; (FC-170) 7.00 x 16 in.; (J-100, J-200) 6.70 x 15 in.; (J-210) 7.60 x 15 in.; (J-300) 7.10 x 15 in.; (J-320) 7.50 x 16 in.; (Other J Series models) 7.00 x 16 in.

TECHNICAL

Three speed synchromesh transmission. Single-plate dry-disc clutch. Semi-floating rear axle. Four-wheel hydraulic brakes. Steel disc wheels. 4x4 models have hypoid, semi-floating front axle and two-speed transfer case with ratios of 1.00:1 and 2.46:1.

OPTIONS

(CJ/DJ): Soft top; metal cab top. Four-speed transmission.

(ALL OTHER MODELS): Air conditioning. Power steering. Overdrive. Four-speed transmission. Rearview mirror. Radio. Antenna. Ramsey or Koenig winches for front, rear or bed mount. Warn or Cutlass selective drive hubs. Canfield wrecker for Universals, 4x4 pickup, or Forward Control models. Meyer angle dozers. Jeep-A-Trench. Tailgate loader for 600 lb. or 1,000 lb. rated models. Deluxe cab on Forward Control models. Fresh air heater. Two-tone paint. Front bumper guards. Directional signals. E-Z-Eye glass. Windshield washer. FC-150 front air vent. FC-150 double passenger seat. Oil bath air cleaner. Oil filter. High-altitude cylinder head (no charge). Powr-Lok rear differential. Heavy-duty rear axle. Heavy-duty springs and shock absorbers. Transmission brake. Hot-climate radiator. Variable and constant-speed governors. Various size and type tires including whitewalls in available sizes. Draw-bar. Stabilizer bar. Rear bumperettes. Automatic transmission in Travelalls and Gladiators. Full wheel discs.

Wagoneer's looks were greatly improved in late 1965 when this new grille design was introduced. Gladiators continued to feature the old keystone grille design.

By special arrangement, every float in the presidential inaugural parade held January 20, 1965, in Washington, D.C., was towed by a Jeep CJ-5.

The newest entries in the low priced delivery market were the DJ-5 and DJ-6 Dispatchers, two-wheel-drive versions of the CJ-5 and CJ-6. With their introduction, the DJ-3A was discontinued.

Jeep Wagoneer saw some major product improvements during 1965. The biggest news was the option of a 327-cid V-8 engine built by American Motors. Dubbed the "Vigilante" V-8 (imagine using a name like that today!), in standard form the engine produced 250 hp, a huge increase over the 140-hp Tornado six, and was just the thing to bring new buyers into the showrooms. The new V-8 was also offered in Gladiator trucks and the Panel Delivery wagon. Along with the new V-8 came a new automatic transmission, the Turbo Hydra-Matic unit produced by General Motors.

Midway through the year, Wagoneers and Gladiators also got a new standard six-cylinder engine. Called the Hi-Torque OHV-6, it was a tough 232-cid, seven-main bearing, inline six produced by American Motors. It produced 145-hp and 215 lbs.-ft. of torque. Endowed with rugged construction and velvety smoothness, this was perhaps the finest six-cylinder engine on the market. With the Hi-Torque OHV-6's introduction, the Jeep OHC six-cylinder engine was no longer offered on J Series vehicles.

There was other power train news. Late in the season (August 24, 1965) came the official announcement that the Jeep Universal vehicles (Jeep CJ and DJ models) would get a new engine option. This was the potent "Dauntless" V-6, a GM design used in Buick cars since the early 1960s. Jeep purchased the engines from Buick for installation in its Universal (CJ) models. Since off-road hot-rodders had been installing the Buick V-6 in Jeeps for several years, it was not a big job for the company to do it on a production basis. With the new engine, Jeep Universal's available power more than doubled. The V-6 produced 160-hp and 225 lbs.-ft. of torque from 225-cid, compare with the standard Hurricane engine's 75 hp, and transformed the small Jeep into a smooth, pleasant, and fast machine. Enthusiastic owners even reported being able to do four-wheel burnouts. The Dauntless engine was available in all CJ-5, CJ-6, DJ-5, and DJ-6 models, including the Tuxedo Park series.

This was the last year for the FC series in America. Apparently, a small number of 1965 model FC trucks were produced for the U.S. market towards the end of 1964. The FC would find new life in India, however, and remain in production for many more years. The newest entries in the low-priced delivery market were the DJ-5 and DJ-6 Dispatchers, which were two-wheel-drive versions of the CJ-5 and CJ-6.

This was the final year during which the Jeep CJ-3B was available in the domestic market. With the CJ-5 and CJ-6 offering so much more vehicle for so little extra cost, it made sense to consolidate the lineup. However, the tough old CJ-3B would continue on in overseas markets for many more years. This was also the final year in which the old-style Jeep station wagons and pickup trucks were produced in the U.S., though, like most old Jeep models, they would continue in overseas markets. Late in 1965, the Jeep Gladiator J-200 and J-300 truck models became known respectively as the Gladiator J-2000 and J-3000.

Despite deliveries of 16,000 military trucks during the year, the backlog of government orders soared to $420 million. The U.S. Postal Service took delivery of additional Fleetvans. These were a new generation of Fleetvans, the FJ-6, which had a more angular body style. The FJ-6 model is quite rare today.

For the year, Kaiser Jeep Corporation reported sales of $311,122,000, which was a substantial increase over 1964. However, this increase was entirely in the military vehicles business. Because of lower retail sales of Jeep vehicles, manufacturing operations actually lost money for the year. Kaiser Jeep's profit derived from payments received from its overseas affiliates. The income from foreign investments totaled $5.9 million, substantial enough so the company was able to report an operating profit of $4.9 million—quite a drop from the prior year. Oddly enough, management blamed the reduced Jeep retail sales on the product improvements it had introduced, saying that good customer response to the new models "... gave dealers some difficulty in disposing of the inventory of prior models. This resulted in a decline in domestic vehicle sales until the inventory adjustment was accomplished in the fourth quarter." The division noted that the four-wheel-drive market was getting more competitive. Jeep, after all, had been almost alone in the market from 1945 up to 1961, when International introduced its Scout.

NOTABLE FOR 1965: The Kaiser Jeep name was added to hood sides or fenders of all models this year. New for 1965 was the DJ-5. It was a 4x2-type vehicle used primarily for light-duty courier service, and would soon be added to the U.S. Postal Service fleet. It had a modified suspension system and could be ordered with left- or right-hand drive. There was also a full steel cab with sliding side doors and a rear door. A single bucket seat was provided for the operator. Joining the new 81-inch-wheelbase DJ-5 was a 101-in.-wheelbase DJ-6. A new postal Fleetvan, the FJ-6, was also introduced this year. The utility-type Jeep station wagons, panels and pickups carried "Kaiser Jeep" badges this season. The L6-226 models disappeared and the L-head six-cylinder engine was used only for the FC-170 trucks. This was the final appearance of the F-134 line. Forward Control models remained available in 1/2-ton (FC-150) and 1-ton (FC-170) configurations. They were little changed, except for addition of Kaiser-Jeep nameplates.

Kaiser-Jeep nameplates replaced the Jeep name on the front fender sides of Wagoneers and Gladiators. There were two separate series of Gladiators this year. The first was comprised of the J-200, J-210, J-300, J-220, J-310, J-320, J-230, and J-330 lines, all of which were carried over from 1964 with no changes in prices, weights or other specifications. For data on these trucks, refer to the 1964 listings for the same models. The second series of Gladiators was comprised of the J-2500, J-2600, J-3500, J-3600, J-2700, J-3700, J-2800, and J-3800 lines. These trucks had the same general styling as the early Gladiators and used the same 230-cid six-cylinder engine as standard equipment. A new option was a 327-cid V-8. The GVW ratings for the later series were also slightly higher, in most cases, than the comparable models in the original Gladiator series.

I.D. DATA: Serial number located in the same locations as before. The new Gladiators used model numbers identical to those for the "old" Gladiators, except for the alphabetical suffix. Codes for other models were the same as 1964. Engine numbers located in the same places.

Model	Body Type	Price	Weight
CJ-3B — 1/4-Ton — 4x4 — 80-in. w.b.			
8105	Jeep Universal	$2,117	2,132 lbs.
CJ-5 — 1/4-Ton — 4x4 — 81-in. w.b.			
8305	Jeep Universal	$2,211	2,163 lbs.
8322	Tuxedo Park	$2,306	2,163 lbs.
CJ-6 — 1/2-Ton — 4x4 — 101-in. w.b.			
8405	Jeep Universal	$2,306	2,225 lbs.
8422	Tuxedo Park	$2,401	2,225 lbs.
DJ-5 — 1/4-Ton — 4x2 — 81-in. w.b.			
8201	Soft Top	$1,518	1,709 lbs.
8203	Hardtop	$1,747	2,004 lbs.
8505	Special	$1,744	1,823 lbs.
DJ-6 — 1/2-Ton — 4x2 — 101-in. w.b.			
8505	Soft Top	$1,818	1,823 lbs.
Fleetvan — 1/2-Ton — Four-cyl — 4x2 — Delivery Van			
FJ-6	Fleetvan (postal)	—	—
Series F-134 — 1/2-Ton — 104.5-in. w.b.			

4112	Station Wagon (4x2)	$2,357	2,858 lbs.
4212	Utility Wagon (4x4)	$3,030	3,093 lbs.
4215	Traveler (4x4)	$3,302	3,077 lbs.
4113	Panel Delivery (4x2)	$2,143	2,746 lbs.
4213	Panel Delivery (4x4)	$2,741	2,893 lbs.

Series F-134 — 1-Ton — 118-in. w.b.

4307	Pickup (4x4)	$2,514	3,065 lbs.

Series 6-230 — 1/2-Ton — 104.5-in. w.b.

6412	Station Wagon (4x2)	$2,596	3,047 lbs.
6512	Utility Wagon (4x4)	$3,263	3,307 lbs.
6513	Panel Delivery (4x4)	$2,973	3,028 lbs.
6413	Panel Delivery (4x2)	$2,377	3,147 lbs.

Series 6-230 — 1-Ton — 4x4 — 118-in. w.b.

6606	Chassis & Cab	$2,619	2,872 lbs.
6607	Pickup	$2,744	3,238 lbs.
6608	Stake	$2,831	3,373 lbs.

Series FC-150 — 1/2-Ton — 4x4 — 81-in. w.b.

9209	Chassis & Cab	$2,735	2,764 lbs.
9209	Pickup	$2,853	3,020 lbs.
9209	Platform Stake	$,2954	3,187 lbs.

Series FC-170 — 1-Ton — 4x4 — 103.5-in. w.b.

9309	Chassis & Cab	$3,056	2,901 lbs.
9309	Pickup	$3,192	3,331 lbs.
9309	Platform Stake	$3399	3,564 lbs.

Series FC-170HD — 1-Ton — 6x6 — 103.5-in. w.b.

9325	Chassis & Cab	$3,547	3,561 lbs.

Series J-100 — 1/2-Ton — 4x2 — 110-in. w.b.

1314	4d Wagoneer	$2,701	3,480 lbs.
1312	2d Wagoneer	$2,658	3,453 lbs.
1314C	4d Custom Wagoneer	$2,896	3,515 lbs.
1312C	2d Custom Wagoneer	$2,853	3,488 lbs.
1313	Panel Delivery	$2,511	3,253 lbs.

Series J-100 — 1/2-Ton — 4x4 — 110-in. w.b.

1414	4d Wagoneer	$3,449	3,623 lbs.
1412	2d Wagoneer	$3,395	3,596 lbs.
1414C	4d Custom Wagoneer	$3,644	3,658 lbs.
1412C	2d Custom Wagoneer	$3,590	3,631 lbs.
1413	Panel Delivery	$3,082	3,396 lbs.

Series J-2500 — 1/2-Ton — 4x2 — 120-in. w.b.

2306W	Chassis & Cab	$2,149	2,919 lbs.
2306W	Thriftside Pickup	$2,250	3,214 lbs.
2306W	Townside Pickup	$2,277	3,322 lbs.

Series J-2500 — 1/2-Ton — 4x4 — 120-in. w.b.

2406W	Chassis & Cab	$2,802	3,128 lbs.
2406W	Thriftside Pickup	$2,903	3,423 lbs.
2406W	Townside Pickup	$2,930	3,531 lbs.

Series J-2600 — 1/2-Ton — 4x2 — 120-in. w.b.

2306X	Chassis & Cab	$2,263	3,060 lbs.
2306X	Thriftside Pickup	$2,364	3,355 lbs.
2306X	Townside Pickup	$2,390	3,463 lbs.

Series J-2600 — 1/2-Ton — 4x4 — 120-in. w.b.

2406X	Chassis & Cab	$2,923	3,269 lbs.
2406X	Thriftside Pickup	$3,024	3,564 lbs.
2406X	Townside Pickup	$3,050	3,672 lbs.

Series J-3500 — 1/2-Ton — 4x2 — 126-in. w.b.

3306W	Chassis & Cab	$2,168	2,943 lbs.
3306W	Thriftside Pickup	$2,282	3,263 lbs.
3306W	Townside Pickup	$2,309	3,371 lbs.

Series J-3500 — 1/2-Ton — 4x4 — 126-in. w.b.

3406W	Chassis & Cab	$2,821	3,152 lbs.
3406W	Thriftside Pickup	$2,935	3,472 lbs.
3406W	Townside Pickup	$2,962	3,580 lbs.

Series J-3600 — 1/2-Ton — 4x2 — 126-in. w.b.

3306X	Chassis & Cab	$2,282	3,081 lbs.

3306X	Thriftside Pickup	$2,396	3,401 lbs.
3306X	Townside Pickup	$2,423	3,509 lbs.
3306X	Platform Stake	$2,620	3,785 lbs.

Series J-3600 — 1/2-Ton — 4x4 — 126-in. w.b.

3406X	Chassis & Cab	$2,942	3,081 lbs.
3406X	Thriftside Pickup	$3,056	3,401 lbs.
3406X	Townside Pickup	$3,083	3,509 lbs.
3406X	Platform Stake	$3,280	3,785 lbs.

Series J-2700 — 3/4-Ton — 4x2 — 120-in. w.b.

2306Y	Chassis & Cab	$2,422	3,147 lbs.
2306Y	Thriftside Pickup	$2,523	3,442 lbs.
2306Y	Townside Pickup	$2,549	3,550 lbs.
2306Y	Platform Stake	$2,748	3,803 lbs.

Series J-2700 — 3/4-Ton — 4x4 — 120-in. w.b.

2406Y	Chassis & Cab	$3,087	3,356 lbs.
2406Y	Thriftside Pickup	$3,188	3,651 lbs.
2406Y	Townside Pickup	$3,215	3,759 lbs.
2406Y	Platform Stake	$3,393	4,012 lbs.

Series J-3700 — 3/4-Ton — 4x2 — 126-in. w.b.

3306Y	Chassis & Cab	$2,441	3,168 lbs.
3306Y	Thriftside Pickup	$2,555	3,488 lbs.
3306Y	Townside Pickup	$2,582	3,596 lbs.
3306Y	Platform Stake	$2,779	3,872 lbs.

Series J-3700 — 3/4-Ton — 4x4 — 126-in. w.b.

3406Y	Chassis & Cab	$3,106	3,377 lbs.
3406Y	Thriftside Pickup	$3,220	3,697 lbs.
3406Y	Townside Pickup	$3,247	3,805 lbs.
3406Y	Platform Stake	$3,444	4,081 lbs.

Series J-2800 — 1-Ton — 4x4 — 120-in. w.b.

2406Z	Chassis & Cab	$3,770	3,789 lbs.
2406Z	Platform Stake	$4,163	4,534 lbs.

Series J-3800 — 1-Ton — 4x4 — 126-in. w.b.

3406Z	Chassis & Cab	$3,788	3,822 lbs.
3406Z	Platform Stake	$4,203	4,620 lbs.

NOTE: Explanation of "J" series model number suffix: W=5,000-lb. GVW; X=6,000-lb. GVW; Y=7,000-lb. GVW; Z=8,600-lb. GVW.

PRODUCTION: The company did not report total production, but it is estimated that 108,574 vehicles were produced. The company reported production of 16,000 heavy-duty military trucks at its South Bend, Indiana, plant.

ENGINES

(CJ/FC-150/FJ-6 FOUR): Inline. F-head. Cast-iron block. Bore & stroke: 3 3/8 x 4 3/8 in. Displacement: 134.2 cid. Compression ratio: 7.4:1. Brake hp: 75 at 4000 rpm. Torque: 114 lbs.-ft. at 2000 rpm. Solid valve lifters. Carburetor: Carter.

(FC-170 SIX): Inline. L-head. Six-cylinder. Cast-iron block. Bore & stroke: 3 3/16 x 4 3/8 in. Displacement: 226.2 cid. Compression ratio: 6.86:1 (7.3:1 optional). Brake hp: 105 at 3600 rpm. Torque: 190 lbs.-ft. at 1,400 rpm. Solid valve lifters. Carburetor: Carter.

(6-230/J-SERIES SIX): Overhead cam. Inline. Cast-iron block. Bore & stroke: 3.34 x 4.38 in. Displacement: 230 cid. Compression ratio: 8.5:1. Brake hp: 140 at 4000 rpm. Torque: 210 lbs.-ft. at 1,750 rpm. Solid valve lifters. Carburetor: Carter model two-barrel.

(6-230/J-SERIES ECONOMY OPTION SIX): Inline. Overhead camshaft. Cast-iron block. Bore & stroke: 3.344 x 4.375 in. Displacement: 230.5 cid. Compression ratio: 7.5:1. Brake hp: 133 at 4000 rpm. Torque: 199 lbs.-ft. at 2400 rpm. Solid valve lifters. Carburetor: Carter model two-barrel.

(OPTIONAL V-8): Overhead valve. Cast-iron block. Bore & stroke: 4.00 x 3.25 in. Displacement: 327 cid. Brake hp: 250 at 4700 rpm. Torque: 340 lbs.-ft. at 2600 rpm. Hydraulic valve lifters. Carburetor: Carter.

(STANDARD WAGONEER/GLADIATOR SIX [midyear change]): Inline. Overhead valve. Cast-iron block. Bore & stroke: 3.75 x 3.51 in. Displacement: 232 cid. Compression ratio: 8.5:1. Brake hp: 145 @ 4300 rpm. Torque: 215 lbs.-ft. @ 1600 rpm. Seven main bearings. Hydraulic valve lifters. Carburetor: one barrel.

CHASSIS

For wheelbase see chart above. Overall length: (CJ-3B) 129.9 in.; (CJ-5) 135.5 in.; (CJ-6) 155.5 in.; (F-134/L6-226/6-230) 1/2-ton 176.2 in.; 1-ton 183.7 in.; (FC-150) 147.3 in.; (FC-170) 181.4 in.; (J-100) 183.66 in.; (Fleetvan) 154 in. Front tread: (CJ-3B) 48.4 in.; (CJ-5) 48.4 in.; (CJ-6) 48.4 in.; (F-134, L6-226, 6-230) 1/2-ton: 57 in.; 1-ton: 57 in.; (FC-150) 57 in.; (FC-170) 63.4 in.; (J-100) 57 in.; (Fleetvan) 48 9/16 in. Rear tread: (CJ-3B) 48.4 in.; (CJ-5) 48.4 in.; (CJ-6) 48.4 in.;(F-134/L6-226/6-230) 1/2-ton: 57 in.; 1-ton: 63.5 in.; (FC-150) 57 in.; (FC-170) 63.8 in.; (J-100) 57 in.; (Fleetvan) 48 9/16 in. Tires: (CJ-all models) 6.00 x 16 in.; (Fleetvan) 6.70 x 15; (F-134/L6-226/6-230) 1/2-ton 4x2: 6.70 x 15 in.; 1/2-ton 4x4: 7.00 x 15 in.; 1-ton 7.00 x 16 in.; (FC-150) 7.00 x 15 in.; (FC-170) 7.00 x 16 in.; (J-100, J-200) 6.70 x 15 in.; (J-210) 7.60 x 15 in.; (J-300) 7.10 x 15 in.; (J-320) 7.50 x 16 in.; (Other J Series models) 7.00 x 16 in.

TECHNICAL

Three-speed synchromesh transmission. Semi-floating rear axle. Four-wheel hydraulic brakes. Steel disc wheels. 4x2 models have I-beam front axle. 4x4 models have hypoid, semi-floating front axle, and two-speed transfer case with ratios of 1.00:1 and 2.46:1.

OPTIONS

(CJ/DJ) Soft top, metal cab top. Four-speed transmission.

(OTHER MODELS): Air conditioning. Power steering. Overdrive. Four-speed transmission. Rearview mirror. Radio. Antenna package. Ramsey or Koenig winches for front, rear or bed mount. Free wheeling front hubs. Wrecker body for 4x4 pickup or Forward Control models. Meyer angle dozers. Jeep-A-Trench. Tailgate loader for 600-lb. or 1,000-lb. rated models. Deluxe cab on Forward Control models. Heater. Two-tone paint. Front bumper guards. E-Z-Eye glass. Windshield washer. FC-150 front air vent. FC-150 double passenger seat. Oil bath air cleaner. Oil filter. High-altitude cylinder head (no charge). Powr-Lok rear differential. Heavy-duty rear axle. Heavy-duty springs and shock absorbers. Transmission brake. Hot-climate radiator. Variable and constant-speed governors. Draw-bar. Stabilizer bar. Rear bumperettes. Automatic transmission in Travelalls and Gladiators. Full wheel discs.

**Inside and out the Super Wagoneer set new standards for luxury
in four-wheel-drive vehicles.**

In December of 1965, Jeep dealers began receiving a new Wagoneer model that in retrospect was one of the most pioneering vehicles ever. First shown as a concept vehicle at several autos shows earlier in the year, the so-called "Super Wagoneer" was a loaded version of the Wagoneer, more luxurious than any previous four-wheel-drive vehicle had ever been. Standard equipment included a 270-hp four-barrel version of the 327-cid Vigilante V-8, Turbo Hydra-Matic transmission, power steering, power brakes, air conditioning, tilt steering wheel, bucket seats, fancy carpeting, power tailgate window, mag-style wheel covers, whitewall tires, vinyl-covered roof, and distinctive antique-gold trim panels spanning the full length of the body sides. Kaiser Jeep said the Super Wagoneer "constituted a unique and dramatic approach to the station wagon market" and was "...designed for the prestige buyer who is rapidly becoming aware of the safety and other advantages of four-wheel drive." The Super Wagoneer should be considered the template for the SUVs of the 1990s and 2000s.

All Wagoneers got a new front-end look that year. The full-width grill introduced in late 1965 greatly changed the Wagoneers' entire frontal appearance, making them look lower, wider, and more car-like. The company called it the "action look."

Several important safety items were introduced on Wagoneer and Gladiator, including an impact-resistant windshield, padded instrument panel and sun visors, seatbelts, outside mirrors, dual windshield wipers and washers, back-up lights, four-way flashers, a dual-circuit brake system, and self-adjusting brakes.

During the year arrangements were made for the

**The 1966 CJ-5s were almost identical to the 1965
models. They were available
for a starting price of $2,284**

DaimlerChrysler photo

purchase of the production line tooling for Buick's V-6 engine. Buick realized demand for its six-cylinder models wasn't growing, so it wanted to phase out the engine. Kaiser Jeep, however, needed the V-6 for its CJ series, so it decided to produce it in its own plants. Plans were to move the assembly operations to Toledo, with production beginning there in late 1967. Although the CJ-3B continued in production for overseas markets, it was no longer offered in the U.S.

The Super Wagoneer (1966 model shown) was the most luxurious four-wheel-drive wagon that had ever been offered up to that time.

Willys Overland Brazil (WOB) sold 68,479 vehicles during its fiscal year and Industrias Kaiser Argentina (IKA) sold 52,055, making them the two largest automotive manufacturers in South America. By that time Jeep owned 38 percent of WOB and 31 percent of IKA.

The company reported record sales of $322,924,000 for 1966. Kaiser Jeep's profits improved materially, to $7.18 million. Although dollar volume of domestic sales was about the same as 1965, and export sales were down 23 percent, sales to the U.S. government increased 23 percent to $178.8 million. Additional Fleetvans were delivered to the Postal Service. The South Bend plant produced 25,000 heavy-duty military trucks in the 2 1/2- and 5-ton classes. The backlog of government orders stood at $470 million.

Significantly, the company also mentioned that another domestic manufacturer had brought out an entry in the light four-wheel-drive market. Though not mentioned by name, it was Ford's new Bronco. Jeep's domination of the light four-wheel-drive market was being attacked now by two large competitors—International Harvester and Ford—and more were on the way.

NOTABLE FOR 1966: The 1966 CJ and DJ vehicles looked like 1965 models. There were no significant changes. Now in their last season, the Jeep Forward Control models were unchanged in appearance, features, or models. Two-door Panel Deliveries shared the Gladiator's keystone grille. Four-door Wagoneers had a full-width grille.

I.D. DATA: Serial number located on left front door hinge pillar post and left firewall. The VIN consists of from nine to 11 symbols. The first five symbols indicate series and body style. The last five or six are sequential production numbers. Engine numbers located on right-hand front of block.

Model	Body Type	Price	Weight
CJ-5 — 1/4-Ton — 4x4 — 81-in. w.b.			
8305	Jeep CJ-5 Universal	$2,284	2,163 lbs.
CJ-5A — 1/4-Ton — 4x4 — 81-in. w.b.			
8322	CJ-5 Tuxedo Park	$2,379	2,163 lbs.
CJ-6 — 1/4-ton 4x4 — 101-in. w.b.			
8405	Jeep CJ-6 Universal	$2,379	2,225 lbs.
CJ-6A — 1/4-Ton — 4x4 — 101-in. w.b.			
8422	CJ-6 Tuxedo Park	$2,475	2,225 lbs.
DJ-5 — 1/4-Ton — 4x2 — 81-in. w.b.			
8505	Dispatcher	$1,744	1,823 lbs.
DJ-6 — 1/2-Ton — 4x2 — 101-in. w.b.			
8201	Soft Top	$1,519	1,709 lbs.
8203	Hardtop	$1,748	2,004 lbs.
Fleetvan — 1/2-Ton — Four-cyl — 4x2 — Delivery Van			
FJ-6	Fleetvan (postal)	—	—
Series J-100 — 1/2-Ton — 4x2 — 110-in. w.b.			
1314	4d Wagoneer	$2,838	3,480 lbs.
1312	2d Wagoneer	$2,794	3,453 lbs.
1314C	4d Custom Wagoneer	$3,033	3,515 lbs.
1312C	2d Custom Wagoneer	$2,989	3,488 lbs.
1313	Panel Delivery	$2,650	3,253 lbs.
Series J-100 — 1/2-Ton — 4x4 — 110-in. w.b.			
1414	4d Wagoneer	$3,585	3,623 lbs.
1412	2d Wagoneer	$3,531	3,596 lbs.
1414C	4d Custom Wagoneer	$3,780	3,658 lbs.
1412C	2d Custom Wagoneer	$3,726	3,631 lbs.
1413	Panel Delivery	$3,223	3,396 lbs.
1414D	4d Super Wagoneer	$5,943	4,241 lbs.
Series J-2500 — 1/2-Ton — 4x2 — 120-in. w.b.			
2306W	Chassis & Cab	$2,207	2,919 lbs.
2306W	Thriftside Pickup	$2,308	3,214 lbs.
2306W	Townside Pickup	$2,335	3,322 lbs.
Series J-2500 — 1/2-Ton — 4x4 — 120-in. w.b.			
2406W	Chassis & Cab	$2,861	3,128 lbs.
2406W	Thriftside Pickup	$2,961	3,423 lbs.
2406W	Townside Pickup	$2,988	3,531 lbs.
Series J-2600 — 1/2-Ton — 4x2 — 120-in. w.b.			
2306X	Chassis & Cab	$2,321	3,060 lbs.
2306X	Thriftside Pickup	$2,421	3,355 lbs.
2306X	Townside Pickup	$2,448	3,463 lbs.
2306X	Platform Stake	$2,626	3,716 lbs.

The 1966 Wagoneer offered a choice of V-8 or six-cylinder engines.

Series J-2600 — 1/2-Ton — 4x4 — 120-in. w.b.

2406X	Chassis & Cab	$2,981	3,269 lbs.
2406X	Thriftside Pickup	$3,082	3,564 lbs.
2406X	Townside Pickup	$3,109	3,672 lbs.
2406X	Platform Stake	$3,287	3,925 lbs.

Series J-3500 — 1/2-Ton — 4x2 — 126-in. w.b.

3306W	Chassis & Cab	$2,226	2,943 lbs.
3306W	Thriftside Pickup	$2,340	3,263 lbs.
3306W	Townside Pickup	$2,367	3,371 lbs.

Series J-3500 — 1/2-Ton — 4x4 — 126-in. w.b.

3406W	Chassis & Cab	$2,879	3,152 lbs.
3406W	Thriftside Pickup	$2,994	3,472 lbs.
3406W	Townside Pickup	$3,021	3,580 lbs.

Series J-3600 — 1/2-Ton — 4x2 — 126-in. w.b.

3306X	Chassis & Cab	$2,340	3,081 lbs.
3306X	Thriftside Pickup	$2,454	3,401 lbs.
3306X	Townside Pickup	$2,481	3,509 lbs.
3306X	Platform Stake	$2,678	3,785 lbs.

Series J-3600 — 1/2-Ton — 4x4 — 126-in. w.b.

3406X	Chassis & Cab	$3,000	3,290 lbs.
3406X	Thriftside Pickup	$3,114	3,610 lbs.
3406X	Townside Pickup	$3,141	3,718 lbs.
3406X	Platform Stake	$3,338	3,994 lbs.

Series J-2700 — 3/4-Ton — 4x2 — 120-in. w.b.

2306Y	Chassis & Cab	$2,480	3,147 lbs.
2306Y	Thriftside Pickup	$2,580	3,442 lbs.
2306Y	Townside Pickup	$2,607	3,550 lbs.
2306Y	Platform Stake	$2,785	3,803 lbs.

Series J-2700 — 3/4-Ton — 4x4 — 120-in. w.b.

2406Y	Chassis & Cab	$3,146	3,356 lbs.
2406Y	Thriftside Pickup	$3,246	3,651 lbs.
2406Y	Townside Pickup	$3,273	3,759 lbs.
2406Y	Platform Stake	$3,451	4,012 lbs.

Series J-3700 — 3/4-Ton — 4x2 — 126-in. w.b.

3306Y	Chassis & Cab	$2,498	3,168 lbs.
3306Y	Thriftside Pickup	$2,613	3,488 lbs.
3306Y	Townside Pickup	$2,640	3,596 lbs.
3306Y	Platform Stake	$2,837	3,872 lbs.

Series J-3700 — 3/4-Ton — 4x4 — 126-in. w.b.

3406Y	Chassis & Cab	$3,164	3,377 lbs.
3406Y	Thriftside Pickup	$3,279	3,697 lbs.
3406Y	Townside Pickup	$3,305	3,805 lbs.
3406Y	Platform Stake	$3,502	4,081 lbs.

Series J-2800 — 1-Ton — 4x4 — 120-in. w.b.

2406Z	Chassis & Cab	$3,831	3,789 lbs.
2406Z	Platform Stake	$4,223	4,534 lbs.

Series J-3800 — 1-Ton — 4x4 — 126-in. w.b.

3406Z	Chassis & Cab	$3,849	3,822 lbs.
3406Z	Platform Stake	$4,264	4,620 lbs.

PRODUCTION/SALES: The company reported production of 25,000 heavy-duty military trucks at its South Bend, Indiana, plant. U.S. retail sales were 37,891 for calendar year 1966. The firm did not report total vehicle production, but it is estimated that 99,623 vehicles were produced.

ENGINES

(CJ/DJ//FJ FOUR): Inline. F-head. Cast-iron block. Bore & stroke: 3 1/8 in. x 4 3/8 in. Displacement: 134.2 cid. Compression ratio: 7.4:1. Brake hp: 75 at 4000 rpm. Torque: 114 lbs.-ft. at 2000 rpm. Solid valve lifters. Carburetor: Carter.

(CJ/DJ OPTIONAL V-6): Overhead valve. Bore & stroke: 3.75 in. x 3.40 in. Displacement: 225 cid. Compression ratio: 9.0:1. Brake hp: 155 at 4400 rpm. Torque: 225 lbs.-ft. at 2400 rpm. Four main bearings. Hydraulic valve lifters. Carburetor: Carter model two-barrel.

(STANDARD WAGONEER/GLADIATOR SIX [midyear change]): Inline. Overhead valve. Cast-iron block. Bore & stroke: 3.75 x 3.51 in. Displacement: 232 cid. Compression ratio: 8.5:1. Brake hp: 145 @ 4300 rpm. Torque: 215 lbs.-ft. @ 1600 rpm. Seven main bearings. Hydraulic valve lifters. Carburetor: one barrel.

(OPTIONAL WAGONEER/GLADIATOR V-8):

Overhead valve. Cast-iron block. Bore & stroke: 4.00 x 3.25 in. Displacement: 327 cid. Brake hp: 250 at 4700 rpm. Torque: 340 lbs.-ft. at 2600 rpm. Hydraulic valve lifters.

(SUPER WAGONEER V-8): Overhead valve. Cast-iron block. Bore & stroke: 4.00 x 3.25 in. Displacement: 327 cid. Brake hp: 270 at 4700 rpm. Torque: 340 lbs.-ft. at 2600 rpm. Hydraulic valve lifters.

CHASSIS

For wheelbase see chart above. Overall length:(CJ-5) 135.5. in.; (CJ-6) 155.5 in.; (J-100) 183.66 in.; (Fleetvan) 154 in. Front tread: (CJ-5) 48.4 in.; (CJ-6) 48.4 in.; (F-134, L6-226, 6-230) 1/2-Ton: 57 in.; 1-Ton: 57 in.; (J-100) 57 in.; (Fleetvan) 48-9/15 in. Rear tread: (CJ-5) 48.4 in.; (CJ-6) 48.4 in.; (J-100) 57 in.; (Fleetvan) 48 9/16 in. Tires: (CJ-all models) 6.00 x 16 in.; (Fleetvan) 6.70 x 15 in.; (J-100, J-200) 6.70 x 15 in.; (J-210) 7.60 x 15; (J-300) 7.10 x 15 in.; (J-320) 7.50 x 16 in.; (Other J Series) 7.00 x 16 in.

TECHNICAL

Three-speed synchromesh transmission. Semi-floating rear axle. Four-wheel hydraulic brakes. Steel disc wheels. 4x2 models have I-beam front axle. 4x4 models have hypoid, semi-floating front axle and two-speed transfer case with ratios of 1.00:1 and 2.46:1.

OPTIONS

(CJ/DJ): Soft top, metal cab. Four-speed transmission.

(OTHER MODELS): Air conditioning. Power steering. Overdrive. Four-speed transmission. Rearview mirror. Radio. Antenna package. Ramsey or Koenig winches for front, rear, or bed mount. Warn or Cutlass selective drive hubs. Canfield wrecker for Universals and 4x4 pickup. Meyer angle dozers. Jeep-A-Trench. Tailgate loader for 600-lb. or 1,000-lb. rated models. Heater. Two-tone paint. Front bumper guards. E-Z-Eye glass. Windshield washer. Powr-Lok rear differential. Heavy-duty rear axle. Heavy-duty springs and shock absorbers. Draw-bar. Stabilizer bar. Rear bumperettes. Automatic transmission in Travelalls and Gladiators. Full-wheel discs. V-6 engine (optional on CJ/DJ).

Although at first glance this looks like a CJ-5, it is actually a Jeep M38-A1 (also known as an MD).

**The 1967 Jeepster Commando roadster with its optional pull-off soft top.
The base Jeepster roadster came standard with no top at all.**

In January 1967, Kaiser Jeep introduced the new Jeepster vehicles. The major new product line was comprised of a single fancy Jeepster convertible model, plus three lower-priced Jeepster Commando models—a roadster, pickup, and station wagon. Jeepster Commando came in direct response to International's modern-looking Scout four-wheel-drive vehicle and offered the same flexibility of body types. The Commando station wagon's top, for instance, could be unbolted to reveal a comfortable open roadster. The pickup truck's top likewise was removable. The roadster came with no top as standard equipment, but a removable soft top was available at extra cost. Interiors were plain, but upgraded trim was optional. Standard power train for all models was the 75-hp Hurricane four-cylinder hooked up to a three-speed transmission and four-wheel drive. Unlike Scout, Jeepster offered no two-wheel-drive models. Built on basically the same 101-in.

wheelbase as the CJ-6, Commandos offered more interior space than a CJ-5, more storage room, greater carrying capacity, better ride, better handling, and the security of steel doors. The Dauntless V-6 engine was a popular option, as was the Turbo Hydra-Matic transmission. Power steering wasn't available, but Commandos were fairly easy to steer regardless.

The single Jeepster model in the line, the one that wasn't part of the Commando series, was a true convertible. Unlike the Commando roadster, which had a pull-off soft top, the Jeepster convertible had a conventional folding soft top, manually operated as standard equipment with an optional power soft top. The Jeepster convertible was the top of the Jeepster line, and featured unique exterior trim pieces to delineate the two-tone paint in a style that was very similar to the old Willys Jeepster. The Jeepster convertible also offered a

Here are two of the three models offered in the 1967 Jeepster Commando series. For 1967 the Commando didn't offer a true convertible, only a roadster (left and middle), a station wagon (right), and a pickup (not shown). If you wanted a real convertible, you had to buy the Jeepster (see page 95).

Like the Commando wagon, the Jeepster Commando came with a removable top.

Bill Belk photo

Bill Belk photo

The 1967 Commando had few interior options to choose from. The three-speed transmission with floor-mounted shifter was standard.

Bill Belk photo

The Jeepster Commando pickup offered an optional 225-cid V-6. This nice 1967 truck belongs to Bill Belk of Culver, Indiana.

unique rear panel that held a rear mounted spare tire. Among other unique features: fancier interior trim, a trunk, and sporty optional wheel covers.

For many years there has been a folk legend going around to the effect that the Kaiser Jeep Jeepster was an updated and improved version of the old Willys Jeepster, and was assembled using the old Jeepster's tooling. That is not the case. The new Jeepster shared virtually nothing with the old, save the name and heritage. Nearly every part is different. True, the base engines were related, but the new Jeepster was a four-wheel-drive machine, while the old Jeepster was two-wheel only. The old model was created to appeal to traditional passenger car buyers, while the new Jeepster recognized the fact that traditional cars were not for everyone and that off-road driving could be a form of fun in and of itself.

Also in January, production commenced on a $91 million contract for four-wheel-drive military cargo trucks and ambulances. These new M715 and M725

models were developed by Jeep and were based on the Gladiator civilian truck. Oddly enough, the new military trucks used the overhead-cam six instead of the more powerful and reliable AMC engines. The contract was increased to a total of 28,000 units, with 10,400 delivered during 1967. Indications are that the Jeep Fleetvan went out of production this year.

In August, Henry J. Kaiser passed away at the age of 85, and his son, Edgar, became chairman of the board of Kaiser Industries.

Kaiser Jeep Corporation turned in the best financial year in its history in 1967. Sales rose to $470,731,000, up 41 percent from a year earlier, and the operating profit doubled to $14,530,000. The increases were mainly the result of greatly increased military orders. The war in Vietnam was escalating, and many new vehicles were needed. In addition to the company's operating profits, Kaiser Jeep also made a profit of $16.4 million on the sale of its two biggest overseas affiliates:

Willys Overland Brazil and Industrias Kaiser Argentina. WOB was sold to Ford Motor Company, which would continue the production of Willys cars for many years, and also Jeep vehicles, which would be labeled as Ford Jeeps. IKA was sold to Renault, which renamed the unit IKA-Renault. Production of Jeep vehicles and Rambler cars likewise continued.

One item mentioned in the company's annual report was small, but important. Kaiser Jeep admitted to stockholders that the company's profitability was dependent on high-volume military production. This was an admission that the firm was no longer doing well in the retail business, despite all the new products it had launched since 1963. In fact, of the $470 million in sales that year, $302 million came from government orders. Jeep was falling behind in the retail market.

The sale of its two South American affiliates generated a huge amount of cash, which allowed the parent company to reduce its debt burden. However, it also meant that the tremendous profits those two firms generated would no longer contribute to the Kaiser Jeep bottom line. Since retail operations were not doing well, it was easy to figure what would happen to the company if military orders dried up. The big problem was that war obviously couldn't last forever, and then a day of reckoning would be at hand.

NOTABLE FOR 1967: Jeep CJ-5 and CJ-6 continued as the mainstays of the 1/4-ton utility vehicle lineup. Also available were the two-wheel-drive DJ-5 and DJ-6. The base engine in all models was the 134.2-cid/75-hp F-head four-cylinder engine. Optional in all Jeep Universals was the 225-cid 90-degree V-6, now rated at 160 hp. This was the final year for the Tuxedo Park CJs. All-new Jeepster and Jeepster Commando models were introduced in January 1967. Jeepster came in only one model, an up-level convertible, while Jeepster Commando came in three models: roadster, station wagon, and pickup truck. All were 4x4 models with the 134.2-cid/75-hp four-cylinder as base engine. The 225-cid/160-hp V-6 was optional. Jeepster Commando paint options were: Sprucetip Green, President Red, Empire Blue, Gold Beige, Glacier White, and Prairie Gold.

For model year 1967 there was some paring down of models in the Wagoneer/Gladiator range. This was accomplished by eliminating nearly all 4x2 models, except in the J-100 series. The base engine for all series was the 232-cid overhead-cam six-cylinder with 145 hp. The 327-cid V-8 was optional.

I.D. DATA: Serial number located on left front door hinge pillar post and left firewall. The VIN consists of from nine to 11 symbols. The first four or five symbols indicate series and style. The last five or six are sequential production numbers.

Perhaps the most collectible Jeep of the 1960s is the highline Jeepster.

Model	Body Type	Price	Weight
CJ-5 — 1/4-Ton — 4x4 — 81-in. w.b.			
8305	Jeep CJ-5	$2,361	2,163 lbs.
CJ-5A — 1/4-Ton — 4x4 — 81-in. w.b.			
8322	CJ-5 Tuxedo Park	$2,458	2,163 lbs.
CJ-6 — 1/2-Ton — 4x4 — 101-in. w.b.			
8405	Jeep CJ-6	$2,457	2,217 lbs.
CJ-6A — 1/2-Ton — 4x4 — 101-in. w.b.			
8422	CJ-6 Tuxedo Park	$2,553	2,217 lbs.
DJ-5 — 1/4-Ton — 4x2 — 81-in. w.b.			
8505	Dispatcher	$1,821	1,823 lbs.
DJ-6 — 1/4-Ton — 4x2 — 101-in. w.b.			
8605	Dispatcher	$1,917	1,956 lbs.
Jeepster — 1/4-Ton — 4x4 — 101-in. w.b.			
8701	Convertible	$3,186	2,724 lbs.
Jeepster Commando — 1/4-Ton — 4x4 — 101-in. w.b.			
8705F	Station Wagon	$2,749	2,673 lbs.
8705	Roadster	$2,466	2,461 lbs.
8705H	Pickup	$2,548	2,610 lbs.
Series J-100 — 1/2-Ton — 4x2 — 110-in. w.b.			
1314	4d Wagoneer	$2,953	3,497 lbs.
1312	2d Wagoneer	$2,909	3,470 lbs.
1314C	4d Custom Wagoneer	$3,150	3,532 lbs.
1312C	2d Custom Wagoneer	$3,106	3,505 lbs.
1313	Panel Delivery	$2,783	3,270 lbs.
Series J-100 — 1/2-Ton — 4x4 — 110-in. w.b.			
1414	4d Wagoneer	$3,702	3,654 lbs.
1412	2d Wagoneer	$3,648	36,27 lbs.
1414C	4d Custom Wagoneer	$3,898	3,689 lbs.
1412C	2d Custom Wagoneer	$3,844	3,662 lbs.
1413	Panel Delivery	$3,357	3,427 lbs.
1414D	Super Wagoneer	$6,048	4,241 lbs.
Series J-2500 — 1/2-Ton — 4x4 — 120-in. w.b.			
2406W	Chassis & Cab	$2,957	3,096 lbs.
2406W	Thriftside Pickup	$3,058	3,391 lbs.
2406W	Townside Pickup	$3,085	3,499 lbs.

Model	Body Type	Price	Weight
Series J-2600 — 1/2-Ton — 4x4 — 120-in. w.b.			
2406X	Chassis & Cab	$3,078	3,237 lbs.
2406X	Thriftside Pickup	$3,178	3,532 lbs.
2406X	Townside Pickup	$3,205	3,640 lbs.
2406X	Platform Stake	$3,383	3,893 lbs.
Series J-2700 — 3/4-Ton — 4x4 — 120-in. w.b.			
2406Y	Chassis & Cab	$3,242	3,324 lbs.
2406Y	Thriftside Pickup	$3,343	3,619 lbs.
2406Y	Townside Pickup	$3,369	3,727 lbs.
2406Y	Platform Stake	$3,548	3,980 lbs.
Series J-2800 — 1-Ton — 4x4 — 120-in. w.b.			
2406Z	Chassis & Cab	$3,920	3,757 lbs.
2406Z	Platform Stake	$4,312	4,502 lbs.
Series J-3500 — 1/2-Ton — 4x2 — 126-in. w.b.			
3406W	Chassis & Cab	$2,976	3,120 lbs.
3406W	Thriftside Pickup	$3,091	3,440 lbs.
3406W	Townside Pickup	$3,117	3,548 lbs.
Series J-3600 — 1/2-Ton — 4x4 — 126-in. w.b.			
3406X	Chassis & Cab	$3,096	3,258 lbs.
3406X	Thriftside Pickup	$3,211	3,578 lbs.
3406X	Townside Pickup	$3,238	3,686 lbs.
3406X	Platform Stake	$3,435	3,962 lbs.
Series J-2700 — 3/4-Ton — 4x4 — 126-in. w.b.			
3406Y	Chassis & Cab	$3,261	3,345 lbs.
3406Y	Thriftside Pickup	$3,375	3,665 lbs.
3406Y	Townside Pickup	$3,402	3,773 lbs.
3406Y	Platform Stake	$3,599	4,049 lbs.
Series J-3800 — 1-Ton — 4x4 — 126-in. w.b.			
3406Z	Chassis & Cab	$3,938	3,790 lbs.
3406Z	Platform Stake	$4,353	4,588 lbs.

PRODUCTION/SALES: The company did not report total vehicle production. However, the firm did report production of 30,000 heavy-duty military trucks at its South Bend, Indiana, plant. The company also noted that 10,400 M715/M725 military vehicles were produced

This 1967 Gladiator Townside pickup is owned by Lynn Tammaro of Dubline, Pennsylvania. The truck featured the standard 232-cid six-cylinder engine with three-speed transmission and four-wheel drive.

Lynn Tammaro photo

This is the top of the Jeepster line: the Jeepster convertible. The body moldings and two-tone paint recall the fancy Willys Jeepster of 1948-1951. The Jeepster convertible is a really fun collectible car, combining four-wheel drive with the ease of (optional) automatic transmission, a power top, and V-6 power.

in Toldeo. Jeep's U.S. retail sales were 39,470 for calendar year 1967. Excluding sales to U.S. military and government agencies, (and vehicles produced by W/O Brazil and IKA) the company sold 61,300 Jeeps worldwide.

ENGINES

(CJ/DJ/COMMANDO FOUR): Inline. F-head. Cast-iron block. Bore & stroke: 3 1/8 in. x 4 3/8 in. 134.2 cid displacement. Compression ratio: 7.4:1. Brake hp: 75 at 4000 rpm. Torque: 114 lbs.-ft. at 2000 rpm. Solid valve lifters.

(OPTIONAL CJ/DJ/COMMANDO SIX): Overhead valve. Bore & stroke: 3.75 in. x 3.40 in. Displacement: 225 cid. Compression ratio: 9.0:1. Brake hp: 155 at 4400 rpm. Torque: 225 lbs.-ft. at 2400 rpm. Four main bearings. Hydraulic valve lifters.

(STANDARD WAGONEER/GLADIATOR SIX [midyear change]): Inline. Overhead valve. Cast-iron block. Bore & stroke: 3.75 x 3.51 in. Displacement: 232 cid. Compression ratio: 8.5:1. Brake hp: 145 @ 4300 rpm. Torque: 215 lbs.-ft. @ 1600 rpm. Seven main bearings. Hydraulic valve lifters. Carburetor: one barrel.

(OPTIONAL WAGONEER/GLADIATOR V-8): Overhead valve. Cast-iron block. Bore & stroke: 4.00 x 3.25 in. Displacement: 327 cid. Brake hp: 250 at 4700 rpm. Torque: 340 lbs.-ft. at 2600 rpm. Hydraulic valve lifters.

(SUPER WAGONEER V-8): Overhead valve. Cast-iron block. Bore & stroke: 4.00 x 3.25 in. Displacement: 327 cid. Brake hp: 270 at 4700 rpm. Torque: 340 lbs.-ft. at 2600 rpm. Hydraulic valve lifters.

CHASSIS

For wheelbase see chart above. Overall length: (CJ-5) 135.5. in.; (CJ-6) 155.5 in.;(J-100) 183.66 in. Front tread:(CJ-5) 48.4 in.; (CJ-6) 48.4 in.; (J-100) 57 in.; (Fleetvan) 48 9/16 in. Rear tread: (CJ-5) 48.4 in.; (CJ-6) 48.4 in.; (J-100) 57 in.; (Fleetvan) 48 9/16 in. Tires: (CJ) 6.00 x 16 in.; (J-100, J-200) 6.70 x 15 in.; (J-210) 7.60 x 15; (J-300) 7.10 x 15 in.; (J-320) 7.50 x 16 in.; (Other J Series) 7.00 x 16 in. (Jeepster Commando): Wheelbase: 101 in. Cargo area: 63.8 in. Tires: 7.35 x 15 in.

TECHNICAL

Three-speed synchromesh transmission. Semi-floating rear axle. 4x2 models have I-beam front axle. 4x4 models have hypoid, semi-floating front axle and two-speed transfer case with ratios of 1.00:1 and 2.46:1. (Jeepster Commando): Three-speed synchromesh transmission. Floor-mounted gearshift lever. Single-plate clutch with torsional dampening. Axles: Hypoid gears, full-floating front, semi-floating rear. Overall ratio: 3.54:1.

OPTIONS

(CJ/DJ): Soft top, metal cab top. Four-speed transmission.

(OTHER MODELS): Air conditioning. Power steering. Overdrive. Four-speed transmission. Rearview mirror. Radio. Antenna package. Ramsey or Koenig winches for front or rear. Selective drive hubs. Canfield wrecker body. Meyer angle dozers. Tailgate loader for 600-lb. or 1,000-lb. rated models. Two-tone paint. Front bumper guards. Powr-Lok rear differential. Heavy-duty rear axle. Heavy-duty springs and shock absorbers. Draw-bar. Stabilizer bar. Rear bumperettes. Automatic transmission in Travelalls and Gladiators. Full-wheel discs.

The 1968 Super Wagoneer continued to be the plushest, most luxurious four-wheeler in America.

There were several product improvements and revisions for 1968. The two-wheel-drive Wagoneer models were dropped with an emphasis directed solely at the four-wheel-drive wagons. A new Custom V-8 Wagoneer model was slotted in between the base Wagoneer and the full-boat Super Wagoneer. During the year, the AMC 250-hp/327-cid Vigilante V-8 was replaced by a 230-hp/350-cid Buick V-8, though the 270-hp four-barrel version of the Vigilante 327-cid V-8 apparently continued to be used in Super Wagoneer models.

The Jeepster line received a new convertible model in the Commando series. In the prior year only the top-line Jeepster offered a true convertible model—the only open vehicle in the Commando line was a roadster with a pull-off top. The new Commando convertible's top wasn't the same as on the Jeepster. It was a full-length top since the Commando convertible lacked the small trunk lid seen on the Jeepster convertible. Despite the new model, Jeepster sales fell for the year, helping to drag total retail Jeep sales down 3 percent.

The new V-6 engine line reached full production during 1968, providing a good supply of the popular engines for buyers of Jeep CJs and Jeepsters. A marine version of the engine was also developed and Jeep began selling it to a leading boat manufacturer.

Although retail sales were down for the year, Kaiser Jeep recorded the best sales in its history, $476,983,000, and an operating profit of $14,530,000. The results came about because of continued high-volume production of military vehicles. For the year, 62 percent of dollar sales involved government orders. The Toledo plant was operating profitably because, along with civilian Jeeps, it was producing the M715 and M725 military trucks. The company noted that because the M715/725 contract would be completed by the first quarter of 1969, profitability that year would be dependent on continued high production of military trucks and economies being effected at the Toledo plant.

NOTABLE FOR 1968: The 1968 Universal Jeeps were generally the same as in 1967. All models gained a few pounds when government-mandated safety equipment was added to the vehicles, along with emissions-control hardware. The Jeepster Commando line for 1968 included a new convertible model, priced lower than the top-line Jeepster convertible. There was also a redesign of the name badges on the hood, and newly styled wheel covers. Jeepster engine options were the same as in 1967. A Turbo Hydra-Matic transmission was available with the optional V-6. Wagoneers and Gladiators saw some additional trimming of models. Gone from the long-wheelbase series was the flared-rear-fender

For 1968, a real convertible was added to the Jeepster Commando series, though it wasn't nearly as fancy as the up-level Jeepster convertible, which was still offered.

Thriftside pickup trucks. This reduced the model count to a total of eight Wagoneers and 24 Gladiators. Wagoneers came only in 4x4 form. There was one new Wagoneer, called the Custom V-8, which joined the Super Wagoneer in a separate sub-series. They represented the marque's luxury models. A camper package for J-3600 Gladiators was a $267 option.

I.D. DATA: Serial number located on left front door hinge pillar post and left firewall. The VIN consists of from nine to 11 symbols. The first four or five symbols indicate series and body style. The last five or six are sequential production numbers. Starting serial numbers: (CJ-5) 8305S or 8305015 or 8305C15-228800 and up. (CJ-5A) 8322S-17423 and up. (CJ-6) 8405015 or 8405S-33935 and up. (CJ-6A) 8422S-10462 and up. (DJ-5) 8505015 or 8505S-12261 and up. (DJ-6) 8605015 or 8605S-11461 and up. (Series 8700) 15-19027 and up. (Convertible) 8701-12215 and up. (Pickup) 8705H15-19027 and up. (Wagoneers) 1414017 or 1414S-205868 and up; 1412017 or 1412S-200358 and up; 1414017 or 1414CS-200621 and up; 1412C17 or 1412CS-200015 and up; 1414D19 or 1414DS-101078 and up; 1414X19-30001 and up; 1413S-200583 and up (V-8 100060 and up). (Gladiator) 2406W17 or 2406WS-202456 and up (V-8 101447 and up); 2406X1or 2406XS-20257 and up (V-8 101447 and up); 2406Y17 or 2460Y or 2406YS-201297 and up (V-8 100235 and up); 2406Z17 or 2406Z or 2406ZS-200020 and up (V-8 100010 and up); 3406W17 or 3406WS-21022 and up (V-8 101794 and up); 3406X17 or 3406XS-200669 and up (V-8 102974 and up); 3406Y17 or 3406Y or 3406YS-200725 up (V-8 100514 and up); 3406Z17 or 3406ZN or 3406ZS-200150 and up (V-8 100139 and up).

Model	Body Type	Price	Weight
CJ-5 — 1/4-Ton — 4x4 — 81-in. w.b.			
8305	Jeep Universal	$2,683	2,212 lbs.
CJ-6 — 1/2-Ton — 4x4 — 101-in. w.b.			
8405	Jeep Universal	$2,778	2,274 lbs.
DJ-5 — 1/4-Ton — 4x2 — 81-in. w.b.			
8505	Jeep Dispatcher	$2,153	1,872 lbs.
DJ-6 — 1/4-Ton — 4x2 — 101-in. w.b.			
8605	Jeep Dispatcher	$2,249	2,005 lbs.

Model	Body Type	Price	Weight
Jeepster — 1/4-Ton — 4x4 — 101-in. w.b.			
8701	Convertible	$3,186	2,724 lbs.
Jeepster Commando — 1/4-Ton — 4x4 — 101-in. w.b.			
8702	2d Convertible	$3,442	2,853 lbs.
8705F	Station Wagon	$3,005	2,722 lbs.
8705	Roadster Coupe	$2,730	2,510 lbs.
8705H	Pickup Truck	$2,817	2,659 lbs.
Series J-100 — 1/2-Ton — 4x4 — 110-in. w.b.			
1414S	4d Wagoneer	$3,869	3,710 lbs.
1412S	2d Wagoneer	$3,815	3,683 lbs.
1414CS	4d Custom Wagoneer	$4,065	3,745 lbs.
1412CS	2d Custom Wagoneer	$4,011	3,718 lbs.
1413S	Panel Delivery	$3,457	3,483 lbs.
Series J-100 V-8 — 1/2-Ton — 4x4 — 110-in. w.b.			
1414D	Super Wagoneer	$6,163	4,263 lbs.
1414X	4d Custom Wagoneer	$5,671	3,907 lbs.
Series J-2500 — 1/2-Ton — 4x4 — 120-in. w.b.			
2406W	Chassis & Cab	$3,119	3,152 lbs.
2406W	Thriftside Pickup	$3,225	3,447 lbs.
2406W	Townside Pickup	$3,253	3,555 lbs.
Series J-2600 — 1/2-Ton — 4x4 — 120-in. w.b.			
2406X	Chassis & Cab	$3,240	3,293 lbs.
2406X	Thriftside Pickup	$3,345	3,588 lbs.
2406X	Townside Pickup	$3,373	3,696 lbs.
2406X	Platform Stake	$3,560	3,949 lbs.
Series J-2700 — 3/4-Ton — 4x4 — 120-in. w.b.			
2406Y	Chassis & Cab	$3,404	3,380 lbs.
2406Y	Thriftside Pickup	$3,510	3,675 lbs.
2406Y	Townside Pickup	$3,538	3,785 lbs.
2406Y	Platform Stake	$3,725	4,036 lbs.
Series J-2800 — 1-Ton — 4x4 — 120-in. w.b.			
2406Z	Chassis & Cab	$3,996	3,813 lbs.
2406Z	Platform Stake	$4,411	4,558 lbs.
Series J-3500 — 1/2-Ton — 4x4 — 126-in. w.b.			
3406W	Chassis & Cab	$3,138	3,176 lbs.
3406W	Townside Pickup	$3,286	3,604 lbs.
Series J-3600 — 1/2-Ton — 4x4 — 126-in. w.b.			
3406X	Chassis & Cab	$3,258	3,314 lbs.
3406X	Townside Pickup	$3,407	3,742 lbs.
3406X	Platform Stake	$3,614	4,018 lbs.
Series J-3700 — 3/4-Ton — 4x4 — 126-in. w.b.			
3406Y	Chassis & Cab	$3,423	3,401 lbs.
3406Y	Townside Pickup	$3,571	3,829 lbs.
3406Y	Platform Stake	$3,778	4,105 lbs.
Series J-3800 — 1-Ton — 4x4 — 126-in. w.b.			
3406Z	Chassis & Cab	$4,015	3,846 lbs.
3406Z	Platform Stake	$4,429	4,644 lbs.

PRODUCTION/SALES: The company reported production of 28,300 heavy-duty military trucks at its South Bend, Indiana, plant. The firm also revealed that 16,200 M715/M725 military vehicles were produced in the Toledo, Ohio, plant. U.S. Jeep retail sales were 38,235 for calendar year 1968. The firm did not report total vehicle production, but stated that 59,600 Jeep vehicles were sold worldwide, exclusive of military and governmental sales.

ENGINES

(CJ/DJ/COMMANDO FOUR): Inline. F-head. Cast-iron block. Bore & stroke: 3 1/8 in. x 4 3/8 in. Displacement: 134.2 cid. Compression ratio: 7.4:1. Brake hp: 75 at

4000 rpm. Torque: 114 lbs.-ft. at 2000 rpm. Solid valve lifters. A four-cylinder diesel with 3.5 x 5 in. bore and stroke was optional on CJ models.

(OPTIONAL CJ/DJ/COMMANDO V-6): Overhead valve. Bore & stroke: 3.75 in. x 3.40 in. Displacement: 225 cid. Compression ratio: 9.0:1. Brake hp: 155 at 4400 rpm. Torque: 225 lbs.-ft. at 2400 rpm. Four main bearings. Hydraulic valve lifters.

(STANDARD WAGONEER/GLADIATOR SIX [midyear change]): Inline. Overhead valve. Cast-iron block. Bore & stroke: 3.75 x 3.51 in. Displacement: 232 cid. Compression ratio: 8.5:1. Brake hp: 145 @ 4300 rpm. Torque: 215 lbs.-ft. @ 1600 rpm. Seven main bearings. Hydraulic valve lifters. Carburetor: one barrel.

(OPTIONAL WAGONEER/GLADIATOR V-8): Overhead valve. Cast-iron block. Bore & stroke: 4.00 x 3.25 in. Displacement: 327 cid. Brake hp: 250 at 4700 rpm. Torque: 340 lbs.-ft. at 2600 rpm. Hydraulic valve lifters.

(SUPER WAGONEER V-8): Overhead valve. Cast-iron block. Bore & stroke: 4.00 x 3.25 in. Displacement: 327 cid. Brake hp: 270 at 4700 rpm. Torque: 340 lbs.-ft. at 2600 rpm. Hydraulic valve lifters.

CHASSIS

For wheelbase see chart above. Overall length: (CJ-5) 135.5 in.; (CJ-6) 155.5 in.; (J-100) 183.66 in. Front tread: (CJ-5) 48.4 in.; (CJ-6) 48.4 in.; (J-100) 57 in.; Rear tread: (CJ-5) 48.4 in.; (CJ-6) 48.4 in.; (J-100) 57 in.; Tires: (CJ-all models) 6.00 x 16 in.; (J-100, J-200) 6.70 x 15; in. (J-210) 7.60 x 15 in.; (J-300) 7.10 x 15; (J-320) 7.50 x 16; in. (Other J Series) 7.00 x 16 (Jeepster Commando): Wheelbase: 101 in. Cargo area: 63.8 in. Tires: 7.35 x 15 in.

TECHNICAL

Three-speed synchromesh transmission Semi-floating rear axle. 4x2 models have I-beam front axle. 4x4 models have hypoid, semi-floating front axle and two-speed transfer case with ratios of 1.00:1 and 2.46:1. (Jeepster Commando): Synchromesh transmission. Speeds: 3F/1R. Floor-mounted gearshift lever. Single-plate dry-disc clutch with torsional dampening. Axles: Hypoid gears, full-floating front, semi-floating rear. Overall ratio: 3.54:1.

OPTIONS

(CJ/DJ): Soft top, metal cab top. Four-speed transmission.

(OTHER MODELS): Air conditioning. Power steering. Four-speed transmission. Rearview mirror. Radio w/antenna. Winch. Free-wheeling hubs. Two-tone paint. Front bumper guards. Powr-Lok rear differential. Heavy-duty rear axle. Heavy-duty springs and shock absorbers. Draw-bar. Stabilizer bar. Rear bumperettes. Automatic transmission in Travelalls and Gladiators. Full-wheel discs.

The Jeep M715 military truck was derived from the civilian Gladiator. Introduced in 1967, it became one of the Army's prime workhorse vehicles.

With its go-anywhere capability, the Jeep CJ-5 was always a favorite of hunters and sportsmen.

Company management reached an understanding on a number of key points this year.

First of all, it realized that the market for recreational vehicles was rapidly growing, and in 1969 the company introduced new products, new innovations, and new marketing efforts in an attempt to capture some additional business. A 132-in.-wheelbase Gladiator truck was designed to accommodate a large camper unit that would appeal to outdoorsmen and their families. This was a big roomy unit and one of the nicest on the market. Combined with Gladiator's rugged four-wheel drive, this was one camper that could travel *far* off road. Besides the big camper, Jeep also offered a lighter-weight camper unit for the 126-in.-wheelbase, 6,000-lb. GVW chassis, plus a choice of box-type camper shells—hard or soft fabric tent-like tops.

An El Dorado camper unit for the CJ-5, manufactured by Honorbuilt Division of Ward Manufacturing, was also offered. It was a small, two-wheeled affair that could be mounted onto the rear of a CJ-5 equipped with a half cab and V-6 engine, making the combined unit a six-wheeler, which was necessary for stability on such a small vehicle. Jeep boasted the CJ camper could hold a family of four, and indeed it could, though how comfortably is a matter for debate. There was one double bed and two seats that each opened to a single bed. There was also a sink, stove, toilet, icebox , and a wardrobe closet. There was even a furnace.

Jeep Wagoneers were marketed as superb tow vehicles for family travel trailers, while Jeepsters were pitched to folks who preferred pop-up campers. And all Jeep vehicles were idal for hauling boats. Jeep produced a recreational vehicles catalog titled "The Great Jeep Escape" to show off the many uses of what it called the "Jeep Recreational Fleet."

According to some sources, the fancy Jeepster model wasn't offered this year, though there is some disagreement about that. Most sources agree that the Super Wagoneer was no longer offered. Two-wheel-drive Gladiator trucks were no longer offered, as Jeep began to concentrate more on its four-wheel-drive vehicles.

Another important point that Jeep management also realized was that the market for sporty off-road vehicles was beginning to open up, so it introduced a limited-edition sport version of its CJ-5 Universal. Called the "462," it included four-wheel drive, a V-6 engine, two bucket seats, a swing-out spare tire carrier, roll bar, skid plates, ammeter and oil gauges, and Polyglas tubeless tires. Full-wheel covers were available to dress up the wheels.

But the biggest point which Kaiser Industries management came to realize this year was something that went to the root of their very being: They really didn't want to be in the automobile business. Management had tried to find a buyer for Jeep as far back as 1960, then tried again in the mid-1960s. Roy D. Chapin Jr. of American Motors Corporation had tried twice to convince AMC management to buy Jeep. In the years since then Chapin worked his way up the corporate ladder and had become AMC chairman. He and Edgar Kaiser agreed to meet so they could discuss terms for AMC buying Jeep. The deal wouldn't close until early 1970. It was a long time coming, but Jeep was about to finally have an owner that really understood the retail business. For Jeep, a whole new era was about to open.

NOTABLE FOR 1969: To conform with federal safety regulations, Jeep CJs had new side-marker lamps this year. They were mounted to the sides of the hood and rear quarter of the body. New side-marker lights were the main styling change on Jeepsters. Wagoneer and Gladiator were also little-changed for 1969. All Wagoneers were four-door models. New side-marker lamps were added to the sides of the front and rear fenders. The Gladiator 1-ton trucks on both the 120- and 126-in. wheelbase were dropped. The J-3800 chassis was still available, but was down-rated to 3/4-ton and an 8,000 lbs. GVW. A camper package was optional.

I.D. DATA: Serial number located on left front door hinge pillar post and left firewall. The VIN consists of from nine to 11 symbols. The first four to six indicated series and body style. The last five or six are sequential production numbers. Starting serial numbers: (CJ-5) 8305015 or 8305C15-244728 and up. (CJ-6) 8405015-35264 and up. (DJ-5) 8505015-12871 and up. (Jeepster Convertible) 8701015-12545 and up. (Commandos) 15-28002 and up; (Convertible) 15-10001 and up; (Pickup) 8705H15-28002 and up. (J-2500) 2406W17-202937 and up; (J-2600) 2406X17-202823 and up; (J-2700) 2406Y17-203184 and up; (J-3500) 3406W17-201152 and up; (J-3600) 3406X17-200866 and up; (J-3700) 3406Y17-200848 and up; (J-3800) 3407Z19-300001 and up.

Model	Body Type	Price	Weight
CJ-5 — 1/4-Ton — 4x4 — 81-in. w.b.			
8305	Jeep Universal	$2,823	2,212 lbs.
CJ-6 — 1/2-Ton — 4x4 — 101-in. w.b.			
8405	Jeep Universal	$2,918	2,274 lbs.
DJ-5 — 1/4-Ton — 4x2 — 81-in. w.b.			
8505	Jeep Dispatcher	$2,292	1,872 lbs.
Jeepster — 1/4-Ton — 4x4 — 101-in. w.b.			
8701	Convertible	$3,537	2,773 lbs.
Jeepster Commando — 1/4-Ton — 4x4 — 101-in. w.b.			
8702	2d Convertible	$3,005	2,707 lbs.
8705F	Station Wagon	$3,113	2,722 lbs.
8705	Roadster Coupe	$2,824	2,510 lbs.
8705H	Pickup	$2,914	2,659 lbs.
Series J-100 — 1/2-Ton — 4x4 — 110-in. w.b.			
14140	Wagoneer (six-cyl)	$4,145	3,710 lbs.
1414C	Custom Wagoneer (six-cyl)	$4,342	3,745 lbs.
1414X	Wagoneer (V-8)	$5,671	3,907 lbs.
1414D	Custom Wagoneer (V-8)	$6,163	4,263 lbs.
Series J-2500 — 1/2-Ton — 4x4 — 120-in. w.b.			
2406W	Chassis & Cab	$3,243	3,152 lbs.
2406W	Thriftside Pickup	$3,348	3,447 lbs.
2406W	Townside Pickup	$3,376	3,555 lbs.

An unusual Jeep CJ camper option offered enough room for comfortable weekend camping. The camper could be set up as a freestanding unit so the CJ could be used for trips to town or exploring the wilderness.

A unique, limited edition model, the "462" was Jeep's first attempt to produced a small sport performance model. This would be a very desirable vehicle to find today.

Series J-2600 — 1/2-Ton — 4x4 — 120-in. w.b.

2406X	Chassis & Cab	$3,363	3,293 lbs.
2406X	Thriftside Pickup	$3,469	3,588 lbs.
2406X	Townside Pickup	$3,497	3,696 lbs.
2406X	Stake	$3,684	3,949 lbs.

Series J-2700 — 3/4-Ton — 4x4 — 120-in. w.b.

2406Y	Chassis & Cab	$3,528	3,380 lbs.
2406Y	Thriftside Pickup	$3,633	3,675 lbs.
2406Y	Townside Pickup	$3,661	3,783 lbs.
2406Y	Stake	$3,849	4,036 lbs.

Series J-3500 — 1/2-Ton — 4x4 — 126-in. w.b.

3406W	Chassis & Cab	$3,261	3,176 lbs.
3406W	Townside Pickup	$3,410	3,604 lbs.

Series J-3600 — 1/2-Ton — 4x4 — 126-in. w.b.

3406X	Chassis & Cab	$3,382	3,314 lbs.
3406X	Townside Pickup	$3,530	3,742 lbs.
3406X	Stake	$3,737	4,018 lbs.

Series J-3700 — 3/4-Ton — 4x4 — 126-in. w.b.

3406Y	Chassis & Cab	$3,546	3,401 lbs.
3406Y	Townside Pickup	$3,695	3,829 lbs.
3406Y	Stake	$3,902	4,105 lbs.

Series J-3800 — 3/4-Ton — 4x4 — 126-in. w.b.

3406Z	Chassis & Cab	$4,184	3,792 lbs.

PRODUCTION/SALES: The company did not report total vehicle production for the calendar year. However, subsequent reports reveal that for the period of October 1, 1968 to September 30 1969, which corresponded with American Motors' fiscal year, a total of 93,171 vehicles were produced. U.S. Jeep retail sales were 33,963 for calendar year 1969.

ENGINES

(STANDARD CJ/DJ/COMMANDO FOUR) Inline. F-head. Cast-iron block. Bore & stroke: 3 1/8 x 4 3/8 in. Displacement: 134.2 cid. Compression ratio: 7.4:1.

The 1969 Wagoneers offered more luxury and comfort features than other four-wheel-drive wagons, and occupied a unique position in the market.

The 1969 Jeep CJ-5 with Dauntless V-6 engine was a rugged workhorse.

Brake hp: 75 at 4000 rpm. Torque: 114 lbs.-ft. at 2000 rpm. Solid valve lifters.

(OPTIONAL CJ/DJ/COMMANDO V-6): Overhead valve. Bore & stroke: 3.75 in. x 3.40 in. Displacement: 225 cid. Compression ratio: 9.0:1. Brake hp: 155 at 4400 rpm. Torque: 225 lbs.-ft. at 2400 rpm. Four main bearings. Hydraulic valve lifters.

(STANDARD WAGONEER/GLADIATOR SIX [midyear change]): Inline. Overhead valve. Cast-iron block. Bore & stroke: 3.75 x 3.51 in. Displacement: 232 cid. Compression ratio: 8.5:1. Brake hp: 145 @ 4300 rpm. Torque: 215 lbs.-ft. @ 1600 rpm. Seven main bearings. Hydraulic valve lifters. Carburetor: one barrel.

(OPTIONAL WAGONEER/GLADIATOR V-8): Overhead valve. Cast-iron block. Bore & stroke: 4.00 x 3.25 in. Displacement: 327 cid. Brake hp: 250 at 4700 rpm. Torque: 340 lbs.-ft. at 2600 rpm. Hydraulic valve lifters.

(SUPER WAGONEER V-8): Overhead valve. Cast-iron block. Bore & stroke: 4.00 x 3.25 in. Displacement: 327 cid. Brake hp: 270 at 4700 rpm. Torque: 340 lbs.-ft. at 2600 rpm. Hydraulic valve lifters.

CHASSIS

For wheelbase see chart above. Overall length: (CJ-5) 135.5 in.; (CJ-6) 155.5 in.; (J-100) 183.66 in. Front tread: (CJ-3B) 48.4 in.; (CJ-5) 48.4 in.; (CJ-6) 48.4 in.; (J-100) 57 in.; (Fleetvan) 48 9/16 in. Rear tread: (CJ-5)

48.4 in.; (CJ-6) 48.4 in.; (J-100) 57 in.; (Fleetvan) 48 9/16 in. Tires: (CJ all) 6.00 x 16 in.; (J-100, J-200) 6.70 x 15 in.; (J-210) 7.60 x 15 in.; (J-300) 7.10 x 15 in.; (J-320) 7.50 x 16; (Other J Series) 7.00 x 16 (Jeepster Commando): Wheelbase: 101 in. Cargo area: 63.8 in. Tires: 7.35 x 15 in.

TECHNICAL

(CJ/DJ) Three-speed synchromesh transmission. Floor-mounted gearshift lever. Semi-floating rear axle. 4x2 models have I-beam front axle. 4x4 models have hypoid, semi-floating front axle, and two-speed transfer case with ratios of 1.00:1 and 2.46:1. (Jeepster Commando): Three-speed synchromesh transmission. Floor-mounted gearshift lever. Single-plate dry-disc clutch with torsional dampening. Axles: Hypoid gears, full-floating front, semi-floating rear. Overall ratio: 3.54:1. Four-wheel hydraulic brakes.

OPTIONS

(CJ/DJ): Soft top. Metal cab top. Four-speed transmission. V-6 engine.

(OTHER MODELS): Air conditioning. Power steering. Four-speed transmission. Rearview mirror. Radio. Winch. Free wheeling front hubs. Two-tone paint. Front bumper guards. Powr-Lok rear differential. Heavy-duty rear axle. Heavy-duty springs and shock absorbers. Transmission brake. Draw-bar. Stabilizer bar. Rear bumperettes. Automatic transmission in Travelalls and Gladiators. Full-wheel discs. V-6 engine.

AMERICAN MOTORS JEEP VEHICLES
1970-1979

Jeep began a new chapter in its corporate life in 1970. Now a wholly owned subsidiary of American Motors Corporation—America's "Last Independent" automaker—Kaiser Jeep was renamed Jeep Corporation. At the time of the buyout many hardcore Jeep enthusiasts bemoaned the union, fearing AMC would water down the Jeep product and turn it into a shadow of its former self. Concerns centered primarily on Jeep's ruggedness and durability and the worry that it would be compromised in an effort to reduce costs.

Looking back, we can see those fears were ungrounded. In fact, AMC turned Jeep into a proud, profitable, high-volume producer of four-wheel-drive vehicles. The 1970s would see a new birth of Jeep greatness. AMC decided the best way to put things on the right track would be by splitting Jeep into two companies: AM General, which would concentrate on military, government, and commercial vehicles; and Jeep Corporation, which would focus on the potentially lucrative retail market.

Buying Jeep was a bold idea, but AMC Chairman Roy D. Chapin Jr. was a bold man. And unlike some of his predecessors, he truly loved Jeeps. Chapin wanted to see Jeep Corporation achieve greater successes than ever before. How his dream worked out can be seen in the year-by-year summation that follows.

Quite rare and very desirable is the 1970 Jeep CJ-5 Renegade I. These can be identified by the unique hood stripe that identifies it as a Renegade I. 1970 is the only year this limited edition model was produced.

The purchase of Kaiser Jeep Corporation by American Motors was completed in February 1970. For approximately $70 million, AMC now had a truck division. Most importantly, AMC vowed to make Jeep a strong competitor in the retail market.

As a mid-year change, Jeep Wagoneers got a new grille that was handsome and more car-like than before. In June, a new electric sliding steel sunroof became available, priced at $460 extra. It included a vinyl-covered roof in a choice of black, white, brown, or light saddle. The AMC 232-cid six-cylinder engine, which had replaced the Tornado OHC back in late 1965, continued as the standard engine, and the Buick 350-cid V-8 was optional.

At the beginning of the 1970 model year Jeep trucks looked the same as the 1969 models, but partway through the year a new grille was introduced. This was simply the old Wagoneer grille used from 1965-1969. Even so, it greatly improved and modernized the Gladiator's appearance. New two-tone paint

combinations were also available. Trucks offered a side-mounted spare tire, with outside mounting on the passenger side of the bed between the door and the rear wheel opening where, unfortunately, it could cause troubles in tight maneuvers.

Targeted more toward recreational users, and showing the influence of the prior year's "462" model, Jeep Universals (CJ-5 and CJ-6) offered new racing stripes on the hood. Other options were: wheel covers, under-dash radio (AM only), roll bar, swing-away spare tire carrier, and a rear step bumper. Of course, work equipment, including salt spreaders, rotary brooms, snow plows, and power take-off units, was also available.

Jeepster Commandos got power steering as a new option. Of the four Commando models offered (roadster, convertible, pick-up and station wagon), the wagon was the most popular by far. There is some question as to whether the top-line Jeepster convertible was offered this year. Some reference books list it, but it doesn't appear in any of the sales literature. It's likely that any that sold as 1970 models were really leftover 1969s that were simply re-titled as 1970s.

There were several exciting new Jeeps this year. A concept vehicle dubbed the Jeep XJ001 was a two-passenger four-wheel-drive sports car, V-8-powered and quite unlike any Jeep seen before. Created under the direction of Jeep stylist Jim Angers, it was a one-off show car that didn't make it into production.

The excitement created by the 1969 462 model encouraged Jeep to offer another limited-production specialty Jeep this year. Called the Renegade I, it was pretty exciting for the time. Eight-inch-wide steel wheels were painted white and held big 6.70 x 15-in. Polyglas tires. Putting such large wheels and tires on a sport utility vehicle was extremely unusual for the time. The Dauntless V-6 engine was standard, along with a three-speed manual transmission. A standard roll bar and unique hood stripes with Renegade I logo gave it a tough look, but it was the loud paint choices that really set this Jeep apart. The limited supply of Renegade I models was quickly sold out.

The sales slogan this year was "The Two-Car Cars," meaning to own a Jeep was like having two cars: a work vehicle and a fun vehicle. AMC reported Jeep retail sales for 1970 were 30,551 units, which accounted for approximately 20 percent of the U.S. four-wheel-drive market.

NOTABLE FOR 1970: Although Jeep's share of the market had fallen as other competitors had entered this field, its 20-percent share was strong enough to serve as a base to re-establish Jeep as a sales leader. American Motors' new product development group was assigned the task of developing new Jeep models while making improvements in the current line. For 1970, the only noticeable change to be found were new grilles for Wagoneers and Gladiators.

I.D. DATA: The VIN is located on the left front door hinge pillar and left firewall. The VIN has 13 symbols. The first five digits indicate series and style. The sixth and seventh designate engine type. The last six digits are sequential serial numbers. The starting number varies per model.

Model	Body Type	Price	Weight
CJ-5 — 1/4-Ton — 4x4 — 81-in. w.b.			
8305	Jeep CJ-5	$2,930	2,212 lbs.
8305	CJ-5 Renegade I Lim. Ed.	—	—
CJ-6 — 1/4 Ton — 4x4 — 101-in. w.b.			
8405	Jeep CJ-6	$3,026	2,274 lbs.
DJ-5 — 1/4-Ton — 4x2 — 81-in. w.b.			
8505	Jeep DJ-5	$2,396	1,872 lbs.
DJ-6 — 1/4 Ton — 4x2 — 101-in. w/b.			
8605	Jeep DJ-6	—	—

Note: Although the DJ-6 remained in production through 1973, it does not appear in U.S. sales literature and apparently was offered only in overseas markets. Therefore it will not appear in listings after 1970.

A side view of the limited production Renegade I. Note the V-6 badge below the Jeep name on the side panel. Not all Renegade I models came with the optional wheel covers shown. Plain painted wheels were standard equipment. The standard roll bar was an unusual feature for the time; most CJ's were sold without it.

Jeepster Commando — 1/4-Ton — 4x4 — 101-in. w.b.

8705F	2d Station Wagon	$3,208	2,722 lbs.
8705C	2d Roadster	$2,917	2,510 lbs.
8705H	Pickup	$3,014	2,659 lbs.
8702	Convertible	$3,328	2,787 lbs.

Jeep Wagoneer — 4x4 — 110-in. w.b.

1414	4d Station Wagon	$4,284	3,710 lbs.
1414C	4d Station Wagon	$4,526	3,745 lbs.
1414X	4d Custom Station Wagon	$5,876	3,907 lbs.

Series J-2500 — 1/2-Ton — 4x4

2406W17	Chassis & Cab	$3,361	3,152 lbs.
2406W17	Thriftside Pickup	$3,488	3,447 lbs.
2406W17	Townside Pickup	$3,516	3,555 lbs.

Series J-2600 — 1/2-Ton — 4x4

2406X17	Chassis & Cab	$3,483	3,293 lbs.
2406X17	Thriftside Pickup	$3,610	3,588 lbs.
2406X17	Townside Pickup	$3,638	3,696 lbs.
2406X17	Platform Stake	$3,804	3,949 lbs.

Series J-2700 — 1/2-Ton — 4x4

2406Y17	Chassis & Cab	$3,649	3,380 lbs.
2406Y17	Thriftside Pickup	$3,776	3,675 lbs.
2406Y17	Townside Pickup	$3,804	3,783 lbs.
2406Y17	Platform Stake	$3,790	4,036 lbs.

Series J-3500 — 1/2-Ton — 4x4

3406W17	Chassis & Cab	$3,381	3,176 lbs.
3406W17	Townside Pickup	$3,544	3,604 lbs.

Series J-3600 — 1/2-Ton — 4x4

3406X17	Chassis & Cab	$3,505	3,314 lbs.
3406X17	Townside Pickup	$3,667	3,742 lbs.
3406X17	Platform Stake	$3,860	4,018 lbs.

Series J-3700 — 1/2-Ton — 4x4

3406Y17	Chassis & Cab	$3,668	3,401 lbs.
3406Y17	Townside Pickup	$3,831	3,829 lbs.
3406Y17	Platform Stake	$4,024	4,105 lbs.

Series J-3800 — 1/2-Ton — 4x4

3407Z19	Chassis & Cab	$4,320	3,792 lbs.

Series J-4500 — 1/2-Ton — 4x4

3408W17	Chassis & Cab	$3,381	3,130 lbs.
3408W17	Townside Pickup	$3,544	3,558 lbs.

Series J-4600 — 3/4-Ton — 4x4

3408X17	Chassis & Cab	$3,505	3,268 lbs.
3408X17	Townside Pickup	$3,668	3,696 lbs.

Series J-4700 — 3/4-Ton — 4x4

3408Y17	Chassis & Cab	$3,668	3,355 lbs.
3408Y17	Townside Pickup	$3,831	3,783 lbs.

PRODUCTION/SALES: For the fiscal year AMC reported production of 93,171 Jeep vehicles, down nearly 6,000 units from the same period in 1969. U.S. Jeep retail sales were 30,842 for calendar year 1970.

ENGINES

(STANDARD CJ/DJ/JEEPSTER & COMMANDO FOUR): Inline. F-head. Cast-iron block. Bore & stroke: 3.125 x 4.375 in. Displacement: 134.2 cid. Compression ratio: 6.9:1. Brake hp: 72 at 4000 rpm. Torque: 114 lbs.-ft. at 2000 rpm. Three main bearings. Mechanical valve lifters. Carburetor: one-barrel.

(STANDARD [EXCEPT CJ/DJ/JEEPSTER/COM-MANDO] SIX): Overhead valve. Inline. Cast-iron block. Bore & stroke: 3.75 x 3.51 in. Displacement: 232 cid.

Compression ratio: 8.5:1. Brake hp: 145 at 4300 rpm. Torque: 215 lbs.-ft. at 1600 rpm. Seven main bearings. Hydraulic valve lifters. Carburetor: one-barrel.

(OPTIONAL CJ/DJ/ JEEPSTER & COMMANDO V-6): Overhead valve. Cast-iron block. Bore & stroke: 3.75 x 3.40 in. Displacement: 225 cid. Compression ratio: 9.0:1. Brake hp: 160 at 4200 rpm. Torque: 235 lbs.-ft. at 2400 rpm. Hydraulic valve lifters. Carburetor: two-barrel.

(OPTIONAL ALL MODELS [EXCEPT CJ/DJ/-JEEPSTER & COMMANDO] V-8): Overhead-valve. Cast-iron block. Bore & stroke: 3.8 x 3.85 in. Displacement: 350 cid. Compression ratio: 9.0:1. Brake hp: 230 at 4400 rpm. Torque: 314 lbs.-ft. at 2600 rpm. Five main bearings. Hydraulic valve lifters. Carburetor: two-barrel.

CHASSIS

(CJ-5): Wheelbase: 81 in. Overall length: 133 in. Front tread: 48.25 in. Rear tread: 48.25 in. Tires: 6.00 x 16 in.

(CJ-6): Wheelbase: 101 in. Tires: 6.00 x 16 in.

(DJ-5): Wheelbase: 80 in. Overall length: 126 in. Front tread: 48.25 in. Rear tread: 48.25 in. Tires: 6.85 x 15 in.

(JEEPSTER & COMMANDO): Wheelbase: 101 in. Overall length: 168.5 in. Tires: 7.35 x 15 in.

(WAGONEER): Wheelbase: 110. Tires: 7.75 x 15 in.

(J-2500/J-2600/J-2700): Wheelbase: 120 in. Overall length: 193.6 in. Front tread: 63.5 in. Rear tread: 63.8 in. Tires: (J-2500) 8.25 x 15; (J-2600) 7.00 x 16; (J-2700) 7.50 x 16 in.

(J-3500/J-3600/J-3700): Wheelbase: 126 in. Tires: (J-3500) 8.25 x 15; (J-3600) 7.00 x 16; (J-3700) 7.50 x 16 in.

(J-3800/J-4500/J-4600/J-4700): Wheelbase: 132 in. Overall length: 205.6 in. Front tread: 63.9 in. Rear tread: 64.4 in. Tires: (J-3800) 7.50 x 16; (J-4500) 8.25 x 15; (J-4600) 7.00 x 16; (J-4700) 7.50 x 15 in.

TECHNICAL

Three-speed synchromesh transmission. Semi-floating rear axle (1/2-ton models); Full-floating rear axle (all others). Hydraulic, four-wheel, drum brakes. Pressed-steel wheels.

OPTIONS

Rear bumper. Rear step bumper. AM radio. Clock. Camper package. West Coast mirror. Automatic transmission. Power steering. Four-speed manual transmission.

Perhaps the rarest of all Jeep vehicles is the 1971 Hurst Jeepster. It's not even known for certain exactly how many of these special edition Jeepsters were produced, but the number mentioned most often is about 100. This beautiful example is owned by photographer Denise Coulson.

The first year AMC owned Jeep, 1970, the company wasn't able to exert much influence on the product. Major product changes involve engineering, testing, and proving grounds testing, and all of that takes time. However, in the second year under new management the Jeep product line showed some marked changes. Although Jeep traditionalists eyed them suspiciously, the changes and improvements were all aimed at creating a better Jeep.

Wagoneers got new engines this year. AMC's larger 258-cid/150-hp six-cylinder became the base engine, while AMC's 304-cid/210-hp and 360-cid/245-hp V-8s were optional. The Buick 350 V-8s were no longer offered. Wagoneer also got substantial upgrading in the areas of noise control, ride smoothness, and handling. As the top-of-the-line Jeep product, AMC was pouring resources into Wagoneer to make it a greater success.

Jeep Gladiator trucks got the same engine lineup as Wagoneer, base 258-cid six-cylinder, and optional 304 and 360 V-8s. Three truck models were listed—J-2000, J-4000, and the Camper Truck, an 8,000-lb. GVW model which came with the 360-cid/245-hp V-8, four-speed

transmission, heavy-duty cooling, heavy-duty battery, and heavy-duty springs and shock absorbers included in its $4,218 base price.

Jeepster Commando was mostly unchanged this year. The line consisted of the roadster, pickup and station wagon models. Neither the Commando convertible, nor Jeepster convertible was offered. Power steering and brakes were available, as was air conditioning. Two new limited-production Jeepsters were offered this year, both of them station wagon models. The Jeepster Commando SC-1 introduced in the spring of 1971 was a sporty wagon painted Butterscotch Gold with a white top. Black rally stripes incorporated the SC-1 logo. Standard features included a radio, aluminum wheel covers, luggage rack, V-6 engine, and special trim. The other special wagon was the Hurst/Jeepster Special, a joint product of Jeep Corporation and Hurst Performance. Red and blue rally stripes were on the cowl and tailgate, a special hood scoop with built-in lighted tachometer was featured, plus full wheel covers, wide-tread tires, and a choice of Hurst's Dual-Gate shifter with automatic transmission or Hurst T-handle shifter with the manual gearbox. The only engine available was the V-6. It's not known how many Hurst Jeepsters were built, but the most common estimate is about 100 total.

The Jeep CJ-5 again offered a limited-edition model; this time designated the Renegade II. For 1971, beautiful aluminum alloy wheels were standard equipment, greatly enhancing its sporty appearance. Renegade colors this year included Mint Green, Baja Yellow, and Riverside Red, which mid-year was switched to Big Bad Orange. Production figures are vague, but it's believed that 600 Renegade IIs were built. One source claims the breakdown was 200 Mint Green, 200 Baja Yellow, 50 Riverside Red, and 150 Big Bad Orange.

The Jeep DJ-5 two-wheel-drive model continued to be listed as part of the lineup, but it didn't appear in the regular sales catalog and was hardly mentioned.

"It takes guts to cut car prices when others are raising theirs. Jeep guts." So read one Jeep ad, which went on to claim that the company had reduced prices

on trucks and V-6-powered CJs. Jeep was using "Jeep Guts" as an overall theme, and also was including the phrase "The Toughest 4-Letter Word on Wheels" as a tag line.

In March 1971, AMC spun off Jeep's old General Products Division into a new wholly owned subsidiary known as AM General. From that point on the military and government vehicles business would no longer be handled by Jeep, but would come under AM General's purview. This corporate change was hardly mentioned at the time, but it was a major turning point in Jeep's history. The division whose brand name was the most famous product to come out of World War II would no longer build military vehicles.

For the 1971 fiscal year ending September 30, 1971 Jeep retailed 37,124 units.

NOTABLE FOR 1971: No appearance changes were made for either the Jeep CJ or J Series trucks for 1971. Early in 1971, the AMC 304-cid and 360-cid V-8 engines

Hurst Jeepsters were equipped with the V-6 engine and Hurst shifter. If automatic transmission was ordered, the shifter used was the Hurst Dual-Gate, which is what this vehicle has. A hood scoop and rally stripes were standard. Apparently, all of the Hurst Jeepsters were equipped with hardtops.

became optional for the J Series, while the AMC 258-cid six-cylinder became their standard power plant.

I.D. DATA: The VIN is located on the left front door hinge pillar and left firewall. The VIN has 13 symbols. The first five digits indicate series and style. The sixth and seventh designate engine type. The last six digits are sequential serial numbers. The starting number varies per model.

Model	Body Type	Price	Weight
CJ-5 — 1/4-Ton — 4x4			
8305	Jeep CJ-5	$2,886	2,112 lbs.
8305	CJ-5 Renegade II: Lim. Ed	—	—
CJ-6 — 1/4-Ton — 4x4			
8405	Jeep CJ-6	$2,979	2,274 lbs.
DJ-5 — 1/4-Ton — 4x2			
8505	Jeep DJ-5	$2,382	1,872 lbs.
Jeep Wagoneer — 4x4 — 110-in. w.b.			
1414	4d Station Wagon	$4,447	3,661 lbs.
1414C	4d Custom Station Wagon	$4,526	3,696 lbs.
Jeepster Commando — 4x4			
8705F	2d Station Wagon	$3,546	2,802 lbs.
8705O	2d Roadster	$3,297	2,590 lbs.
N/A	2d SC-1 Station WagonLimited Edition		—
N/A	2d Hurst Station WagonLimited Edition		—
8705H	Pickup	$3,291	2,659 lbs.
J-2000 — 5,000-lb. GVW — 4x4			
2406W17	Chassis & Cab	$3,251	3,125 lbs.
2406W17	Thriftside Pickup (7 ft.)	$3,406	3,420 lbs.
2406W17	Townside Pickup (7 ft.)	$3,406	3,528 lbs.
J-4000 — 5,000-lb. GVW — 4x4			
3408W17	Chassis & Cab	$3,281	3,151 lbs.
3408W17	Townside Pickup (8 ft.)	$3,443	3,579 lbs.
J-4000 — 6,000-lb. GVW — 4x4			
3408X17	Chassis & Cab	$3,405	3,289 lbs.
3408X17	Townside Pickup (8 ft.)	$3,567	3,717 lbs.
J-4000 — 7,000-lb. GVW — 4x4			
3408Y17	Chassis & Cab	$3,567	3,378 lbs.
3408Y17	Townside Pickup (8 ft.)	$3,729	3,806 lbs.
J-4000 — 8,000-lb. GVW Camper Truck — 4x4			
3407Z19	Chassis & Cab	$4,218	3,806 lbs.
3407Z19	Townside Pickup (8 ft.)	$4,370	4,294 lbs.

PRODUCTION/SALES: American Motors did not provide a production total, but noted U.S. retail sales of 37,124 Jeeps during the fiscal year, and 38,979 for calendar year 1971. Export sales numbers were not provided. This year, AMC spun off the miltary and governmental vehicle side of the business (including postal vehicles) into a new company called AM General. Therefore, from 1971 on all production or sales figures will be strictly for non-military, non-governmental vehicles only, except for any coincidental municipal fleet business generated by Jeep dealers.

For 1971, the hot new limited edition CJ was the Renegade II. The side stripe was changed to reflect the "II" designation, and stylish aluminum wheels were standard equipment. This model is quite rare today.

Here are three of only about 600 Renegade II models that were built for 1971.

ENGINES

(STANDARD CJ/DJ/JEEPSTER COMMANDO FOUR): Inline. F-head. Cast-iron block. Bore & stroke: 3 1/8 x 4 3/8 in. Displacement: 134.2 cid. Compression ratio: 6.9:1. Brake hp: 72 at 4000 rpm. Torque: 114 lbs.-ft. at 2000 rpm. Three main bearings. Mechanical valve lifters. Carburetor: one-barrel.

(OPTIONAL CJ/DJ/ JEEPSTER COMMANDO V-6): Overhead-valve. Bore & stroke: 3.75 x 3.4 in. Displacement: 225 cid. Brake hp: 160 at 4200 rpm.

(STANDARD WAGONEER/J-2000 TRUCKS SIX): Overhead valve. Inline. Cast-iron block. Bore & stroke: 3.75 x 3.5 in. Displacement: 232 cid. Brake hp: 145 at 4300 rpm.

(STANDARD J SERIES SIX [mid-year change]): Overhead valve. Cast-iron block. Bore & stroke: 3.75 x 3.9 in. Displacement: 258 cid. Compression ratio: 8.0:1. Brake hp: 110 at 3500 rpm. Torque: 195 lbs.-ft. at 2000 rpm. Seven main bearings. Hydraulic valve lifters. Carburetor: Carter one-barrel model YF.

(OPTIONAL J SERIES V-8 [mid-year change]): Overhead valve. Cast-iron block. Bore & stroke: 3.75x 3.44 in. Displacement: 304 cid. Compression ratio: 8.4:1. Hp: 210 @ 4400 rpm. Torque: 300 lbs.-ft. @ 2600 rpm. Hydraulic valve lifters.

(OPTIONAL J-SERIES V-8 [mid-year change]): Overhead valve. Cast-iron block. Bore & stoke: 4.08 x 3.44 in. Displacement: 360 cid. Compression ratio: 8.5:1. Hp: 245 @ 4400 rpm. Torque: 365 lbs.-ft. @ 2600 rpm. Hydraulic valve lifters. Carburetor: two-barrel.

(STANDARD CAMPER TRUCK/OPTIONAL WAGONEER/OTHER TRUCKS V-8): Overhead valve. Cast-iron block. Bore & stroke: 3.8 x 3.85 in. Displacement: 350 cid. Brake hp: 230 at 4400 rpm.

CHASSIS

(CJ-5): Wheelbase: 81 in. Overall length: 133 in. Front tread: 48.25 in. Rear tread: 48.25 in. Tires: 6.00 x 16 in.

(CJ-6): Wheelbase: 101 in. Tires: 6.00 x 16 in.

(DJ-5): Wheelbase: 81 in. Overall length: 133 in. Tires: 6.85 x 15 in.

(J-100): Wheelbase: 110 in. Overall length: 183.66 in. Width: 75.60 in. Tires: 7.75 x 15 in.

(3700): Wheelbase: 101 in. Overall length: 168.5. Tires: 7.35 x 15 in.

(JEEPSTER AND COMMANDO): Wheelbase: 101 in. Overall length: 168.4 in. Height: 64.2 in. Front tread: 50 in. Rear tread: 50 in. Tires: 7.35 x 15 in.

(J-2500): Wheelbase: 120 in. Overall length: 193.6 in. Front tread: 63.5 in. Rear tread: 63.8 in. Tires: 8.25 x 15 in.

(J-3800/J-4500/J-4600/J-4700/J-4800): Wheelbase: 132 in. Overall length: 205.6 in. Front tread: 63.9 in. Rear tread: 64.4 in. Tires: (J-4500) 8.25 x 15; (J-4600) 7.00 x 16 in.; (J-4700) 7.50 x 16 in.; (J-4800) 7.50 x 16 in.

The SC-1 was another limited edition version of the Jeepster Commando. The roof rack, wheel covers, rally stripes, and Butterscotch Gold paint combined to make a very attractive vehicle.

The good-looking 1971 Jeep Wagoneer.

TECHNICAL

Three-speed synchromesh transmission. Single-plate, dry-disc clutch. Semi-floating rear axle (1/2-ton trucks, CJ/DJ); full-floating rear axle (all others). Four-wheel drum brakes. Pressed-steel wheels.

OPTIONS

Rear bumper. Rear step bumper. AM radio. Clock. Cigar lighter. Camper package. V-8 engine. Power steering. Four-speed transmission. Turbo Hydra-Matic transmission. 225-cid V-6 engine (CJ & Commando). CJ camper.

AMC engineer Carl Chakmakian demonstrates the 1971 Jeep CJ-5 at a new vehicle announcement show for dealers.

During 1971, AMC began a program of incorporating its engines in the Jeep line, starting with the senior models. Jeep Wagoneers and Gladiators now came with an AMC 258-cid six as standard equipment, with 304- and 360-cid V-8s optional.

V-8 power was available even on plain CJ-5s.

AMC's influence on Jeep became more pronounced this year and the product improvements were numerous. In fact, product-wise this was one of the most significant years in Jeep's history up to that point.

Jeep CJ-5 and CJ-6 received AMC engines this year. The 100-hp/232-cid inline six replaced the ancient Hurricane as standard equipment, with a 258-cid/110-hp six optional. Bigger news was the availability of an optional 304-cid V-8 producing 150 hp. We should note here that in 1972 manufacturers used a different method of rating horsepower. They switched to net horsepower instead of gross horsepower, and the result was lower official horsepower ratings than prior years. However, actual, usable power was mostly unchanged. The new engines were more powerful than the ones they replaced, and much smoother, too. The four-cylinder Jeep engine in particular was a hoary old mill long past its prime, while the V-6, though powerful, was much rougher running than any of the AMC engines. Also, the seven main bearing AMC sixes were among the most reliable and durable engines on earth. The Jeep four-cylinder engine remained available for overseas markets.

In order for the new power plants to fit under the hood, the CJ's wheelbase needed to be lengthened slightly, to 84 in. for the CJ-5 and 101 in. for the CJ-6. That meant that some areas of the body would have to be retooled—the hood and front fenders primarily. AMC retooled without changing the appearance of the Jeep, in order to preserve its unique character. In fact, to improve quality several parts of the body got large new one-piece stampings to replace multiple parts. A fixed tailgate area with a rear-mounted spare tire was a new option—the regular fold-down tailgate remained standard. Heftier axles were fitted this year along with bigger brakes, a wider track, and a higher-capacity heater-defroster system. A recirculating ball steering system replaced the old cam-and-lever steering, and power steering became available for the first time, along with power brakes. Suspended brake and clutch pedals debuted.

The limited-edition Jeep Renegade returned this year and was called simply the Renegade with no Roman numeral designation. This was the best Renegade yet because its standard equipment included the 304-cid

V-8, roll bar, Trac-Lok differential, and H78 x 15 whitewall tires with 7-in.-wide cast-aluminum wheels. Colors this year were: Renegade Yellow, Renegade Orange, and a bright, sparkling purple dubbed Renegade Plum.

The Jeepster Commando became the Jeep Commando this year and boasted many new features. Styling was revised with new front-end sheet metal. The look was slab-sided and more conventional. Smooth front fenders replaced the CJ-style units used formerly. Commandos looked much like the Ford Bronco. The wheelbase grew from 101 to 104 in. Commando got the same new engine lineup as the CJ. The 232-cid six was standard, 258-cid six and 304-cid V-8 optional, and the Commando had the same chassis improvements, better steering, brakes etc. The interior was new and boasted more leg, hip, and elbow room, an elliptical steering wheel to enhance knee room, and molded foam bucket seats. The automatic transmission now used a column shifter. A larger 16.5-gallon gas tank was new.

On the J Series pickups, the Gladiator name was dropped and the line was called simply the Jeep Truck. Six models were offered: J-2500 and J-3500 on a 120-inch wheelbase; and J-4500, J-4600, J-4700, and J-4800 on a 132-inch wheelbase. All were four-wheel drive. The J-4700 and J-4800 came with a 360-cid V-8 as standard, while the others came with a 258-cid six standard, and 304-cid or 360-cid V-8s optional.

Jeep Wagoneers for 1972 offered a standard interior that included full carpeting and a rear seat- both of which were optional on most competitors' SUVs.

For the fiscal year ending September 30, Jeep retailed 46,000 vehicles.

NOTEABLE FOR 1972: Although the F-head four-cylinder was still offered for export, the standard CJ engine now was AMC's 232-cid six-cylinder. The 258-cid six-cylinder and 304-cid V-8 engines were available as options. CJ-5 and CJ-6 now had longer wheelbases and increased length. Front and rear treads were increased by 3 and 1.5 in., respectively. There was a new Dana model 30 open-end front axle and a rear axle with a capacity of 3,000 lbs., which was 500 lbs. greater than the unit used in 1971. Use of a Dana model 20 transfer case reduced overall noise and provided smoother shifting. Also new were a larger diameter clutch, improved heater, and suspended clutch and brake pedals. Jeep Commando had a longer wheelbase and the same engine lineup as CJs. Commando was equipped with an open-ended front axle, larger brakes, and increased capacity clutch. Changes to the Commando's interior included repositioned front seats and reshaped rear wheel housings. J Series trucks could now be ordered with a 6,000-lb. GVW capacity on the 120-in.-wheelbase chassis. Common to all J-trucks were larger clutches and brakes. No styling changes were made, but interiors featured new seat trim patterns.

The 1972 CJ-5 Renegade came with a 304-cid V-8 as standard equipment. Although still a limited edition model, it did not carry a numeric designation like it predecessors.

I.D. DATA: The VIN is located on the left front door hinge pillar and left firewall as before, but the format was changed. The VIN still has 13 symbols. The first indicates Jeep Corp. The second indicates model year. The third indicates transmission, drive train and assembly plant. The fourth and fifth indicate series or model. The sixth symbol identifies body style. The seventh symbol indicates model type and GVW. The eighth symbol indicates the engine. Engine codes were: E=232-cid six-cylinder; A=258-cid six-cylinder; H=304-cid V-8; N=360-cid V-8. The next five symbols are the sequential production number.

Model	Body Type	Price	Weight
CJ-5 — 1/4-Ton — 4x4			
8305	Jeep CJ-5	$2,955	2,437 lbs.
8305	CJ-5 Renegade Limited Edition	—	—
CJ-6 — 1/4-Ton — 4x4			
8405	Jeep CJ-6	$ 3,045	2,499 lbs.
DJ-5 — 1/4-Ton — 4x2			
8505	Jeep DJ-5	$2,475	2,255 lbs.
Jeep Commando — 1/4-Ton — 4x4			
8705F	Station Wagon	$3,408	3,002 lbs.
87050	Roadster	$3,257	2,790 lbs.
8705II	Pickup	$3,284	2,939 lbs.
Jeep Wagoneer — 1/4-Ton — 4x4			
1414	4d Station Wagon	$4,398	3,808 lbs.
1414C	4d Custom Station Wagon	$4,640	3,843 lbs.
J-2500 — 5,000-lb. GVW — 4x4			
2406W	Chassis & Cab	$3,181	3,272 lbs.
2406W	Thriftside Pickup	$3,328	3,567 lbs.
2406W	Townside Pickup	$3,328	3,675 lbs.
J-2600 — 6,000-lb. GVW — 4x4			
2406X	Thriftside Pickup	$3,449	3,689 lbs.
2406X	Townside Pickup	$3,449	3,797 lbs.
J-4500 — 5,000-lb. GVW — 4x4			
3408W	Chassis & Cab	$3,210	3,298 lbs.
3408W	Townside Pickup	$3,365	3,726 lbs.
J-4600 — 6,000-lb. GVW — 4x4			
3408X	Chassis & Cab	$3,331	3,436 lbs.
3408X	Townside Pickup	$3,486	3,864 lbs.
J-4700 — 7,000-lb. GVW — 4x4			
3408Y	Chassis & Cab	$3,698	3,732 lbs.
3408Y	Townside Pickup	$3,853	4,160 lbs.
J-4800 — 8,000-lb. GVW — 4x4			
3407Z	Chassis & Cab	$4,107	4,013 lbs.
3407Z	Townside Pickup	$4,262	4,441 lbs.

PRODUCTION/SALES: American Motors reported fiscal year U.S. retail sales of 46,000 units. U.S. Jeep retail sales were 51,621 for calendar year 1972. No figures were provided for export sales.

ENGINES

(STANDARD CJ/DJ/COMMANDO SIX): Inline, OHV six-cylinder. Cast-iron block. Bore & stroke: 3.75 x 3.5 in. Displacement: 232 cid. Brake hp: 145 at 4300 rpm. Torque: 185 lbs.-ft. at 1800 rpm. Seven main bearings. Hydraulic valve lifters. Carburetor: One-barrel.

(STANDARD: WAGONEER/ J-2500, J-2600, J-4500, J-4600, OPTIONAL CJ/DJ/COMMANDO SIX): Overhead valve. Inline. Cast-iron block. Bore & stroke: 3.75 x 3.9 in. Displacement: 258 cid. Compression ratio: 8.0:1. Brake hp: 110 at 3500 rpm. Torque: 195 lbs.-ft. at 2000 rpm. Seven main bearings. Hydraulic valve lifters. Carburetor: Carter one-barrel model YF.

(OPTIONAL WAGONEER/J-2500, J-4500, J-4600, CJ AND COMMANDO V-8): Overhead valve. Cast-iron block. Bore & stroke: 3.75 x 3.44 in. Displacement: 304 cid. Compression ratio: 8.4:1. Net hp: 150 at 4400 rpm.

The 1972 Wagoneer was a popular vehicle for families that enjoyed camping in the great outdoors.

Here's an interesting piece of optional equipment—a push front bumper, used by a service station for moving stuck vehicles. Note this 1972 CJ-5 is also equipped with the optional steel cab, right-hand mirror, whitewall tires, free-wheeling front hubs, and front-mounted winch.

Net torque: 245 lbs.-ft. at 2500 rpm. Five main bearings. Hydraulic valve lifters. Carburetor: Autolite two-barrel model 2100.

(STANDARD J-4700, J-4800; OPTIONAL WAGONEER/J-2500, J-2600, J-4500, J-4600 V-8): Overhead valve. Cast-iron block. Bore & stroke: 4.08 x 3.44 in. Displacement: 360 cid. Compression ratio: 8.5:1. Net hp: 175 at 4000 rpm. Net torque: 285 lbs.-ft. at 2400 rpm. Five main bearings. Hydraulic valve lifters. Carburetor: Autolite two-barrel.

CHASSIS

(CJ-5): Wheelbase: 84 in. Overall length: 138.9 in. Front tread: 51.5 in. Rear tread: 50 in. Tires: (with 232-cid six) 8.45 x 15 in.; (with 258-cid six) H78 x 15 in.; (with V-8) 6.00 x 16 in.

(CJ-6): Wheelbase: 104 in. Overall length: 158.9 in. Front tread: 51.5 in. Rear tread: 50 in. Tires: 7.35 x 15 in.

(DJ-5): Wheelbase: 84 in. Overall length: 138.9 in. Tires: 7.35 x 15 in.

(COMMANDO): Wheelbase: 104 in. Overall length: 174.5 in. Front tread: 51.5 in. Rear tread: 50 in. Tires: 7.35 x 15 in.

(WAGONEER): Wheelbase: 110 in. Overall length: 183.66 in. Width: 75.6 in.

(J-2500/J-2600): Wheelbase: 120 in. Overall length: 193.6 in. Front tread: 63.5 in. Rear tread: 63.8 in. Tires: (J-2500) 8.25 x 15 in.; (J-2600) 7.00 x 16 in..

(J-4500/J-4600/J-4700/J-4800): Wheelbase: 132 in. Overall length: 205.6 in. Front tread: 63.9 in. Rear tread: 64.4 in. Tires: (J-4500) 8.25 x 15; (J-4600) 7.00 x 16 in.; (J-4700) 7.50 x 16 in.; (J-4800) 7.50 x 16 in.

TECHNICAL

(CJ-5, CJ-6): Three-speed synchromesh transmission. Floor-mounted gearshift. Single-plate, dry-disc clutch.

(COMMANDO SERIES): Manual synchromesh transmission. Speeds: 3F/1R. Floor-mounted gearshift. Single-plate, dry-disc clutch.

(J SERIES): Three-speed synchromesh transmission. (1/2-ton trucks, DJ-5, CJ-5, CJ-6) semi-floating rear axle; (all others) full-floating rear axle. Drum brakes. Pressed-steel wheels.

OPTIONS

Power steering. Power brakes. V-8 engine. Four-speed transmission. Turbo Hydra-Matic transmission. Air conditioning. Heavy-duty shocks.

This 1973 Jeep CJ-5 is shown with optional chrome front bumper, full wheel covers, and white sidewall tires. This was considered sporty equipment for an off-roader!

The 1973 model year was notable for several things, but probably most important was the introduction of a revolutionary new four-wheel-drive system. Called Quadra-Trac, it was a full-time system, meaning it didn't need to be disengaged when driven on hard, paved surfaces. Combined with automatic transmission, it eliminated the need for a driver to do anything differently from a conventional vehicle, greatly improving Jeep's market appeal. Quadra-Trac was available only with automatic transmission on Jeep J Series trucks (5,000- and 6,000-lb. GVW versions) and Wagoneers.

In addition to Quadra-Trac, Jeep trucks also got a new optional cap for the pickup bed, an aluminum cab-height unit with side and rear windows. It was normally priced at $200, but during the year the factory ran a promotion offering it at no extra charge on J-4500 and J-4600 models. New double-walled pickup boxes and a new tailgate were introduced. A new instrument panel also debuted, and dashboard, steering column, steering wheel and floor mats were now color-coordinated. A 360-cid, four-barrel V-8 rated at 195 hp was available.

Jeep Wagoneer this year continued to include the 258-cid six as the standard engine, but offered the 360-cid V-8 in two versions: with two-barrel carburetor producing 175 hp, or with four-barrel putting out 195 hp. The 304 wasn't offered. Like Jeep trucks, Wagoneers got a redesigned instrument panel. Interior trim was more luxurious, too.

Jeep CJ also got a new instrument panel this year. Although it was still a flat piece of painted sheet metal, it was a little less stark than before and much more user friendly. Gauges were easier to read. New clutch linkage for easier operation was also introduced. A fuel tank skid plate became standard equipment, and new F-78 x 15 four-ply tires were standard this year. Jeep CJs were offered in nine exterior colors.

The Renegade special edition model was offered again and was more popular than ever. Production was limited and Renegades weren't available until January 1973. Due to the overwhelming popularity of the Renegade, AMC decided to offer a second limited edition, the CJ-5 Super Jeep. Features included: special body stripes, a custom interior, L78 x15 tires, a standard 258-cid six-cylinder engine, fender lip extensions, and chrome front bumper. Most sources indicate that the Super Jeep was a one-year-only model.

Jeep Commando showed few changes this year. Like CJ, Commando's standard tires were upgraded to the F-78 x 15 size this year. Stronger axle joints were introduced.

AMC had a great year in 1973, and reported Jeep retail sales at almost 67,000 units—a 44-percent increase. It was the fourth consecutive year of sales increases under AMC.

NOTABLE FOR 1973: J Series trucks had new double-wall side panels for the bed, a wider tailgate (operable with one hand) and a new clutch linkage that required less maintenance. The interior featured a redesigned instrument panel with increased padding and easier-to-read gauges. Big news for the J Series was the availability of the full-time Quadra-Trac four-wheel drive option. Quadra-Trac allowed all four wheels to operate at their own speeds. Key to the system was a limited-slip differential that transmitted power to the front and rear axles. CJs were given a new instrument panel with a large center gauge encompassing the speedometer and the temperature and fuel gauges. Mounted to the left and right of this unit were the ammeter and oil pressure gauges. Beginning in January 1973, the Jeep CJ-5 Renegade was available with a standard 304-cid V-8, H78 x 16 tires on styled wheels, racing stripes, fender lip extensions, dual mirrors and visors, a custom vinyl interior, rear-mounted spare tire, plus transmission and fuel tank skid plates. For its last year of production, Jeep Commando was given upgraded tires and new axle joints.

I.D. DATA: VIN located on the left front door hinge pillar and left firewall. VIN still has 13 symbols. The first indicates Jeep Corp. The second indicates model year. The third indicates transmission, drive train and assembly plant. The fourth and fifth indicate series or model. The sixth symbol identifies body style. The seventh symbol indicates model type and GVW. The eighth symbol indicates the engine. Engine codes were: E=232-cid six-cylinder; A=258-cid six-cylinder; H=304-cid V-8; N=360-cid V-8; P=360-cid V-8; Z=401-cid V-8. The next five symbols are the sequential production number.

Model	Body Type	Price	Weight
CJ-5 — 1/4-Ton — 4x4			
83	CJ-5	$3,862	2,450 lbs.
83	CJ-5 Renegade Limited Edition	—	—
CJ-6 — 1/4-Ton — 4x4			
84	Jeep	$3,176	2,510 lbs.
DJ-5 — 1/4-Ton — 4x2			
85	Jeep	$2,606	2,270 lbs.
Jeep Commando — 1/2-Ton — 4x4			
89	2d Station Wagon	$3,506	3,010 lbs.
87	2d Roadster	$3,355	2,800 lbs.
88	Pickup	$3,382	2,950 lbs.

Jeep Wagoneer — 4x4			
14	4d Standard Station Wagon	$4,501	3,810 lbs.
15	4d Custom Station Wagon	$4,739	3,850 lbs.
Series J-2500 — 5,000-lb. GVW — 4x4			
25	Thriftside Pickup	$3,353	3,570 lbs.
25	Townside Pickup	$3,353	3,715 lbs.
Series J-2600 — 6,000-lb. GVW — 4x4			
26	Chassis & Cab	$3,327	3,395 lbs.
26	Thriftside Pickup	$3,474	3,690 lbs.
26	Townside Pickup	$3,474	3,835 lbs.
Series J-4500 — 5,000-lb. GVW — 4x4			
45	Chassis & Cab	$3,235	3,300 lbs.
45	Townside Pickup	$3,390	3,760 lbs.
Series J-4600 — 6,000-lb. GVW — 4x4			
46	Chassis & Cab	$3,356	3,435 lbs.
46	Townside Pickup	$3,511	3,895 lbs.
Series J-4700 — 7,000-lb. GVW — 4x4			
47	Chassis & Cab	$3,723	3,730 lbs.
Series J-4800 — 8,000-lb. GVW — 4x4			
48	Chassis & Cab	$4,132	4,015 lbs.
48	Townside Pickup	$4,287	4,475 lbs.

PRODUCTION/SALES: American Motor reported fiscal-year U.S. retail sales of 67,000 units. U.S. Jeep retail sales were 68,430 for calendar year 1973. No figures were provided for export sales.

ENGINES

(STANDARD: COMMANDO/DJ/CJ-5/CJ-6 SIX): Overhead valve. Inline. Cast-iron block. Bore & stroke: 3.75 x 3.5 in. Displacement: 232 cid. Compression ratio: 8.0:1. Brake hp: 145 at 4300 rpm. Torque: 215 lbs.-ft. at 1600 rpm. Net hp: 100 at 3600 rpm. Torque: 185 lbs.-ft. at 1800 rpm. Seven main bearings. Hydraulic valve lifters. Carburetor: Single Carter one-barrel model YF.

(STANDARD WAGONEER/J-2500/J-4500/J-4600 — OPTIONAL: CJ & COMMANDO SIX): Overhead valve. Inline. Cast-iron block. Bore & stroke: 3.75 x 3.9 in. Displacement: 258 cid. Compression ratio: 8.0:1. Net hp: 110 at 3500 rpm. Net torque: 195 lbs.-ft.@ 2000 rpm. Seven main bearings. Hydraulic valve lifters. Carburetor: Single Carter one-barrel model YF.

(STANDARD CJ-5 RENEGADE — OPTIONAL COMMANDO/CJ-5/CJ-6 V-8): Overhead valve. Cast-iron block. Bore & stroke: 3.75 x 3.44 in. Displacement:

The Rugged 1973 Jeep J-4000 truck.

304 cid. Compression ratio: 8.4:1. Net hp: 150 at 4200 rpm. Net torque: 245 lbs.-ft. at 2500 rpm. Five main bearings. Hydraulic valve lifters. Carburetor: Single two-barrel.

(STANDARD J-4700/J-4800; OPTIONAL WAGONEER/J-2500/J-2600/J-4500/J-4600 V-8): Overhead valve. Cast-iron block. Bore & stroke: 4.08 x 3.44 in. Displacement: 360 cid. Compression ratio: 8.5:1. Net hp: 175 at 4000 rpm. Net torque: 285 lbs.-ft. at 2400 rpm. Five main bearings. Hydraulic valve lifters. Carburetor: single two-barrel.

(OPTIONAL WAGONEER J-2500/J-2600/J-4500/J-4700/J-4800 V-8): Overhead-valve. Cast-iron block. Bore & stroke: 4.08 x 3.44 in. Displacement: 360 cid. Compression ratio: 8.5:1. Net hp: 195 at 4400 rpm. Net torque: 295 lbs.-ft. at 2900 rpm. Five main bearings. Hydraulic valve lifters. Carburetor: single four-barrel.

CHASSIS

(WAGONEER): Wheelbase: 110 in. Overall length: 183.66 in. Width: 75.6 in.

(COMMANDO): Wheelbase: 104 in. Overall length: 174.5 in. Front tread: 51.5 in. Rear tread: 50.0 in. Tires: F78 x 15 in.

(J-2500): Wheelbase: 120 in. Overall length: 193.6 in. Front tread: 63.5 in. Rear tread: 63.8 in. Tires: F78 x 15 in.

(J-2600): Wheelbase: 120 in. Overall length: 193.6 in. Front tread: 63.5 in. Rear tread: 63.8 in. Tires: 7.00 x 16 in.

(J-4500): Wheelbase: 132 in. Overall length: 205.6 in. Front tread: 63.9 in. Rear tread: 64.4 in. Tires: F78-15 in.

(J-4600): Wheelbase: 132 in. Overall length: 205.6 in. Front tread: 63.9 in. Rear tread: 64.4 in. Tires: 7.00 x 16 in.

(J-4700): Wheelbase: 132 in. Overall length: 205.6 in. Front tread: 63.9 in. Rear tread: 64.4 in. Tires: 7.50 x 16 in.

(J-4800): Wheelbase: 132 in. Overall length: 205.6 in. Front tread: 63.9 in. Rear tread: 64.4 in. Tires: 7.50 x 16 in.

(CJ-5): Wheelbase: 84 in. Overall length: 138.9 in. Front tread: 51.5 in. Rear tread: 50 in. Tires: F78 x 15 in.

(CJ-6): Wheelbase: 104 in. Overall length: 158.9 in. Front tread: 51.5 in. Rear tread: 50 in. Tires: F78 x 15 in.

TECHNICAL

(CJ-5, CJ-6): Three-speed manual synchromesh transmission. Floor-mounted gearshift. Semi-floating rear axle. Hydraulic drum brakes. Pressed-steel wheels.

(COMMANDO): Three-speed manual transmission. Floor-mounted gearshift. Semi-floating rear axle.

(J-2500/J-2600/J-4500/J-4600/J-4700/J-4800): Three-speed manual transmission. (J-4800: 4F/1R). Column-mounted gearshift (J-4800: floor-mounted).

OPTIONS

Chrome front bumper (CJ/Commando). Chrome rear bumper. AM Radio. Electric clock. Cigar lighter. Wheel covers. Full-width split front seat. Tinted glass. Air conditioning. Special Decor Group. Bucket seats with center armrest (J Series). West Coast Mirrors (J Series). Courtesy lights. Outside passenger side mirror. Dual horns (J Series). Tonneau cover (J trucks). Rear step bumper (J Series). Two-tone paint (J Series). Wood-grain trim (J Series). Safari top (Commando Roadster/CJ). Metal top (CJ). Fabric top (CJ). Front bucket seats (CJ). Rear bench seat (Commando). Power brakes. 304-cid V-8. 258-cid six. Four-speed manual transmission. Power brakes. Power steering. Heavy-duty springs. Heavy-duty shock absorbers. Heavy-duty alternator. Heavy-duty battery. Trac-Lok differential. Semi-automatic front hubs. Heavy-duty cooling system. Power take-off. Reserve fuel tank (J Series).

The 1973 CJ-5 Super Jeep is somewhat mysterious. It's not known how many were produced, but probably not very many. Although some reference books insist that this model was produced again in 1976, most evidence suggests the CJ-5 Super Jeep was offered only in 1973.

Even after 12 years on the market, the Jeep truck was a good-looking alternative to the "Big Three" rigs.

The Commando was dropped this year and replaced by a new wagon called the Jeep Cherokee. The company called its new sporty wagon "A Jeep and a Half." The Cherokee was a clever adaptation of the Wagoneer. It came only in two-door models; no problem since the Wagoneer had once offered a two-door, so the tooling was already there.

Cherokee got a new roof (or more correctly new side windows) that gave it an all-new sporty look. Two models were offered—standard Cherokee and Cherokee S. Standard models had front bucket seats, rear bench seat, rubber floor mat, fixed rear side windows, painted bumpers, plain wheels and small hubcaps. Cherokee S came with better seat upholstery, full carpeting, chrome bumpers, flipper-style rear side windows, special instrument panel trim, aluminum wheels, and additional exterior chrome trim. The 258-cid six was standard equipment, with 360- and 401-cid V-8s optional. A three-speed manual transmission was standard, with automatic optional. Conventional part-time four-wheel-drive was standard on all Cherokees, with Quadra-Trac optional.

AMC finally realized that Jeep Renegade's fantastic appeal marked the beginning of a new trend, so Renegade became a regular production model beginning this year. Standard equipment was the 304-cid V-8 with

heavy-duty cooling system, forged-aluminum wheels, stripes, H78 x 15 WSW tires, rear-mounted spare tire, roll bar, passenger safety handle, and oil and amp gauges. Paint choices included exclusive Renegade Yellow or Renegade Plum, plus the regular Jeep production colors. The stripe package was altered this year to give a new look. All CJs benefited from improved body mounts, better brakes, energy-absorbing front and rear bumpers, and improvements to the heating system. A foot-operated parking brake was a welcome new feature.

Jeep Wagoneers were substantially upgraded this year. Standard equipment included a 360-cid two-barrel V-8, Turbo Hydra-Matic transmission, power steering, power disc brakes, and Quadra-Trac full-time four-wheel drive. Standard and Custom models were offered. Custom models included full carpeting and upgraded interior trim. Optional engines included 360-cid four-barrel and 401-cid V-8s. Wagoneer sported a new look this year, with a rich-looking new grille.

Jeep trucks got new model designations for 1974. The J-10 pickup was offered with either a 119-in. or 131-in. wheelbase. The 258-cid six was standard, with 360-cid two-barrel, 360-cid four-barrel, and 401-cid V-8s optional. The J-20 series was available only on the 131-inch wheelbase, and came with the 360-cid two-barrel standard, and offered the 360-cid four-barrel and the

401-cid V-8s as options. The bed was 7 ft. on the 119-in. chassis, 8 ft. on the 131-in. chassis. All Jeep trucks got improved brakes this year.

AMC reported that domestic retail sales of Jeep vehicles climbed to 72,000 during the fiscal year ending September 30.

NOTABLE FOR 1974: Jeep Cherokee was introduced. Wagoneers received a new grille. Jeep Commando was discontinued. Renegade, previously available only on a limited basis, became a regular production model. Quadra-Trac four-wheel drive was offered on all J Series vehicles with either six- or eight-cylinder engines. Improvements included larger brakes and shorter turning radius for the J-trucks.

I.D. DATA: VIN located on the left front door hinge pillar and left firewall. VIN still has 13 symbols. The first indicates Jeep Corp. The second indicates model year. The third indicates transmission, drive train and assembly plant. The fourth and fifth indicate series or model. The sixth symbol identifies body style. The seventh symbol indicates model type and GVW. The eighth symbol indicates the engine. Engine codes were: E=232-cid six-cylinder; A=258-cid six-cylinder; H=304-cid V-8; N=360-cid V-8; P=360-cid V-8; Z=401-cid V-8. The next five symbols are the sequential production number.

Model	Body Type	Price	Weight
CJ-5 — 1/4-Ton — 4x4			
83	Jeep CJ-5	$3,574	2,540 lbs.

CJ-6 — 1/4-Ton — 4x4			
84	Jeep CJ-6	$3,670	2,600 lbs.

Note: Although Jeep CJ-6 remained in production and was available through dealers, it did not appear in the regular U.S. catalog offerings.

Cherokee — 4x4			
16	2d Station Wagon	$4,161	3,870 lbs.
17	2d "S" Station Wagon	$4,724	3,870 lbs.
Wagoneer — 4x4			
14	4d Station Wagon	$5,406	4,270 lbs.
15	4d Custom Station Wagon	$5,704	4,290 lbs.
J-10 — 1/2-Ton — 4x4			
25	Townside Pickup (SWB)	$3,776	3,770 lbs.
45	Townside Pickup (LWB)	$3,837	3,820 lbs.
J-20 — 3/4-Ton — 4x4			
46	Townside Pickup (LWB)	$4,375	4,390 lbs.

PRODUCTION/SALES: American Motors reported fiscal-year sales of 72,000 units. For the calendar year Jeep retail sales were 67,110 for 1974. No figures were provided for export sales.

ENGINES

(STANDARD CJ SIX): Overhead valve. Inline. Cast-iron block. Bore & stroke: 3.75 x 3.50 in. Displacement: 232 cid. Compression ratio: 8.0:1. Net hp: 100 at 3600 rpm. Net torque: 185 lbs.-ft. at 1800 rpm. Seven main bearings. Hydraulic valve lifters. Carburetor: One-barrel.

(STANDARD CJ-5 RENEGADE; OPTIONAL OTHER CJ V-8): Overhead valve. Cast-iron block. Bore & stroke: 3.75 x 3.44 in. Displacement: 304 cid. Compression

The new Cherokee arrived in 1974, giving Jeep a more competitive offering in the sport utility wagon market.

The 1974 Jeep truck with a simple cap for the bed.

ratio: 8.4:1. Net hp: 150 at 4200 rpm. Net torque: 245 lbs.-ft. at 2500 rpm. Five main bearings. Hydraulic valve lifters. Carburetor: two-barrel.

(STANDARD CHEROKEE & J-10; OPTIONAL CJ SIX): Overhead valve. Inline. Cast-iron block. Bore & stroke: 3.85 x 3.90 in. Displacement: 258 cid. Compression ratio: 8.0:1. Net hp: 110 at 3500 rpm. Torque: 195 lbs.-ft. at 2000 rpm. Seven main bearings. Hydraulic valve lifters. Carburetor: One-barrel.

(STANDARD WAGONEER & J-20; OPTIONAL CHEROKEE & J-10 V-8): Overhead valve. Cast-iron block. Bore & stroke: 4.08 x 3.44 in. Displacement: 360 cid. Compression ratio: 8.5:1. Net hp: 175 at 4000 rpm. Net torque: 285 lbs.-ft. at 2400 rpm. Five main bearings. Hydraulic valve lifters. Carburetor: Two-barrel.

(OPTIONAL WAGONEER/CHEROKEE & ALL TRUCKS V-8): Overhead valve. Cast-iron block. Bore & stroke: 4.17 x 3.68 in. Displacement: 401 cid. Net hp: 235 at 4600 rpm. Five main bearings. Hydraulic valve lifters. Carburetor: four-barrel.

CHASSIS

(CJ-5): Wheelbase: 84 in. Overall length: 138.9 in. Front tread: 51.5 in. Rear tread: 50 in. Tires: F78 x 15 in.

(CJ-6): Wheelbase: 104 in. Overall length: 158.9 in. Front tread: 51.5 in. Rear tread: 50 in. Tires: F78 x 15 in.

(CHEROKEE): Wheelbase: 109 in. Overall length: 183.7 in. Tires: F78 x 15 in.

(WAGONEER): Wheelbase: 109 in. Overall length: 183.7 in. Tires: F78 x 15 in.

DaimlerChrysler photo

The Wagoneer remained a competent family hauler in 1974.

In 1974, the CJ-5 Renegade became a regular production model, with a standard 304-cid V-8 engine.

(J-10 SHORT BED): Wheelbase: 118.7/130.7 in. Overall length: 192.5/204.5 in. Height: 69.3/69.1 in. Front tread: 63.3 in. Rear tread: 63.8 in. Tires: G78 x 15 in.

(J-20 & J-10 LONG BED): Wheelbase: 130.7 in. Overall length: 204.5 in. Height: 70.7 in. Front tread: 63.3 in. Rear tread: 63.8 in. Tires: 8.00 x 16.5 in.

OPTIONS

258-cid six-cylinder engine (CJ). 360-cid V-8 or 401-cid V-8 (J Series). 304-cid V-8 (CJ-5, standard on Renegade). Four-speed transmission. Renegade Package. Wagoneer wood-grain trim. CJ metal cab. Power disc brakes for J Series. Power brakes for CJ. Quadra-Trac full-time four-wheel drive (J Series).

After the Cherokee debuted, Jeep began moving Wagoneer even further upscale.

Jeep Renegade for 1975 was a great-looking machine. Note the Levi's denim trim.

The country was suffering through a recession in 1975, with many workers laid off from their jobs. That hurt sales of just about everything. Jeep sales were affected, but not that much.

Jeep CJs got improved exhaust systems, stronger frames, better engine insulation, a new electric wiring harness for easier service, plus new standard equipment that included a passenger-side bucket seat and electronic ignition. Windshield frames were now painted body color rather than black. A new Levi's-look seat trim in blue or tan was standard on Renegades and optional on other CJ-5s. Renegades got a new hood stripe, too. The AM radio was now available as a factory-installed option, where previously it had been strictly dealer installed. As before, all Renegades came with the 304-cid V-8 engine.

Cherokees offered many new options, including: AM/FM radio with four speakers, rear window defogger,

and cruise control (which Jeep called Cruise Command). Cherokees also got four new interior trim colors, new springs and shock absorbers, plus electronic ignition. As before, Cherokees were offered in a single two-door body style, with two models—standard and "S."

A new trim package was added to the Jeep truck line. Called the Pioneer, it was available on both J-10 and J-20 models. The package included attractive wood-grain exterior trim, thick carpeting, chrome front bumper, wood-grain instrument panel trim, bright exterior window moldings and hubcaps, dual horns, and a cigar lighter. Bucket seats were available on all Custom pickups, along with aluminum wheels. Electronic ignition was a new standard feature.

The top of the Jeep lineup was still the Wagoneer, and the best Wagoneer was the Custom. Wagoneer Customs were treated to several new features, including wood-grain trim on the instrument panel and interior door panels. A new optional exterior wood-grain side treatment was especially attractive. Wagoneer enhancements included new shocks and springs to improve ride quality.

Domestic sales of Jeep vehicles fell slightly due to the recession. The company reported wholesale sales to its dealers of 69,289, down from 69,795 in 1974. In April, the 400,000th Jeep vehicle produced by AMC came off the assembly line.

NOTEABLE FOR 1975: At midyear, the Cherokee Chief was introduced at the Detroit Auto Show. It featured a wider track, fat tires and special trim. New Cherokee options included Cruise Command speed control, AM/FM quadraphonic sound system, and a rear window defogger. CJ models offered Levi's spun-nylon upholstery. Renegade had new body stripes. Added to the CJ option list was a factory-installed AM radio with a weatherproof case. J Series pickup trucks were available with a new Pioneer trim package consisting of wood-grain exterior trim, deep-pile carpeting, pleated fabric seats, chrome front bumpers, bright exterior window moldings, deluxe door trim pads, bright wheel covers (J-10), bright hubcaps (J-20), dual horns, locking glove box, cigar lighter, wood-grain instrument cluster trim, and bright armrest overlays.

I.D. DATA: VIN located on the left front door hinge pillar and left firewall. VIN still has 13 symbols. The first indicates Jeep Corp. The second indicates model year. The third indicates transmission, drive train and assembly plant. The fourth and fifth indicate series or model. The sixth symbol identifies body style. The seventh symbol now indicates the engine. Engine codes were: E=232-cid six-cylinder; A=258-cid six-cylinder; H=304-cid V-8; N=360-cid V-8; P=360-cid V-8; Z=401-cid V-8. The next six symbols are the sequential production number, beginning at 000001.

Model	Body Type	Price	Weight
CJ-5 — 1/4-Ton — 4x4 — 84-in. w.b.			
83	Jeep CJ-5	$4,099	2,648 lbs.
CJ-6 — 1/4-Ton — 4x4 — 104-in. w.b.			
84	Jeep CJ-6	$4,195	2,714 lbs.

Note: Jeep CJ-6 remained in production and was available through dealers, although it is mentioned only briefly in the regular U.S. sales catalog.

Model	Body Type	Price	Weight
Cherokee — 4x4			
16	2d Station Wagon	$4,851	3,657 lbs.
17	2d "S" Station Wagon	$5,399	3,677 lbs.
Wagoneer — 4x4			
14	4d Standard Station Wagon	$6,013	4,240 lbs.
15	4d Custom Station Wagon	$6,246	4,256 lbs.
J-10 — 1/2-Ton — 4x4 — 119/131-in. w.b.			
25	Townside Pickup (SWB)	$4,228	3,712 lbs.
45	Townside Pickup (LWB)	$4,289	3,770 lbs.
J-20 — 3/4-Ton — 4x4 — 131-in. w.b.			
46	Townside Pickup	$4,925	4,333 lbs.

PRODUCTION/SALES: American Motors reported fiscal-year U.S. wholesale sales (sales to its dealers) of 69,300 units. Combined fiscal-year retail sales for the

1975 Jeep Cherokee had numerous refinements for 1975, including new springs and shocks, plus optional cruise control, AM/FM stereo radio with four speakers, and a rear window defogger.

U.S. and Canada were 67,711. During calendar year 1975, Jeep retail sales were 68,834. No figures were provided for export sales, but the company stated that Jeep export sales doubled in the time since AMC took over.

ENGINES

(STANDARD CJ-5/CJ-6 SIX): Overhead valve. Inline. Cast-iron block. Bore & stroke: 3.75 x 3.50 in. Displacement: 232 cid. Compression ratio: 8.0:1. Net hp: 100 at 3600 rpm. Net torque: 185 lbs.-ft. at 1800 rpm. Seven main bearings. Hydraulic valve lifters. Carburetor: one-barrel.

(STANDARD RENEGADE — OPTIONAL CJ-5/CJ-6 V-8): Overhead valve. Cast-iron block. Bore & stroke: 3.75 x 3.44 in. Displacement: 304 cid. Compression ratio: 8.4:1. Net hp: 150 at 4200 rpm. Net torque: 245 lbs.-ft. at 2500 rpm. Seven main bearings. Hydraulic valve lifters. Carburetor: two-barrel.

(STANDARD CHEROKEE & J-10 — OPTIONAL CJ-5/CJ-6 SIX): Overhead valve. Inline. Cast-iron block. Bore & stroke: 3.75 x 3.9 in. Displacement: 258 cid. Compression ratio: 8.0:1. Net hp: 110 at 3500 rpm. Torque: 195 lbs.-ft. at 2000 rpm. Seven main bearings. Hydraulic valve lifters. Carburetor: one-barrel. (Note: This engine was not available in California where a four-barrel version of the 360 cid V-8 was standard.

(STANDARD: WAGONEER & J-20 — OPTIONAL CHEROKEE & J-10): Overhead valve. Cast-iron block. Bore & stroke: 4.08 x 3.44 in. Displacement: 360 cid. Compression ratio: 8.5:1. Net hp: 175 at 4000 rpm. Net torque: 285 lbs.-ft. at 2400 rpm. Five main bearings. Hydraulic valve lifters. Carburetor: two-barrel.

(OPTIONAL CHEROKEE/WAGONEER/J-10/J-20 V-8): Overhead valve. Cast-iron block. Bore & stroke: 4.08 x 3.44 in. Displacement: 360 cid. Net hp: 195 at 4400 rpm. Five main bearings. Hydraulic valve lifters. Carburetor: four-barrel.

(OPTIONAL CHEROKEE/WAGONEER/J-10/J-20 V-8): Overhead valve. Cast-iron block. Bore & stroke: 4.17 x 3.68 in. Displacement: 401 cid. Net hp: 235 at 4600 rpm. Five main bearings. Hydraulic valve lifters. Carburetor: four-barrel.

CHASSIS

(WAGONEER/CHEROKEE): Wheelbase: 109 in. Overall length: 183.7 in. Tires: F78 x 15 in.

(CJ-5): Wheelbase: 84 in. Overall length: 138.9 in. Height: 69.5 in. Front tread: 51.5 in. Rear tread: 50 in. Tires: F78 x 15 in.

(CJ-6): Wheelbase: 104 in. Overall length: 158.9 in. Height: 68.3 in. Front tread: 51.5 in. Rear tread: 50.0 in. Tires: F78 x 15 in.

(J-10 SWB): Wheelbase: 119 in. Overall length: 193.6 in. Height: 65.9 in. Front tread: 63.1 in. Rear tread: 64.9 in. Tires: H78 x 15 in.

(J-20/J-10 LWB): Wheelbase: 131 in. Overall length: 205.6 in. Height: 71.3 in. Front tread: 64.8 in. Rear tread: 66.1 in. Tires: (J-10) H78-15; (J-20/6,500-lb. GVW) 8.00 x 16.5; (J-20/7,200-lb. GVW) 8.75 x 16.5 in.

TECHNICAL

(CJ-5/CJ-6): Three-speed manual transmission. Floor-mounted gearshift. Semi-floating rear axle. Overall ratio: 3.73:1, (optional) 4.27:1. Manual four-wheel drum brakes. Pressed-steel, five-bolt wheels.

(CHEROKEE/WAGONEEER/J-10/J-20): Fully synchronized three-speed manual transmission. Floor-mounted gearshift. Clutch: (J-10) 10.5 in., 106.75-sq. in. area, (J-20) 11.0 in., 110.96-sq. in. area. (J-10) Semi-floating rear axle; (J-20) full-floating rear axle. Overall ratio: (J-10) 3.54, 4.09:1; (J-20) 3.73:1, 4.09:1 optional. Brakes: (J-10) hydraulic, 11 in. x 2 in.; (J-20) front power disc, 12.5 in. Wheels: (J-10) six-bolt; (J-20) eight-bolt steel disc.

OPTIONS

(CJ-5): Rear bumperettes. AM radio. CB radio. Cigar lighter and ashtray. Swing-out tire carrier. Roll bar. Power steering. Four-speed transmission. Power brakes. Rear seat. Renegade package. Padded instrument panel (standard with Renegade package). Passenger safety Rail. Air conditioning. 304-cid V-8. Tachometer. Metal top (full or half). Push bumper. Outside passenger mirror. Rear Trak-Lok differential. Heavy-duty battery and alternator. Heavy-duty cooling system. Cold climate group. Heavy-duty springs and shock absorbers.

(WAGONEER/CHEROKEE): 360-cid V-8 engine. Wood-grain (wagon). Quadra-Trac full-time four-wheel-drive. Automatic transmission. Rear Trak-Lok differential (not available with Quadra-Trac). Heavy-duty battery and alternator. Heavy-duty cooling system. Cold climate group. Heavy-duty springs and shock absorbers.

(J-10/J-20): Rear bumper. Rear step bumper. Bumper guards with nerf strips. AM, AM/FM stereo radios. Air conditioning. Sliding rear window. Cruise control. Power steering. Tilt steering wheel. Steel-belted radial tires (not available for J-20). Tinted glass. Custom trim package. Light group. Convenience group. Wheel covers (J-10). Outside passenger mirror. Two-tone paint. Aluminum cargo cap. Automatic transmission. Auxiliary fuel tank. Quadra-Trac. Rear Trak-Lok differential (not available with Quadra-Trac). Camper special package. Heavy-duty battery and alternator. Four-speed transmission. Heavy-duty cooling system. Cold climate group. Heavy-duty springs and shock absorbers. Helper springs.

With its two-tone paint and bed cover, this 1975 Jeep truck would make a nice all-around collectible today.

The Jeep Cherokee Chief set a new standard for sporty appearance in a four-wheel-drive wagon and was one of the hottest-selling vehicles of that era.

There was very big news for Jeep lovers this year. A new CJ model debuted—the most important one in more than 20 years. The CJ-7 was a longer, roomier version of the CJ-5. The Jeep CJ-7 boasted a 93.5-in. wheelbase, 10 in. longer than the CJ-5 (which this year was listed as having an 83.5-in. wheelbase, instead of the 84-in. wheelbase ascribed to it since 1972). The 10 extra inches of wheelbase provided extra legroom up front, more legroom for rear seat passengers, plus carrying space behind the rear seat for the first time.

With CJ-7, automatic transmission and Quadra-Trac were offered for the first time on a CJ vehicle, and that was extremely important. It meant anybody could drive a Jeep CJ, opening up CJ ownership to many more drivers. Jeep said CJ-7 was "the new easy way to drive tough." Door openings were much bigger, too, which was also important because many tall or heavy drivers simply couldn't get into a CJ-5 comfortably. With CJ-7, entry and egress was greatly improved. Stability and handling were better than the CJ-5, and ride smoothness was greatly improved as well. CJ-7s offered a new optional fiberglass hardtop with steel doors. Unlike some aftermarket steel tops, these doors had conventional exterior door handles, roll-down windows, and interior trim panels. It was a good-looking top, with rounded

corners and large window areas, and was available in black or white. *Pick-up Van & 4WD* magazine named CJ-7 "Four Wheel Drive Vehicle of the Year."

Jeep Renegade was offered in both CJ-5 and CJ-7 versions. New features on Renegades this year were: courtesy lights under the dash, an 8-in. day/night mirror, sports steering wheel, and a bright rocker panel molding. A new instrument panel overlay greatly improved the dashboard look. However, beginning this year, the Renegade became in essence a sport appearance package with the V-8 engine optional, not standard equipment.

All CJ vehicles benefited this year from a new frame with splayed side rails that were wider in the back than in front. This allowed for wider-spaced rear springs, improving stability. The new frame also got stronger cross-members and an integral skid plate to protect the engine and transmission. A dash-mounted clock and tachometer were optional this year, replacing the former column-mounted tachometer. With the introduction of the CJ-7, the old CJ-6 model was dropped from the U.S. lineup, though it continued to be built for overseas markets.

Cherokee refinements this year included new

forward-pivoting driver and passenger seats for easier rear seat access. New trim was featured on seats, doors, and interior quarter panels. Like CJ, Cherokee this year got a new frame with splayed rails and stronger cross members. New multi-leaf springs and shocks provided a smoother ride. A new Cherokee Chief model was cataloged, and it was especially interesting because it featured wider axles for an aggressive, wide-track look. Included on the Cherokee Chief were five 10 x 15-in. Tracker A-T Goodyear tires with raised white lettering, mounted on 8-in.-wide slot-style wheels painted white, 3.54 axle ratio, plus exterior striping and blackout paint treatment for the rear side window panels. The Cherokee Chief had debuted partway through the 1975 model year as a show vehicle displayed at the Detroit Auto Show. Steel fender lip extensions, borrowed from the truck line, were welded on to provide room for the wider axles, bigger tires, and 8-in.-wide wheels that came standard on the Chief. The factory referred to this version of the chassis as the "wide-wheel" model.

The Jeep Wagoneer continued to be offered in standard and Custom models. Like the Cherokee, Wagoneer got an improved frame design. The optional wood-grain side treatment on Wagoneer this year was smaller than before, and less attractive.

The popular Jeep Pioneer package returned, and was joined midway through the season by a new J-10 Honcho—a sport appearance package that included white slotted wheels, big A-T tires with raised white letters, special stripes, Levi's denim interior, and a rear step bumper. Jeep trucks also got the frame improvements seen on other J Series vehicles.

Jeep's parent company, AMC, lost $46 million for the year because of falling sales of its passenger cars. Sales of Jeep vehicles to dealers, on the other hand, were 92,798 compared to 69,289 the year before. Retail sales were pegged at 95,718 for the U.S. and Canada, which was a huge improvement.

NOTABLE FOR 1976: The new CJ-7 debuted. With a 93.5-in. wheelbase, CJ-7 offered more front and rear legroom, more cargo space, and wider door openings. Wagoneers featured a rugged new frame. Cherokee Chief became a regular production model this season. The CJ frame was upgraded with splayed side rails (wider in front than back) to allow for wider spacing of the rear springs. In addition, the frame had stronger cross-

members and an integral skid plate. J Series trucks also had a new frame with splayed rear side rails, hold-down mounts, springs, and shocks.

I.D. DATA: VIN located on the left front door hinge pillar and left firewall. VIN still has 13 symbols. The first indicates Jeep Corp. The second indicates model year. The third indicates transmission, drive train and assembly plant. The fourth and fifth indicate series or model. The sixth symbol identifies body style. The seventh symbol indicates the engine. Engine codes were: E=232 cid six-cylinder; A=258-cid six-cylinder; H=304-cid V-8; N=360-cid V-8; P=360-cid V-8. Z=401-cid V-8. The next six symbols are the sequential production number beginning at 000001.

Model	Body Type	Price	Weight
CJ-5 — 1/4-Ton — 4x4 — 84-in. w.b.			
83	Jeep CJ-5	$4,199	2,641 lbs.
CJ-6 — 1/4 ton 4x4			
84	Jeep CJ-6*	—	—

*Note: Although Jeep CJ-6 remained in production this year, apparently it was sold only in overseas markets. Because of this, CJ-6 models will not appear in this book after this year.

Model	Body Type	Price	Weight
CJ-7 — 1/4-Ton — 4x4 — 94-in. w.b.			
93	Jeep CJ-7	$4,299	2,683 lbs.
Cherokee — 4x4			
16	2d Station Wagon	$5,258	3,918 lbs.
17	2d Wide Wheel Chief	$5,806	3,938 lbs.
Wagoneer — 4x4			
14	4d Standard Wagon	$6,339	4,329 lbs.
15	4d Custom Wagon	$6,572	4,345 lbs.
J-10 — 1/2-Ton — 4x4 — 119/131-in. w.b.			
25	Townside Pickup (SWB)	$4,643	3,773 lbs.
45	Townside Pickup (LWB)	$4,704	3,873 lbs.
J-20 — 3/4-Ton — 4x4 — 131-in. w.b.			
46	Townside Pickup	$5,290	4,285 lbs.

The 1976 Jeep CJ-5 Renegade.

PRODUCTION/SALES: American Motors reported fiscal-year retail sales in the U.S. and Canada of 95,718 units. Jeep U.S. retail sales during calendar year 1976 were reported to be 95,506. Overseas sales were put at 26,500 units.

ENGINES

(STANDARD CJ-5/CJ-7 SIX): Overhead valve. Inline. Cast-iron block. Bore & stroke: 3.75 x 3.50 in. Displacement: 232 cid. Compression ratio: 8.0:1. Net hp: 100 at 3600 rpm. Net torque: 185 lbs.-ft. at 1800 rpm. Seven main bearings. Hydraulic valve lifters. Carburetor: one-barrel.

(OPTIONAL CJ-5/CJ-7 V-8): Overhead valve V-8. Cast-iron block. Bore & stroke: 3.75 x 3.44 in. Displacement: 304 cid. Compression ratio: 8.4:1. Net hp: 150 at 4200 rpm. Net torque: 245 lbs.-ft. at 2500 rpm. Seven main bearings. Hydraulic valve lifters. Carburetor: two-barrel.

(STANDARD CHEROKEE & J-10; OPTIONAL CJ-5/CJ-7 SIX): Overhead valve. Inline. Cast-iron block. Bore & stroke: 3.75 x 3.9 in. Displacement: 258 cid. Compression ratio: 8.0:1. Net hp: 110 at 3500 rpm. Torque: 195 lbs.-ft. at 2000 rpm. Seven main bearings. Hydraulic valve lifters.

(STANDARD WAGONEER & J-20; OPTIONAL J-10 V-8): Overhead valve. Cast-iron block. Bore & stroke: 4.08 x 3.44 in. Displacement: 360 cid. Compression ratio: 8.5:1. Net hp: 175 at 4000 rpm. Net torque: 285 lbs.-ft. at 2400 rpm. Five main bearings. Hydraulic valve lifters. Carburetor: two-barrel.

(OPTIONAL CHEROKEE/WAGONEER/J-10/J-20 V-8): Overhead valve. Cast-iron block. Bore & stroke: 4.08 x 3.44 in. Displacement: 360 cid. Net hp: 195 at 4400 rpm. Five main bearings. Hydraulic valve lifters. Carburetor: four-barrel.

(OPTIONAL CHEROKEE/WAGONEER/J-10/J-20 V-8): Overhead-valve. Cast-iron block. Bore & stroke: 4.17 x 3.68 in. Displacement: 401 cid. Net hp: 235 at 4600 rpm. Five main bearings. Hydraulic valve lifters. Carburetor: four-barrel.

CHASSIS

(WAGONEER/CHEROKEE): Wheelbase: 109 in. Overall length: 183.7 in. Tires: F78 x 15.

(CJ-5): Wheelbase: 83.5 in. Overall length: 138.5 in. Height: 67.6 in. Front tread: 51.5 in. Rear tread: 50 in. Tires: F78 x 15.

(CJ-7): Wheelbase: 93.5 in. Overall length: 147.9 in.

For 1976, Jeep CJ buyers could get this roomy CJ-7 Renegade with optional fiberglass hardtop and steel doors. The CJ-7 could even be had with automatic transmission—the first CJ to offer that convenience.

The great-looking 1976 Jeep Pioneer pickup.

Height: 67.6 in. Front tread: 51.5 in. Rear tread: 50 in. Tires: F78 x 15 in.

(J-10): Wheelbase: 118.7 in. Overall length: 192.5 in. Front tread: (J-10) 63.3 in., (Honcho) 65.4 in. Rear tread: (J-10) 63.8 in., (Honcho) 65.8 in. Tires: H78 x 15 in.

(J-20/J-10 LWB): Wheelbase: 130.7 in. Overall length: 204.5 in. Front tread: 64.6 in. Rear tread: 65.9 in. Tires: (J-10) H78-15; (J-20/6,500-lb. GVW) 8.00 x 16.5; in. (J-20/7,200-lb. GVW) 9.50 x 16.5 in.

TECHNICAL

(WAGONEER/CHEROKEE/J-10/J-20): Three-speed manual transmission. (Automatic transmission in Wagoneer). Floor-mounted gearshift. Clutch: (J-10) 10.5 in. diameter, 106.75 sq. in., (J-20) 11 in. diameter, 110.96 sq. in. Front disc/rear drum brakes.

(CJ-SERIES): Three-speed manual transmission. Floor-mounted gearshift. Semi-floating rear axle. Overall ratio: 3.54:1. Pressed-steel, five-bolt wheels.

OPTIONS

(WAGONEER/CHEROKEE/TRUCKS): 401-cid V-8. Power steering (standard Wagoneer). Turbo Hydra-Matic with Quadra-Trac (standard Wagoneer). Four-speed transmission. Roof rack. Air conditioning. Front bumper guards with nerf strips. Rear step bumper. Convenience group. Light group. Custom trim package. Radios: AM, AM/FM stereo; CB. Forged-aluminum wheels (J-10). Bucket seats (Custom, Pioneer and Honcho). Cruise control. Tilt steering wheel. Sports steering wheel. Leather-wrapped steering wheel. Sliding rear window. Dual low profile mirror. Aluminum cargo cap. Wheel covers. Honcho package. Pioneer package. Automatic transmission. Power front disc brakes. Snow Boss plow package. Winches (mechanical or 12-volt). Auxiliary fuel tank (20 gallon, for long wheelbase only). Rear Trac-Lok differential. Camper package. Fuel tank skid plate. Heavy-duty battery and alternator. Heavy-duty shock absorbers. Heavy-duty springs. Heavy-duty cooling system. Cold climate package. Free-wheeling hubs (not available with Quadra-Trac). Trailer Towing Package.

(CJ SERIES): Rear step bumper. Roll bar. Soft top. Carpeting. Convenience group. Decor group. AM or citizens band radios. Sports steering wheel. Leather-wrapped sports steering wheel. Rear seat. Swing-out tire carrier. Passenger grab rail. Tachometer and Rally clock. Padded instrument panel. Removable hardtop (CJ-7). Outside passenger mirror. Renegade package. Automatic transmission with Quadra-Trac. Quadra-Trac (available on CJ-7 with automatic transmission only). Four-speed manual transmission. Extra-duty suspension system. Front stabilizer bar. Power drum brakes (w/304-cid V-8 only). Low range for Quadra-Trac (CJ-7). Heavy-duty cooling system. Rear Trac-Lok differential. 70-amp battery. Heavy-duty alternator. Cold climate group. Steel-belted radial ply tires. Winches. Snowplow. Free-wheeling hubs.

Here's a great looking truck: the 1977 Jeep J-10 Honcho.

"Welcome to Jeep Country" was one of Jeep's ad themes this year. Interest in sporty four-wheel-drives was growing by leaps and bounds, and over the years Jeep had introduced many appealing new models.

Jeep Renegade came with 9 x 15-in. Goodyear Tracker A-T tires and white spoke wheels, rather than the Suburbanite tires with aluminum wheels formerly used. A new hood stripe was used. Big news for 1977 was a new limited edition Golden Eagle appearance package for CJs. Included in the Golden Eagle were tan Levi's seat upholstery and soft top, unique body striping, full carpeting, gold-painted spoke wheels, 9 x 15-in. Tracker tires, roll bar, tachometer, and decor group. Golden Eagles came only in a special Oakleaf Brown color with a large decal of an eagle on the hood. All CJs this year offered a new optional six-position tilt steering wheel. There were also new manual or power-assisted front disc brakes.

The wide-wheel chassis Cherokee Chief returned for 1977 and its popularity was almost beyond belief. There was a waiting list of buyers as the factory struggled to keep up with demand that continued to grow. Cherokee's lineup was broadened this year with the addition of a new four-door model. As was the case across the Jeep line, there was no change in engine offerings. Cherokee also offered a new two-door wide-wheel model. It came equipped like the base models, but also included 10 x 15-in. Tracker tires and white-spoke wheels, flared fenders, and the 3.54:1 axle ratio.

The Jeep Wagoneer line was consolidated to just one model. It used no trim designation, but was equivalent to the former Custom. Standard equipment included: a 360-cid two-barrel V-8, automatic transmission with Quadra-Trac, power front disc brakes, power steering, bench seats, color-keyed carpeting, and a 22-gallon fuel tank. There was a choice of 11 exterior colors, all baked enamel.

There were few changes to the Jeep pickup line. The Pioneer and Honcho packages continued to be popular. "Jeep Honcho—Mucho Macho" was an extremely effective advertising slogan. The Snow Boss plow package sold well in cold-weather states. During the summer, Jeep showed a prototype pick up dubbed the Jeep "Shorty," which featured flared rear fenders and a step-side bed.

In August, the 100,000th Jeep vehicle of the year, a CJ-5, was sold—a one-year record. In November, the company announced it was building a new plant in Egypt for a joint venture that would assemble Jeeps for Middle Eastern markets. There already was an assembly operation in Israel.

AMC returned to profitability in 1977 largely because of record Jeep production. Sales in the U.S. and Canada during the fiscal year totaled 117,077 vehicles.

NOTABLE FOR 1977: Midyear saw the introduction of the "Golden Eagle" trim package for the CJ-5 and CJ-7, which included special stripes, a roll bar, white-letter off-road tires, and a tachometer. For the first time the CJ models were available with factory air conditioning. A new CJ option was power front disc brakes. CJs had stronger front axles and wheel spindles, plus wider wheels and tires. The frame now had fully boxed side rails. Rear panels were strengthened. A four-door wagon was added to the Cherokee series. J Series trucks got higher standard and optional GVW payload ratings. The standard rating was increased to 6,800 lbs. from 6,500, and the optional ratings were increased by 400 lbs. to 7,200 and 8,000 lbs.

I.D. DATA: VIN located on the left front door hinge pillar and left firewall. VIN still has 13 symbols. The first indicates Jeep Corp. The second indicates model year. The third indicates transmission, drive train and assembly plant. The fourth and fifth indicate series or model. The sixth symbol identifies body style. The seventh symbol indicates the engine. Engine codes were: E=232-cid six-cylinder; A=258-cid six-cylinder; H=304-cid V-8; N=360-cid V-8; P=360-cid V-8; Z=401-cid V-8. The next six symbols are the sequential production number beginning at 000001.

Model	Body Type	Price	Weight
CJ-5 — 1/4-Ton — 4x4 — 84-in. w.b.			
83	Jeep CJ-5	$4,399	2,659 lbs.
CJ-7 — 1/4-Ton — 4x4 — 94-in. w.b.			
93	Jeep CJ-7	$4,499	2,701 lbs.
Cherokee — 4x4			
16	2d Station Wagon	$5,636	3,971 lbs.
17	2d Wide Wheel	$6,059	3,991 lbs.
18	4d Station Wagon	$5,736	4,106 lbs.
Wagoneer — 4x4			
15	4d Station Wagon	$6,966	4,345 lbs.
J-10 — 1/2-Ton — 4x4 — 119/131-in. w.b.			
25	Townside Pickup (SWB)	$4,995	3,826 lbs.
45	Townside Pickup (LWB)	$5,059	3,926 lbs.
J-20 — 3/4-Ton — 4x4 — 131-in. w.b.			
46	Townside Pickup	$5,607	4,285 lbs.

PRODUCTION/SALES: American Motors reported fiscal-year combined U.S. and Canada sales of 117,077 units. Jeep U.S. retail sales during calendar year 1977 were reported to be 115,079. Overseas sales were reported to be 30,323 units.

ENGINES

(STANDARD CJ-5/CJ-7 SIX): Overhead valve. Inline. Cast-iron block. Bore & stroke: 3.75 x 3.50 in. Displacement: 232 cid. Compression ratio: 8.0:1. Net hp: 100 at 3600 rpm. Net torque: 185 lbs.-ft. at 1800 rpm. Seven main bearings. Hydraulic valve lifters. Carburetor: one-barrel.

(OPTIONAL CJ-5/CJ-7 V-8): Overhead valve. Cast-iron block. Bore & stroke: 3.75 x 3.44 in. Displacement: 304 cid. Compression ratio: 8.4:1. Net hp: 150 at 4200 rpm. Net torque: 245 lbs.-ft. at 2500 rpm. Seven main bearings. Hydraulic valve lifters. Carburetor: two-barrel.

(STANDARD CHEROKEE & J-10 — OPTIONAL CJ-5/CJ-7 SIX): Overhead valve. Inline. Cast-iron block. Bore & stroke: 3.75 x 3.9 in. Displacement: 258 cid. Compression ratio: 8.0:1. Net hp: 110 at 3500 rpm. Torque: 195 lbs.-ft. at 2000 rpm. Seven main bearings. Hydraulic valve lifters. Carburetor: one-barrel.

(STANDARD WAGONEER & J-20 — OPTIONAL CHEROKEE & J-10 V-8): Overhead valve. Cast-iron block. Bore & stroke: 4.08 x 3.44 in. Displacement: 360 cid. Compression ratio: 8.5:1. Net hp: 175 at 4000 rpm. Net torque: 285 lbs.-ft. at 2400 rpm. Five main bearings. Hydraulic valve lifters. Carburetor: two-barrel.

(OPTIONAL WAGONEER/CHEROKEE/J-10/J-20 V-8): Overhead valve. Cast-iron block. Bore & stroke: 4.08 x 3.44 in. Displacement: 360 cid. Net hp: 195 at 4400 rpm. Five main bearings. Hydraulic valve lifters. Carburetor: four-barrel.

(OPTIONAL WAGONEER/CHEROKEE/J-10/J-20 V-8): Overhead valve. Cast-iron block. Bore & stroke: 4.17 x 3.68 in. Displacement: 401 cid. Net hp: 235 at 4600 rpm. Five main bearings. Hydraulic valve lifters. Carburetor: four-barrel.

CHASSIS

(WAGONEER/CHEROKEE): Wheelbase: 109 in. Overall length: 183.7 in. Tires: F78 x 15.

CJ-7 Renegade for 1977 was a big seller.

The 1977 Cherokee Chief continued to be one of America's most desired SUVs.

(CJ-5): Wheelbase: 83.5 in. Overall length: 138.5 in. Height: 67.6 in. Front tread: 51.5 in. Rear tread: 50 in. Tires: F78 x 15 in.

(CJ-7): Wheelbase: 93.5 in. Overall length: 147.9 in. Height: 67.6 in. Front tread: 51.5 in. Rear tread: 50 in. Tires: F78 x 15 in.

(J-10): Wheelbase: 118.7 in. Overall length: 192.5 in. Front tread: (J-10) 63.3 in.; (Honcho) 65.4 in. Rear tread: (J-10) 63.8 in.; (Honcho) 65.8 in. Tires: H78 x 15 in.

(J-20/J-10 LWB): Wheelbase: 130.7 in. Overall length: 204.5 in. Front tread: 64.6 in. Rear tread: 65.9 in. Tires: (J-10) F78-15; (J-20/6,800-lb. GVW) 8.00 x 16.5 in.; (J-20/7,600-8,200-lb. GVW) 9.50 x 16.5 in.

TECHNICAL

(WAGONEER/CHEROKEE/J-10/J-20): Three-speed manual transmission. Clutch: (J-10) 10.5-in. diameter. Front disc/rear drum brakes.

TECHNICAL: (CJ Series): Three-speed manual transmission. Floor-mounted gearshift. Semi-floating rear axle. Overall ratio: 3.54:1; 4.09:1. Four-wheel drum brakes. Pressed-steel wheels.

OPTIONS

(WAGONEER/CHEROKEE/TRUCKS): 401-cid V-8. Power steering (standard Wagoneer). Turbo Hydra-Matic with Quadra-Trac (standard Wagoneer). Four-speed transmission. Cherokee Chief package. Roof rack. Air conditioning. Front bumper guards. Rear step bumper. Convenience group. Light group. Custom trim package. AM/FM stereo radio. AM radio. CB radio. Forged aluminum wheels. Bucket seats (Custom, Pioneer and Honcho only). Cruise control. Power steering. Tilt steering wheel. Sports steering wheel. Leather-wrapped steering wheel. Sliding rear window. Dual low profile mirror. Aluminum cargo cap. Wheel covers. Honcho package. Pioneer package. Power front disc brakes (J-10). Snow Boss plow package. Winches. Auxiliary fuel tank. Rear Trac-Lok differential. Camper package. Fuel tank skid plate. Heavy-duty battery and alternator. Heavy-duty shock absorbers. Heavy-duty springs. Heavy-duty cooling system. Cold climate package. Locking hubs (not available with Quadra-Trac). Towing package.

(CJ SERIES): Rear step bumper. Roll bar. Soft top. Carpeting. Convenience group. Decor group. AM radio. Cigar lighter and ashtray. Renegade package. Outside passenger mirror. Center console. Air conditioning. Tachometer and rally clock. Sports steering wheel. Leather wrapped sports steering wheel. Rear seat. Swing-out tire carrier. Padded instrument panel. Removable hardtop (CJ-7). Automatic transmission with Quadra-Trac (CJ-7). Free-wheeling front hubs. Power steering. Power front disc brakes. Steering damper. Front stabilizer bar. Four-speed manual transmission. Heavy-duty suspension. Low-range for Quadra-Trac (CJ-7 only). Heavy-duty cooling system. Rear Trac-Lok differential. 70-amp battery. Heavy-duty alternator. Cold climate group. Winches. Snow plow.

Jeep startled everyone when it introduced the ultra-luxury Wagoneer Limited in 1978. Despite a high price tag, the new Wagoneer model was soon in short supply.

"Jeep wrote the book on 4-wheel drive!" was a popular tag line again this year. CJs got manual front disc brakes as standard equipment, with power assist optional. To show how much the four-wheel-drive market was evolving, H78-15 tires—once considered a high-performance option—became standard equipment on the base CJs. The highly popular Renegade and Golden Eagle packages were largely unchanged.

There were minimal changes to the Jeep Cherokee line for 1978. Cherokee continued to offer the narrow-wheel two- and four-door wagons in base and S models, plus wide-wheel two-doors in base, S and Chief models.

The Jeep CJ line also showed little that was new, other than a few new items of optional equipment and some minor mechanical improvements. The optional 258-cid six now came with a two-barrel carburetor. There was a moon-roof option for the hardtop.

Jeep Wagoneer was where the big news was this year. Jeep introduced a new top-end Wagoneer, the Wagoneer Limited, that was destined to become the most coveted four-wheel-drive wagon in the world. The Wagoneer Limited had just about every conceivable option or accessory as standard equipment: the 360-cid two-barrel V-8, automatic transmission, Quadra-Trac, power steering, power disc brakes, air conditioning, leather trim on the bucket seats, armrest, and door panels, leather-wrapped steering wheel, large wood-grain body-side treatment, radial white-sidewall tires, thick carpeting, roof rack with wood-grain accents, lighted visor vanity mirror, choice of AM/FM/CB or AM/FM/tape player, power tailgate window, cruise control, tilt steering wheel, tinted glass, and improved sound insulation. Wagoneer Limited marked the first time leather upholstery was used in a four-wheel-drive vehicle, and AMC VP of Styling Dick Teague received an award from the Auto Leather Guild in recognition of that milestone.

Jeep trucks came in for some exciting new features this year. A new 10-4 package became available and included 10 x 15-in. outlined white-letter (OWL) Tracker A-T tires on white-spoke wheels, roll bar, rear step bumper, and special two-tone orange 10-4 decal on the body-side panel. There was also a Custom Truck option package that included: a chrome front bumper, bright trim for the door window frames, special vinyl seat upholstery, deluxe door trim panels, instrument panel trim, and hood insulation.

Jeep also added a new Golden Eagle truck package. Like the Honcho package, Golden Eagle was available only on the 119-in. wheelbase J-10 with power steering. Included in the Golden Eagle's list of standard features was: a chrome front bumper, rear step bumper, five 10 x 15-in. Tracker A-T tires mounted on spoke steel wheels painted gold with a black stripe, black roll bar, black grille guard, two off-road driving lights, beige Levi's bucket seats, sports steering wheel, and more.

In independent tests Jeep Quadra-Trac was shown to offer better traction in normal and off-road driving than competing full-time systems from Dodge, Ford, and Chevy. The reason was because of a fundamental difference in design. In Jeep Quadra-Trac, when a wheel begins to lose traction power is diverted to the axle that has the most traction. In competitors' designs, the axle with the least traction got the most power—which of course meant it lost traction faster and more easily.

In April, AMC announced an affiliation with French automaker Renault. Although the initial plan was simply to have AMC sell Renault cars in the U.S., events would cause this association to grow into something neither party wanted.

In July, the 150,000th Jeep vehicle of the model year came down the assembly line, marking the highest level of civilian Jeep production in Jeep Corporation history.

AMC also announced that it would begin assembling Jeeps at its Brampton, Ontario, plant starting in September 1978. The move would boost combined U.S./Canada Jeep production to 200,000 units annually, up from 150,000.

Wholesale sales of Jeep vehicles to its dealers were up again this year to 153,000 vehicles during the fiscal year ending September 30. During the 1978 model year, more than 74,000 Jeeps equipped with Quadra-Trac were produced.

NOTABLE FOR 1978: The new Wagoneer Limited featured a luxury interior, wood-grain exterior trim, and a very comprehensive list of standard equipment. CJ models were fitted with an improved heating system. J Series trucks had an additional 2.5 in. of legroom due to a modified toeboard and relocated accelerator. J-10 GVW rating for the J-10 was moved up to 6,200 lbs.

I.D. DATA: VIN located on the left front door hinge pillar and left firewall. VIN still has 13 symbols. The first indicates Jeep Corp. The second indicates model year. The third indicates transmission, drive train, and assembly plant. The fourth and fifth indicate series or model. The sixth symbol identifies body style. The seventh symbol indicates the engine. Engine codes were: E=232-cid six-cylinder; A=258-cid six-cylinder; C=258-cid six-cylinder; E=232-cid six-cylinder; G=121-cid four-cylinder; H=304-cid V-8; N=360-cid V-8; P=360-cid V-8; Z=401-cid V-8. The next six symbols are the sequential production number, beginning at 000001.

Model	Body Type	Price	Weight
CJ-5 — 1/4-Ton — 4x4 — 84-in. w.b.			
83	Jeep CJ-5	$5,095	2,738 lbs.
CJ-7 — 1/4-Ton — 4x4 — 94-in. w.b.			
93	Jeep CJ-7	$5,195	2,782 lbs.
Cherokee — 4x4			
16	2d Station Wagon	$6,229	3,971 lbs.
17	2d Wide Wheel	$6,675	4,084 lbs.
18	4d Station Wagon	$6,335	4,106 lbs.
Wagoneer — 4x4			
15	4d Station Wagon	$7,695	4,345 lbs.
J-10 — 1/4-Ton — 4x4 — 119/131-in. w.b.			
25	Townside Pickup (SWB)	$5,675	3,831 lbs.
45	Townside Pickup (LWB)	$5,743	3,890 lbs.
J-20 — 3/4-Ton — 4x4 — 131-in. w.b.			
46	Townside Pickup	$6,324	4,269 lbs.

PRODUCTION/SALES: American Motors reported fiscal-year combined U.S. and Canada wholesale sales to its dealers of 152,396 units. Jeep U.S. retail sales during calendar year 1978 were reported to be 161,912. Overseas sales were reportedly 28,271 units.

ENGINES

(STANDARD CJ-5/CJ-7 SIX): Overhead valve. Cast-iron block. Bore & stroke: 3.75 x 3.50 in. Displacement: 232 cid. Compression ratio: 8.0:1. Net hp: 100 at 3600 rpm. Net torque: 185 lbs.-ft. at 1800 rpm. Seven main bearings. Hydraulic valve lifters. Carburetor: one-barrel.

(OPTIONAL CJ-5/CJ-7 SIX): Overhead valve. Cast-iron block. Bore & stroke: 3.75 x 3.9 in. Displacement: 258 cid. Compression ratio: 8.0:1. Net hp: 110 at 3500 rpm. Torque: 195 lbs.-ft. at 2000 rpm. Seven main bearings. Hydraulic valve lifters. Carburetor: one-barrel.

(OPTIONAL CJ-5/CJ-7 V-8): Overhead valve. Cast-

Jeep Wagoneer Limited was the first domestic 4x4 to offer leather interior.

iron block. Bore & stroke: 3.75 x 3.44 in. Displacement: 304 cid. Compression ratio: 8.4:1. Net hp: 150 at 4200 rpm. Net torque: 245 lbs.-ft. at 2500 rpm. Seven main bearings. Hydraulic valve lifters. Carburetor: two-barrel.

(STANDARD CHEROKEE/J-10 SIX): Overhead valve. Cast-iron block. Bore & stroke: 3.75 x 3.9 in. Displacement: 258 cid. Compression ratio: 8.0:1. Net hp: 120 at 3600 rpm. Torque: 195 lbs.-ft. at 2000 rpm. Seven main bearings. Hydraulic valve lifters. Carburetor: two-barrel.

(STANDARD WAGONEER & J-20 — OPTIONAL J-10, CHEROKEE V-8): Overhead valve. Cast-iron block. Bore & stroke: 4.08 x 3.44 in. Displacement: 360 cid. Compression ratio: 8.5:1. Net hp: 175 at 4000 rpm. Net torque: 285 lbs.-ft. at 2400 rpm. Five main bearings. Hydraulic valve lifters. Carburetor: two-barrel. (This was the only engine available on Cherokees sold in California.)

(OPTIONAL WAGONEER/CHEROKEE/J-10/J-20 V-8): Overhead valve. Cast-iron block. Bore & stroke: 4.08 x 3.44 in. Displacement: 360 cid. Net hp: 195 at 4400 rpm. Five main bearings. Hydraulic valve lifters. Carburetor: four-barrel.

(OPTIONAL WAGONEER/CHEROKEE/J-10/J-20 V-8): Overhead valve. Cast-iron block. Bore & stroke: 4.17 x 3.68 in. Displacement: 401 cid. Net hp: 235 at 4600 rpm. Five main bearings. Hydraulic valve lifters. Carburetor: four-barrel.

CHASSIS

(CJ-5): Wheelbase: 83.5 in. Overall length: 138.5 in. Height: 67.6 in. Front tread: 51.5 in. Rear tread: 50 in. Tires: H78 x 15

(CJ-7): Wheelbase: 93.5 in. Overall length: 147.9 in. Height: 67.6 in. Front tread: 51.5 in. Rear tread: 50 in. Tires: H78 x 15

(J-10): Wheelbase: 118.7 in. Overall length: 192.5 in. Front tread: (J-10) 63.3 in.; (Honcho) 65.4 in. Rear tread: (J-10) 63.8 in.; (Honcho) 65.8 in. Tires: H78 x 15.

(J-10/J-20 LWB): Wheelbase: 130.7 in. Overall length: 204.5 in. Front tread: 64.6 in. Rear tread: 65.9 in. Tires: (J-10) F78-15; (J-20/6,800-lb. GVW) 8.00 x 16.5 in.; (J-20/7,600-8,200-lb. GVW) 9.50 x 16.5 in.

(WAGONEER/CHEROKEE): Wheelbase: 108.7 in. Overall length: 186 in. Width: 76 in. Tires: F78 x 15 in.

TECHNICAL

(CHEROKEE/J-10/J-20): Three-speed synchromesh transmission. Floor-mounted gearshift. Clutch: (J-10) 10.5-in. diameter, 106.75 sq. in., (J-20) 11.0-in. diameter, 110.96 sq. in. Power front disc/rear drum brakes.

(CJ SERIES): Three-speed synchromesh transmission. Floor-mounted gearshift. Semi-floating rear axle. Overall ratio: 3.54:1; 4.09:1. Front disc/rear drum brakes. Standard tires on CJ were H78-15 Suburbanite.

OPTIONS

(CJ SERIES): AM radio. Soft top. Levi's soft top. Bucket seats. Vinyl bench seat. Rear seat. Roll bar. Air conditioning. Metal cab (CJ-5). Automatic transmission with Quadra-Trac (CJ-7). Removable front and rear carpet. Convenience group. Decor group. Golden Eagle package. Hardtop (CJ-7). Moon roof for CJ-7 hardtop. Renegade package. Free-wheeling front hubs. Power steering. Four-speed transmission. Extra-duty suspension system. Low-range for Quadra-Trac (CJ-7). Heavy-duty cooling system. Rear Trac-Lok differential. 70-amp battery. Heavy-duty alternator. Cold climate group. Steel-belted radial ply tires. Winches. Snow plow.

(WAGONEER/CHEROKEE): Automatic transmission with Quadra-Trac (standard Wagoneer). Four-speed manual transmission. Snow Boss plow package. Winch. Rear Trac-Lok differential. Heavy-duty battery and alternator. Heavy-duty shock absorbers. Heavy-duty springs. Heavy-duty cooling system. Cold climate package. Trailer towing package.

(J-SERIES): AM Radio. AM/CB radio. AM/FM stereo. AM/FM stereo w/8-track tape player. Sliding rear window. Tinted glass. "10-4" package. Levi's fabric bucket seats. Roll bar. Air conditioning. Brush guard. Pickup box cap. Convenience group. Cruise control. Custom package. Golden Eagle package, (J-10 SWB). Honcho package, (J-10 SWB). Quadra-Trac (available with Turbo Hydra-Matic only).

Jeep Renegade for 1979 was a tremendously popular 4x4.

The final year of the decade was destined to be remembered for a variety of reasons. Jeep was enjoying glorious success, as the popularity of its civilian vehicle line continued to grow.

There were changes in the engine lineup. Jeep CJ-5 and CJ-7 got the 258-cid two-barrel six as standard equipment this year. The 304-cid V-8 was still available as an extra-cost option. On Cherokees and trucks, the 258-cid two-barrel six remained as standard equipment, but the only V-8 engine option was the 360-cid two-barrel. The 360-cid four-barrel and 401-cid V-8s were dropped. Wagoneers had only one engine—the 360-cid two-barrel that came as standard equipment.

The reason for simplifying the engine line-up was two-fold. First, the cost of getting federal certification for each engine/transmission combination was a very time-consuming and costly process. Fewer engine choices would save a lot of money. Second, fuel economy was beginning to worry buyers, so dropping the most powerful engines seemed the smartest thing to do.

There were appearance changes, too. The senior Jeep line of Wagoneer, Cherokee, and trucks all got revised grills with new rectangular headlights, a styling feature that was sweeping the industry.

In January 1979, the company reported it had produced more than 250,000 Jeep vehicles with Quadra-Trac full-time four-wheel drive since the debut of that system in 1973.

In May, the company unveiled a special, limited edition Silver Anniversary CJ-5 model. Built to commemorate the 25th anniversary of the CJ-5, the Silver Anniversary model featured special silver paint, chrome wheels, special seat trim, and a special emblem on the instrument panel.

The company reported net earnings of $83.9 million during the fiscal year ending September 30. However, a fuel crisis and weak economy caused sales to begin to falter during the last quarter. Exceptionally strong sales in the first three quarters help to minimize the fourth-quarter weakness. For fiscal 1979, a total of 207,642 Jeep vehicles were sold to dealers. It was announced that Jeep production in Venezuela was being doubled.

NOTABLE FOR 1979: The CJ Renegade package featured new exterior graphics. Revisions to the J Series trucks consisted of a new front-end appearance with rectangular headlights set in a grille with a slightly protruding center section and vertical blades. The front bumper no longer had a recessed middle portion. Available for all pickups was a stylish new bed enclosure. The Honcho trim package was revised.

I.D. DATA: VIN located on the left front door hinge pillar and left firewall. VIN still has 13 symbols. The first indicates Jeep Corp. The second indicates model year. The third indicates transmission, drive train and assembly plant. The fourth and fifth indicate series or model. The sixth symbol identifies body style. The seventh symbol indicates the engine. Engine codes were: A=258-cid six-cylinder; C=258-cid six-cylinder; E=232-cid six-cylinder; G=121-cid four-cylinder; H=304-cid V-8; N=360-cid V-8. The next six symbols are the sequential production number beginning at 000001.

Model	Body Type	Price	Weight
CJ-5 — 1/4-Ton — 4x4 — 84-in. w.b.			
83	Jeep CJ-5	$5,588	2,623 lbs.
CJ-7 — 1/4-Ton — 4x4 — 94-in. w.b.			
93	Jeep CJ-7	$5,732	2,666 lbs.
Cherokee — 4x4			
16	2d Station Wagon	$7,328	3,653 lbs.
17	2d Wide Stance	$7,671	3,774 lbs.
18	4d Station Wagon	$7,441	3,761 lbs.
Wagoneer — 4x4			
15	4d Station Wagon	$9,065	4,034 lbs.
15	4d Limited	$12,485	4,181 lbs.

J-10 — 1/2-Ton — 4x4 — 119/131-in. w.b.			
25	Townside Pickup (SWB)	$6,172	3,693 lbs.
45	Townside Pickup (LWB)	$6,245	3,760 lbs.
J-20 — 3/4-Ton — 4x4 — 131-in. w.b.			
46	Townside Pickup	$6,872	4,167 lbs.

PRODUCTION/SALES: American Motors reported fiscal-year combined U.S. and Canada wholesale sales (sales to its dealers) of 175,647 units. Jeep U.S. retail sales during calendar year 1979 were reported to be 140,431. Overseas sales were reported to be 31,995 units.

ENGINES

(STANDARD CJ-5/CJ-7/CHEROKEE & J-10 SIX): Overhead valve. Inline. Cast-iron block. Bore & stroke: 3.75 x 3.9 in. Displacement: 258 cid. Compression ratio: 8.0:1. Net hp: 110 at 3500 rpm. Torque: 195 lbs.-ft. at 2000 rpm. Seven main bearings. Hydraulic valve lifters. Carburetor: Two-barrel. (Note: On Cherokees sold in California a 360-cid two-barrel V-8 was standard.)

(OPTIONAL CJ-5/CJ-7 V-8): Overhead valve. Cast-iron block. Bore & stroke: 3.75 x 3.44 in. Displacement: 304 cid. Compression ratio: 8.4:1. Net hp: 150 at 4200 rpm. Net torque: 245 lbs.-ft. at 2500 rpm. Seven main bearings. Hydraulic valve lifters. Carburetor: two-barrel.

(STANDARD WAGONEER & J-20 — OPTIONAL J-10/CHEROKEE): Overhead valve. Cast-iron block. Bore & stroke: 4.08 x 3.44 in. Displacement: 360 cid. Compression ratio: 8.5:1. Net hp: 175 at 4000 rpm. Net torque: 285 lbs.-ft. at 2400 rpm. Five main bearings. Hydraulic valve lifters. Carburetor: two-barrel.

Cherokee Chief was the standard by which other SUVs were judged.

CHASSIS

(CJ-5): Wheelbase: 83.5 in. Overall length: 134.8 in. Height: 67.6 in. Front tread: 51.5 in. Rear tread: 50 in. Tires: H78 x 15 in.

(CJ-7): Wheelbase: 93.5 in. Overall length: 144.3 in. Height: 67.6 in. Front tread: 57.5 in. Rear tread: 50 in. Tires: H78 x 15 in.

(CHEROKEE): Wheelbase: 108.7 in. Overall length: 186 in.

(WAGONEER): Wheelbase: 108.7 in. Overall length: 186 in. Width: 76 in. Tires: F78 x 15 in.

(J-10 SWB): Wheelbase: 118.7 in. Overall length: 192.5 in. Height: 69.3 in. Front tread: 63.3 in. Rear tread: 63.8 in. Tires: H78 x 15 in.

(J-20/J-10 LWB): Wheelbase: 130.7 in. Overall length: 204.5 in. Height: 69.1/70.7 in. Front tread: (J-10) 63.3 in., (J-20) 64.6 in. Rear tread: (J-10) 63.8 in., (J-20) 65.9 in. Tires: (J-10) H78 x 15 in., (J-20) 8.75 x 16.5 in.

TECHNICAL

(CJ-SERIES): Three-speed synchromesh transmission. Floor-mounted gearshift. Front disc/rear drum brakes.

(CHEROKEE/J-10): Three-speed manual transmission. Floor-mounted gearshift. Power front disc/rear drum brakes. Steel disc wheels.

OPTIONS

(CJ SERIES): Renegade package. Golden Eagle package. Soft top (CJ-5/CJ-7). Hardtop (CJ-7). Full metal cab (CJ-5). Removable carpet. AM radio. Moon roof (CJ-7 hardtop). Body-side step. Power disc brakes. Power steering. Tachometer and rally clock. Tilt steering wheel. Air conditioning. Convenience group. Decor group. Wheel covers. Padded instrument panel. Four-speed transmission. 304-cid V-8. Turbo-Hydra-Matic with Quadra-Trac (CJ-7). Four-speed manual transmission. Quadra-Trac low range (CJ-7). Rear Trac-Lok differential. Free-wheeling hubs. Heavy-duty cooling system. Extra-duty suspension package. Heavy-

duty 70-amp battery. Heavy-duty 63-amp alternator. Cold climate group.

(WAGONEER/CHEROKEE): AM/FM stereo. AM/FM stereo w/8-track tape player. Turbo Hydra-Matic with Quadra-Trac (standard Wagoneer). Four-speed manual transmission. Rear Trac-Lok differential. Free-wheeling hubs. Heavy-duty cooling system. Extra-duty suspension system. Heavy-duty shock absorbers. Heavy-duty 70-amp battery. Cold climate group. "Snow Boss" package. Power steering (standard Wagoneer). 360-cid V-8 (standard Wagoneer).

(TRUCKS): Radios: AM, AM/FM, AM/CB, AM/FM/CB, and AM/FM/8-Track. Electric clock. Custom package. Turbo Hydra-Matic with Quadra-Trac. Four-speed manual transmission. Rear Trac-Lok differential. Free-wheeling hubs. Heavy-duty Honcho package. Golden Eagle package. "10-4" package (J-10 short bed). Soft-Feel sport steering wheel. Leather-wrapped sports steering wheel. Aluminum wheels (not available J-20). Wheel covers (not available J-20). Hubcaps (J-20). Convenience group. Air conditioning. Tinted glass. Tilt steering wheel. Cruise control. Light group. Low-profile mirrors. Bucket seats. Rear step bumper. Sliding rear window. Cargo cap. Roll bar. Fuel tank skid plate. Front bumper guards. Brush guards. Floor mats.

Jeep Golden Eagle was another popular trim package, priced higher than the Renegade.

THE GREAT DECADE OF JEEP
1980-1989

The automobile market began to go through great changes during the last half of 1979 and it spilled over into the 1980s with devastating impact. The second fuel crisis hit hard and gasoline prices soared overnight as Americans finally awoke to the fact that fossil fuels are a finite resource. Effects from the gas crisis included economic disruption, inflation, job layoffs, and, for those still able to buy a new automobile, a mad rush to small cars. The four-wheel-drive market went through a dramatic contraction that killed off a few longtime competitors.

During that turbulent decade, it sometimes seemed that Jeep would not be able to survive. The twin blows of high inflation and a fuel crisis were staggering even giant General Motors. How could a small firm like AMC hope to withstand?

In fact, troubles that began even before the decade opened ended up affecting Jeep greatly. Before the close of the decade, Jeep, that recurrent orphan, would have a new corporate parent. Like the previous corporate owners, this new one would lead Jeep into new territories. In the 10 years of the new era, Jeep would falter, stumble, regain its balance, and go on to greater success than ever before.

In the final analysis, the decade of the 1980s would prove to be one of the very best for Jeep, because it would mark another turning point. Jeep's full potential in the retail market was about to be unleashed, as the new corporate owners decided to see exactly how high Jeep sales could soar. The results would be spectacular.

The 1980 CJ-7 with Laredo package was a beautiful machine.

When the new 1980 Jeeps debuted in the fall of 1979, there were a great many changes, although the majority of them involved engineering improvements rather than modifications to the exterior styling. America was suffering through a fuel crisis of major proportions and the public was looking for greatly improved fuel economy in every type of vehicle, especially sport utility vehicles. In order for Jeep to survive, it needed to introduce new engineering that would offer increased fuel economy, and it needed to do so immediately.

Jeep CJs came in for many revisions, the most important of which was a new standard four-cylinder engine purchased from General Motors. A 2.5-liter (151-cid) 82-hp cast-iron mill that GM called the "Iron Duke," the engine was rated at 21 mpg in city driving and 25 mpg in highway use. This marked the first modern U.S. four-wheel-drive vehicle to officially break the 20-mpg barrier—an important accomplishment for Jeep. Jeep dubbed the new four the "Hurricane," recalling the famed Hurricane engine it produced from the 1950s to the 1970s. The 258-cid two-barrel six and 304-cid V-8 were available as extra cost options, though the V-8's popularity was considerably diminished. Free-wheeling front hubs and a full synchromesh four-speed transmission were made standard equipment to improve gas mileage. The four-speed tranny included a conventional road-use first gear, rather than the ultra-low "granny gear" offered previously. Automatic transmission was optional, but this year it included a part-time four-wheel-drive system. Quadra-Trac was no longer available in the CJ series.

In addition to the popular Renegade and Golden Eagle, the Jeep CJ offered an exciting new top-of-the-line Laredo package. Available on CJ-5 and CJ-7, Laredo was sporty, but also offered a large dose of luxury. Included in the package were 15 x 8-in. chrome wheels, plus a chrome grille, front bumper and rear bumperettes, a swing-away spare tire carrier with chrome latch and stop, chrome mirrors, chrome hood latches, special striping, indoor/outdoor carpeting, console with padded top, custom door trim panels, special high-back bucket seats with special trim, a leather-wrapped steering wheel, and more.

A new soft top with steel doors debuted this year for CJ-7, providing for the first time the convenience of conventional roll-down windows in a soft-top CJ.

Jeep pickups likewise offered many improvements. Standard free-wheeling hubs provided better fuel economy. Automatic transmission was offered in conjunction with either part-time four-wheel-drive or an all-new Quadra-Trac full-time system with improved fuel economy. On the J-10, the 258-cid six remained the standard engine, with the 360-cid V-8 optional. J-20s came only with the 360-cid V-8. Although both the J-10 and J-20 now came with a standard four-speed transmission, the J-20 had a true work tranny, with a creeper first gear.

The new Laredo package was also offered on the J-10 trucks and included chrome wheels, grille, rear step bumper, and mirrors, plus special interior trim, and a leather-wrapped steering wheel. Functional features included extra insulation, front sway bar, and bumper guards. All trucks got a new molded plastic fuel tank this year. The Honcho and Custom packages returned, but the Pioneer and 10-4 packages were dropped.

Also debuting this year was a sharp new J-10 Sportside model with a stepside body, balloon rear fenders, black and chrome grille, white-spoke wheels, 10 x 15-in. OWL Tracker AT tires, and floor carpeting.

Cherokee got a front sway bar, four-speed transmission, and free-wheeling hubs as standard equipment. The 258-cid six was the standard engine, and the 360-cid V-8 the only optional engine. Amazingly, a Cherokee six with four-speed was EPA rated at 15 mpg city, 20 highway. Automatic transmission could be had with full- or part-time four-wheel-drive. Cherokee was offered in two-door narrow wheel or wide wheel chassis in base and S versions. The wide-wheel chassis also offered the Chief, Golden Eagle, and new Laredo packages. The Cherokee four door was offered in base and S trim.

Wagoneer continued to be offered in regular Wagoneer and Wagoneer Limited models. However, the tone of the times could be seen in the power trains offered on Wagoneer. The 360-cid V-8 and new Quadra-Trac system were standard equipment, but buyers interested in maximum fuel economy could now order

the 258-cid six, along with either a four-speed manual transmission or automatic with part-time four-wheel drive.

In February, the 1 millionth Jeep produced by American Motors—a CJ-5 Laredo—rolled off the assembly line. Over the previous decade annual production had grown from 36,043 in 1970 to 187,359 in 1979. At midseason two new Golden Hawk limited-edition models became available for a short time. The CJ-5/CJ-7 Golden Hawk and Cherokee Golden Hawk included bold hood decals, gold-painted spoke wheels, Levi's seat trim, halogen fog lamps, and more.

All Jeeps produced in Toledo got better paint jobs beginning this year as a new paint facility began operation. In a new process, Jeep bodies received a negative electrical charge as they moved through a dip tank that was filled with a rust resistant primer, which had a positive charge. The primer thus attached itself to the body via reverse polarity.

However, none of the improvements were enough to offset the economic plight that gripped the nation. The automotive industry saw one of its worst downturns ever, and Jeep suffered along with the rest. In an industry where a 6-percent drop is considered a big problem, Jeep factory sales fell by more than 50 percent. For the calendar year, Jeep sold 77,852 vehicles. American Motors reported a mind-numbing loss for the year of $208 million.

Renault was forced to increase its investment in AMC simply to keep the company from going out of business, and ended up owning 46 percent—effectively a controlling interest—so Jeep's fortunes became increasingly dependent on the whims of a company owned by the French government.

NOTABLE FOR 1980: Throughout the Jeep line transmissions were lighter in weight and more fuel efficient. Most models had free-wheeling front hubs as standard equipment. Quadra-Trac was improved. For CJs, the big news was the new GM built 151-cid, four-cylinder engine that became standard equipment. All CJs came with a roll bar. There was a new soft top with steel doors and roll-up windows, and a new "Laredo" package. J Series models had a more efficient drive train, free-wheeling front hubs, and a new plastic fuel tank.

I.D. DATA: VIN located on the left front door hinge pillar and left firewall. VIN has 13 symbols. The first indicates Jeep Corp. The second indicates model year. The third indicates transmission, drive train, and assembly plant. The fourth and fifth indicate series or model. The sixth symbol identifies body style. The seventh symbol indicates the engine. Engine codes were: B=151-cid four-cylinder engine; C=258-cid six-cylinder engine; H=304-cid V-8; N=360-cid V-8. The next six symbols are the sequential production number beginning at 000001.

Model	Body Type	Price	Weight
CJ-5 — 1/4-Ton — 4x4 — 84-in. w.b.			
83	Jeep CJ-5	$6,195	2,439 lbs.
CJ-7 — 1/4-Ton — 4x4 — 94-in. w.b.			
93	Jeep CJ-7	$6,445	2,464 lbs.
Cherokee — 4x4			
16	2dr Station Wagon	$8,180	3,780 lbs.
17	2dr Wide Wheel	$8,823	3,868 lbs.
18	4dr Station Wagon	$8,380	3,849 lbs.
Wagoneer — 4x4			
15	4dr Station Wgn	$9,732	3,964 lbs.
15	4dr Limited Sta Wgn	$13,653	3,990 lbs.
J-10 — 1/2-Ton — 4x4 — 119/131-in. w.b.			
25	Townside Pickup (SWB)	$6,874	3,714 lbs.
45	Townside Pickup (LWB)	$6,972	3,776 lbs.
J-20 — 3/4-Ton — 4x4 — 131-in. w.b.			
46	Townside Pickup	$7,837	4,246 lbs.

PRODUCTION & SALES: AMC reported U.S. retail sales during calendar year 1980 of 77,852 units.

ENGINES

(STANDARD CJ FOUR): Overhead-valve. Inline. Displacement: 151 cid. Two-barrel carburetor. Cast-iron block. Bore & stroke: 4.00 x 3.00 in. Compression ratio: 8.2:1. Hydraulic valve lifters.

(STANDARD CHEROKEE & J-10 — OPTIONAL CJ AND WAGONEER SIX): Overhead-valve Inline. Two-barrel carburetor. Cast-iron block. Bore & stroke: 3.75 x 3.90 in. Displacement: 258 cid. Compression ratio: 8.0:1. Net hp: 110. Seven main bearings. Hydraulic valve lifters.

(OPTIONAL CJ V-8): Overhead-valve. Cast-iron block. Displacement: 304 cid. Two-barrel carburetor. Bore & stroke: 3.75 x 3.44 in. Compression ratio: 8.4:1. Net hp: 150 at 4200 rpm. Torque: 245 lb.-ft. at 2500 rpm. Seven main bearings. Hydraulic valve lifters.

(STANDARD WAGONEER AND J-20 — OPTIONAL CHEROKEE AND J-10 V-8): Overhead-valve. Displacement: 360 cid. Two-barrel carburetor. Cast-iron block. Bore & stroke: 4.08 x 3.44 in. Compression ratio: 8.25:1. Net hp: 175. Taxable hp: 53.27. Five main bearings. Hydraulic valve lifters.

CHASSIS

(WAGONEER/CHEROKEE): Wheelbase: 108.7 in. Overall length: 186 in. Width: 76 in. Tires: H78-15.

(CJ-5): Wheelbase: 83.5 in. Overall length: 144.3 in. Height: 67.6 in. Front tread: 51.5 in. Rear tread: 50 in. Tires: H78-15

(CJ-7): Wheelbase: 93.5 in. Overall length: 153.2 in. Height: 67.6 in. Front tread: 51.5 in. Rear tread: 50 in. Tires: H78-15

(J-10 SWB): Wheelbase: 118.7 in. Overall length: 192.7 in. Height: 69.3 in. Front tread: 63.3 in. Rear tread: 63.8 in. Tires: H78-15

(J-20/J-10 LWB): Wheelbase: 130.7 in. Overall length: 204.5 in. Height: 69.1/70.7 in. Front tread: (J-10) 63.3 in.; (J-20) 63.3 in. Rear tread: (J-10) 63.8 in.; (J-20) 64.9 in. Tires: (J-10) H78-15; (J-20) 8.75 x 16.5

(J-10 SPORTSIDE): Wheelbase: 118.7 in. Overall length: 196.9 in. Height: 69.1 in. Front tread: 63.3 in. Rear tread: 63.8 in. Tires: H78-15

TECHNICAL

(CJ-SERIES): Four-speed manual transmission. Floor-mounted gearshift. Single-plate, dry-disc clutch. Manual front disc/rear drum brakes. Steel wheels.

(WAGONEER/CHEROKEE/J-SERIES): Four-speed manual transmission. Floor-mounted gearshift. Front disc/rear drum brakes. Pressed-steel wheels.

OPTIONS

(CJ-5/CJ-7): Soft top. Skyview soft top. Top boot. Metal cab (CJ-5). Renegade package. Golden Hawk package. Laredo package. Hardtop (CJ-7). Automatic transmission (CJ-7). 304-cid V-8. 258-cid six-cylinder. Heavy-duty shock absorbers. Heavy-duty cooling system. Snow plows.

(WAGONEER/CHEROKEE): Power steering (standard Wagoneer & wide-wheel Cherokee). Automatic transmission (standard Wagoneer). AM/FM stereo. AM/FM stereo w/tape player. AM/FM stereo CB. Cruise control. Rear window defroster. Tilt steering wheel. Luggage rack. Aluminum wheels (standard Wagoneer Limited). Moon roof. Power door locks. Power windows. Cherokee S package. Cherokee Chief package for model 17. Golden Eagle or Golden Hawk package (Cherokee). Laredo package. 360-cid V-8. Air conditioning. Quadra-Trac (with automatic transmission). Heavy-duty cooling system. Heavy-duty shock absorbers. Heavy-duty battery. Heavy-duty alternator. Cold climate group. Snow Boss package.

(J SERIES TRUCKS): Custom package. Honcho package (model 25). Laredo package, (model 25). Honcho. Automatic transmission. 360-cid V-8. Air conditioning. Quadra-Trac (with automatic transmission). Heavy-duty cooling system. Heavy-duty shock absorbers. Heavy-duty battery. Heavy-duty alternator. Cold climate group. Snow Boss package.

The J-10 Honcho Sportside truck was one of the best-looking trucks Jeep ever produced.

The fuel crisis and high gasoline prices were still in the forefront in 1981 so just about every change to Jeeps this year was made in an effort to improve fuel economy.

CJ fuel economy improved again this year with the four-cylinder engine now rated 22 mpg city and 27 mpg highway. The six also boasted good mileage at 17 city and 24 highway. The 258-cid six had a redesigned thin wall block and plastic valve cover, and weighed 90 lbs less than before. The automatic transmission used with the six now had a lock-up torque converter for better fuel economy. The 304-cid V-8 was again offered, though not in California. A wide-ratio automatic transmission was offered with the four-cylinder engine. The CJ's soft top was offered in four colors, including a new nutmeg color choice. CJ appearance package choices were trimmed back. The Golden Eagle and Golden Hawk packages were no longer offered.

Cherokee, Truck, and Wagoneer models all featured a small air dam beneath the front bumper to funnel air downward for reduced wind resistance. Most of the big Jeeps also got new springs that resulted in a lower height and reduced aerodynamic drag. The automatic transmissions used on the senior Jeeps included a lock-up torque converter, and all big Jeeps got new drag-free front disc brakes. Senior Jeeps also got a new inside hood release as standard equipment. In addition, Jeep trucks were given a new roof panel that eliminated the trademark lip, which previously extended over the windshield.

A handsome new grill appeared on Jeep Cherokee wagons. Cherokee offered both the Laredo and Chief

packages in four-door models for the first time. Both packages were offered on the regular four-door narrow-wheel chassis without flared fenders. Goodyear Viva radial tires became standard equipment on regular Cherokees, and Laredo models now came with Goodyear Wrangler steel-belted radial tires for better fuel economy. Cherokee Chief continued to use Goodyear Tracker AT tires. The Cherokee S models were dropped.

Jeep trucks also got new grilles this year (same as the Cherokees) and the new 258-cid six, which was 90 lbs. lighter. The Laredo package got special emphasis this year. J-20 trucks continued to have the 360-cid V-8 as standard equipment, but according to a factory press release they could be ordered with the six-cylinder if desired.

The Jeep Wagoneer line was expanded with the addition of a third model. The new Wagoneer Brougham was slotted between the base Wagoneer Custom and the full-tilt Wagoneer Limited. All Wagoneers came with the 258-cid six as standard equipment, and radial tires for improved fuel economy. Broughams came with added niceties such as: Coventry Check fabric upholstery, premium door trim panels, wood-grain accents on the instrument panel and steering wheel, a wood-grain body-side molding, and chrome styled wheels. Besides all that, there was additional bright trim on the exterior, plus extra insulation, a lighted visor vanity mirror, roof rack, floor mats, and a power tailgate window. Customs and Broughams came with a four-speed manual transmission and part-time four-wheel-drive as standard equipment, and automatic transmission, with or without Quadra Trac, optionally available. The plush Wagoneer Limited came with Quadra Trac standard.

In March, Jeep unveiled a new compact pickup truck to do battle with the horde of Japanese small trucks that were flooding the market. Called the Scrambler, it was based on the CJ chassis and known internally as the CJ-8. Basically, the Scrambler was a stretched CJ-7. Its wheelbase was 103.5 inches, which was 10 inches longer than a CJ-7. Like the CJ-7, it was offered as an open roadster, soft top, or hardtop. Power trains and standard equipment levels were the same as the other CJ models. Payload capacity was 1,486 lbs., but a major drawback was the 5-ft. pickup bed, which was at least a foot shorter than just about every other truck on the market. Two sport packages were available on the Scrambler. The SR package included almost identical equipment as the Renegade package, while the SL was basically the same as the Laredo package.

Jeep sales fell a little further in the U.S. to 63,275 for the calendar year, although in overseas markets they increased by almost 10,000 units. Jeep's parent company, AMC, reported another loss this year, $138 million.

NOTABLE FOR 1981: Responding to the fuel crisis, Wagoneer offered a 258-cid six as standard equipment (360-cid V-8 was standard in California). Cherokee continued to offer three models. Model 16 was a five-passenger two-door station wagon. Model 17 was the same vehicle in the more popular "wide-wheel" style with fatter wheels and tires. Model 18 was a four-door Cherokee wagon. CJ's standard drive train was the 151-cid four-cylinder with a four-speed manual transmission. Jeep Scrambler (CJ-8) was a new compact pickup. All CJ models included a steering damper and a front sway bar, plus a new front axle assembly with gas-filled upper and lower ball joint sockets. J Series trucks got a new plastic grille, and the roof lip was eliminated. Less noticeable was a standard front air dam.

I.D. DATA: VIN located on the top left surface of the instrument panel. There are 17 symbols. The first three symbols indicate the manufacturer, make and vehicle type. The engine type is indicated by the fourth symbol: B=151-cid four-cylinder; C=258-cid six-cylinder; N=360-cid V-8. The next letter identifies the transmission type. The series and type of vehicle are identified by the sixth and seventh symbols, which are the same as the model number. The eighth character identifies the GVW rating with the next serving as the check digit. Then follows the model year and assembly point codes. The last six digits are sequential production numbers.

Model	Body Type	Price	Weight
CJ-5 — 1/4-Ton — 4x4 — 84-in. w.b.			
85	Jeep CJ-5	$7,240	2,495 lbs.
CJ-7 — 1/4-Ton — 4x4 — 94-in. w.b.			
87	Jeep CJ-7	$7,490	2,520 lbs.
CJ-8 Scrambler 4x4 — 104-in. w.b.			
88	Scrambler CJ-8	$7,288	2,650 lbs.

Cherokee — 4x4			
16	2d Station Wagon	$9,574	3,699 lbs.
17	2d Wide Wheel	$9,837	3,748 lbs.
18	4d Station Wagon	$10,722	3,822 lbs.
Wagoneer — 4x4			
15	4d Station Wagon	$10,464	3,779 lbs.
15	4d Brougham Wagon	—	—
15	4d Limited Wagon	$15,164	3,800 lbs.
J-10 — 1/2-Ton — 4x4 — 119/131-in. w.b.			
25	Townside Pickup (SWB)	$7,960	3702 lbs.
26	Townside Pickup (LWB)	$8,056	3,764 lbs.
J-20 — 3/4-Ton — 4x4 — 131-in. w.b.			
27	Townside Pickup	$8,766	4,308 lbs.

PRODUCTION & SALES: AMC reported U.S. retail sales during calendar year 1981 of 63,275 units. The breakdown was: CJ 30,564; Scrambler 7,840; Cherokee 5,801; Wagoneer 12,554; and trucks 6,516.

ENGINES

(STANDARD CJ & SCRAMBLER FOUR): Inline. Overhead-valve. Displacement151-cid. Two-barrel carburetor. Cast-iron block. Bore & stroke: 4.00 x 3.00 in. Compression ratio: 8.2:1. Hydraulic valve lifters.

(STANDARD WAGONEER/J-10 & CHEROKEE — OPTIONAL CJ & SCRAMBLER SIX): Inline. Overhead-valve. Displacement 258-cid. Two-barrel carburetor. Cast-iron block. Bore & stroke: 3.75 x 3.90 in. Compression ratio: 8.0:1. Net hp: 110. Seven main bearings. Hydraulic valve lifters.

(OPTIONAL CJ V-8): Overhead-valve. 304 cid. Two-barrel carburetor. Cast-iron block. Bore & stroke: 3.75 x 3.44 in. Compression ratio: 8.4:1. Net hp: 150 at 4200 rpm. Torque: 245 lb.-ft. at 2500 rpm. Seven main bearings. Hydraulic valve lifters.

(STANDARD J-20 — OPTIONAL WAGONEER-/CHEROKEE & J-10): Overhead-valve. 360 cid. Two-barrel carburetor. Cast-iron block. Bore & stroke: 4.08 x 3.44 in. Compression ratio: 8.25:1. Net hp: 175. Five main bearings. Hydraulic valve lifters.

TECHNICAL

(CJ/SCRAMBLER): Four-speed manual transmission. Floor-mounted gearshift. Manual front disc/rear drum brakes. Steel wheels.

(WAGONEER/CHEROKEE/J SERIES): Four-speed manual transmission. Floor-mounted gearshift. Front disc/rear drum brakes. Pressed-steel wheels.

CHASSIS

(CJ-5): Wheelbase: 83.5 in. Overall length: 144.3 in. standard or 134.8 in. with rear-mounted spare; Width: 68.6 in. Height with open body, 67.6 in. GVW maximum: 3,700 lbs. Cargo capacity: 10.2 cu. ft. without rear seat. Front overhang: 23.5 in. Rear overhang: 37.3 in.

standard or 27.8 in. with rear-mounted spare. Front suspension: leaf spring on live axle with tube shocks. Rear suspension: leaf springs on live axle with tube shocks. Front brakes: manual discs. Rear brakes: drum. Steering: manual re-circulating ball, 24:1 ratio, 34.1 ft. turning circle. Fuel: 15.5 gallons.

(CJ-7): Wheelbase: 93.5 in. Overall length: 153.2 in. standard or 144.3 in. with rear-mounted spare; Width: 68.6 in. Height with open body, 67.6 in. GVW maximum: 4,100 lbs. Cargo capacity: 13.6 cu. ft. without rear seat. Front overhang: 23.5 in. Rear overhang: 36.2 in. standard or 27.3 in. with rear-mounted spare. Front suspension: leaf spring on live axle with tube shocks. Rear suspension: leaf springs on live axle with tube shocks. Front brakes: manual discs. Rear brakes: drum. Steering: manual re-circulating ball, 24:1 ratio, 38 ft. turning circle. Fuel: 15.5 gallons.

(CJ-8 SCRAMBLER): Wheelbase: 103.5 in. Overall length: 177.3 in. Height: 67.6 in. (70.5 w/hardtop). Front tread: 51.5 in. Rear tread: 50 in. Tires: H78-15 in.

(WAGONEER/CHEROKEE): Wheelbase: 108.7 in. Overall length: 183.5 in. Width: 75.6 in. Height: 65.9 in. GVW maximum: 6,100 lbs. Cargo capacity: 95.1 cu. ft. Front overhang: 29.9 in. Rear overhang: 44.9 in. Front suspension: Leaf springs on live axle with stabilizer bar. Rear suspension: Leaf springs on live axle with tube shocks. Front brakes: power disc. Rear brakes: drum. Steering: Power-assisted; 17.1 ratio. Turning circle: 37.7 ft. Fuel: 20.3 gallons.

(J-10 SWB): Wheelbase: 118.8 in. Overall length: 194 in. Height: 68.5 in. Front tread: 63.3 in. Rear tread: 63.8 in. Tires: H78-15.

(J-10 LWB): Wheelbase: 130.8 in. Overall length: 206 in. Height: 68.3 in. Front tread: 63.3 in. Rear tread: 63.8 in. Tires: H78-15.

(J-10 SPORTSIDE): Wheelbase: 118.8 in. Overall length: 194 in. Height: 69.1 in. Front tread: 63.3 in. Rear tread: 63.8 in. Tires: H78-15.

(J-20): Wheelbase: 130.8 in. Overall length: 206 in. Height: 70.7 in. Front tread: 64.9 in. Rear tread: 65.9 in. Tires: 8.75 x 16.5.

OPTIONS

(CJ-5/CJ-7 SCRAMBLER): Vinyl bucket seats with denim trim. Center console. Rear seat. 258-cid six. 304-cid V-8. California emissions. Rear Trac-Loc. Laredo package (on Scrambler this was called the SL package). Renegade package (on Scrambler this was called the SR package). Power front disc brakes. Power steering. AM radio. AM/FM stereo. 63-amp alternator. Heavy-duty cooling system. Extra-heavy-duty suspension. Front and rear heavy-duty shocks. Body side steps. Draw-Bar. Side-mount spare and removable tailgate. Black or white vinyl soft top. Denim vinyl soft top, blue or nutmeg.

Bumperettes. Front and rear floor carpet. Air conditioning. Convenience group. Halogen fog lamps. Stowage box. Tilt steering wheel. Decor group. Full wheel covers. Chrome-plated 15 x 18-in. styled steel wheels. Automatic transmission (N/A CJ-5). Heavy-duty shock absorbers. Heavy-duty cooling system. Snow plow.

(WAGONEER): Two-tone paint. Special non-recommended color combinations. Vinyl or fabric bucket seat with center armrest. 360-cid V-8. California emissions. Automatic transmission (standard Limited). Quadra-Trac. Snow Boss package. Trailer towing package. Power door locks. Power side windows and door locks. Power tailgate window. Power six-way bucket seats. AM radio. AM/ FM stereo radio with four speakers. AM/FM CB. AM/FM cassette stereo. AM/FM 8-Track. 70-amp heavy-duty alternator. Heavy-duty battery. Heavy-duty cooling system. Extra-duty suspension. Soft Ride suspension. Heavy-duty shocks. Roof rack with adjustable top bars. Sunroof. Bumper guards. Retractable cargo area cover. Extra quiet insulation (Custom). Front and rear protective floor mats. Air conditioning. Tinted glass. Convenience group. Cruise control. Halogen fog lamps. Light group. Remote-control mirrors. Rear window defroster. Tilt steering. Visibility group. Leather sport steering wheel. Forged-aluminum wheels. Cruise control. Engine block heater. Cold climate group.

(CHEROKEE): 360-cid V-8. California emissions. Automatic transmission w/part-time four-wheel drive. Automatic w/Quadra-Trac. Snow Boss package. Trailer towing package. Power tailgate window. Power six-way bucket seats. AM radio. AM/FM stereo radio with four speakers. AM/FM/CB. AM/FM cassette. AM/FM 8-Track. Heavy-duty alternator. Rear window defroster. Cold Climate group. Heavy-duty battery. Heavy-duty cooling system. Extra-duty suspension. Soft Ride suspension. Heavy-duty shocks. Roof rack. Sunroof . Bumper guards. Retractable cargo area cover Carpeted cargo floor and insulation. Front and rear floor mats. Air conditioning. Tinted glass. Convenience group. Cruise control. Halogen fog lamps. Light group. Left- and right-hand remote-control mirrors. Tilt steering. Visibility group. Chrome wheels. Fabric bucket seats. Cherokee Chief package (two-door). Laredo package (two-door). Chrome grille, (standard w/Laredo). Power door locks. Power side windows and door locks. Cold climate package. Fixed center armrest. Rear quarter vent window-two doors (standard w/Cherokee Chief & Laredo). Power sunroof. Soft-Feel steering wheel. Vinyl body-side moldings.

(J SERIES TRUCKS): Two-Tone paint. Fabric bench seat (standard Laredo). Vinyl bucket seats (standard Laredo). 360-cid V-8. California emissions system. Automatic transmission w/part-time four-wheel drive. Automatic transmission w/Quadra-Trac. Sportside package. Honcho Sportside package. Custom package. Honcho package. Laredo package. Cap for Townside box. Painted rear step bumper. Chrome rear step bumper. Townside box delete ($140 credit). Brush guard. 15 x 8 chrome styled wheels. Chrome grille.

The 1982 Honcho had a bold, aggressive look.

Perhaps the most unusual Jeep CJ model ever produced made its debut in 1982. Called the CJ-7 Limited, it was an ultra-luxurious version of the CJ, and was aimed at people stepping down in size from big, conventional SUVs. The CJ-7 Limited offered the fuel economy of the CJ, which was the highest of any domestic four-wheel-drive vehicle, plus an unusually luxurious interior that included Western Weave fabric high-back bucket seats with leather optional, plush carpeting, leather-wrapped steering wheel, and a padded roll bar. Exterior features included body stripes, chrome front bumper, color-keyed spoke-styled wheels, body-color wheel lip extensions, and special hardtop colors. The Limited's standard equipment included AM/FM stereo radio with two speakers, power steering, power brakes, unique shock absorbers and springs, plus a wider track and a specially tuned ride.

The CJ line also offered the Renegade and Laredo packages. New CJ features included an optional five-speed overdrive manual transmission for all models

except CJ-5 with six-cylinder engine. On CJ-7s, the wide-ratio automatic transmission was available for the first time with the six, permitting for a lower axle ratio for improved fuel economy with no lowering of performance, according to Jeep. Low-drag disc brakes were new, as was the optional variable-ratio power steering, the latter of which was introduced into production towards the end of the 1981 run. Five new colors were available this year: Silver Mist Metallic, Slate Blue Metallic, Deep Night Blue, Jamaican Beige, and Sun Yellow. Cruise control was available on manual transmission vehicles for the first time. CJ fuel economy improved again this year to 23 mpg city, 28 mpg highway. Jeep Scrambler shared in the new colors and new mechanical features seen on the CJ line.

Jeep pickups also got a major boost in fuel economy, with the six-cylinder J-10 rated at 18 mpg city and an impressive 25 mpg highway. Power train improvements included the new optional wide-ratio automatic transmission, and the five-speed overdrive manual transmission. As with CJs, a four-speed was standard equipment. The Pioneer trim package returned this year and was available on J-20 and J-10, except Sportside models. the Pioneer package included a rear step bumper, front bumper guards, wheel covers, moldings, tailgate stripes, a dark painted grille, carpeting, and a sport steering wheel. Door and seat rim was Honcho cloth.

Jeep Wagoneer was again offered in Custom, Brougham, and Limited models. The six-cylinder engine was standard on all, with a four-speed manual standard on Customs and Broughams, and automatic standard on Limited. Part-time four-wheel drive was standard on the lesser models, while the Wagoneer Limited came with Quadra-Trac.

Jeep Cherokee was mostly carryover, with the mechanical improvements seen on other J Series vehicles.

In April the company announced a new four-wheel-drive system. Selec-Trac was a full-time four-wheel-drive system that could be switched to two-wheel drive at the flick of a dashboard-mounted lever. Offered only with automatic transmission, Selec-Trac replaced Quadra-Trac.

There was a new limited-edition Jeep model this year. It was a special version of the CJ-7 called the Jeep Jamboree, created to commemorate the 30th anniversary of the legendary Jeep Jamboree on-road event. Jamboree's special features included Topaz Gold exterior paint, Jamboree hood decal and graphics, chrome styled wheels, chrome bumpers, AM/FM stereo radio with CB, overhead driving lamps, electric winch, fire extinguisher, grille guard, brush guard, and carpeting.

For the calendar year, Jeep sold 63,761 vehicles. AMC lost $153 million for the year.

NOTABLE FOR 1982: CJ-7 and Scrambler had a wider front and rear tread. Respective increases were 3.4 and 4.6 inches. CJs & Scramblers were available with a five-speed manual T5 transmission supplied by Warner Gear. Scrambler and CJ-7 also offered a wide-ratio, three-speed automatic transmission with lock-up converter. Scrambler came with a Space-Saver spare tire mounted on the roll bar, instead of on the tailgate. A tailgate-mounted full-sized spare was optional.

Custom Wagoneers came with standard equipment that included: power steering, full wheel covers, carpets, vinyl bench seats, body-side moldings, cargo mat; chrome grille, and electronic ignition. Wagoneer Brougham added cloth or deluxe vinyl upholstery, custom door trim, wood-grained dash trim, power tailgate window, styled wheels, lower tailgate molding, light group, halogen headlights, wood-grain body-side rub strips, convenience options group, and visibility group. Wagoneer Limited also included: full wood-grain

The 1982 Jeep Scrambler was a very good off-roader. Although not many were sold when new, Scrambler is a very collectible vehicle today.

Not many changes were seen on the 1982 Jeep Wagoneer Limited, but its popularity was very strong.

trim, special wood-grained luggage rack; 15-in. forged aluminum wheels, Goodyear Arriva white-sidewall tires, bucket seats; wood-grained door trim, air conditioning, cruise control, tilt steering, premium AM/FM radio, power windows and power door locks.

A new Pioneer Townside package for J-10 and J-20 included all features found in the Custom package, plus upper side scuff molding, tailgate stripes, "Pioneer" decals, dark argent-painted grille, carpeted cab floor, front bumper guards, and full wheel covers (J-10 only), plus several other interior and exterior features. Otherwise, changes to the J Series trucks were minimal. The most important drive train development was the availability of the five-speed gearbox.

I.D. DATA: VIN located on the top left surface of the instrument panel. There are 17 symbols. The first three symbols indicate the manufacturer, make, and vehicle type. The engine type is indicated by the fourth symbol: B=151-cid four-cylinder; C=258-cid six-cylinder; N=360-cid V-8. The next letter identifies the transmission type. The series and type of vehicle are identified by the sixth and seventh symbols, which are the same as the model number. The eighth character identifies the GVW rating with the next serving as the check digit. Then follows the model year (10 symbol C) and assembly point codes. The last six digits are sequential production numbers.

Model	Body Type	Price	Weight
CJ-5 — 1/4-Ton — 4x4 — 84-in. w.b.			
85	Jeep CJ-5	$7,515	2,490 lbs.
CJ-7 — 1/4-Ton — 4x4 — 93.4-in. w.b.			
87	Jeep CJ-7	$7,765	2,556 lbs.
Scrambler — 4x4 — 103.4-in. w.b.			
88	Jeep Scrambler	$7,588	2,694 lbs.
Cherokee — 4x4			
16	2dr Station Wagon	$9,849	3,763 lbs.
17	2dr Wide Wheel	$10,812	3,812 lbs.
18	4dr Station Wagon	$11,647	3,867 lbs.
Wagoneer — 4x4			
15	4dr Station Wagon	$11,114	3,868 lbs.
15	4dr SW Brougham	$12,084	3,868 lbs.
15	4dr SW Limited	$15,964	3,868 lbs.
J-10 — 1/2-Ton — 4x4 — 119/131-in. w.b.			
25	Townside Pickup (SWB)	$8,610	3,656 lbs.
26	Townside Pickup (LWB)	$8,756	3,708 lbs.
J-20 — 3/4-Ton — 4x4 — 131-in. w.b.			
27	Townside Pickup	$9,766	4,270 lbs.

PRODUCTION & SALES: AMC reported U.S. retail sales during calendar year 1982 of 63,761 units. The breakdown was: CJ 29,718; Scrambler 7,138; Cherokee 5,796; Wagoneer 15,547; and trucks 5,562.

ENGINES

(STANDARD SCRAMBLER/CJ FOUR): Displacement: 151 cid. Two-barrel carburetor. Cast-iron block. Bore & stroke: 4.00 x 3.00 in. Compression ratio: 8.2:1. Net hp: 82 at 4000 rpm. Torque: 125 lbs.-ft. at 2600 rpm. Hydraulic valve lifters.

(STANDARD WAGONEER/CHEROKEE/J-10 — OPTIONAL SCRAMBLER/CJ SIX): Overhead-valve. Inline. Displacement: 258 cid. Two-barrel carburetor. Cast-iron block. Bore & stroke: 3.75 x 3.90 in. Compression ratio: 8.3:1. Net hp: 110 at 3000 rpm. Net torque: 205 lbs.-ft. at 1800 rpm. Seven main bearings. Hydraulic valve lifters.

(STANDARD J-20 — OPTIONAL WAGONEER-/CHEROKEE/J-10 V-8): Overhead-valve. Displacement: 360 cid. Two-barrel carburetor. Cast-iron block. Bore & stroke: 4.08 x 3.44 in. Compression ratio: 8.25:1. Net hp: 150 at 3400 rpm. Net torque: 205 lbs.-ft. at 1500 rpm. Five main bearings. Hydraulic valve lifters.

CHASSIS

(CJ-5): Wheelbase: 83.5 in. Overall length: 144.3 in. standard or 134.8 in. with rear-mounted spare; Width: 68.6 in. Height with open body, 67.6 in. GVW maximum: 3,700 lbs. Cargo capacity: 10.2 cu. ft. without rear seat. Front overhang: 23.5 in. Rear overhang: 37.3 in. standard or 27.8 in. with rear-mounted spare. Front suspension: leaf spring on live axle with tube shocks. Rear suspension: leaf springs on live axle with tube shocks. Front brakes: manual discs. Rear brakes: drum. Steering: manual re-circulating ball, 24:1 ratio, 34.1 ft. turning circle. Fuel: 15.5 gallons.

(CJ-7): Wheelbase: 93.5 in. Overall length: 153.2 in. standard or 144.3 in. with rear-mounted spare; Width: 68.6 in. Height with open body, 67.6 in. GVW maximum: 4,100 lbs. Cargo capacity: 13.6 cu. ft. without rear seat. Front overhang: 23.5 in. Rear overhang: 36.2 in. standard or 27.3 in. with rear-mounted spare. Front suspension: leaf spring on live axle with tube shocks. Rear suspension: leaf springs on live axle with tube shocks. Front brakes: manual discs. Rear brakes: drum. Steering: manual re-circulating ball, 24:1 ratio, 38 ft. turning circle. Fuel: 15.5 gallons.

(CJ-8 SCRAMBLER): Wheelbase: 103.5 in. Overall length: 177.3 in. Height: 67.6 in. (70.5 w/hardtop). Front tread: 51.5 in. Rear tread: 50 in. Tires: H78-15

(CHEROKEE): Wheelbase: 108.7 in. Overall length: 183.5 in. Width: 75.6 in. Height: 66.8 in. GVW: 6,100 lbs. maximum. Cargo capacity: 95.1 cu. ft. without rear seat. Front overhang: 29.9 in. Rear overhang: 44.9 in. Front suspension: Leaf springs on live axle with stabilizer bar. Rear suspension: Leaf springs on live axle with tube shocks. Front brakes: power disc. Rear brakes: drum. Steering: Power-assisted; 17.1 ratio. Turning circle: 37.7 ft. Fuel: 20.3 gallons.

(WAGONEER): Wheelbase: 108.7 in. Overall length: 183.5 in. Width: 75.6 in. Height: 65.9 in. GVW maximum: 6,100 lbs. Cargo capacity: 95.1 cu. ft. Front overhang: 29.9 in. Rear overhang: 44.9 in. Front suspension: Leaf springs on live axle with stabilizer bar.

Rear suspension: Leaf springs on live axle with tube shocks. Front brakes: power disc. Rear brakes: drum. Steering: Power-assisted; 17.1 ratio. Turning circle: 37.7 ft. Fuel: 20.3 gallons.

(J-10 SWB): Wheelbase: 118.8 in. Overall length: 194 in. Height: 68.5 in. Front tread: 63.3 in. Rear tread: 63.8 in. Tires: H78 x 15

(J-10 LWB): Wheelbase: 130.8 in. Overall length: 206 in. Height: 68.3 in. Front tread: 63.3 in. Rear tread: 63.8 in. Tires: H78 x 15.

(J-10 SPORTSIDE): Wheelbase: 118.8 in. Overall length: 194 in. Height: 69.1 in. Front tread: 63.3 in. Rear tread: 63.8 in. Tires: H78 x 15.

(J-20): Wheelbase: 130.8 in. Overall length: 206 in. Height: 70.7 in. Front tread: 64.9 in. Rear tread: 65.9 in. Tires: 8.75 x 16.5.

TECHNICAL

Four-speed synchromesh transmission. Floor-mounted gearshift. Single-plate, dry-disc clutch. Front disc/rear drum power brakes. Steel disc wheels.

OPTIONS

258-cid six-cylinder engine (CJ/Scrambler). 360-cid V-8 (standard J-20). Five-speed transmission (n/a J-20). Automatic transmission w/part-time four-wheel drive. Automatic w/Quadra-Trac (n/a CJ/Scrambler). Air conditioning. Heavy-duty alternator. Heavy-duty battery. Bumper accessory package (CJ/Scrambler). Retractable cargo area cover. Townside pickup cap. Cold climate group. Heavy-duty cooling system. Cruise control. Custom package (Townside pickup). Decor group. California emissions system. Tinted glass. Chrome grille. Honcho package, (model 25). Honcho Sportside package (J-10) Sportside package (J-10). Laredo package. Light group. CJ-7 Limited package. Pioneer package (J-10 & J-20). AM radio AM/FM stereo. AM/FM stereo w/CB. AM/FM w/cassette. AM/FM ETR stereo w/cassette. Premium audio system. CJ Renegade package. Roll bar on pickups. Scrambler SL package. Scrambler SR package. Pickup cloth bench seat trim. Cloth bucket seats. Vinyl bucket seats. Dual low-profile mirrors. Heavy-duty shocks. Snow Boss package. Heavy-duty rear springs. Heavy-duty front springs. Power steering (Scrambler and CJ). Tachometer and rally clock, Scrambler and CJ). Hardtop with doors (Scrambler & CJ). Soft top. Scrambler tonneau cover. Visibility group. Wheel covers. Sliding rear window, J-10/J-20. Wood side rails (Scrambler). Chrome styled steel wheels.

The last call for the big Cherokee was in 1983. Sales were very low, so these are rare today.

For 1983 there wasn't a whole lot that was new in the Jeep lineup. The company was busy preparing important new models for 1984, so the existing line got only some minor improvements, some freshening up, and some reshuffling of models.

In the CJ line the CJ-5 was available only in base and Renegade trim, and the Laredo package wasn't offered. The only engine offered in the CJ-5 was the 258-cid six. The four-cylinder was still standard on CJ-7, with the six optional. CJ-7 could be ordered in Laredo trim, in the base and Renegade models, or in the top-of-the-line Limited model. This year automatic transmission was available only in combination with the six-cylinder engine.

Jeep trucks were again offered in J-10 and J-20 models. J-10s on the 119-in. chassis with the standard Townside body were offered in base, Custom, Pioneer and Laredo trim. The J-20 and long-bed J-10s could be had in basic, Custom and Pioneer trim. The Sportside truck was offered only in Honcho trim.

The Cherokee lineup had several changes. The two-door narrow-wheel chassis was offered in base or new Pioneer trim, while the four-door now came only as a Pioneer model. The Cherokee Pioneer package included vinyl or cloth bucket seats, custom door trim panels,

carpeting, sport steering wheel, Argent styled steel wheels with trim rings, P235/75R15 Goodyear Arriva tires, and special decals. It was particularly attractive in the four-door version. The wide-wheel Cherokee two-door offered both Chief and Laredo packages.

Jeep Wagoneer no longer offered the base Custom model. The Brougham was now the base model, as Wagoneer continued to move up the scale in prestige and price. The 258-cid six-cylinder engine continued to be standard equipment, with the trusty old 360-cid V-8 optional. This year automatic transmission with Selec-Trac four-wheel-drive came standard on all Wagoneers.

AMC announced a surprise move into the Chinese market when it purchased a 31.6-percent share in the new Beijing Jeep Corporation. The new company would continue to manufacture an existing Chinese vehicle and would begin to assemble Jeep models as well. It was expected to be Jeep's largest operation outside of North America.

For the calendar year, Jeep sold 82,140 vehicles. The company lost money again in 1983, this time a whopping $146 million net, but Jeep sales were rising and in the fall of 1983 the company at last was able to introduce its long-awaited new compact sport utilities. Because of the dire straits the company was in, these vehicles were the most important new Jeeps since 1940.

NOTABLE FOR 1983: A significant Jeep development was Selec-Trac full-time four-wheel/two-wheel-drive introduced in mid-1982 to replace Quadra-Trac. Selec-Trac included a two-speed transfer case. To engage either two-or four-wheel drive, the driver stopped the vehicle and moved a small lever on the instrument panel. A safety catch was provided to avoid accidental movement of the Selec-Trac lever. Technical refinements to the 258-cid six-cylinder engine included an increase in compression ratio to 9.2:1 from 8.6:1, and the addition of a fuel feedback system and knock sensor to improve performance and efficiency. Appearance changes were held to a minimum. CJ Renegade and Scrambler SR trim packages got new stripes.

I.D. DATA: VIN located on the top left surface of the instrument panel. There are 17 symbols. The first three symbols indicate the manufacturer, make, and vehicle type. The engine type is indicated by the fourth symbol: B=151-cid (2.5-liter) four-cylinder; C=258-cid (4.2-liter) six-cylinder; N=360-cid (6.0-liter) V-8; U=150-cid (2.5-liter) four-cylinder. The next letter identifies the transmission type. The series and type of vehicle are identified by the sixth and seventh symbols, which are the same as the model number. The eighth character identifies the GVW rating with the next serving as the check digit. Then follows the model year (10th symbol D) and assembly point codes. The last six digits are sequential production numbers.

Model	Body Type	Price	Weight
CJ-5 — 1/4-Ton — 4x4 — 83.4-in. w.b.			
85	Jeep CJ-5	$7,515	2,490 lbs.
CJ-7 — 1/4-Ton — 4x4 — 93.4-in. w.b.			
87	Jeep CJ-7	$6,995	2,556 lbs.
Scrambler -4x4 — 103.4-in. w.b.			
88	Scrambler	$6,765	2,694 lbs.
Cherokee — 4x4			
16	2d Station Wagon	$10,315	3,763 lbs.
17	2d Wide Wheel	$10,812	3,812 lbs.
18	4d Station Wagon	$11,647	3,867 lbs.
Wagoneer — 4x4			
15	4d Brougham Wagn	$13,173	3,868 lbs.
15	4d Limited Wagon	$16,889	3,868 lbs.
J-10 — 1/2-Ton — 4x4 — 119/131-in. w.b.			
25	Townside Pickup (SWB)	$9,082	3,716 lbs.
26	Townside Pickup (LWB)	$9,227	3,778 lbs.
J-20 — 3/4-Ton — 4x4 — 131-in. w.b.			
27	Townside Pickup	$10,117	4,335 lbs.

PRODUCTION & SALES: AMC reported U.S. retail sales during calendar year 1983 of 82,140 units, which included some 1984 models. The breakdown was: CJ 36,308; Scrambler 4,678; Cherokee (SJ and XJ) 12,894; Wagoneer (SJ and XJ) 23,997; and trucks 4,263.

ENGINES

(STANDARD CJ-7 & SCRAMBLER FOUR): Overhead-valve. Inline. Displacement: 151 cid. Two-barrel carburetor. Cast-iron block. Bore & stroke: 4.0 x 3.0 in. Compression ratio: 9.6:1. Net hp: 92. Five main bearings. Hydraulic valve lifters.

(STANDARD CJ-5/J-10/CHEROKEE/WAGONEER — OPTIONAL CJ-7 & SCRAMBLER SIX): Overhead-valve. Inline. Displacement: 258 cid. Two-barrel carburetor. Cast-iron block. Bore & stroke: 3.75 x 3.90 in. Compression ratio: 9.2:1. Net hp: 102 at 3000 rpm. Torque: 204 lbs.-ft. at 1650 rpm. Seven main bearings. Hydraulic valve lifters.

(STANDARD J-20 — OPTIONAL CHEROKEE-/WAGONEER/J-10 V-8): Overhead-valve. Displacement: 360 cid. Two-barrel carburetor. Cast-iron block. Bore & stroke: 4.08 x 3.44 in. Net hp: 170 at 4000 rpm. Torque: 280 lbs.-ft. at 2400 rpm. Five main bearings. Hydraulic valve lifters.

CHASSIS

(CJ-5): Wheelbase: 83.4 in. Overall length: 142.9 in. standard. Width: 68.6 in. Height with open body, 69.3 in. Front tread: 52.4 in. (53.9 in. with styled wheels). Rear tread: 50.5 in. GVW maximum: 3,700 lbs. Cargo capacity: 10.2 cu. ft. without rear seat. Front overhang: 23.5 in. Rear overhang: 37.3 in. standard, or 27.8 in. with rear-mounted spare. Front suspension: leaf spring w/tube shocks. Rear suspension: leaf springs on live axle with tube shocks. Front brakes: manual discs. Rear brakes: drum. Steering: manual recirculating ball, 24:1 ratio, 34.1-ft. turning circle. Fuel: 15.5 gallons. Tires: G78 x 15.

(CJ-7): Wheelbase: 93.4 in. Overall length: 153.5 in. standard or 144.3 in. with rear-mounted spare; Width: 68.6 in. Front tread: 55.8 in. Rear tread: 55.1 in. Height with open body, 69.3 in. GVW maximum: 4,100 lbs. Cargo capacity: 13.6 cu. ft. without rear seat. Front overhang: 23.5 in. Rear overhang: 36.2 in. standard or 27.3 in. with rear-mounted spare. Front suspension: leaf spring with tube shocks. Rear suspension: leaf springs on live axle with tube shocks. Front brakes: manual discs. Rear brakes: drum. Steering: manual re-circulating ball, 24:1 ratio, 38-ft. turning circle. Fuel: 15.5 gallons. Tires: G78 x 15.

(CJ-8 SCRAMBLER): Wheelbase: 103.4 in. Overall length: 168.9 in. Height: 69.5 in. (70.5 w/hardtop). Front tread: 55.8 in. Rear tread: 55.1 in. Tires: G78 x 15

(CHEROKEE): Wheelbase: 108.7 in. Overall length: 183.5 in. Width: 75.6 in. Height: 66.8 in. GVW: 6,100 lbs. maximum. Cargo capacity: 95.1 cu. ft. without rear seat. Front overhang: 29.9 in. Rear overhang: 44.9 in. Front suspension: Leaf springs on live axle with stabilizer bar. Rear suspension: Leaf springs on live axle with tube shocks. Front brakes: power disc/rear drum. Steering: Power assisted; 17.1 ratio. 37.7-ft. turning circle: Fuel: 20.3 gallons.

(WAGONEER): Wheelbase: 108.7 in. Overall length:

The ultimate four-wheel-drive wagon was the beautiful Grand Wagoneer.

183.5 in. Width: 75.6 in. Height: 65.9 in. GVW maximum: 6,100 lbs. Cargo capacity: 95.1 cu. ft. Front overhang: 29.9 in. Rear overhang: 44.9 in. Front suspension: Leaf springs on live axle with stabilizer bar. Rear suspension: Leaf springs on live axle with tube shocks. Front brakes: power disc. Rear brakes: drum. Steering: Power assisted; 17.1 ratio. Turning circle: 37.7 ft. Fuel: 20.3 gallons.

CHASSIS

(MODEL 25): Wheelbase: 118.7 in. Overall length: 192.5 in. Height: 67.4 in. Front tread: 64 in. Rear tread: 63.8 in. Tires: P225-75R15.

(MODEL 26): Wheelbase: 130.7 in. Overall length: 204.5 in. Height: 67.5 in. Front tread: 66 in. Rear tread: 65.8 in. Tires: P225-75R15.

(MODEL 27): Wheelbase: 130.7 in. Overall length: 204.5 in. Height: 67.6 in. Front tread: 64.6 in. Rear tread: 65.9 in. Tires: 8.75 x 16.5.

TECHNICAL

Four-speed manual transmission. Floor-mounted gearshift. Front disc/rear drum power brakes. Steel disc wheels.

OPTIONS

(WAGONEER/CHEROKEE): Automatic transmission (standard Wagoneer). Five-speed transmission. AM/FM stereo, (standard-Wagoneer Limited). AM/FM stereo with tape. Cruise control, (standard Wagoneer Limited). Rear window defroster, (standard Wagoneer Limited). Tilt steering wheel (standard Wagoneer Limited). Roof rack (standard Wagoneer Limited). Aluminum wheels (standard Wagoneer Limited). Sunroof. Power sunroof. Power door locks. Power windows. Power seats (standard Wagon Limited). Laredo package. Pioneer package. 360-cid V-8 engine. Air conditioning.

(CJ/SCRAMBLER): Renegade package (CJ). Laredo package (CJ). Limited package (CJ-7). Scrambler SR Sport package. Scrambler SL Sport package. Soft top. Hardtop. Automatic transmission. Five-speed manual transmission. 258-cid six-cylinder engine (Standard CJ-5).

(J10/J20): Custom package. Pioneer package. Laredo package. Automatic transmission. Five-speed manual transmission. 360-cid V-8. Air Conditioning.

The 1984 Custom Wagoneer offered the full size of an SJ Jeep at an attractive price tag of $15,995.

This was a great year for Jeep. The big excitement was the debut of the first all-new Jeep vehicles in more than 20 years. In September 1983, Jeep introduced its new generation of sport utility vehicles, which were collectively called the Jeep SportWagons. Internally the new Jeep line was referred to as the XJ series. Reporters soon began using that term, and it stuck.

Ever since the gas crisis and economic troubles had begun back in the latter half of 1979, it had been necessary to continually increase Jeep's fuel efficiency. Mechanical enhancements to the existing Jeep line delivered important fuel economy improvements, but even more was needed. The four-wheel-drive market was on its knees, and the only thing that would bring buyers back to the showrooms was a new vehicle that addressed fuel economy concerns.

The new Jeeps were outstanding! While retaining the old Cherokee and Wagoneer nameplates, they introduced new state-of-the-art technology, some of which has yet to be matched by competitors even today. In designing the all-new vehicles, Jeep was able to retain about 90 percent of the interior room of the former wagons, while at the same time dramatically reducing weight and bulk. The 101.4-in. wheelbase, although the longest among compact SUVs, was 7.3 in. less than the J Series Cherokee/Wagoneer. The of 165.3-in. length was 21 in. shorter, and the width was reduced by 4.3 in. The basic six-cylinder Wagoneer was now 2,971 lbs., versus 4,221 lbs. for the old-style Wagoneer. A big part of that weight loss came from a switch to unibody construction instead of the old-fashion body and frame formerly used. This extremely rigid construction, which Jeep called UniFrame, included a stamped steel frame member welded to the underside for added strength. A new one-piece fiberglass liftgate replaced the old-fashion tailgate.

Cherokee was offered in base, Chief, and Pioneer models. Wagoneer came in basic and Wagoneer Limited models. Cherokee was offered in two body styles—two-door wagon and four-door wagon. Wagoneer came only in the four-door style. These were the first four-door compact four-wheel-drive wagons on the market. Jeep's competitors didn't think a four-door sport utility made sense, but Jeep officials believed the market would soon be comprised primarily of four-doors. As before, Cherokee was aimed at families looking for a sporty model, while Wagoneer was targeted to luxury buyers.

Cherokee/Wagoneer width was 2 in. greater than Chevy Blazer and 4 in. more than Ford Bronco II, providing much better interior room. The Jeep wagons were five-passenger vehicles, while the Chevy and Ford offerings held only four passengers. Jeep's innovative pedestal-mounted front seats allowed more foot room for rear seat passengers. The all-new instrument panel featured a climate control system that was fully integrated for the first time on a Jeep vehicle. Also used for the first time on a Jeep was curved side glass, to maximize interior room.

With the arrival of the XJ Wagoneer, the Wagoneer Limited was renamed the Grand Wagoneer.

The standard engine was an all-new 2.5-liter (150-cid) four-cylinder designed and built by AMC. Based on the 258-cid six, the new four was designed from the start as a truck engine, and was built to meet truck-type endurance standards. It was introduced into production at the tail end of the 1983 model year, showing up first in Jeep CJs and AMC Eagle cars. A new 2.8-liter V-6 engine purchased from GM was optional. A four-speed manual transmission was standard equipment, with automatic transmission or five-speed manual optional. The standard four-wheel-drive system was new Command Trac shift-on-the-fly part-time four-wheel drive, and Selec-Trac was optional with either automatic or five-speed transmission. Fuel economy was outstanding. The four-cylinder Cherokee was rated at an amazing 24 mpg city and 33 mpg highway.

Another innovation was the new Quadra-Link front suspension, which utilized a conventional solid front axle for durability plus coil springs for a smooth ride. As a result, the new Jeeps rode better than Chevy or Ford while still providing better ground clearance than either.

As could be expected, the rest of the Jeep lineup was carryover this year, with few changes. The CJ-5 was no longer offered, its demise marked by a small run of 1983 models. The new AMC 2.5-liter four was the standard engine for both CJ-7 and Scrambler. CJ-7 continued to offer Renegade and Laredo packages, but the Limited model was no longer offered. Jeep trucks got a new color-keyed instrument panel borrowed from the Wagoneer, and continued to offer Pioneer and Laredo packages. The Honcho package was discontinued, as well as the good-looking Sportside balloon fender model.

There was still a market for full-size wagons, and in that market the former Wagoneer Limited had been the king. For 1984, what had previously been known as the Wagoneer Limited became the Grand Wagoneer. It was the flagship of the Jeep line. The 258-cid six and Selec-Trac were the standard power team, though the 360-cid V-8 was ordered on most. Standard equipment included power six-way seats, door locks, windows and outside mirrors, leather upholstery, clearcoat metallic paint and six-speaker am/fm/cassette radio. A 5,000-lb. towing package, 5.9-liter V-8, and power moonroof were optional.

Two special value packages were offered for a limited time. The CJ-7 package included: special charcoal metallic paint, soft top in black or white, high-back denim seats, chrome bumper and rear bumperettes, and styled steel wheel with Wrangler Mud and Snow (M&S) tires. The J-Series Wagoneer Custom included automatic transmission with part-time four-wheel drive, air conditioning, AM/FM stereo, wheel covers, carpeting, bucket seats, and more for just $15,995.

Jeep Cherokee won the Triple Crown of four-wheel-drive commendations by being named "4x4 of the Year" by 4Wheel & Off-Road magazine, Four-Wheeler magazine and Off-Road magazine. Jeep sales nearly doubled, with calendar-year sales of 153,801 vehicles. The new Jeeps helped AMC return to profitability, with a net profit of $15.4 million reported for the year.

NOTABLE FOR 1984: All-new down-sized Cherokee and Wagoneer Sportwagons (the XJ series) nearly doubled the retail sales of Jeep vehicles by the end of the year. Cherokee came in two-door and four-door versions, while Wagoneer came as a four-door only. The XJs were 21 in. shorter, 6 in. narrower, 4 in. lower and 1,000 lbs. lighter than the senior-line Grand Wagoneer (SJ Series). Significant to the future of Jeep vehicles was the introduction of an all-new 2.5-liter four-cylinder engine. Jeep's 4.2-liter (258-cid) inline six continued as the base engine for Grand Wagoneer and J-10 pickups.

I.D. DATA: VIN located on the top left surface of the instrument panel. There are 17 symbols. The first three symbols indicate the manufacturer, make, and vehicle type. The engine type is indicated by the fourth symbol: U=150-cid (2.5-liter) four-cylinder; W=173-cid (2.8-liter) V-6; C=258-cid (4.2-liter) six-cylinder; N=360-cid (5.9-liter) V-8. The next letter identifies the transmission type. The series and type of vehicle are identified by the sixth and seventh symbols, which are the same as the model number. The eighth character identifies the GVW rating with the next serving as the check digit. Then follows the model year (10th symbol E) and assembly point codes. The last six digits are sequential production numbers.

Here's a Scrambler with the top and doors removed. Despite being almost the only soft-top pickup on the market, sales never amounted to much.

Model	Body Type	Price	Weight
CJ-7 1/4 — Ton — 4x4 — 93.4-in. w.b.			
87	Jeep CJ-7	$7,563	2,598 lbs.
Scrambler — 4x4 — 103.4-in. w.b.			
88	Jeep Scrambler	$7,563	2,679 lbs.
Cherokee — Four-cyl — 4x4			
77	2d Station Wagon	$9,995	2,817 lbs.
78	4d Station Wagon	$10,295	2,979 lbs.
Cherokee — V-6 — 4x4			
77	2d Station Wagon	$10,300	2,963 lbs.
78	4d Station Wagon	$10,600	3,023 lbs.
Wagoneer — Four-cyl — 4x4			
75	4d Station Wagon	$12,444	3,047 lbs.
75	4d Limited Wagon	$17,076	3,222 lbs.
Wagoneer — V-6 — 4x4			
75	4d Station Wagon	$12,749	3,065 lbs.
75	4d Limited Wagon	$17,381	3,240 lbs.
Grand Wagoneer — V-8 — 4x4			
15	4d Station Wagon	$19,306	4,221 lbs.
J-10 Pickup — Six-cyl — 1/2-Ton — 4x4 — 118.8/130.7-in. w.b.			
25	Townside (SWB)	$9,967	3,724 lbs.
26	Townside (LWB)	$10,117	3,811 lbs.
J-20 Pickup — V-8 — 3/4-Ton — 4x4 — 130.7-in. w.b.			
27	Townside Pickup	$11,043	4,323 lbs.

PRODUCTION & SALES: AMC reported U.S. retail sales during calendar year 1984 of 153,810 units. The breakdown was: CJ 39,547; Scrambler 2,826; Cherokee (XJ) 69,057; Wagoneer (XJ) 19,886; Grand Wagoneer (and the small number of SJ Wagoneer Custom special value models that were produced) 19,081; trucks 3,404.

ENGINES

(STANDARD CHEROKEE XJ/WAGONEER XJ/CJ-7/SCRAMBLER FOUR): Inline. Overhead-valve. Displacement: 150.4 cid. One-barrel carburetor. Cast-iron block. Bore & stroke: 3.875 x 3.188 in. Compression ratio: 9.2:1. Net hp: 86 at 3650 rpm. Net torque: 132 lbs.-ft. at 3200 rpm. Five main bearings. Hydraulic valve lifters.

(OPTIONAL CHEROKEE/WAGONEER V-6): Inline. Overhead-valve. Displacement: 173 cid. Two-barrel carburetor. Bore & stroke: 3.50 x 2.99 in. Compression ratio: 8.5:1.

(STANDARD GRAND WAGONEER/J-10 — OPTIONAL CJ-7/SCRAMBLER SIX): Inline. Overhead-valve. Displacement: 258 cid. Two-barrel carburetor. Cast-iron block. Bore & stroke: 3.75 x 3.90 in. Compression ratio: 9.2:1. Net hp: 102 at 3000 rpm. Net torque: 204 lbs.-ft. at 1650 rpm. Seven main bearings. Hydraulic valve lifters.

(STANDARD J-20 — OPTIONAL GRAND WAGONEER/J-10 V-8): Inline. Overhead-valve. Displacement: 360 cid. Two-barrel carburetor. Cast-iron block. Bore & stroke: 4.08 x 3.44 in. Net hp: 175. Five main bearings. Hydraulic valve lifters.

CHASSIS

(CJ-7): Wheelbase: 93.4 in. Width: 65.3 in. Overall

Offered only in 1984, the CJ-7 value model was an attempt to boost lagging sales of CJs. The suggested retail price was $8813.

length: 153.2 in. Height: 70.9 in. Front tread: 55.8 in. Rear tread: 55.1 in. Tires: P205/75R15.

(SCRAMBLER): Wheelbase: 103.4 in. Width: 65.3 in. Overall length: 166.2 in. Height: 70.8 in. Front tread: 55.8 in. Rear tread: 55.1 in. Tires: P205/75R15.

(CHEROKEE XJ): Wheelbase: 101.4 in. Width: 69.3 in. Overall length: 165.3 in. Height: 64.1 in.

(WAGONEER XJ): Wheelbase: 101.4 in. Width: 70.5 in. Overall length: 165.3 in. Height: 64.1 in.

(GRAND WAGONEER): Wheelbase: 108.7 in. Width: 74.8 in. Overall length: 186.4 in. Height: 66.4 in. Tires: P225/75R15.

(J-10/MODEL 25): Wheelbase: 118.7 in. Width: 78.9 in. Overall length: 194 in. Height: 69 in. Front tread: 64.0 in. Rear tread: 63.8 in. Tires: P225/75R15.

(J-10/MODEL 26): Wheelbase: 130.7 in. Width: 78.9 in. Overall length: 206 in. Height: 69 in. Front tread: 64.0 in. Rear tread: 63.8 in. Tires: P225/75R15.

(J-20): Wheelbase: 130.7 in. Width: 78.9 in. Overall length: 206 in. Height: 70 in. Front tread: 64.6 in. Rear tread: 65.9 in. Tires: 8.25 x 16.5 in.

TECHNICAL

Transmissions: four-speed (standard Cherokee, J-10, CJ, Scrambler), five-speed (standard Wagoneer base, optional Cherokee, CJ, Scrambler and J-10), automatic (standard Wagoneer Limited, Grand Wagoneer and J-20, optional others). Front disc/rear drum brakes.

(CHEROKEE/WAGONEER XJ): Quadra-Link front suspension. Two "shift-on-the-fly" two-wheel-drive/four-wheel-drive systems. UniFrame construction. Power front disc brakes/rear drum. Stabilizer bars front and rear.

OPTIONS

(WAGONEER XJ/CHEROKEE XJ/GRAND WAGONEER): Automatic transmission (standard Grand Wagoneer & Wagoneer Limited) AM/FM stereo, (standard Wagoneer, Limited) AM/FM stereo tape player (standard Grand Wagoneer). Cruise control, (standard Grand Wagoneer). Rear window defroster, (standard Grand Wagoneer and Limited). Tilt steering wheel, (standard Grand Wagoneer and Limited). Luggage rack, (standard on Grand Wagoneer and Limited). Aluminum wheels, (standard on Grand Wagoneer and Limited). Power sunroof (Grand Wagoneer). Power door locks, (standard Grand Wagoneer and Limited). Power windows, (standard Grand Wagoneer and Limited). Power seats, (standard in Grand Wagoneer and Limited). Cherokee Chief package. Pioneer package. 360-cid V-8 (Grand Wagoneer & J-10).

(CJ): Automatic transmission. Power steering. Air conditioning. HD suspension. HD cooling. AM/FM or AM/FM w/tape. Renegade package. Scrambler SR Sport package. Hardtop.

(PICKUPS): Pioneer package. Laredo package. Automatic transmission. Power steering. air conditioning. HD suspension. HD cooling. AM/FM or AM/FM w/tape.

Jeep Cherokee and Wagoneer models were all new in 1984. Dubbed the XJ series, they were smaller, lighter, and more fuel efficient than prior models, yet provided about 90 percent of the interior room of the old ones.

Jerry Heasley photo

The 1985 Grand Wagoneer got a host of new interior amenities and a new suspension system. The 258-cid six was standard with an optional 360-cid V-8 available.

Jeep Cherokee and Wagoneer grew more popular with each passing month and for 1985 got several new features and some interesting refinements. A new 85-hp four-cylinder turbo diesel engine was optional and offered in all states except California. The 2.1 diesel, built by Renault, provided decent acceleration coupled with class-leading fuel economy. AMC projected it would deliver 31 mpg in city driving and 36 mpg highway when matched to the five-speed transmission. An automatic transmission was also available. However, mid-year changes mandated by the EPA required automakers to reduce reported averages by 10 percent so that actual mileage would be closer to what the label mileage was.

Selec-Trac now featured shift-on-the-fly capability—a major improvement. A new keyless entry remote locking system debuted and was one of the first on a production vehicle. Jeep Cherokee also now offered a Laredo package. In the spring, a new two-wheel-drive version of the Cherokee became available in both two- and four-door models. The two-wheel-drive models were the first from Jeep in many years, and were aimed at buyers in southern states where four-wheel drive had much less appeal, and yet where sport utility wagons were popular. Jeep offered the two-wheelers in base and

Pioneer trim levels. Also arriving around the same time were Cherokees with special Spring Special Pioneer trim, which included contrasting dark and light blue paint, blue denim interior, and styled wheels.

The CJ-7 was again mostly carryover. The Scrambler got a new Laredo package to replace the former Scrambler SL package, and both CJ and Scrambler got new high-back bucket seats as standard equipment. The Jeep J Series truck line was trimmed again. The J-10 119-in.-wheelbase model was no longer offered. Power train offerings were likewise reduced. The six now came only with a four-speed transmission. If a buyer wanted an automatic they had to purchase the V-8 engine, too.

Jeep Grand Wagoneer got a host of new features for 1985. A fold-up feature for the center armrest, and the addition of a third front seat belt, made Grand Wagoneer a six-passenger vehicle. A new suspension system included front and rear track bars, lower-friction leaf springs, and a longer sway bar. The 258-cid six continued as the standard engine with the 360-cid V-8 optional. Jeep's new shift-on-the-fly four-wheel-drive capability came as standard equipment on all Grand Wagoneers.

Something not seen in many years returned to the lineup for 1985—a two-wheel-drive Jeep. The two-wheel-drive Cherokee was aimed at buyers in warm climates where four-wheel-drive was not a big attraction. Response was very good and Jeep has offered two-wheel-drive vehicles ever since.

Production of Jeep Cherokees began in China in the fall of 1985. It was a major accomplishment and marked the first time a modern U.S. vehicle would be produced in China.

Jeep's parent company, AMC, slipped back into losses this year, losing $125 million because sales of its Renault cars had fallen. Jeep sales, on the other hand, continued to climb. The company sold 181,389 in the U.S. during 1985.

NOTEABLE FOR 1985: CJ-7 offered a new optional fold and tumble rear seat. CJ-7 Laredo and Renegade featured new exterior tape stripes, three new exterior colors, and one new interior color. High-back bucket seats were now standard. J Series trucks were unchanged. A two-wheel-drive Cherokee was released at midyear.

I.D. DATA: VIN located on the top left surface of the instrument panel. There are 17 symbols. The first three symbols indicate the manufacturer, make and vehicle type. The engine type is indicated by the fourth symbol: B=126-cid (2.1-liter) OHC-4 turbo diesel; U=150-cid

The 1985 Jeep Renegade offered soft- and hardtop models.

(2.5-liter) four-cylinder; W=173-cid (2.8 liter) V-6; C=258-cid (4.2-liter) six-cylinder; N=360-cid (5.9-liter) V-8. The next letter identifies the transmission type. The series and type of vehicle are identified by the sixth and seventh symbols, which are the same as the model number. The eighth character identifies the GVW rating with the next serving as the check digit. Then follows the model year (10th symbol F) and assembly point codes. The last six digits are sequential production numbers.

Model	Body Type	Price	Weight
CJ-7 — 1/4-Ton — 4x4 — 93.5-in. w.b.			
87	Jeep	$7,282	2,601 lbs.
Scrambler — 4x4 — 103.5-in. w.b.			
88	Jeep	$7,282	2,701 lbs.
Cherokee — Four-cyl — 4x2			
73	2d Station Wagon	$9,195	2,777 lbs.
74	4d Station Wagon	$9,766	2,828 lbs.
Cherokee — Four-cyl — 4x4			
77	2d Station Wagon	$10,405	2,923 lbs.
78	4d Station Wagon$	$10,976	2,984 lbs.
Cherokee — V-6 — 4x2			
73	2d Station Wagon	$9,544	2,852 lbs.
74	4d Station Wagon	$10,115	2,903 lbs.
Cherokee — V-6 — 4x4			
77	2d Station Wagon	$10,754	2,998 lbs.
78	4d Station Wagon	$11,325	3,059 lbs.
Wagoneer — Four-cyl — 4x4			
75	4d Station Wagon	$13,255	3,063 lbs.
75	4d Limited Wagon	$17,953	3,222 lbs.
Wagoneer — V-6 — 4x4			
75	4d Station Wagon	$13,604	3,106 lbs.
75	4d Limited Wagon	$18,302	3,265 lbs.
Grand Wagoneer — Six-cyl — 4x4			
15	4d Station Wagon	$20,462	4,228 lbs.
J-10 Pickup — 1/2-Ton — 4x4 — 131-in. w.b.			
26	Pickup	$10,311	3,799 lbs.
J-20 Pickup — 3/4-Ton — 4x4 — 131-in. w.b.			
27	Pickup	$11,275	4,353 lbs.

PRODUCTION & SALES: AMC reported U.S. retail sales during calendar year 1985 of 182,389 units.

ENGINES

(STANDARD CJ-7/SCRAMBLER/CHEROKEE XJ/-WAGONEER XJ FOUR): Inline. Overhead valve. Cast-iron block. Bore & stroke: 3.88 x 3.19 in. Displacement: 150 cid. Compression ratio: 9.2:1. Net hp: 86 at 3650 rpm. Net torque: 132 lbs.-ft. at 3200 rpm. Five main bearings. Hydraulic valve lifters. One-barrel carburetor.

(OPTIONAL WAGONEER XJ/CHEROKEE XJ V-6): Overhead valve. Bore & stroke: 3.50 x 2.99 in. Displacement: 173 cid. Compression ratio: 8.5:1. Two-barrel carburetor.

(OPTIONAL CHEROKEE XJ/WAGONEER XJ FOUR): Overhead-valve. Inline. Overhead cam. Turbocharged diesel. Bore & stroke: 2.99 x 3.56 in.

The top of the 1985 CJ line was the handsome CJ-7 Laredo.

Hp: 85. Displacement: 126 cid. Compression: 21.5:1. Fuel system: Indirect injection.

(STANDARD GRAND WAGONEER/J-10 — OPTIONAL CJ-7/SCRAMBLER SIX): Overhead valve. Inline. Cast-iron block. Bore & stroke: 3.75 x 3.90 in. Displacement: 258 cid. Compression ratio: 9.2:1. Net hp: 102 at 3000 rpm. Net torque: 204 lbs.-ft. at 1650 rpm. Seven main bearings. Hydraulic valve lifters. Two-barrel carburetor.

(STANDARD J-20/OPTIONAL — J-10/GRAND WAGONEER V-8): Overhead valve. Cast-iron block. Bore & stroke: 4.08 x 3.44 in. Displacement: 360 cid. Compression ratio: 8.25:1. Taxable hp: 53.27. Five main bearings. Hydraulic valve lifters. Two-barrel carburetor.

CHASSIS

(CJ-7): Wheelbase: 93.4 in. Overall length: 153.2 in. Height: (hardtop) 71 in.; (open) 69.1 in. Front tread: 55.8 in. Rear tread: 55.1 in. Tires: P205/75R15 Arriva steel belted.

(SCRAMBLER): Wheelbase: 103.4 in. Width: 65.3 in. Overall length: 166.2 in. Height: 70.8 in. Front tread: 55.8 in. Rear tread: 55.1 in. Tires: P205/75R15.

(CHEROKEE XJ): Wheelbase: 101.4 in. Width: 69.3 in. Overall length: 165.3 in. Height: 64.1.

(WAGONEER XJ): Wheelbase: 101.4 in. Width: 70.5 in. Overall length: 165.3 in. Height: 64.1.

(GRAND WAGONEER): Wheelbase: 108.7 in. Width: 74.8 in. Overall length: 186.4 in. Height: 66.4 in. Tires: P225/75R15.

(J-10): Wheelbase: 130.7 in. Width: 78.9 in. Overall length: 206 in. Height: 69 in. Front tread: 64 in. Rear tread: 63.8 in. Tires: P225/75R15.

(J-20): Wheelbase: 130.7 in. Width: 78.9 in. Overall length: 206 in. Height: 70 in. Front tread: 64.6 in. Rear tread: 65.9 in. Tires: 8.25 x 16.5.

TECHNICAL

(CJ-7/SCRAMBLER): Four-speed manual transmission. Floor-mounted gearshift. Manual front disc/rear drum brakes. 15 x 6-in., five-bolt pressed-steel wheels.

(J-10): Four-speed manual transmission. Floor-mounted gearshift. Power front disc/rear drum brakes. 15 x 6-in. pressed-steel wheels.

(J-20): Automatic transmission. Speeds: 3F/1R. Column-mounted gearshift. Power front disc/rear drum brakes. 16.5 x 6-in. pressed-steel wheels.

(CHEROKEE): Four-speed manual transmission. Floor-mounted gearshift. Quadra-Link front suspension. Shift-on-the-fly two-wheel drive/four-wheel drive. UniFrame construction. Power front disc brakes/rear drum. Stabilizer bars front and rear.

(WAGONEER): Three-speed automatic transmission. Column-mounted gearshift. Power front disc/rear drum brakes. Shift-on-the-fly two-wheel drive/four-wheel drive.

OPTIONS

(CJ-7/SCRAMBLER): Renegade package. Laredo package. Variable-ratio power steering (required with air conditioning. Five-speed manual transmission with overdrive. Power front disc brakes. Cold climate group. Heavy-duty alternator. Heavy-duty battery. Heavy-duty cooling system. Automatic/part-time four-wheel drive (n/a with four-cylinder) Rear Trac-Lok differential. Heavy-duty shock absorbers. Extra-duty suspension package. Chrome rear step bumper (Scrambler only, standard Laredo). Rear bumperettes (standard Laredo). Outside passenger side mirror. Body-side step. Vinyl soft top. AM radio. AM-FM Stereo. AM-FM stereo/cassette. Hardtop. Air conditioning (n/a with four-cylinder) Cruise Control. Fog lamps (clear lens). Halogen headlights. Extra Quiet Insulation (hardtop only). Styled steel chrome wheels. Styled steel painted wheels. Carpeting (front and rear) (standard Laredo). Center console (standard Laredo). Convenience group (base model only, standard all others). Decor group (standard Renegade). Fold and tumble rear seat (CJ-7, standard Renegade and Laredo). Soft-Feel sport steering wheel (standard Renegade). Leather-wrapped steering wheel (standard Laredo). Rear storage box. Tilt steering wheel.

(PICKUPS): Heavy-duty alternator. Heavy-duty battery. Cold climate group. Heavy-duty cooling system. GVW options: 8,400-lb. GVW (J-20); 6,200-lb. GVW (J-10). Rear Trac-Lok differential. Heavy-duty shock absorber. Extra heavy-duty springs. AM radio. AM-FM stereo/electronically tuned. AM/FM with cassette. Automatic transmission. 5.9-liter V-8 engine. Pioneer package. White styled wheels. Visibility group. Tilt steering wheel (n/a with manual transmission). Light group. Insulation package. Protective floor mats. Grain vinyl bench seat. Soft-Feel sport steering wheel. Leather-wrapped steering wheel. Chrome front grille. Dual low-profile exterior mirrors. Sliding rear window. Air conditioning. Convenience group.

(WAGONEER/CHEROKEE): Stereo tape. Cruise control (standard Grand Wagoneer). Tilt steering wheel (standard Grand Wagoneer). Custom wheel covers. Power sunroof (Grand Wagoneer) Power door locks (standard Grand Wagoneer). Power windows (standard Grand Wagoneer). Power seat (standard Grand Wagoneer). Cherokee Chief package. Cherokee Laredo package. Cherokee Pioneer package. Turbo diesel engine. Six-cylinder engine (standard Grand Wagoneer). Power steering. Air conditioning (standard Grand Wagoneer).

Jeep CJ-7 Laredo for 1986

The debut of a new compact pickup gave Jeep some very exciting news for 1986. Called Comanche, it was derived from the Cherokee platform. Comanche was available in both two- and four-wheel-drive versions. Long-wheelbase models were offered for this first year only. Like the Cherokee, Comanche featured UniFrame design and Quadra-Link suspension with a solid front axle. Comanche also boasted the longest wheelbase of any compact truck, a 7-ft.-4-in. double-wall pickup box, plus standard 15-in. wheels and tires. Other standard equipment included power brakes, 2.5-liter engine, four-speed transmission and a 16-gallon fuel tank. The 2.8 V-6 and 2.1 diesel engines were optional, as were the five-speed manual and three-speed automatic transmissions. Three trim series were offered: base Custom, mid-range X, and top-line XLS. Customs were aimed primarily at business or commercial users and included durable vinyl interiors, plus black moldings, grille, window trim, and fender flares. The X offered bright trim moldings, upgraded interior trim, AM radio and sport steering wheel. Comanche XLS upgraded the interior and exterior trim further still. The Jeep Scrambler was dropped.

The Jeep 2.5-liter four-cylinder was redesigned to incorporate throttle-body single-point fuel injection. Horsepower increased from 105 to 117. This engine was standard on Jeep Comanche, Cherokee, and Wagoneer. Jeep CJ-7 continued to use the carbureted four.

Jeep Cherokee now offered an "Off-Highway Vehicle" package that included high-pressure gas shocks painted yellow, five P225/75R15 OWL Wrangler tires, white-spoke wheels, a 4.10:1 axle ratio, and a high-ground-clearance suspension. Wagoneer got completely new front-end styling with stacked rectangular headlamps. The Trac-Lok limited-slip rear differential was now available with Selec-Trac as well as Command-Trac. The turbo diesel engine was offered only with the five-speed gearbox. Laredo trim was offered on the two-wheel-drive Cherokee.

Grand Wagoneers got a new grille and a stand-up hood ornament, as well as an improved Jensen sound system. Grand Wagoneers and Jeep trucks both got a new steering wheel with column-mounted controls and a new instrument panel. CJ-7s had little that was new. With the introduction of the new Comanche, the Jeep Scrambler was discontinued.

In a surprise move, the Jeep CJ series reached the end of the line in 1986, with final production scheduled for January. The final CJ-7s offered were a small batch dubbed the Collector's Edition CJ. There was a new

The Grand Wagoneer got a new grille treatment for 1986, and some new controls and styling inside

DaimlerChrysler photo

vehicle being readied to replace the CJ, and it would debut as a 1987 model.

Jeep sold 207,514 vehicles for the calendar year. All these new Jeep products were good for business but, unfortunately, they were unable to offset the parent company's problems in the passenger car field. AMC reported another loss for 1986 and major changes were just over the horizon.

NOTEABLE FOR 1986: There were no significant changes in the small run of CJ-7 that were produced. Jeep CJ-7 production ended in January 1986. J Series trucks had little appearance change other than new graphics. Base engines were the 4.2-liter six in the 1/2-ton J-10, and the 5.9-liter V-8 in the 3/4-ton J-20.

I.D. DATA: VIN located on the top left surface of the instrument panel. There are 17 symbols. The first three symbols indicate the manufacturer, make and vehicle type. The engine type is indicated by the fourth symbol: B=126-cid (2.1-liter) overhead-cam four-cylinder turbo diesel; H=150-cid (2.5-liter) four-cylinder TBI engine; W=173-cid (2.8-liter) V-6; C=258-cid (4.2-liter) six-cylinder; N=360-cid (5.9-liter) V-8. The next letter identifies the transmission type. The series and type of vehicle are identified by the sixth and seventh symbols, which are the same as the model number. The eighth character identifies the GVW rating with the next serving as the check digit. Then follows the model year (10th symbol G) and assembly point codes. The last six digits are sequential production numbers.

Model	Body Type	Price	Weight
CJ-7 — 1/4-Ton — 4x4 — 93.5-in. w.b.			
87	Jeep CJ-7	$7,500	2,596 lbs.
Cherokee — Four-cyl — 4x2			
73	2d Station Wagon	$9,335	2,751 lbs.
74	4d Station Wagon	$9,950	2,802 lbs.
Cherokee — Four-cyl — 4x4			
77	2d Station Wagon	$10,695	2,917 lbs.
78	4d Station Wagon	$11,320	2,968 lbs.
Cherokee-V-6 — 4x2			
73	2d Station Wagon	$9,772	2,847 lbs.
74	4d Station Wagon	$10,387	2,898 lbs.

Cherokee — V-6 — 4x4			
77	2d Station Wagon	$11,132	3,013 lbs.
78	4d Station Wagon	$11,757	3,064 lbs.
Wagoneer — Four-cyl — 4x4			
75	4d Station Wagon	$13,360	3,039 lbs.
75	4d Limited Wagon	$18,600	3,234 lbs.
Wagoneer V-6 — 4x4			
75	4d Station Wagon	$14,607	3,104 lbs.
75	4d Limited Wagon	$19,037	3,299 lbs.
Grand Wagoneer — Six-cyl — 4x4			
15	4d Station Wagon	$21,350	4,252 lbs.
Comanche — 1/2-Ton — 4x2 — 120-in. w.b.			
66	Pickup	$7,049	2,931 lbs.
Comanche — 1/2-Ton — 4x4 — 120-in. w.b.			
65	Pickup	$8,699	30,98 lbs.
J-10 — 1/2-Ton — 4x4 — 131-in. w.b.			
26	Pickup	$10,870	3,808 lbs.
J-20 — 3/4-Ton — 4x4 — 131-in. w.b.			
27	Pickup	$12,160	4,388 lbs.

PRODUCTION & SALES — AMC reported US retail sales during calendar year 1986 of 207,515 units.

ENGINES

(STANDARD CJ-7 FOUR): Inline. Overhead-valve. Cast-iron block. Bore & stroke: 3.88 x 3.19 in. Displacement: 150 cid. Compression ratio: 9.2:1. Net hp: 86 at 3650 rpm. Net torque: 132 lbs.-ft. at 3200 rpm. Five main bearings. Hydraulic valve lifters. One-barrel carburetor.

(STANDARD CHEROKEE/WAGONEER/COMMAN- CHE FOUR): Inline. Overhead-valve. Cast-iron block. Bore & stroke: 3.88 x 3.19 in. Displacement: 150 cid/2.5L. Compression ratio: 9.2:1. Brake hp: 117 at 5000 rpm. Hydraulic valve lifters. Throttle body injection (EFI). Torque: 135 lbs.-ft. at 3500 rpm.

(OPTIONAL CHEROKEE/WAGONEER/COMMAN- CHE V-6): Cast-iron block. Bore & stroke: 3.5 x 2.99 in. Displacement: 173 cid/2.8 liter. Brake hp: 115 at 4800 rpm. Taxable hp: 29.45. Hydraulic valve lifters. Two-

The basic CJ-7 could be dressed up with optional spoke wheel, OWL tires.

The 1986 Cherokee two-door Pioneer was a popular model. This particular version is a two-wheel-drive model.

barrel carburetor. Torque 150 lbs.-ft. at 2100 rpm.

(TURBO DIESEL — OPTIONAL CHEROKEE-/WAGONEER/COMMANCHE FOUR): Inline. Overhead-valve. Cast-iron block. Bore & stroke: 2.99 x 3.5 in. Displacement: 126 cid/2.1 liter. Hydraulic valve lifters. Turbocharged.

(STANDARD J-10/GRAND WAGONEER — OPTIONAL CJ-7 SIX): Inline. Overhead-valve. Cast-iron block. Bore & stroke: 3.75 x 3.9 in. Displacement: 258 cid/4.2 liter. Compression ratio: 9.2:1. Brake hp: 112 at 3000 rpm. Hydraulic valve lifters. Two-barrel carburetor. Torque 210 lbs.-ft. at 3000 rpm.

(STANDARD J-20 — OPTIONAL J-10/GRAND WAGONEER V-8): Cast-iron block. Bore & stroke: 4.08

x 3.44 in. Displacement: 360 cid/5.9 liter. Hydraulic valve lifters. Four-barrel carburetor.

CHASSIS

(CJ-7): Wheelbase: 93.5 in. Overall length: 153.2 in. Height: (hardtop) 71 in. Front tread: 55.8 in. Rear tread: 55.1 in. Tires: P205/75R15.

(WAGONEER XJ): Wheelbase: 101.4 in. Width: 70.5 in. Overall length: 165.3 in. Height: 64.1 in.

(CHEROKEE XJ): Wheelbase: 101.4 in. Width: 69.3 in. Overall length: 165.3 in. Height: 64.1 in.

(COMANCHE): Wheelbase: 119.6 in. Overall length: 194 in. Width: 71.7 in. Height: 63.7 in. (4x2 and 4x4).

(GRAND WAGONEER): Wheelbase: 108.7 in. Width: 74.8 in. Overall length: 186.4 in. Height: 66.4 in. Tires: P225/75R15.

(J-10/J-20): Wheelbase: 131 in. Overall length: 206 in. Height: 70.7 in. Front tread: 63.3 in. Rear tread: 63.8 in.

TECHNICAL

(CJ-7): Four-speed manual transmission. Floor-shift. Manual front disc/rear drum brakes. 15 x 6-in., five-bolt pressed-steel wheels.

(J-10): Four-speed manual transmission. Floor-mounted gearshift. Power front disc/rear drum brakes. 15 x 6-in. pressed-steel wheels.

A two-wheel-drive Cherokee Pioneer four-door with optional alloy wheels.

The Jeep Comanche Custom for 1986 was a nice-size truck, stylish and very powerful.

(J-20): Automatic transmission. Column-mounted gearshift. Power front disc/rear drum brakes. 16.5 x 6-in. pressed-steel wheels.

(CHEROKEE): Four-speed manual transmission. Floor-mounted gearshift. Quadra-Link front suspension. Shift-on-the-fly two-wheel drive/four-wheel drive. UniFrame construction. Power front disc brakes/rear drum. Stabilizer bars front and rear.

(WAGONEER): Three-speed automatic transmission. Column-mounted gearshift. Power front disc/rear drum brakes. Shift-on-the-fly two-wheel drive/four-wheel drive.

(COMANCHE): Four-speed manual transmission. Front disc/rear drum. Wheels: 15 x 6-in. five-bolt pressed-steel wheels.

OPTIONS

(CJ-7): Renegade package. Laredo package. Variable-ratio power steering. Five-speed manual transmission. Power front disc brakes. Cold climate group. Heavy-duty alternator. Heavy-duty battery. Heavy-duty cooling system. Automatic/part-time four-wheel-drive (n/a w/four-cylinder) Rear Trac-Lok differential. Heavy-duty shock absorbers. Extra-duty suspension package. Soft ride suspension. Rear bumperettes. Outside passenger side mirror. Body-side step. Vinyl soft top. AM radio. AM/FM stereo. AM/FM stereo/cassette. Hardtop. Air conditioning (n/a four-cylinder). Cruise control. Fog lamps. Extra Quiet Insulation (hardtop only). Styled steel chrome wheels. Styled steel painted wheels. Carpeting (front and rear). Center console (standard Laredo). Convenience group (base model only, standard all others). Decor group (standard Renegade, n/a for Laredo). Fold and tumble rear seat (standard Renegade and Laredo) CJ-7 only. Soft-Feel sport steering wheel. Leather-wrapped steering wheel (standard on Laredo). Rear storage box. Tilt steering wheel.

(WAGONEER/CHEROKEE): AM/FM stereo tape. Cruise control (standard Grand Wagoneer). Tilt steering wheel (standard Grand Wagoneer). Power sunroof (Grand Wagoneer). Power door locks (standard Grand Wagoneer). Power windows (standard Grand Wagoneer). Power seat (standard Grand Wagoneer). Cherokee Chief package. Cherokee Laredo package. Cherokee Pioneer package. Turbo diesel engine. Six-cylinder engine (standard Grand Wagoneer). Power steering (standard Grand Wagoneer). Air conditioning (standard Grand Wagoneer).

(COMANCHE): "X" package. "XLS" package. 2.8-liter six-cylinder engine. 2.1-liter turbo diesel engine. 2,205-lb. payload package. Power steering w/17.5:1 ratio. P225/75R15 radial tires. 24-gallon fuel tank. Automatic transmission. Selec-Trac 4x4 system. 4:11.1 rear axle ratio.

(J-SERIES PICKUPS): Heavy-duty alternator. Heavy-duty battery. Cold climate group. Heavy-duty cooling system. Rear Trac-Lok differential. Heavy-duty shock absorber. Heavy-duty springs. AM radio. AM/FM stereo/electronically tuned. AM/FM with cassette. Automatic transmission. 5.9-liter V-8 engine (standard J-20). White styled wheels. Visibility group. Tilt steering wheel (n/a with manual transmission). Light group. Insulation package. Protective floor mats. Grain vinyl bench seat. Dual low-profile exterior mirrors. Sliding rear window. Air conditioning. Convenience group.

The all-new Jeep Wrangler was introduced in May 1986 as a 1987 model. Many Jeep traditionalists bemoaned the rectangular headlamps and bent "V" grille, but no one could argue with the many improvements in ride, handling, and build quality.

This was destined to be another critical year for Jeep. There was important product news across the board. The replacement for the CJ-7 was announced in May 1986 as an early 1987 model. Dubbed the Wrangler, at first glance it appeared to be nothing more than a CJ-7 with a bent grille and rectangular headlights. But Wrangler was an entirely new product.

Though still using a separate body/frame design, Wrangler was a significantly improved vehicle and shared a number of chassis components with the XJ Cherokee line. Front and rear axles from the Cherokee gave Wrangler the widest track in its class. Wrangler also got Cherokee's steering system, brakes, hydraulic clutch, wheels, tires, and shift-on-the-fly transfer case. Wrangler's power train was significantly upgraded. The base engine was the fuel-injected 2.5-liter four from the XJ series, rated at 117 hp @ 5000 rpms and capable of delivering 18 mpg city and 20 mpg highway. The 258-cid carbureted six was optional. A five-speed transmission was now standard equipment, with a three-speed automatic optional with the six-cylinder engine only.

Suspension included track bars and multi-leaf springs front and rear.

Off-road testing on the ultra-rugged Rubicon Trail proved that Wrangler was as competent as any Jeep, while at the same time its on-road ride was significantly improved over CJ's. Wrangler was available in base, Sport Décor, and Laredo versions. Standard equipment on base models included power brakes, high-back bucket seats, mini front carpet mat, padded roll bar, soft top with metal half doors, a swing-away rear tailgate with integral spare tire mount, P215/75R15 tires, tinted windshield, and a fold & tumble rear seat. The Sports Decor option added AM/FM mono radio, black carpeting on the inner cowl sides, Wrangler hood decals and lower body-side stripes, Goodyear Wrangler All Terrain radial tires, full-size spare tire, and a convenience group. The Laredo model included Buffalo grain vinyl seat trim, front and rear carpeting, center console, extra quiet insulation, leather-wrapped sports steering wheel, and special door trim panels. Laredo exterior trim included chrome front bumper, rear bumperettes, grille,

Jeep XJs got a very powerful engine this year. The hot new 4.0-liter was designed and built by AMC. It produced 173 hp, which was unusually high for that era. This is the 1987 Wagoneer Limited.

headlamp bezels, and tow hooks. Aluminum wheels and OWL tires were part of the package, too. The wheel flares were color-keyed, and full-length mudguards with integrated body sidesteps were also included. For the first time, Laredo was offered only as a hardtop, and it included deep tinted glass. Full-color ads featured a stylish cowboy asleep in his red Wrangler at dawn. The advertising theme this year was "The possibilities are endless." In Canada, Wrangler was marketed as the Jeep YJ.

There was big news in the Jeep Comanche line, too. A short-wheelbase model with a 6-ft. cargo box was now offered at an attractively low price. Built on a 113-in.wheelbase, the shortbed two-wheel-drive Comanche base model included 15-in. wheels and tires, special SporTruck striping, and the most powerful standard engine in its class—the 2.5-liter fuel-injected four rated at 121 hp. At $6,495, it was the lowest-priced Jeep vehicle that year, and an amazing value at more than $1,000 lower in price than a Dodge Dakota. Comanche trim levels were completely reworked this year, with the new series being base, Pioneer, Chief, and Laredo. Base was about the same as the previous Custom, while the Pioneer was a step up in trim. Chief was the sport package and offered very similar equipment to the Cherokee Chief. Laredo was the top line, and included luxury features such as wingback bucket seats, bright grille, and special trim on the instrument panel.

From a competitive standpoint, the most important news this year was the announcement of a new six-cylinder engine for the XJ vehicles (Cherokee, Wagoneer, and Comanche). The old GM-supplied V-6 engine was discontinued. Cherokee, Wagoneer, and Comanche offered an inline 4.0-liter (242-cid) six-cylinder engine dubbed the Power Tech Six. The new engine showcased important new state-of-the-art engine technology, including new multi-port sequential fuel injection. Rated at an impressive 173 hp and 220 lbs.-ft. of torque, it offered the largest engine displacement of

any compact SUV. Overnight the Jeeps became by far the most powerful vehicles in their class. In combination with this new powerhouse was the standard five-speed manual or a new optional four-speed automatic transmission offering both power and comfort modes. In the power mode the transmission up-shifted at a higher rpm under hard acceleration, while the comfort mode operated with a more conservative and economical shift schedule. The Renault-built 2.1-liter diesel engine continued to be available on two-wheel-drive long-bed Comanche trucks, and four-wheel-drive Cherokee and Wagoneers, with manual transmission only.

The Cherokee line saw a new Limited model added in mid-1987. The Cherokee Limited was aimed at a very substantial segment of the population that desired the luxury features of the Jeep Wagoneer and Wagoneer Limited, but wanted them in a vehicle with Cherokee's youthful, sporty image. Cherokee Limited featured gold accent body striping, gold inserts on the lower-body moldings, and gold cast-aluminum wheels. Fender flares, front air dam, headlight bezels, bumpers, and grille were all color-keyed. Rear side windows and liftgate window had deep tinted glass. Standard equipment included: leather wingback bucket seats with six-way power adjustment, plush carpeting, the 4.0-liter six, four-speed automatic transmission, air conditioning, Command-Trac shift-on-the-fly four-wheel-drive, power steering, brakes, windows, side mirrors and door locks, power radio antenna, cruise control, tilt wheel and AM/FM/stereo cassette. At announcement time the Cherokee Limited was offered only in a four-door model.

Grand Wagoneer got a new standard engine this year in the 360-cid V-8. Michelin "Tru Seal" P235/75R15 self-sealing radial tires were another new standard feature, and Jeep was the first vehicle manufacturer to offer them as standard equipment. There were no significant changes on Jeep J Series trucks.

In August, after nearly a decade of trying to solve its myriad problems, Renault sold American Motors to

Wrangler offered new thinking for the traditional tailgate. It swung sideways instead of down, and incorporated a spare tire carrier rather than having a separate carrier as prior Jeeps had.

Chrysler Corporation in a deal estimated to cost $1.1 billion. Chrysler wasn't very interested in AMC's passenger car business, but bought the company primarily for its Jeep Corporation subsidiary. AMC had done pretty well for Jeep; from annual production of less than 35,000 vehicles the company was now producing over 200,000 annually. And from a producer of mostly work-related agricultural devices, the product line had developed into one of the most respected and coveted vehicles in the world. For 1987 Jeep sold 208,440 vehicles.

With Chrysler's marketing muscle and vastly greater financial reserves and engineering organization, Jeep was bound to grow even larger. But, as history had shown, it would take some time to see any real changes.

NOTABLE FOR 1987: The biggest news of the year was the acquisition of American Motors by Chrysler Corporation. Jeep output reached record levels. The GM-sourced 2.8-liter V-6 formerly used in the XJs was replaced with a high-output 4.0-liter inline six-cylinder designed and built by AMC. Bore and stroke were 3.875 and 3.44 inches, yielding 242 cid. The engine was fed with multi-port sequential fuel injection, featuring full electronic control of all engine functions. The Grand Wagoneer continued as Jeep's ultimate premium sport utility vehicle. The 5.9-liter V-8 engine was now standard equipment.

I.D. DATA: The VIN has 17 characters. The first three symbols indicate the country of origin, manufacturer, and type. The fourth indicates the engine type. The fifth indicates the transmission type. The sixth, and seventh indicate the series and type of vehicle, which are the same as the model number. The eighth indicates the GVW rating. The ninth is a check digit. The 10th (a letter) indicates model year (1987=H). The 11th indicates the assembly plant. The remaining numbers indicate the sequential production number starting with 000001 at each plant.

With its new optional 4.0-liter six, the Jeep Cherokee Chief had the power to go with its aggressive looks. Jeep was the undisputed horsepower champ this year. Ford and GM had nothing that came close to Jeep's Power Tech six for performance.

Model	Body Type	Price	Weight
Wrangler — 1/4-Ton — Four-cyl — 93.4-in. w.b.			
81	Jeep	$8,396	2,868 lbs.
Wrangler — 1/4-Ton — Six –cyl — 93.4-in. w.b.			
81	Jeep	$9,899	3,022 lbs.
Cherokee — Four-cyl — 4x2			
73	2d Station Wagon	$12,452	2,936 lbs.
74	4d Station Wagon	—	—
Cherokee — Four-cyl — 4x4			
77	2d Station Wagon	—	—
78	4d Station Wagon	$13,047	2,983 lbs.
Wagoneer — Four-cyl — 4x4			
75	4d Station Wagon	$15,930	3,083 lbs.
Wagoneer — Six-cyl — 4x4			
75	4d Station Wagon	$15,634	4,598 lbs.
76	4d Limited Station Wagon	$20,503	4,598 lbs.
Grand Wagoneer — V-8 — 4x4			
15	4d Station Wagon	$24,521	4,509 lbs.
Comanche — 1/2-Ton — Four-cyl			
66	LBx Pickup, 4x2	$7,860	2,955 lbs.
64	SBx Pickup, 4x2	$6,495	2,897 lbs.
65	LBx Pickup, 4x4	$10,325	3,129 lbs.
63	SBx Pickup, 4x4	$8,960	3,071 lbs.
J-10 — 1/2-Ton — Six-cyl — 4x4			
26	Pickup	$12,392	3,790 lbs.
J-20 — 3/4-Ton — V-8 — 4x4			
27	Pickup	$13,746	4,386 lbs.

PRODUCTION & SALES: The company reported U.S. retail sales during calendar year 1987 of 208,440 units.

(STANDARD WRANGLER/CHEROKEE, WAGONEER/COMANCHE FOUR): Inline. Overhead valve. Cast-iron block. Bore & stroke: 3.88 x 3.19 in. Displacement: 150 cid (2.5 liters). Compression ratio: 9.2:1. Brake hp: 117 at 5000 rpm. Torque: 135 lbs.-ft. at 3500 rpm. Throttle body fuel injection (TBI). VIN code E.

(STANDARD WAGONEER LIMITED — OPTIONAL CHEROKEE/ WAGONEER/COMANCHE SIX): Inline. Overhead valve. Cast-iron block. Bore & stroke: 3.88 x 3.41 in. Displacement: 242 cid (4.0 liter). Compression ratio: 9.2:1. Brake hp: 173 at 4500 rpm. Torque: 220 lbs.-ft. at 2500 rpm. Multi-port fuel injection (MFI). VIN code M.

(TURBO DIESEL — OPTIONAL CHEROKEE-/WAGONEER/COMANCHE FOUR): Inline. Overhead valve. Cast-iron block. Bore & stroke: 2.99 x 3.50 in. Displacement: 126 cid (2.1 liter). Taxable hp: 18.34. Fuel injection. VIN code B.

(STANDARD J-10 — OPTIONAL WRANGLER SIX): Inline. Overhead valve. Cast-iron block. Bore & stroke: 3.75 x 3.90 in. Displacement: 258 cid (4.2 liter). Compression ratio: 9.2:1. Brake hp: 112 at 3000 rpm. Torque: 210 lbs.-ft. at 3000 rpm. Two-barrel carburetor. VIN code C.

(STANDARD J-20, GRAND WAGONEER —

OPTIONAL J-10 V-8): Cast-iron block. Bore & stroke: 4.08 x 3.44 in. Displacement: 360 cid (5.9 liters). Hp: 144. Two-barrel carburetor. VIN code N.

CHASSIS

(WRANGLER YJ): Wheelbase: 93.5 in. Overall length: 152 in. Height (with hardtop): 69.3 in. Width: 66 in. Tread: front and rear, 58 in. Tires: P215/75R15.

(CHEROKEE & WAGONEER XJ): Wheelbase: 101 in. Overall length: 165.3 in. Width: 70.5 in. Height: 63.4 in. (4x2), 63.3 in. (4x4).

(COMANCHE): Wheelbase: 113 in. (short box), 119.6 in. (long box). Overall length: 179.2 in. (short box), 194 in. (long box). Width: 71.7 in. Height: 63.7 in. (4x2 and 4x4).

(GRAND WAGONEER): Wheelbase: 108.7 in. Overall length: 186.4 in. Width: 74.8 in. Height: 66.4 in. Tires: P225/75R15 WSW.

(J-10/J-20): Wheelbase: 131 in. Overall length: 206 in. Width: 78.9 in. Height: 69 in. (J-10), 70 in. (J-20). Tread: front and rear, 63.3 and 63.8 in. Tires: P225/75R15 BSW (J-10), 8.25 x 16.5 in. steel-belted radial (J-20).

TECHNICAL

(CHEROKEE XJ): UniFrame construction. Five-speed manual transmission. Floor shift. Semi-floating rear axle. Power front disc/rear drum brkaes. Shift-on-the-fly four-wheel-drive.

(WAGONEER XJ): UniFrame construction. Four-speed automatic transmission with overdrive. Column-mounted gearshift. Semi-floating rear axle. Power front disc/rear drum brakes. Shift-on-the-fly four-wheel-drive.

(GRAND WAGONEER): Automatic transmission. Column-mounted gearshift. Semi-floating rear axle. Brakes: front disc with rear drum, power assisted. Selec-Trac shift-on-the-fly full-time four-wheel-drive.

(COMANCHE): Four-speed manual transmission (standard on base and Pioneer, five-speed standard all others). Floor shift. Semi-floating rear axle; final drive ratio, 3.73:1. Power front disc/rear drum brakes.

(J-10): Four-speed manual transmission. Floor mounted gearshift. Semi-floating rear axle; final drive ratio, 2.73:1. Power front disc/rear drum brakes.

(J-20): Automatic transmission. Column-mounted gearshift. Full-floating rear axle; final drive ratio, 3.73:1. Front disc brakes with rear drum, power assisted. Selec-Trac shift-on-the-fly full-time four-wheel-drive system.

OPTIONS

(WRANGLER): 4.2-liter two-barrel six-cylinder engine. Three-speed automatic transmission. Hardtop (standard with Laredo). Tilt steering. Sport decor group includes standard features plus: AM/FM radio, black side cowl carpet, Wrangler hood decals, lower body-side stripes; P215/75R15 Goodyear Wrangler tires; conventional spare tire with lock, Convenience group. Laredo hardtop group includes: richer interior trim; AM/FM radio, Buffalo-grain vinyl upholstery, front and rear carpeting, center console, extra-quiet insulation, leather-wrapped Sport steering wheel, special door trim panels and map pockets, chrome front bumper, rear bumperettes, grille panel, headlight bezels, tow hooks, color-keyed wheel flares, full-length mud guards, integrated steps, deep tinted glass, door mirrors, hood and body side stripes, Convenience group; 15 x 7 in. aluminum wheels; P215/75R15 Goodyear Wrangler RWL radial tires, spare tire and matching aluminum spare wheel. Rear Trac-Lok differential. Air conditioning. Extra-quiet insulation. Full-carpets. Halogen fog lamps. Power steering. Cruise control (six-cylinder only). Electric rear window defogger (hardtop). Heavy-duty suspension. Heavy-duty cooling. Aluminum wheels. Off-Road equipment package.

(CHEROKEE XJ): Pioneer, Cherokee Chief, and Laredo trim packages. Power-Tech 4.0-liter inline six-cylinder engine. Four-speed automatic transmission. AM/FM stereo. AM/FM stereo with tape player. Cruise control. Tilt steering wheel. Sunroof. Power door locks. Power windows. Power seats. Power steering. Air conditioning. Rear window defroster. Luggage rack. Aluminum wheels. Selec-Trac fulltime four-wheel drive.

(WAGONEER XJ): Power-Tech 4.0-liter inline six-cylinder engine. AM/FM stereo tape player. Sunroof. Four-speed automatic transmission. AM/FM stereo. Rear window defroster. Cruise control. Tilt steering wheel. Power door locks. Power windows. Power seats. Power steering. Air conditioning. Lluggage rack. Aluminum wheels. Selec-Trac full-time four-wheel drive.

(GRAND WAGONEER): Power sunroof.

(COMANCHE): SporTruck, Pioneer, Chief, and Laredo trim packages. Power-Tech 4.0-liter inline six-cylinder engine. Four-speed automatic transmission. AM/FM stereo. AM/FM stereo with tape player. Cruise control. Tilt steering wheel. Power door locks. Power windows. Power seats. Power steering. Air conditioning. Rear window defroster. Luggage rack. Aluminum wheels.

(J-10/J-20): Heavy-duty alternator. Heavy-duty battery. Cold climate group. Heavy-duty cooling system. Rear Trac-Lok differential. Heavy-duty shock absorbers. Heavy-duty springs. AM radio. AM/FM stereo. AM/FM cassette. Automatic transmission. 5.9-liter V-8 engine (standard J-20). White-spoke styled wheels. Visibility group. Tilt steering wheel (n/a with manual transmission). Light group. Insulation package. Bright grille. Bright wheel covers. Floor mats. Grain vinyl bench seat. Dual low-profile exterior mirrors. Sliding rear window. Air conditioning. Convenience group.

Here's a great looking truck! The 1988 Comanche Chief.

There wasn't much of anything Chrysler could do that would have a substantial impact on the Jeep product this model year. As always, it takes time to engineer and tool up a new or greatly altered vehicle, so for this first full year of Chrysler ownership there hadn't been enough time to change anything. Not that there was any need to. The potent Power Tech Six engine, which this year was rated at 177 hp and 224 lbs.-ft. of torque, kept Jeep ahead of the pack. In power and engineering features, the 1988 Jeep vehicles were now so far ahead of the competition that Jeep was enjoying a groundswell of consumer interest and record vehicle sales. *4Wheel & Off-Road* named Cherokee its 4x4 of the Year.

There were new Wrangler, Comanche and Cherokee Olympic Edition models, each of them equipped with a six-cylinder engine, (4.2-liter for Wrangler, 4.0-liter PowerTech Six for the others) aluminum wheels, and special stripes and decals.

Cherokee Limited added a two-door model and was offered in four exterior colors: Classic Black, Colorado Red, Dover Gray, and Grenadine Metallic. The Limited included a low-gloss black and body-color grille, body-color bumpers, fender flares, and front air dam, and a black nerf strip with gold insert on the bumpers. Of course, leather wingback bucket seats and a full complement of power equipment was all standard. The Jeep Wagoneer base model was discontinued and the XJ Wagoneer was offered only as a Limited model.

Wrangler introduced an important new model, the Sahara, available in khaki or coffee exterior colors. Sahara included unique tape stripes and decals, khaki-colored spoke wheels, khaki soft or hardtop, and unique khaki-colored interior trim. There was also a new low-priced Wrangler designed to compete with newly arrived budget-priced Japanese four-wheel-drive utility vehicles that were flooding the market—principally the Suzuki Samurai. The Wrangler S model was priced at an incredibly low $8,995. It offered a lot for the money, but to ensure it wouldn't cannibalize sales of other more profitable Wrangler models, the option list was very limited. Standard equipment included the 2.5-liter four-cylinder engine and five-speed manual transmission. Front high-back bucket seats, a soft top with steel half doors, OWL radial tires, and argent steel wheels pretty much completed the list of standard features. The very short option list included power steering, hardtop, carpeting, radios, and a rear seat. Neither the six-cylinder engine, nor the automatic transmission was available on the S. Only five exterior colors were offered: Pearl White, Classic Black, Sand Dune Yellow, Colorado Red, and Coffee.

Comanche added a new model, too. The tough-looking Comanche Eliminator was a two-wheel-drive performance sport truck aimed at the youth market. Offered only on the 113-inch wheelbase short-bed model, the Eliminator came equipped with a five-speed transmission and the Power-Tech Six. It featured bold tape striping, and eight-slot painted grille, color-keyed fender flares, and silver-painted bumpers front and rear.

Roger Scheffer photo

The 1988 Wrangler came in Laredo, Sahara and S models. The Laredo, like this one owned by Roger Scheffer of West Unity, New Hampshire, was equipped with a standard hardtop.

In 1988, Jeep introduced a new model, the Wrangler Sahara, which became one of the most popular Wranglers ever.

The Wrangler hardtop has always been a favorite with sportsmen and off-road enthusiasts.

Eliminator colors were Classic Black, Colorado Red, or Dover Gray metallic. A new Pioneer trim level was also offered on all Comanche models, while the Chief package was available only on four-wheel-drive short-bed models.

There was even some product news for the Grand Wagoneer. It had a new AM/FM/MPX stereo with Dolby, plus an optional electric sunroof that included an integral air deflector.

Among Jeep aficionados there is some uncertainty as to whether any 1988 J Series trucks were actually built. Evidence seems to indicate a small number were produced. The factory released pricing and ordering information in July 1987, around the time the merger was going through. The company then issued an updated version of the ordering information in November 1987—something it was hardly likely to do if it didn't intend to produce the vehicles. It's very likely that some Jeep dealers ordered a supply of trucks during that July-November ordering period. At any rate, pictures and specifications exist of the 1988 truck. According to the initial Jeep ordering guide, the 1988 J-10s offered a six-cylinder engine as standard equipment. The 360 V-8 was standard on the J-20 and optional on J-10. However, in the later version of the ordering guide, both J-10 and J-20 are equipped with the 360-cid V-8 as the standard engine, and that was the only engine offered. Automatic transmission was also standard equipment on both.

In September, it was announced that Chrysler would invest $24 million to increase Jeep production capacity

This front view of Wrangler highlights its aggressive looks and wide wheels bulging under wheel flares.

to 403,000 units. The expansion would help Jeep meet strong U.S. demand as well as help increase its exports to 37,000 annually, up from 20,000 exported in the 1988 model year. It would be a simple thing for the company to afford, since Jeep executives were privately telling reporters that AMC/Jeep would have turned a $200-million profit even if Chrysler had not bought the company. Jeep sold a whopping 253,454 vehicles in 1988.

NOTABLE FOR 1988: The Wagoneer line was trimmed down to a single Wagoneer Limited model. Wrangler offered a new Sahara trim package, consisting of a khaki-colored soft top and steel spoke wheels, Bumper Accessory Package, dual outside mirrors, fog lamps, unique tape striping, and special body-side and spare tire cover logos. Laredo and Sport Decor packages were carried over. Comanche got an upgraded rear suspension for an increased payload capacity of up to 1,475 lbs. and

Long-bed Comanche trucks make good haulers.

GVW rating of 4,615 lbs.

I.D. DATA: The VIN has 17 characters. The first three symbols indicate the country of origin, manufacturer, and vehicle type. The fourth indicates the engine type. The fifth indicates the transmission type. The sixth and seventh indicate the series and type of vehicle, which are the same as the model number. The eighth indicates the GVW rating. The ninth is a check digit. The 10th (a letter) indicates model year (1988=J). The 11th indicates the assembly plant. The remaining numbers indicate the sequential production number starting with 000001 at each plant.

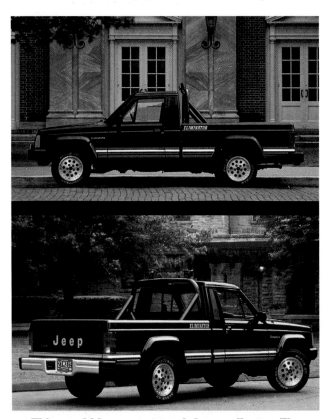

This would be a great truck for a collector. The Comanche Eliminator was one sport truck that had the power to go with its looks.

Model	Body Type	Price	Weight
Wrangler — Four-cyl — 1/4-Ton — 4x4			
81	Jeep Wrangler	$10,595	3,022 lbs.
81	Jeep Wrangler S	$8,995	2,914 lbs.
Cherokee — Four-cyl — 4x2			
73	2d Station Wagon	$11,600	2,716 lbs.
74	4d Station Wagon	$12,212	2,716 lbs.
Cherokee — Four-cyl — 4x4			
77	2d Station Wagon	$12,952	2,937 lbs.
78	4d Station Wagon	—	—
Wagoneer Limited — Six-cyl — 4x4			
75	4d Station Wagon	$22,340	3,080 lbs.
Grand Wagoneer — V-8 — 4x4			
15	4d Station Wagon	$25,253	4,505 lbs.
Comanche — 1/2-Ton — Four-cyl			
63	SB Pickup 4x4	—	—
64	SB Pickup 4x2	$7,787	2,914 lbs.
65	LB Pickup 4x4	$10,410	3,129 lbs.
66	LB Pickup 4x2	$7,528	2,810 lbs.
J-10 — 1/2-Ton — V-8 — 4x4			
26	Pickup	$12,392	3,790 lbs.
J-20 — 3/4-Ton — V-8 — 4x4			
27	Pickup	$13,746	4,386 lbs.

PRODUCTION & SALES: The company reported U.S. retail sales during calendar year 1988 of 253,454 units.

ENGINES

(STANDARD WRANGLER/CHEROKEE/COMANCHE FOUR): Overhead valve. Inline. Cast-iron block. Bore & stroke: 3.88 x 3.19 in. Displacement: 150 cid (2.5 liters). Compression ratio: 9.2:1. Brake hp: 117 at 5000 rpm. Torque: 135 lbs.-ft. at 3500 rpm. Throttle body fuel injection (TBI). VIN code E.

(STANDARD WAGONEER LIMITED/COMANCHE ELIMINATOR; OPTIONAL CHEROKEE/OTHER COMANCHES SIX): Overhead valve. Inline. Cast-iron

Jeep's volume seller in the 1980s was the Cherokee. This is a 1988 model.

block. Bore & stroke: 3.88 x 3.41 in. Displacement: 242 cid (4.0 liter). Compression ratio: 9.2:1. Brake hp: 173 at 4500 rpm. Torque: 220 lbs.-ft. at 2500 rpm. Multi-port fuel injection (MFI). VIN code M.

(OPTIONAL WRANGLER SIX): Overhead valve. Inline. Cast-iron block. Bore & stroke: 3.75 x 3.90 in. Displacement: 258 cid (4.2 liter). Compression ratio: 9.2:1. Brake hp: 112 at 3000 rpm. Torque: 210 lbs.-ft. at 3000 rpm. Two-barrel carburetor. VIN code C. (Note: It's possible some early J-10s were equipped with this engine.)

(STANDARD GRAND WAGONEER/J-10/J-20 V-8): Cast-iron block. Bore & stroke: 4.08 x 3.44 in. Displacement: 360 cid (5.9 liter). Hp: 144. Two-barrel carburetor. VIN code N. (Note: Early editions of the vehicle ordering guide indicate that J-10 may have come standard with the 4.2-liter six initially; but the V-8 later became the standard and only engine.)

CHASSIS

(WRANGLER YJ): Wheelbase: 93.5 in. Overall length: 152 in. Height (with hardtop): 69.3 in. Width: 66 in. Tread: front and rear, 58 in. Tires: P215/75R15 RWL.

(CHEROKEE AND WAGONEER XJ): Wheelbase: 101 in. Overall length: 165.3 in. Width: 70.5 in. Height: 63.4 in. (4x2), 63.3 in. (4x4).

(GRAND WAGONEER): Wheelbase: 108.7 in. Overall length: 186.4 in. Width: 74.8 in. Height: 66.4 in. Tires: P225/75R15 WSW.

(COMANCHE): Wheelbase: 113 in. (short box), 119.6 in. (long box). Overall length: 179.2 in. (short box), 194 in. (long box). Width: 71.7 in. Height: 63.7 in. (4x2 and 4x4).

Cherokee was very compact, yet had a spacious interior.

(J-10/J-20): Wheelbase: 131 in. Overall length: 206 in. Width: 78.9 in. Height: 69 in. (J-10), 70 in. (J-20). Tread: front and rear, 63.3 and 63.8 in.

TECHNICAL

(WRANGLER): Five-speed manual transmission. Floor shift. Semi-floating rear axle. Standard overall drive ratio: 4.11:1. Brakes: front disc with rear drum, power assisted. Command-Trac shift-on-the-fly part-time four-wheel drive.

(CHEROKEE XJ): UniFrame construction. Five-speed manual transmission. Floor shift. Semi-floating rear axle. Power front disc/rear drum brakes.

(WAGONEER LIMITED): UniFrame construction. Four-speed automatic transmission with overdrive. Column-mounted gearshift. Semi-floating rear axle. Power front disc/rear drum brakes. Command-Trac shift-on-the-fly part-time four-wheel drive.

(GRAND WAGONEER): Three-speed automatic transmission. Column-mounted gearshift. Shaft drive. Semi-floating rear axle. Brakes: front disc with rear drum, power assisted. Selec-Trac shift-on-the-fly full-time four-wheel-drive system.

The Wagoneer Limited for 1988 had plenty of class and elegance.

(COMANCHE): Selective synchromesh five-speed manual transmission. Floor-mounted controls. Single-plate, dry-disc clutch. Shaft drive. Semi-floating rear axle; final drive ratio: 3.73:1. Brakes: front disc with rear drum, power assisted. (4x4 model 65 only): Command-Trac shift-on-the-fly part-time four-wheel-drive system.

OPTIONS

(WRANGLER YJ): Carbureted 4.2-liter six-cylinder engine. Three-speed automatic transmission. Hardtop (standard with Laredo). Tilt steering. Sport Decor group, includes: most standard features, plus AM/FM monaural radio, black side cowl carpet, special Wrangler hood decals, special Wrangler lower body-side stripes, P215/75R15 Goodyear all-terrain Wrangler tires, conventional size spare with lock, and Convenience group. Laredo Hardtop group, includes: richer interior trim, AM/FM monaural radio, Buffalo-grain vinyl upholstery, front and rear carpeting, center console, extra-quiet insulation, leather-wrapped sport steering wheel, special door trim panels and map pockets, chrome front bumper, rear bumperettes, grille panel, headlight bezels, tow hooks, color-keyed wheel flares, full-length mud guards, integrated steps, deep tinted glass, OSRV door mirrors, bumper accessory package,

**Two-door sport utility vehicles were still very popular in 1988.
The best-looking one was the Jeep Cherokee Chief.**

Cherokee Limited was aimed at buyers who wanted the sporty connotations of the Cherokee name and the luxury of the Wagoneer Limited.

special hood and body side stripes, Convenience group, 15 x 7 in. aluminum wheels; P215/75R15 Goodyear Wrangler RWL radial tires, spare tire, and matching aluminum spare wheel. Rear Trac-Lok differential. Air conditioning. Extra-quiet insulation. Full-carpets. Halogen fog lamps. Power steering. Cruise control (six-cylinder only). Leather-wrapped sport steering wheel. Electric rear window defogger (hardtop). Heavy-duty suspension. Heavy-duty cooling. Aluminum wheels. Off-Road equipment package. Conventional spare tire. Metallic exterior paints.

(CHEROKEE XJ): Pioneer, Eliminator, Chief, and

Cherokee Pioneer was a dress-up option for people who wanted a look that was a bit less flamboyant than Cherokee Chief.

Laredo trim packages. Power-Tech 4.0-liter inline six-cylinder engine. Four-speed automatic transmission. AM/FM stereo. AM/FM stereo with tape player. Cruise control. Tilt steering wheel. Manual sunroof. Power sunroof. Power door locks. Power windows. Power seats. Power steering. Air conditioning. Rear window defroster. Luggage rack. Aluminum wheels.

(WAGONEER LIMITED): AM/FM Stereo with tape player. Power sunroof. Limited trim package (includes the following that are otherwise optional): Power-Tech 4.0-liter inline six-cylinder engine. Four-speed automatic transmission. AM/FM stereo. Rear window defroster. Cruise control. Tilt steering wheel. Power door locks. Power windows. Power seats. Power steering. Air conditioning. Luggage rack. Aluminum wheels.

(GRAND WAGONEER): Power sunroof.

(COMANCHE): SporTruck, Pioneer, Chief, and Laredo trim packages. Power-Tech 4.0-liter inline six-cylinder engine (standard. in Eliminator). Four-speed automatic transmission. AM/FM stereo. AM/FM stereo with tape player. Cruise control. Tilt steering wheel. Manual sunroof. Power sunroof. Power door locks. Power windows. Power seats. Power steering. Air conditioning. Rear window defroster. Luggage rack. Aluminum wheels.

The Wrangler Islander was new for 1989. It was a moderately priced sport dress-up package with unique graphics.

For 1989 Jeep continued its leadership role in pioneering new technology. Cherokee and Wagoneer models introduced another first in the four-wheel-drive market: a four-wheel anti-lock brake system, fully operational in four-wheel drive. Designed by Bendix, Jeep's optional anti-lock brake system was unique in the sport utility/light truck industry. Other anti-lock brake systems worked on the rear wheels only, and none operated in the four-wheel-drive mode. The brakes were optional on Wagoneer Limited and Cherokee models equipped with the 4.0-liter six, four-speed automatic transmission and Selec-Trac full-time four-wheel drive.

Cherokee was offered in base, Sport, Pioneer, Laredo, and Limited versions, while Wagoneer was offered only as a Limited model. Cherokee's standard equipment was substantially upgraded this year, with five-speed transmission, power steering, and the extra-capacity fuel tank now standard on all models. Laredos also got tachometers, roof racks and bumper guards as new standard features. The Cherokee Sport was a value model, with unique exterior stripe, 10-spoke aluminum wheels, 4.0-liter engine, and five-speed transmission. Automatic transmission was optional. All Cherokees got upgraded interior trim. New colors included Sand, Sand Metallic, Dark Vivid Red and, for Cherokee Limited, Pearl White—an especially popular choice.

Jeep Wrangler offered a new Islander model replacing the Sport Decor group. Islanders featured special graphics on the hood, doors, and spare tire cover. Standard equipment included: soft top, high back bucket seats, full carpeting, P215/75R15 OWL tires with six-spoke steel wheels, the standard 2.5-liter engine, and five-speed transmission. Islander was available in Malibu Yellow, Bright Red, Pearl White and Pacific Blue. The 4.2-liter six was optional. Other Wrangler models were the S, base, Sahara, and Laredo. AM radio became standard on all Wranglers, except the S. Power steering was now standard on Sahara and Laredo, and Laredo also got fog lamps added to its standard equipment.

Wrangler Islander offered youthful appearance and bright, attractive exterior colors. Many of these models are still on the road.

Comanche showed little that was new, but received upgraded standard equipment with the addition of tinted glass and a larger fuel tank. Interior trim was upgraded, and Pioneer models now included power steering as standard equipment. Special option discount packages were offered to generate interest. Comanche short-bed models included the base SporTruck, Pioneer, and Eliminator, while the long-bed models were offered in base and Pioneer trim.

Additions to the list of standard equipment for Wagoneer Limited included the extra capacity fuel tank, fog lamps, keyless entry system, electric remote outside mirrors, and a tachometer.

Grand Wagoneers received some additional standard equipment. A "keyless entry" remote locking system was added to the long list of standard features. Inside, Grand Wagoneer got a new overhead console that included interior lights, sunglass holder, compass, garage door opener, and outside temperature indicator. A new rear window wiper/washer was also added to the standard equipment list.

A seven-year, 70,000-mile power-train warranty was included with every 1989 Jeep vehicle.

It was a good year for Jeep, with some 249,170 vehicles sold. The decade to come would see Chrysler introduce completely new vehicles, the first all-new Jeeps designed by Chrysler technicians, and the last new Jeeps designed by American Motors. The 1990s would be an exciting decade.

NOTABLE FOR 1989: Trim packages remained virtually unchanged on Cherokee and Wagoneer lines. These models now offered the industry's first light-duty truck four-wheel anti-lock brake system, made by Bendix, available with the 4.0-liter engine. Wrangler added a new model, the Islander, which included a soft top, silver-painted steel six-spoke wheels with P215/75R15 raised-white letter tires, full carpeting, door map pockets, unique stripes, and special body-side and spare tire cover logos. It was offered in: Red, Pearl White, Malibu Yellow, and Pacific Blue.

I.D. DATA: The VIN has 17 characters. The first three symbols indicate the country of origin (1=U.S., 2=Canada), manufacturer (J=Jeep/Eagle Div.), and type (4=multipurpose, 6=incomplete, 7=truck). The fourth indicates the gross vehicle weight rating. The fifth indicates the model line (J=4x4 Cherokee and Comanche, N=Wagoneer, S=Grand Wagoneer, T=4x2 Cherokee and Comanche, Y=Wrangler). The sixth indicates the series (1=standard, 2=base, 3=Islander-/Pioneer, 4=Sahara, 5=Grand/Laredo, 6=Eliminator-/Sport, 7=Limited). The seventh indicates the body style (6=pickup, 7=two-door wagon, 8=four-door wagon, 9=open body). These last three symbols are the models indicated in detail below. The eighth indicates the engine. The ninth is a check digit. The 10th (a letter) indicates model year (1989=K). The 11th indicates the

assembly plant (B and J=Brampton, Ontario, L, P, and T=Toledo, Ohio). The remaining numbers indicate the sequential production number starting with 000001 at each plant.

Model	Body Type	Price	Weight
Wrangler — 1/4-Ton — Four-cyl — 4x4			
Y19	Wrangler	$11,457	2,936 lbs.
Y59	Wrangler Laredo HT	$15,302	3,062 lbs.
Cherokee — Four-cyl — 4x2			
T17	2d station wagon	$12,809	2,853 lbs.
T18	4d station wagon	$13,631	2,908 lbs.
Cherokee — Four-cyl — 4x4			
J17	2d station wagon	$14,150	3,043 lbs.
J18	4d station wagon	$14,964	3,082 lbs.
Wagoneer Limited — Six-cyl — 4x4			
N78	4d station wagon	$23,890	3,491 lbs.
Grand Wagoneer — V-8 — 4x4			
S58	4d station wagon	$27,284	4,470 lbs.
Comanche — 1/2-Ton — Four-cyl			
T16	2d P/U, SB 4x2	$8,192	2,988 lbs.
T16	2d P/U, LB 4x2	$9,020	3,006 lbs.
J16	2d P/U, SB 4x4	$11,162	3,082 lbs.
J16	2d P/U, LB 4x4	$11,848	3,181 lbs.

PRODUCTION & SALES: The company reported U.S. retail sales during calendar year 1989 of 249,170 units.

ENGINES

(STANDARD WRANGLER/CHEROKEE/COMANCHE FOUR): Inline. Overhead valve. Cast-iron block. Bore & stroke: 3.88 x 3.19 in. Displacement: 150 cid (2.5 liters). Compression ratio: 9.2:1. Brake hp: 117 at 5000 rpm. Torque: 135 lbs.-ft. at 3500 rpm. Throttle-body fuel injection (TBI). VIN code E.

(STANDARD WAGONEER LIMITED/COMANCHE ELIMINATOR — OPTIONAL CHEROKEE/OTHER COMANCHE SIX): Inline. Overhead valve. Cast-iron block. Bore & stroke: 3.88 x 3.41 in. Displacement: 242 cid (4.0 liters). Compression ratio: 9.2:1. Brake hp: 173 at 4500 rpm. Torque: 220 lbs.-ft. at 2500 rpm. Multi-port fuel injection (MFI). VIN code L.

(OPTIONAL WRANGLER SIX): Inline. Overhead-valve. Cast-iron block. Bore & stroke: 3.75 x 3.90 in. Displacement: 258 cid (4.2 liters). Compression ratio: 9.2:1. Brake hp: 112 at 3000 rpm. Torque: 210 lbs.-ft. at 3000 rpm. Two-barrel carburetor. VIN code T.

(STANDARD GRAND WAGONEER V-8): Cast-iron block. Bore & stroke: 4.08 x 3.44. Displacement: 360 cid (5.9 liters). Hp: 144. Two-barrel carburetor. VIN code 7.

CHASSIS

(WRANGLER): Wheelbase: 93.5 in. Overall length: 152 in. Height (with hardtop): 69.3 in. Width: 66 in. Tread: front and rear, 58 in. Tires: P215/75R15 RWL.

(CHEROKEE & WAGONEER): Wheelbase: 101 in.

Wrangler S was the lowest-priced Wrangler for 1989.

Overall length: 165.3 in. Width: 70.5 in. Height: 63.4 in. (4x2), 63.3 in. (4x4).

(GRAND WAGONEER): Wheelbase: 108.7 in. Overall length: 186.4 in. Width: 74.8 in. Height: 66.4 in. Tires: P225/75R15 WSW.

(COMANCHE): Wheelbase: 113 in. (short box), 119.6 in. (long box). Overall length: 179.2 in. (short box), 194 in. (long box). Width: 71.7 in. Height: 63.7 in. (4x2 and 4x4).

TECHNICAL

(WRANGLER): Five-speed manual transmission. Floor shift. Semi-floating rear axle. Standard overall drive ratio: 4.11:1. Power front disc/rear drum brakes. Command-Trac shift-on-the-fly part-time four-wheel drive.

(CHEROKEE): UniFrame construction. Five-speed manual transmission. Floor shift. Semi-floating rear axle. Power front disc/rear drum brakes.

(WAGONEER LIMITED): UniFrame construction. Four-speed automatic transmission with overdrive. Column-mounted gearshift. Semi-floating rear axle. Brakes: front disc with rear drum, power assisted, with ABS.

(GRAND WAGONEER): Three-speed automatic transmission. Column-mounted gearshift. Semi-floating rear axle. Selec-Trac shift-on-the-fly full-time four-wheel drive.

Wrangler Sahara's popularity continued to grow as the 1980s came to a close.

(COMANCHE): Five-speed manual transmission. Floor shift. Semi-floating rear axle. Final drive ratio: 3.73:1. Power front disc/rear drum brakes. 4x4 models have Command-Trac shift-on-the-fly part-time four-wheel drive.

OPTIONS

(WRANGLER): Carbureted 4.2-liter six-cylinder engine. Three-speed automatic transmission. Rear Trac-Lok differential. Air conditioning. Extra-quiet insulation. Full carpets. Halogen fog lamps. Power steering. Cruise control (six-cylinder only). Leather-wrapped sport steering wheel. Electric rear window defogger (hardtop). Heavy-duty suspension. Heavy-duty cooling. Aluminum wheels. Off-Road Equipment package. Conventional spare tire. Hardtop (standard w/Laredo). Tilt steering. Sport Decor group, includes most standard features, plus: AM/FM monaural radio, 15 x 7-in. aluminum wheels, special Wrangler hood decals and lower body-side stripes, P215/75R15 Goodyear Wrangler tires, and conventional spare with lock, tow hooks, and deep tinted glass.

(CHEROKEE): Pioneer, Chief, and Laredo trim packages. Power-Tech 4.0-liter inline six-cylinder engine. Four-speed automatic transmission. AM/FM stereo. AM/FM stereo with tape player. Cruise control. Tilt steering wheel. Manual sunroof. Power sunroof. Power door locks. Power windows. Power seats. Power steering. Air conditioning. Rear window defroster. Luggage rack. Aluminum wheels.

(WAGONEER LIMITED): Power sunroof. AM/FM stereo w/tape player. Limited trim package (includes the following which are otherwise optional): Power-Tech 4.0-liter inline six-cylinder engine, four-speed automatic transmission, AM/FM stereo, rear window defroster, cruise control, tilt steering wheel, power door locks,

power windows, power seats, power steering, air conditioning, luggage rack, aluminum wheels, Command-Trac full-time four-wheel drive.

(GRAND WAGONEER): Power sunroof.

(COMANCHE): SporTruck, Pioneer, Chief, and Laredo trim packages. Power-Tech 4.0-liter inline six-cylinder engine (standard in Eliminator). Four-speed automatic transmission. AM/FM stereo. AM/FM stereo with tape player. Cruise control. Tilt steering wheel. Manual sunroof. Power sunroof. Power door locks. Power windows. Power seats. Power steering. Air conditioning. Rear window defroster. Luggage rack. Aluminum wheels.

The Comanche Pioneer long-bed pickup for 1989.

**The Comanche Sportruck was low-priced and offered extraordinary value for the money.
It's surprising it didn't sell in greater volume.**

CHRYSLER AND DAIMLERCHRYSLER JEEPS
1990-1999

By the time the 1990s had commenced, Chrysler was beginning to exert a stronger influence on the Jeep product line. Chrysler officials fully understood Jeep's tremendous potential and were rapidly expanding Jeep production to match increased sales efforts. Marketing plans were set that would spark increased demand for Jeep vehicles. At the same time, the company was signing on many new dealers who were stronger, better-financed representatives from within the Chrysler dealer organization.

Chrysler management realized it had gotten hold of the crown jewels of the SUV market, and it fully expected to generate huge profits. The market was becoming more competitive, but Jeep had always been a leader and Chrysler intended to keep it that way. However, the new sport wagon that was being developed by AMC at the time of the merger was going to have to be delayed for a few years, because Chrysler needed to fund an expensive redesign of its popular minivans. Until the new Jeep was introduced, the company would have to soldier on with variations of its existing products.

Wrangler Islander for 1990 offered sporty looks at a reasonable price and was a very popular model.

When the 1990 Jeep line debuted there wasn't much new, just minor detail changes. The five Wrangler models were Wrangler S, Base, Islander, Sahara, and Laredo. Wranglers, which were built in Brampton, Ontario Canada, had new high-back bucket seats with improved front-seat lateral support, AM/FM stereo standard on all models except the bottom-line Wrangler S. New features included door locks for soft-top models with steel doors, a 20-gallon tank on Sahara and Laredo, plus additional options available on the lowest-priced Wranglers. Hardtops now came with a rear window wiper/washer included. As was the case in 1989, the 2.5-liter four-cylinder engine was rated at more horsepower than the 4.2-liter six (117 hp vs. 112 hp).

Cherokee saw little that was new. There were a few new exterior colors, a standard AM/FM electronically tuned (ET) radio plus three-point seat belts for the rear seat. An overhead console was a new option. On March 22, 1990, the 1 millionth Jeep XJ—a red 1990 Cherokee

Limited—was driven off the assembly line in Toledo, Ohio. In its seven years of production, the XJ had become one of the most admired vehicles in the world, a perennial best seller, and Chrysler's top-selling export to Europe.

Jeep Wagoneer was still offered, and the company bragged that its buyers had a median income of $106,000, which was the highest of any domestic model in the industry. Wagoneer got mostly the same bunch of improvements seen on the Cherokee, i.e. new colors, overhead console and rear seat three-point belts. A stereo radio had already become standard equipment.

The beautiful Grand Wagoneer, now in its 28th year on the market, had little to offer that was new. Three exterior colors, a flash-to-pass feature, and a side marker turn signal flash were new, and that was it. Jeep Comanche added a four-wheel-drive version of its Eliminator, plus some new exterior color choices.

Jeep sales tumbled in 1990, falling to 196,863 for the year. Increasing competition, particularly from Ford and GM, was eating into Jeep's market share.

NOTABLE FOR 1990: Equipment, trim, and styling were mostly carryover. Wrangler's standard equipment now included a standard AM/FM stereo radio, except on Wrangler S. A 20-gallon fuel tank was made standard on Laredo and Sahara. Cherokees and Wagoneer Limiteds got standard three-point rear seatbelts this year. Wagoneer Limited and Grand Wagoneer got a new overhead console that provided additional storage and digital displays of compass direction and outside temperature.

I.D. DATA: The VIN has 17 characters. The first three symbols indicate the country of origin (1=USA, 2=Canada), manufacturer (J=Jeep/Eagle Division), and type (4=multipurpose, 6=incomplete, 7=truck). The fourth indicates the Gross Vehicle Weight Rating. The fifth indicates the model line (J=4x4 Cherokee and Comanche, N=Wagoneer, S=Grand Wagoneer, T=4x2 Cherokee and Comanche, Y=Wrangler). The sixth indicates the series (1=standard, 2=base, 3=Islander-/Pioneer, 4=Sahara, 5=Grand/Laredo, 6=Eliminator-/Sport, 7=Limited). The seventh indicates the body style (6=pickup, 7=two-door wagon, 8=four-door wagon, 9=open body). These last three symbols are the models indicated in detail below. The eighth indicates the engine. The ninth is a check digit. The 10th (a letter) indicates model year (1990=L). The 11th indicates the assembly plant (B and J=Brampton, Ontario, L, P, and T=Toledo, Ohio). The remaining numbers indicate the sequential production number starting with 000001 at each plant.

Model	Body Type	Price	Weight
Wrangler YJ — 1/4-Ton — Four-cyl — 4x4			
Y19	Wrangler S	$9,843	2,940 lbs.
Y29	Wrangler Base	$12,049	2,940 lbs.
Y39	Wrangler Islander	$12,795	2,940 lbs.
Y49	Wrangler Sahara	$13,927	2,940 lbs.
Y45	Wrangler Laredo (six-cyl)	$16,193	3,066 lbs.
Cherokee — Four-cyl — 4x2			
T17	2d station wagon	$13,670	2,832 lbs.
T18	4d station wagon	$14,545	2,892 lbs.
Cherokee — Four-cyl — 4x4			
J17	2d station wagon	$14,945	3,033 lbs.
J18	4d station wagon	$15,820	3,076 lbs.
Wagoneer Limited — Six-cyl — 4x4			
N78	4d station wagon	$25,145	3,453 lbs.
Grand Wagoneer — V-8 — 4x4			
S58	4d station wagon	$28,455	4,499 lbs.
Comanche — 1/2-Ton — Four-cyl			
T16	2d Pickup 4x2 shortbed	$8,445	2,895 lbs.
T16	2d Pickup 4x2 longbed	$9,325	2,986 lbs.
J16	2d Pickup 4x4 shortbed	$11,545	3,084 lbs.
J16	2d Pickup 4x4 longbed	$12,245	3,182 lbs.

PRODUCTION/SALES: As reported in the industry trade paper the *Automotive News*, Jeep's U.S. sales for the calendar year were 196,863.

ENGINES

(STANDARD WRANGLER, CHEROKEE, COMANCHE FOUR): Inline. Overhead valve. Cast-iron block. Bore & stroke: 3.88 x 3.19 in. Displacement: 150 cid (2.5 liters). Compression ratio: 9.2:1. Brake hp: 117 at 5000 rpm. Torque: 135 lbs.-ft at 3500 rpm. Throttle-body fuel injection (TBI). VIN code E.

(STANDARD WAGONEER LIMITED, COMANCHE ELIMINATOR; OPTIONAL CHEROKEE, OTHER COMANCHES SIX): Inline. Overhead valve. Cast-iron block. Bore & stroke: 3.88 x 3.41 in. Displacement: 242 cid (4.0-liters). Compression ratio: 9.2:1. Brake hp: 173 at 4500 rpm. Torque: 220 lbs.-ft at 2500 rpm. Multi-port fuel injection (MFI). VIN code L.

(STANDARD WRANGLER LAREDO — OPTIONAL OTHER WRANGLERS SIX): Inline. Overhead valve. Cast-iron block. Bore & stroke: 3.75 x 3.90 in. Displacement: 258 cid (4.2 liters). Compression ratio: 9.2:1. Brake hp: 112 at 3000 rpm. Torque: 210 lbs.-ft. at 3000 rpm. Two-barrel carburetor. VIN code T.

(STANDARD GRAND WAGONEER V-8): Cast-iron block. Bore & stroke: 4.08 x 3.44 in. Displacement: 360 cid (5.9 liters). Brake hp: 144. Two-barrel carburetor (VIN code 7).

CHASSIS

(WRANGLER): Wheelbase: 93.5 in. Overall length: 152 in. Height (with hardtop): 69.3 in. Width: 66 in. Tread: front and rear, 58 in. Tires: P215/75R15.

(CHEROKEE AND WAGONEER): Wheelbase: 101 in. Overall length: 165.3 in. Width: 70.5 in. Height: 63.4 in. (4x2), 63.3 in. (4x4).

(GRAND WAGONEER): Wheelbase: 108.7 in. Overall length: 186.4 in. Width: 74.8 in. Height: 66.4 in. Tires: P225/75R15 WSW.

(COMANCHE): Wheelbase: 113 in. (short box), 119.6 in. (long box). Overall length: 179.2 in. (short box), 194 in. (long box). Width: 71.7 in. Height: 63.7 in. (4x2 and 4x4).

TECHNICAL

(WRANGLER): Five-speed manual transmission Floor shift. Semi-floating rear axle. Standard ratio: 4.11:1. Brakes: front disc with rear drum, power assisted. Command-Trac shift-on-the-fly part-time 4x4 system.

(CHEROKEE): UniFrame construction. Five-speed manual transmission. Floor shift-disc clutch. Semi-floating rear axle. Power front disc/rear drum brakes. 4x4 models include Command-Trac shift-on-the-fly part-time 4x4 system.

The high-volume model in the Jeep line continued to be the exceptionally popular Cherokee. This vehicle is a 1990 two-door Sport.

(WAGONEER LIMITED): UniFrame construction. Four-speed automatic transmission with overdrive. Column-mounted gearshift. Semi-floating rear axle. Power front disc/rear drum brakes. Selec-Trac shift-on-the-fly full-time 4x4 system.

(GRAND WAGONEER): Three-speed automatic transmission. Column-mounted gearshift. Semi-floating rear axle. Power front disc/rear drum brakes. Selec-Trac shift-on-the-fly full-time 4x4 system.

(COMANCHE): Five-speed manual transmission. Floor shift. Semi-floating rear axle. Fnal drive ratio: 3.73:1. Power front disc/rear drum brakes. 4x4 models have Command-Trac shift-on-the-fly part-time 4x4 system as standard.

OPTIONS

(WRANGLER YJ): Three-speed automatic transmission. Hardtop (standard with Laredo). Tilt steering. AM/FM monaural radio. Front and rear carpeting. Center console. Extra quiet insulation. Leather-wrapped sport steering wheel. Rear bumperettes. P215/75R15 Goodyear Wrangler OWL radial tires. Rear Trac-Lok differential. Air conditioning. Fog lamps. Power steering (standard Laredo and Sahara). Cruise control (Six-cylinder only). Electric rear window defogger (hardtop). Heavy-duty suspension. Heavy-duty cooling. Aluminum wheels. Off-Road equipment package. Conventional spare tire.

(CHEROKEE): Sport, Pioneer, Limited, and Laredo option groups. Power-Tech 4.0-liter inline six-cylinder engine. Four-speed automatic transmission. AM/FM stereo. AM/FM stereo cassette. Cruise control. Tilt steering wheel. Power door locks, power windows, power seats. Power steering. Air conditioning. Rear window defroster. Luggage rack. Aluminum wheels. Selec-Trac full-time 4x4.

(WAGONEER LIMITED): AM/FM stereo cassette. Sunroof. Full-size spare tire. Four-wheel ABS.

(GRAND WAGONEER): Power sunroof.

(COMANCHE): Pioneer, Laredo, and Eliminator option packages. Power-Tech 4.0-liter inline six-cylinder engine (standard in Eliminator). Four-speed automatic transmission. AM/FM stereo. AM/FM stereo with tape player. Cruise control. Tilt steering wheel. Power steering. Air conditioning. Aluminum wheels.

The 1991 Wrangler S, Jeep's import fighter, continued to offer tremendous value for the money.

This year Jeep was celebrating its 50th year as a brand, dating back to 1941 and its inception as a military machine. The light truck market was experiencing an off year in 1991 and everybody was struggling to sell vehicles. The Jeep product line for 1991 didn't have anything really new or exciting to spark a sales revival, and had to rely on energetic marketing efforts in order to avert disaster. Those efforts worked, and in the end Jeep managed to hold its own in a down market, selling 177,775 vehicles.

One thing missing this year was the XJ Wagoneer Limited. It had been dropped from the lineup at the end of the 1990 model year due to slow sales. However, Cherokee Limited offered just about everything the XJ Wagoneer did, so customers wouldn't miss out on anything except the Wagoneer name. And for that they could turn to the Grand Wagoneer, because the top-line Jeep was still in the lineup and still looking good in this, its 29th year in the market.

Jeep Wrangler finally dropped the 4.2-liter six, replacing it with the modern 4.0-liter six seen in other Jeeps. In Wranglers, this engine developed 180 hp—the most power in its class and quite an increase over the 258-cid six. Also dropped was the Laredo model. In its place Jeep added a new Wrangler Renegade. Equipped with the 4.0-liter six, gas-charged shocks, power steering, all-terrain tires, 15 x 8-in. five-hole aluminum wheels, body-color bumpers and wheel flares, reclining bucket seats, and unique exterior trim, Renegade was an aggressive-looking machine. All other Wranglers came standard with a revised 2.5-liter four that now put out 123 hp. The Renegade was priced at $16,525, while the Wrangler S started at $9,910.

Jeep Cherokee Sport now offered a four-door model in addition to the popular two-door model. Base Cherokees got the upgraded four-cylinder engine as standard equipment, while all other Cherokees came with an upgraded 4.0-liter six that was rated at 190 hp. The Cherokee Pioneer was dropped, as was the two-door, two-wheel-drive Laredo. However, the Cherokee line got a new high-end four-wheel-drive model called the Briarwood. It came with imitation wood side paneling similar to the discontinued Wagoneer Limited. The main purpose behind the Briarwood was to offer a Wagoneer Limited-type of product to make sure no sales would be lost. Cherokee Briarwood was priced at $24,229, a little bit below Cherokee Limited's $24,749 sticker.

As before, Comanche continued to be the lowest-priced Jeep vehicle. The base SporTruck short-bed two-wheel-drive model was sticker priced at $8,767. The lowest-priced four-wheel-drive Comanche was the base long-bed priced at $12,534.

A new factory was built in 1991 on historic Jefferson Avenue in downtown Detroit, and it was there that an all-new Jeep was going to be produced. In November, factory workers began assembling pre-production models to test the assembly process. It was known that the new vehicle would be a sport utility wagon, but what it would look like or be like was unknown.

NOTABLE FOR 1991: Output of the 4.0-liter inline six-cylinder engine used in XJ models was increased this year to 190 hp. The 2.5-liter four used in the base-level Cherokees and Comanches was now rated at 130 hp. The Wagoneer Limited and Cherokee Pioneer were discontinued. The Wrangler Renegade package featured a standard 180-hp version of the 4.0-liter six.

I.D. DATA: The VIN has 17 characters. The first three symbols indicate the country of origin (1=USA, 2=Canada), manufacturer (J=Jeep/Eagle Division), and type (4=multipurpose, 6=incomplete, 7=truck). The fourth indicates the gross vehicle weight rating. The fifth indicates the model line (J=4x4 Cherokee and Comanche, S=Grand Wagoneer, T=4x2 Cherokee and Comanche, X=Grand Cherokee 4x2, Y=Wrangler, Grand Cherokee 4x4). The sixth indicates the series (1=standard/S, 2=base/SE, 3=Islander/Pioneer, 4=Sahara, 5=Grand/Laredo, 6=Eliminator/Sport/Renegade/SE, 7=Limited/Briarwood/Country, 8=Grand Wagoneer). The seventh indicates the body style (6=pickup, 7=two-door wagon, 8=four-door wagon, 9=open body). These last three symbols are the models indicated in detail below. The eighth indicates the engine. The ninth is a check digit. The 10th (a letter) indicates model year (1991=M). The 11th indicates the assembly plant (J=Brampton, Ontarioa, L and P=Toledo, Ohio). The remaining numbers indicate the sequential production number starting with 000001 at each plant.

Model	Body Type	Price	Weight
Wrangler YJ — 1/4-Ton — 4x4			
Y19	Wrangler	$10,355	2,935 lbs.
Y29	Wrangler Base	$12,653	2,934 lbs.
Y39	Wrangler Islander	—	2,936 lbs.
Y49	Wrangler Sahara	—	2,936 lbs.
Y59	Wrangler Renegade	—	2,936 lbs.

Cherokee — Four-cyl — 4x2			
T17	2d station wagon	$14,287	2,844 lbs.
T18	4d station wagon	$15,164	2,886 lbs.

Cherokee — Four-cyl — 4x4			
J17	2d station wagon	$15,732	3,016 lbs.
J18	4d station wagon	$16,609	3,057 lbs.

Note: Beginning this year, Cherokee Sport, Laredo, Briarwood, and Limited were considered models rather than packages.

Grand Wagoneer — V-8 — 4x4			
S58	4d station wagon	$29,695	4,499 lbs.

Comanche — 1/2-Ton — Four-cyl			
T16	2d Pickup 4x2 shortbed	$8,767	2,895 lbs.
T16	2d Pickup 4x2 longbed	$9,884	2,986 lbs.
J16	2d Pickup 4x4 shortbed	$12,249	3,084 lbs.
J16	2d Pickup 4x4 longbed	$12,979	3,182 lbs.

PRODUCTION/SALES: As reported in the industry trade paper the *Automotive News*, U.S. Jeep sales for the calendar year were 177,775.

ENGINES

(STANDARD WRANGLER, CHEROKEE, COMANCHE FOUR): Inline. Overhead valve. Cast-iron block. Bore & stroke: 3.88 x 3.19. Displacement: 150 cid (2.5 liters). Compression ratio: 9.2:1. Brake hp: 130 at 5250 rpm (123-hp Wrangler). Throttle body fuel injection (TBI). VIN Code P.

(STANDARD CHEROKEE SPORT, LAREDO, BRIARWOOD & LIMITED; WRANGLER RENEGADE & COMANCHE ELIMINATOR — OPTIONAL: OTHER WRANGLER & COMANCHE SIX): Inline. Overhead valve. Cast-iron block. Bore & stroke: 3.88 x 3.41 in. Displacement: 242 cid (4.0-liters). Compression ratio: 9.2:1. Brake hp: 190 at 4750 rpm (180 hp in Wranglers). Multi-port fuel injection (MFI). VIN Code S.

Jeep Cherokee Sport was available in either two- or four-door versions for 1991. With little new in the way of product news, Jeep relied on the appeal of value models like Cherokee Sport to maintain sales.

Howard Rummel photo

**The Grand Wagoneer had its swan song in 1991. This truck is owned by
Howard Rummel of Lenoir, North Carolina.**

(STANDARD GRAND WAGONEER V-8): Cast-iron block. Bore & stroke: 4.08 x 3.44 in. Displacement: 360 cid (5.9 liters). Brake hp: 144 at 3200 rpm. Two-barrel carburetor. VIN Code 7.

CHASSIS

WRANGLER: Wheelbase: 93.5 in. Overall length: 153.0 in. Height (with hardtop): 69.3 in. Width: 66 in. Tread: front and rear, 58 in. Tires: P215/75R15 RWL.

(CHEROKEE): Wheelbase: 101 in. Overall length: 165.3 in. Width: 70.5 in. Height: 63.4 in. (4x2), 63.3 in. (4x4).

(GRAND WAGONEER): Wheelbase: 108.7 in. Overall length: 186.4 in. Width: 74.8 in. Height: 66.4 in. Tires: P225/75R15 WSW.

(COMANCHE): Wheelbase: 113 in. (short box), 119.6 in. (long box). Overall length: 179.2 in. (short box), 194 in. (long box). Width: 71.7 in. Height: 63.7 in. (4x2 and 4x4).

TECHNICAL

(WRANGLER): Five-speed manual transmission. Floor shift. Semi-floating rear axle. Standard drive ratio: 4.11:1. Power front disc/rear drum brakes. Command-Trac shift-on-the-fly part-time 4x4 system.

(CHEROKEE): UniFrame construction. Five-speed manual transmission. Floor shift. Semi-floating rear axle. Power front disc/rear drum brakes. 4x4 models include Command-Trac shift-on-the-fly part-time 4x4 system.

(CHEROKEE BRIARWOOD): Four-speed auto-matic

transmission. Power front disc/rear drum brakes. Selec-Trac shift-on-the-fly full-time four-wheel drive.

(COMANCHE): Five-speed manual transmission. Floor shift. Semi-floating rear axle. Final drive ratio: 3.55:1. Power front disc/rear drum brakes. 4x4 models include Command-Trac shift-on-the-fly part-time four-wheel drive as standard.

OPTIONS

(WRANGLER): Three-speed automatic transmission. Hardtop. Tilt steering. Rear Trac-Lok differential. Air conditioning. Extra-quiet insulation. Full-carpets. Halogen fog lamps. Power steering. Cruise Control (six-cylinder only). Leather-wrapped sport steering wheel. Electric rear window defogger (hardtop). Heavy-duty suspension. Heavy-duty cooling. Aluminum wheels. Off-Road equipment package. Conventional spare tire.

(CHEROKEE): Laredo, Sport, Limited, and Briarwood option groups. Four-speed automatic transmission. AM/FM stereo. AM/FM stereo with tape player. Cruise control. Tilt steering wheel. Manual sunroof. Power door locks. Power windows. Power seats. Power steering. Air conditioning. Rear window defroster. Luggage rack. Aluminum wheels. Selec-Trac full-time 4x4. ABS.

(GRAND WAGONEER): Power sunroof.

(COMANCHE): Pioneer and Eliminator option packages. Power-Tech 4.0-liter inline six-cylinder engine (standard in Eliminator). Four-speed automatic transmission. AM/FM stereo. AM/FM stereo cassette. Cruise control. Tilt steering wheel. Power steering. Air conditioning.

The 1992 Cherokee Laredo was one of the more popular models in the Jeep lineup, offering sporty looks and luxury in a compact SUV.

In December 1991, Jeep began production of a police version of the Cherokee four-door. Available in either two- or four-wheel-drive models, the police Cherokee package included reinforced suspension, anti-lock brakes, larger tires, a 120-mph speedometer, and a column-mounted shift lever. Equipped with the mighty Jeep 4.0-liter six, in closed-course tests, the Cherokee

police vehicle trailed the fastest sedan, the Chevy Caprice V-8, by just 1.4 seconds. Sales were expected to total only a few thousand per year.

For 1992 the Cherokee Sport could be ordered with an optional sunroof. Base Cherokees were now given full carpeting as standard equipment.

The Jeep Comanche Sport package got a new design for the body stripes, and the full-length console now came with a new detachable double cup holder. Comanche sales were dropping, so discounts on Olympic packages were substantially increased.

The Wrangler line got the most improvements. On Islander and Sahara models the 4.0 six-cylinder engine became standard equipment. Sahara models also got a new look with low-luster paints, a choice of Sand (tan) or Sage Green that had the look and feel of primer paints. It was a most unusual look and one that many shoppers didn't find appealing. All Wranglers benefited from new three-point rear seat belts.

At the end of Wrangler model year production on April 24, the Brampton, Ontario, plant at which they were assembled was permanently closed and production was moved to the reopened Toledo-Stickney Avenue plant, commencing with the 1993 model year.

The Comanche line offered Base, Sport, Pioneer and Eliminator models, and this year the 4.0-liter six was standard on Pioneer as well as Eliminator models.

One thing noticeably missing from the 1992 Jeep lineup was the SJ or senior Jeep Grand Wagoneer. Sales of the big Jeep had been falling for the prior few years, but that wasn't the only reason for dropping the Grand Wagoneer. Jeep had an all-new sport utility wagon coming out in the spring and needed to focus as much attention as possible on that vehicle. Since it was larger than the XJ Cherokee, it was likely the new SUV would soon displace the Grand Wagoneer anyway. The decision was made to drop the Grand Wagoneer at the end of the 1991 model run. However, it appears that a small batch of 1992 Grand Wagoneers was produced, though they were not listed in sales literature. Most sources indicate about 300 were assembled. It's not known why they were built, but in all likelihood the company had some orders leftover and decided to fill them. One other possibility is that they were built for overseas markets, though reportedly a few of them have been found in the U.S.

During the year, Chrysler went to court to get back the rights to use of the Jeep name in Brazil. Those rights had been sold to Ford when that company purchased Willys Overland Brazil in 1967. Ford had continued building Jeeps in Brazil until 1983. Since then, Ford's Brazilian operations had merged with VW's to form a new company known as Autolatina, and that firm considered itself the heir to the Jeep name in Brazil.

In January 1992, production of the new Jeep wagon began at the all-new Jefferson North plant in Detroit. The new vehicle was designated as a 1993 model, which was completely appropriate considering how radically new it was. Jeep sales climbed dramatically for the year, mainly due to the new vehicle, sales of which began midway through 1992. For the year, a total of 268,724 Jeep vehicles were sold.

Jeep had been struggling to overcome stiff competition from the Ford Explorer and the Chevy and GM SUVs but with the new Jeep coming it would reach new heights of success and prestige.

NOTABLE FOR 1992: There were no appreciable changes to either the Wrangler or the Comanche. Cherokee trim levels offered were Base, Sport, Laredo, Briarwood, and Limited.

I.D. DATA: The VIN has 17 characters. The first three symbols indicate the country of origin (1=USA, 2=Canada), manufacturer (J=Jeep/Eagle Division), and type (4=multipurpose, 6=incomplete, 7=truck). The fourth indicates the gross vehicle weight rating. The fifth indicates the model line (J=4x4 Cherokee and Comanche, S=Grand Wagoneer, T=4x2 Cherokee and Comanche, X=Grand Cherokee 4x2, Y=Wrangler, Grand Cherokee 4x4). The sixth indicates the series (1=standard/S, 2=base/SE, 3=Islander/Pioneer, 4=Sahara, 5=Grand/Laredo, 6=Eliminator/Sport /Renegade/SE, 7=Limited/Briarwood/Country, 8=Grand Wagoneer). The seventh indicates the body style (6=pickup, 7=two-door wagon, 8=four-door wagon, 9=open body). These last three symbols are the models indicated in detail below. The eighth indicates the engine. The ninth is a check digit. The 10th (a letter) indicates model year (1992=N). The 11th indicates the assembly plant (J=Brampton, Ontario, L and P=Toledo, Ohio). The remaining numbers indicate the sequential production number, starting with 000001, at each plant.

Model	Body Type	Price	Weight
Wrangler YJ — 1/4-Ton — 4x4			
Y19	Wrangler	$11,030	2,843 lbs.
Y29	Wrangler Base	$13,374	2,936 lbs.
Y39	Wrangler Islander	—	2,936 lbs.
Y49	Wrangler Sahara	—	3,066 lbs.
Y59	Wrangler Renegade	—	3,066 lbs.
Cherokee — Four-cyl — 4x2			
T17	2d Station Wagon	$14,831	2,808 lbs.
T18	4d Station Wagon	$16,317	2,985 lbs.
Cherokee — Four-cyl — 4x4			
J17	2d Station Wagon	$15,842	3,005 lbs.
J18	4d Station Wagon	$17,327	3,028 lbs.
Comanche — 1/2-Ton —Four-cyl			
T16	2d Pickup 4x2 shortbed	$9,679	2,898 lbs.
T16	2d Pickup 4x2 longbed	$10,376	2,985 lbs.
J16	2d Pickup 4x4 shortbed	$12,696	3,075 lbs.
J16	2d Pickup 4x4 longbed	$13,427	3,188 lbs.

PRODUCTION/SALES: As reported in the industry trade paper the *Automotive News*, Jeep's U.S. retail sales for the calendar year were 268,724.

ENGINE

(STANDARD WRANGLER, CHEROKEE, COMANCHE FOUR): Inline. Overheadvalve. Cast-iron block. Bore & stroke: 3.88 x 3.19 in. Displacement: 150 cid (2.5 liters). Compression ratio: 9.2:1. Brake hp: 130 at 5250 rpm. (123 hp in Wrangler) Throttle body fuel injection (TBI). VIN code P.

(STANDARD ALL CHEROKEE EXCEPT BASE; COMANCHE PIONEER AND ELIMINATOR; WRANGLER ISLANDER, SAHARA AND RENEGADE — OPTIONAL BASE WRANGLER AND ALL OTHER COMANCHES SIX): Inline. Overhead-valve. Cast-iron block. Bore & stroke: 3.88 x 3.41 in. Displacement: 242 cid (4.0-liters). Compression ratio: 9.2:1. Brake hp: 190 at 4750 rpm (180 hp in Wranglers). Multi-port fuel injection (MFI). VIN code S.

CHASSIS

(WRANGLER): Wheelbase: 93.5 in. Overall length: 153.0 in. Height (with hardtop): 69.3 in. Width: 66 in. Tread: front and rear, 58 in. Tires: P215/75R15 RWL.

(CHEROKEE): Wheelbase: 101 in. Overall length: 165.3 in. Width: 70.5 in. Height: 63.4 in. (4x2), 63.3 in. (4x4).

(COMANCHE): Wheelbase: 113 in. (short box), 119.6 in. (long box). Overall length: 179.2 in. (short box), 194 in. (long box). Width: 71.7 in. Height: 63.7 in. (4x2 and 4x4).

TECHNICAL

(WRANGLER): Five-speed manual transmission. Floor shift. Semi-floating rear axle. Standard drive ratio: 4.11:1. Front disc/rear drum brakes. Command-Trac shift-on-the-fly part-time four-wheel drive.

(CHEROKEE): UniFrame construction. Five-speed manual transmission. Floor shift. Semi-floating rear axle. Power front disc/rear drum brakes. Command-Trac shift-on-the-fly part-time four-wheel drive.

(CHEROKEE LIMITED & BRIARWOOD): Four-speed automatic transmission; speeds. Semi-floating rear axle. Brakes: front disc with rear drum, power assisted. Command-Trac shift-on-the-fly part-time four-wheel drive.

(COMANCHE): Five-speed manual transmission. Floor shift. Semi-floating rear axle. Final drive ratio: 3.73:1. Power front disc/rear drum brakes. 4x4 models include Command-Trac shift-on-the-fly part-time four-wheel drive.

OPTIONS

(WRANGLER): Three-speed automatic transmission. Hardtop. Tilt steering. Rear Trac-Lok differential. Air conditioning. Extra-quiet insulation. Full-carpets. Fog lamps. Power steering. Cruise control (six-cylinder only). Leather-wrapped Sport steering wheel. Electric rear window defogger (hardtop). Heavy-duty suspension. Heavy-duty cooling. Aluminum wheels. Off-Road equipment package. Conventional spare tire.

(CHEROKEE): Sport, Laredo, Briarwood and Limited option groups. Power-Tech 4.0-liter inline six-cylinder engine. Four-speed automatic transmission. AM/FM stereo. AM/FM stereo cassette. Cruise control. Tilt steering wheel. Power door locks. Power windows. Power seats. Air conditioning. Rear window defroster. Luggage rack. Aluminum wheels.

(COMANCHE): Sport, Pioneer, and Eliminator. Power-Tech 4.0-liter six-cylinder engine (standard Eliminator). Four-speed automatic transmission. AM/FM stereo. AM/FM stereo with tape player. Cruise control. Tilt steering wheel. Air conditioning.

In 1993, Jeep tried to resurrect the Grand Wagoneer name on the Grand Cherokee platform. Although attractive and undeniably luxurious, it failed to sell in significant numbers.

The first 1993 Jeep to debut was the last one conceived by American Motors engineers—the all-new Grand Cherokee. It debuted midyear in 1992 as an early 1993 model. Known internally as the ZJ, (because it came after the XJ Cherokee and YJ Wrangler) it was a masterpiece of design. As Engineering VP Francois Castaing noted, Grand Cherokee set a new standard for on-road ride, handling, and comfort while at the same time holding firmly to Jeep's hard-won reputation for off-road ability.

It was a quantum leap forward in SUV design. Like the XJ Cherokee, Grand Cherokee used UniFrame (unibody) construction but the new structure was stiffer and stronger. The Grand Cherokee was larger than the old Cherokee, yet still trim and nimble. Setting new standards for safety, Grand Cherokee was the first SUV to offer a driver's-side airbag. All Grand Cherokees came with four-wheel drive and four-wheel anti-lock brakes as standard equipment. A unique multi-link suspension system featured coil springs on all four wheels for the smoothest ride of any four-wheeler, yet a solid front axle ensured Jeep's off-road capability would be second to none.

The 4.0 six-cylinder engine was standard. In early production, the only transmission offered was an

automatic, but before long a five-speed manual transmission went into production. Base and Laredo models came with a standard five-speed transmission. A four-speed automatic gearbox was standard on Limited, optional on the others. The 4.0-liter six combined with the four-speed automatic transmission received an EPA fuel economy rating of 15 mpg city and 20 mpg highway—very good for a large, powerful sport wagon. A 22.7-gallon fuel tank was standard.

Grand Cherokee was offered in three models, Base, Laredo and Limited. The Base models didn't prove very popular and not many are seen today. They are easy to spot because they were the only Grand Cherokees that don't have lower body cladding.

Three different four-wheel-drive systems were available. Command-Trac shift-on-the-fly part-time four-wheel drive was standard on Base and Laredo models. Selec-Trac full-time four-wheel-drive was optional. Grand Cherokee Limited models came with Quadra-Trac full-time four-wheel-drive, and this system was also available as an extra-cost option on Base and Laredo models.

Ride and handling set new standards. During suspension development and testing, renowned race car driver Emerson Fittipaldi served as a consultant to Chrysler Corporation, and his efforts showed up in a vehicle with handling characteristics that rivaled European sports sedans.

The new Jeeps were the first to offer an optional compact disc player. Grand Cherokee also introduced an automatic temperature control system, the first on a domestic SUV. It came only on Limited models. Air conditioning was standard equipment on the Limited and was extra-cost on Base and Laredo models. Grand Cherokee was also the first Jeep to use the new non-hazardous R-134a refrigerant for its A/C system.

The new Grand Cherokee was an instant hit with the public and the most exciting sport utility vehicle on the market. As one magazine said "the Ford Explorer, in one fell swoop, has become yesterday's news." *Petersen's 4-Wheel & Off-Road* magazine named Grand Cherokee "4x4 of the Year"—just one of many accolades it received.

Because of the amount of work involved in bringing out the Grand Cherokee, the rest of the Jeep line was mostly carryover. They debuted that fall, which was the usual introduction time but of course, it was many months after Grand Cherokee's early intro. Since Grand Cherokee was slotted in the upper levels of the four-wheel-drive market, the XJ Cherokee line was reshuffled to give more emphasis on lower priced models. Base, Sport, and a new Country model were offered. The Country was the top of the Cherokee line, but in keeping with Cherokee's role as a lower-priced vehicle it wasn't nearly as fancy as the old Limited had been. Cherokee Country included a body-color grille and headlight bezels. Inside, there was wood-grain trim on the instrument panel and upper door area. Cherokee Sport now came with cheaper standard wheels, a five-spoke styled steel design. Aluminum wheels were optionally available. The four-cylinder engine continued as standard on base Cherokees, while the Sport and Country came with the 4.0-liter. A stainless-steel exhaust system was new.

Wranglers were offered in the usual S, Base, Sport, and Renegade models, and offered optional four-wheel anti-lock brakes on models equipped with the 4.0-liter engine. Like other Jeeps, Wrangler's exhaust system now was stainless steel.

It was the end of the line for Jeep Comanche trucks. They were dropped due to slow sales.

Around the same time that the 1993 Jeep Cherokee and Wrangler models were being introduced, a V-8 engine became available on Grand Cherokee. The engine was the 5.2 liter 220 hp Chrysler V-8, sturdy and smooth, and with it, Grand Cherokee became the first compact sport utility wagon to offer V-8 power. Buyers flocked to it. A two-wheel-drive Grand Cherokee also joined the line, available as a six-cylinder model only.

Another new Jeep model debuted that fall. Called the Grand Wagoneer, it was a thinly disguised Grand Cherokee. Equipped with a standard V-8 and a long list of luxury features, the Grand Wagoneer even had imitation wood-grain panels. It captured some of the aura of the old Grand Wagoneer, but apparently not enough—it didn't find many buyers.

The 1993 Grand Cherokee Laredo set a new standard for capability in SUVs.

**For 1993, Jeep Wrangler could be had in 'S', base, Sport or Renegade versions.
This is the popular Sport model.**

Not that there was any concern. Jeep sales hit a new record this year with 408,323 units sold. The outlook for the future was even brighter.

NOTABLE FOR 1993: The all-new Grand Cherokee was introduced on April 19, 1992. Design work had begun under AMC well before the Chrysler takeover. Grand Cherokee was available in three trim levels, Base, Laredo, and Limited. Initially the only power plant available was the 4.0-liter inline six. The ZJ-based Grand Wagoneer that debuted some months afterwards was offered in a single premium model. By the start of the regular model year, a 5.2-liter V-8 (Chrysler 318 cid) was available as standard equipment in Grand Wagoneers, and optional equipment in the Grand Cherokee. Additionally, a two-wheel-drive Grand Cherokee was added to the line. There were no appreciable changes to the Wrangler. Cherokee's three trim levels were the Base, Sport, and Country.

I.D. DATA: The VIN has 17 characters. The first three symbols indicate the country of origin (1=USA, 2=Canada), manufacturer (J=Jeep/Eagle Division), and type (4=multipurpose). The fourth indicates the gross vehicle weight rating. The fifth indicates the model line (J=4x4 Cherokee, S=Grand Wagoneer, T=4x2 Cherokee, X=Grand Cherokee 4x2, Y=Wrangler, Grand Cherokee 4x4). The sixth indicates the series (1=standard/S, 2=base/SE, 3=Islander, 4=Sahara, 5=Grand/Laredo, 6=Sport/Renegade/SE, 7=Limited/Country, 8=Grand Wagoneer). The seventh indicates the body style (6=pickup, 7=two-door wagon, 8=four-door wagon, 9=open body). These last three symbols are the models indicated in detail below. The eighth indicates the engine. The ninth is a check digit. The tenth (a letter) indicates model year (1993=P). The eleventh indicates the assembly plant (C=Jefferson, L and P=Toledo, Ohio).

The remaining numbers indicate the sequential production number, starting with 000001, at each plant.

Model	Body Type	Price	Weight
Wrangler YJ — 1/4-Ton — 4x4			
Y19	Wrangler	$11,410	2,935 lbs.
Y29	Wrangler Base	$13,828	2,935 lbs.
Y39	Wrangler Sport	—	2,936 lbs.
Y49	Wrangler Sahara	—	3,080 lbs.
Y59	Wrangler Renegade	—	3,080 lbs.
Cherokee Base — Four-cyl — 4x2			
T17	2d Station Wagon	$12,622	2,808 lbs.
T18	4d Station Wagon	$13,622	2,850 lbs.
Cherokee Base — Four-cyl — 4x4			
J17	2d Station Wagon	$14,107	2,985 lbs.
J18	4d Station Wagon	$15,117	3,028 lbs.
Cherokee Sport — Six-cyl — 4x2			
T17	2d Station Wagon	—	—
T18	4d Station Wagon	—	—
Cherokee Sport — Six-cyl — 4x4			
J17	2d Station Wagon	—	—
J18	4d Station Wagon	—	—
Cherokee Country — Six-cyl — 4x2			
T17	2d Station Wagon	—	—
T18	4d Station Wagon	—	—
Cherokee Country — Six-cyl — 4x4			
J17	2d Station Wagon	—	—
J18	4d Station Wagon	—	—
Grand Cherokee — Six-cyl — 4x2			
X28	4d SUV, Base	—	—
Grand Cherokee — Six-cyl — 4x4			
Z28	4d SUV, Base	$20,185	3,574 lbs.
Z58	4d SUV, Laredo	$21,369	3,574 lbs.
Z78	4d SUV, Limited	$28,925	3,574 lbs.
Grand Wagoneer — V-8 — 4x4			
Z88	4d SUV	$29,826	3,901 lbs.

NOTE: A total of 121,835 Cherokees of all models were built (62.5 percent equipped with 4x4).

PRODUCTION/SALES: As reported in the industry trade paper the *Automotive News*, Jeep's US retail sales for the calendar year were 408,323.

ENGINES

(STANDARD WRANGLER, WRANGLER BASE, WRANGLER SPORT, CHEROKEE BASE FOUR): Inline. Overhead-valve. Cast-iron block. Bore & stroke: 3.88 x 3.19 in. Displacement: 150 cid (2.5 liters). Compression ratio: 9.2:1. Brake hp: 130 at 5250 rpm. (123 hp in Wrangler). Throttle body fuel injection (TBI). VIN code P.

(STANDARD CHEROKEE SPORT & COUNTRY, GRAND CHEROKEE, WRANGLER SAHARA & RENEGADE SIX): Inline. Overhead-valve. Cast-iron block. Bore & stroke: 3.88 x 3.41 in. Displacement: 242 cid (4.0-liters). Compression ratio: 9.2:1. Brake hp: 190 at 4750 rpm (180 hp in Wranglers). Multi-port fuel injection (MFI). VIN code S.

(STANDARD GRAND WAGONEER — OPTIONAL GRAND CHEROKEE V-8): Overhead valve. Cast-iron block. Bore & stroke: 3.91 x 3.31 in. Displacement: 318 cid (5.2 liters). Compression ratio: 9.2:1. Brake hp: 220 at 4800 rpm. Torque: 285 lbs.-ft. at 3600 rpm. Multi-port fuel injection (MFI). VIN code Y.

CHASSIS

(WRANGLER): Wheelbase: 93.5 in. Overall length: 153.0 in. Height (with hardtop): 69.3 in. Width: 66 in. Tread: front and rear, 58 in. Tires: P215/75R15.

(CHEROKEE): Wheelbase: 101 in. Overall length: 165.3 in. Width: 70.5 in. Height: 63.4 in. (4x2), 63.3 in. (4x4).

(GRAND CHEROKEE/GRAND WAGONEER): Wheelbase: 105.9 in. Overall length: 176.7 in. Width: 69.2 in. Height: 64.9 in.

TECHNICAL

(WRANGLER): Five-speed manual transmission. Floor shift. Semi-floating rear axle. Standard drive ratio: 4.11:1. Power front disc/rear drum brakes. Command-Trac shift-on-the-fly part-time four-wheel drive.

(CHEROKEE): UniFrame construction. Five-speed manual transmission. Floor shift. Semi-floating rear axle. Power front disc/rear drum brakes. 4x4 models include Command-Trac shift-on-the-fly part-time four-wheel drive.

(GRAND CHEROKEE): UniFrame construction. Quadra-Coil four-wheel coil suspension. Five-speed manual transmission with overdrive. Floor-mounted gearshift. Brakes: four-wheel disc with ABS.

(GRAND WAGONEER): UniFrame construction. Quadra-Coil four-wheel coil suspension. Four-speed automatic transmission with overdrive. Brakes: four-wheel disc with ABS. Quadra-Trac full-time four-wheel drive.

OPTIONS

(WRANGLER): Three-speed automatic transmission. Hardtop. Tilt steering. Rear Trac-Lok differential. Air conditioning. Fog lamps. Heavy-duty suspension. Heavy-duty cooling. Aluminum wheels. Conventional spare tire.

(CHEROKEE): Power-Tech 4.0-liter inline six-cylinder engine (optional on Base, standard all other Cherokees). Four-speed automatic transmission. AM/FM stereo. AM/FM cassette. Cruise control. Tilt steering wheel.

The basic Cherokee for 1993 came with a four-cylinder engine as standard equipment.

Jeep Cherokee Sport for 1993 included a standard 4.0-liter six-cylinder engine. The standard wheels this year were a less-expensive steel spoke design, though alloy wheels could be ordered for an extra charge.

Power door locks. Power window. Power seats. Power steering. Air conditioning. Rear window defroster. Luggage rack. Aluminum wheels. Selec-Trac full-time four-wheel-drive.

(GRAND CHEROKEE): 5.2-liter V-8 (4x4 only). Selec-Trac or Quadra-Trac full-time four-wheel-drive (Quadra-Trac standard on Grand Cherokee Limited). AM/FM cassette. Fog lamps. Power sunroof. Four-speed automatic transmission. AM/FM stereo. Rear window defroster. Cruise control. Tilt steering wheel. Power door locks. Power windows. Power seats. Air conditioning (standard on Limited). Roof rack.

(GRAND WAGONEER): Fog lamp/skid plate group. Up-Country suspension. Trac-Lok rear differential. Power sunroof.

The 1993 Jeep Grand Cherokee Limited was one of the best SUVs in the world, a remarkable blend of engineering and design.

The only real problem Jeep had with the 1994 Grand Cherokee Laredo was building enough of them to meet the overwhelming demand.

When the 1994 Jeep lineup was unveiled in the fall of 1993 there was one model missing. The Grand Wagoneer, cobbled together from Grand Cherokee mechanicals, didn't make the cut. It had simply failed to attract enough buyers.

According to press release material, Jeep Cherokee offered a new optional three-speed automatic transmission in combination with the four-cylinder engine. The 4.0 six got a revamped torque converter for increased performance. A center high-mounted stoplight (CHMSL) was a new feature, along with new guard beams in the doors and a sturdier roof with increased crush resistance. Cherokee's air conditioner now used the modern R-134a refrigerant. There was a new type of Cherokee for 1994, though it was considered an option package rather than a separate model. The Right Hand Drive Postal Carrier Group option was available on both two-wheel-drive and four-wheel-drive Cherokees, in two-door and four-door versions. This new option group made Cherokee ideal for the thousands of rural letter carriers who had to buy their own delivery vehicles.

Wrangler also offered an automatic transmission /four-cylinder engine combo, and got the new A/C refrigerant and the 4.0's new torque converter. Wrangler's soft top was redesigned for easier operation. A CHMSL was added to Wranglers, along with two new exterior colors: Brilliant Blue Pearl-Coat and Dark Blue Pearl-Coat. Late in the model year, an optional Add-A-Trunk was made available.

Grand Cherokee's base model was now called the

SE, and as before, it was the only Grand Cherokee that didn't come with lower body cladding. The Limited model now included four-wheel disc brakes as standard equipment, with ABS of course, and all Grand Cherokees got new guard beams in the doors. Removable rear seat head rests were new, as was an upgraded cassette player with four speakers, integrated child seat, and a valet key and lock system.

Jeep Grand Cherokee was a runaway success. At mid-year it was announced that Jeep was adding a third shift to its Jefferson North assembly plant to boost Grand Cherokee production from 267,000 units up to 315,000 annually. For the year Jeep sold 436,445 vehicles. It was a very good year.

NOTABLE FOR 1994: A three-speed automatic transmission was available with the 2.5-liter four-cylinder. Base models were renamed SE. Grand Wagoneer was discontinued.

I.D. DATA: The VIN has 17 characters. The first three symbols indicate the country of origin (1=USA, 2=Canada), manufacturer (J=Jeep/Eagle Division), and type (4=multipurpose). The fourth indicates the gross vehicle weight rating. The fifth indicates the model line (J=4x4 Cherokee, S=Grand Wagoneer, T=4x2 Cherokee, X=Grand Cherokee 4x2, Y=Wrangler, Grand Cherokee 4x4). The sixth indicates the series (1=standard/S, 2=SE, 3=Islander, 4=Sahara, 5=Grand/Laredo, 6=Sport/Renegade/SE, 7=Limited/Country, 8=Grand Wagoneer). The seventh indicates the body style (6=pickup, 7=two-door wagon, 8=four-door wagon, 9=open body). These last three symbols are the models indicated in detail below. The eighth indicates the engine. The ninth is a check digit. The 10th (a letter) indicates model year (1994=R). The 11th indicates the assembly plant (C=Jefferson, L and P=Toledo, Ohio). The remaining numbers indicate the sequential production number starting with 000001 at each plant.

Model	Body Type	Price	Weight
Wrangler YJ — 1/4-Ton — 4x4			
YJ	Wrangler S	$11,975	2,935 lbs.
YJ	Wrangler SE	$15,039	2,935 lbs.
YJ	Wrangler Sahara	—	—
YJ	Wrangler Renegade	—	—
Cherokee SE — Four-cyl — 4x2			
T17	2d Station Wagon	$13,572	2,876 lbs.
T18	4d Station Wagon	$14,582	2,928 lbs.
Cherokee SE — Four-cyl — 4x4			
J17	2d Station Wagon	$15,057	3,042 lbs.
J18	4d Station Wagon	$16,067	3,090 lbs.
Cherokee Sport — Six-cyl — 4x2			
T17	2d Station Wagon	—	—
T18	4d Station Wagon	—	—
Cherokee Sport — Six-cyl — 4x4			
J17	2d Station Wagon	—	—
J18	4d Station Wagon	—	—
Cherokee Country — Six-cyl — 4x2			
T17	2d Station Wagon	—	—
T18	4d Station Wagon	—	—
Cherokee Country — Six-cyl — 4x4			
J17	2d Station Wagon	—	—
J18	4d Station Wagon	—	—
Grand Cherokee — Six-cyl — 4x2			
ZJ	4d Sport Wagon SE	—	—
Grand Cherokee — Six-cyl — 4x4			
ZJ	4d Sport Wagon SE	$23,443	3,574 lbs.
ZJ	4d Sport Wagon Laredo	—	—
ZJ	4d Sport Wagon Limited	—	—

NOTE 1: A total of 66,141 Wranglers of all models were built.
NOTE 2: A total of 116,653 Cherokees of all models were built (64.3 percent equipped with 4x4).
NOTE 3: A total of 225,281 Grand Cherokes of all models were built (87.5 percent equipped with 4x4).

PRODUCTION/SALES: As reported in the industry trade paper the *Automotive News*, Jeep's U.S. retail sales for the calendar year were 436,445.

ENGINES

(STANDARD WRANGLER S & SE, CHEROKEE SE FOUR): Inline. Overhead-valve. Cast-iron block. Bore & stroke: 3.88 x 3.19 in. Displacement: 150 cid (2.5 liters). Compression ratio: 9.2:1. Brake hp: 130 at 5250 rpm. (123 hp in Wrangler). Throttle body fuel injection (TBI). VIN code P.

(STANDARD WRANGLER SPORT & RENEGADE, CHEROKEE SPORT & COUNTRY, GRAND CHEROKEE — OPTIONAL CHEROKEE, WRANGLER SE SIX): Inline. Overhead valve. Cast-iron block. Bore & stroke: 3.88 x 3.41 in. Displacement: 242 cid (4.0-liter). Compression ratio: 9.2:1. Brake hp: 190 at 4750 rpm (180 hp for Wranglers). Multi-port fuel injection (MFI). VIN code S.

(OPTIONAL GRAND CHEROKEE V-8): Overhead valve. Cast-iron block. Bore & stroke: 3.91 x 3.31 in. Displacement: 318 cid (5.2 liter). Compression ratio: 9.2:1. Brake hp: 220 at 4800 rpm. Torque: 285 lbs.-ft. at 3600 rpm. Multi-port fuel injection (MFI). VIN code Y.

CHASSIS

(WRANGLER): Wheelbase: 93.5 in. Overall length: 153 in. Height (with hardtop): 69.3 in. Width: 66 in. Tread: front and rear, 58 in. Tires: P215/75R15 RWL.

(CHEROKEE): Wheelbase: 101 in. Overall length: 165.3 in. Width: 70.5 in. Height: 63.4 in. (4x2), 63.3 in. (4x4).

(GRAND CHEROKEE): Wheelbase: 105.9 in. Overall length: 176.7 in. Width: 69.2 in. Height: 64.9 in.

TECHNICAL

(WRANGLER): Five-speed manual transmission. Floor shift. Semi-floating rear axle. Standard drive ratio: 4.11:1. Power front disc/rear drum brakes. Command-Trac shift-on-the-fly part-time four-wheel drive.

(CHEROKEE): UniFrame construction. Five-speed manual transmission. Floor shift. Semi-floating rear axle. Power front disc/rear drum brakes. 4x4 models include Command-Trac shift-on-the-fly part-time four-wheel drive.

(GRAND CHEROKEE): UniFrame construction. Quadra-Coil four-wheel coil suspension. Five-speed manual transmission with overdrive. Floor-mounted gearshift. Shaft drive. Brakes: four-wheel disc with ABS.

OPTIONS

(WRANGLER): Three-speed automatic transmission. Hardtop. Tilt steering, Rear Trac-Lok differential. Air conditioning. Extra-quiet insulation. Full-carpets. Halogen fog lamps. Power steering. Cruise control. Rear window defogger (hardtop). Heavy-duty suspension. Heavy-duty cooling. Aluminum wheels. Off-Road suspension. Conventional spare tire.

(CHEROKEE): Power-Tech 4.0-liter inline six-cylinder engine (optional SE, standard other Cherokees). Four-speed automatic transmission. AM/FM stereo. AM/FM cassette. Cruise control. Tilt steering wheel. Power door locks. Power windows. Power seats. Air conditioning. Rear window defroster. Roof rack. Aluminum wheels. Selec-Trac full-time 4x4.

(GRAND CHEROKEE): 5.2-liter V-8 (with 4x4 only). Quadra-Trac. AM/FM cassette. Fog lamps. Power sunroof. Four-speed automatic transmission. Rear window defroster. Cruise control. Tilt steering wheel. Power door locks. Power windows. Power seats. Air conditioning. Roof rack. Aluminum wheels. Fog lamps.

For 1995, Jeep offered the new Rio Grande dress-up package, available on the Wrangler S.

"The earth has music for those who listen" are the opening words in the 1995 Jeep catalog, appropriate for the brand that opened up the great outdoors for so many.

For 1995 Grand Cherokee got some exciting new features. A new Orvis Edition model, inspired by the 139-year-old sporting goods retailer, was an interesting competitor for Ford's Eddie Bauer Explorer. The Grand Cherokee Orvis Edition included such features as Up-Country suspension, Quadra-Trac four-wheel drive, four-wheel disc anti-lock brake system, power front seats upholstered in dark green and champagne leather with roan red accents, and a unique spare tire cover with both zip and flap pockets, plus the Orvis logo. The exterior was Brilliant Moss Green with roan red and maize accents. Special Orvis badging on the body sides provided instant identification.

Other new Grand Cherokee features included a higher torque camshaft on the V-8 engine (now rated at 300 lbs.-ft. of torque), and enhanced emission controls.

Four-wheel disc brakes became standard equipment on Laredo and SE models. The automatic transmission was now standard equipment for all Grand Cherokees; the five speed manual gearbox was no longer offered. New options included a flip-up liftgate window, mini-overhead console with compass, temperature gauge, trip computer and map lights, and asymmetrical off-road tires. Grand Cherokee Limited could now be had in a two-wheel-drive model, but only with the six-cylinder engine.

The XJ Cherokees this year were given a drivers side air bag. Cherokees also got new standard reclining front seats based on the Grand Cherokee design. Dual horns were made standard equipment. The Cherokee lineup included SE and Sport models in either two- or four-door versions, and a Cherokee Country offered only as a four-door model. All were available in either two or four-wheel-drive versions.

Jeep Wrangler was available in just three models: S (base), SE, and Sahara. The Renegade was dropped.

However, Wrangler offered a new sport appearance package and for once it was offered only as a four-cylinder model. Called the Rio Grande, the package was optional only on S Wranglers and included "Pueblo" cloth seats with recliners, full-face-styled steel wheels, Bright Mango exterior paint, and Rio Grande decals. SE models could be ordered with a Sport group that included body-side graphics and body-color side steps. The 2.5-liter four was the only engine offered on the 'S' model, while SE and Sahara models came only with the 4.0-liter six. Automatic transmission was available on all.

Jeep sales slipped a bit this year to 426,628 units, but all in all, it was another successful and gratifying year for Jeep.

NOTABLE FOR 1995: Wrangler got a new Rio Grande package and Sahara had some interior changes. Cherokee now had a driver's side airbag as standard equipment.

I.D. DATA: The VIN has 17 characters. The first three symbols indicate the country of origin (1=USA, 2=Canada), manufacturer (J=Jeep/Eagle Division), and type (4=multipurpose). The fourth indicates the Gross Vehicle Weight Rating. The fifth indicates the model line (J=4x4 Cherokee, S=Grand Wagoneer, T=4x2 Cherokee, X=Grand Cherokee 4x2, Y=Wrangler, Grand Cherokee 4x4). The sixth indicates the series (1=standard/S, 2=SE, 3=Islander, 4=Sahara, 5=Grand/Laredo, 6=Sport/Renegade/SE, 7=Limited/Country, 8=Grand Wagoneer). The seventh indicates the body style (6=pickup, 7=two-door wagon, 8=four-door wagon, 9=open body). These last three symbols are the models indicated in detail below. The eighth indicates the engine. The ninth is a check digit. The tenth (a letter) indicates model year (1995=S). The eleventh indicates the assembly plant (C=Jefferson, L and P=Toledo, Ohio). The remaining numbers indicate the sequential production number starting with 000001 at each plant.

Model	Body Type	Price	Weight
Wrangler YJ — 1/4-Ton — 4x4			
YJ	Wrangler S	—	—
YJ	Wrangler SE	—	—
YJ	Wrangler Sahara	—	—
Cherokee SE — Four-cyl — 4x2			
T17	2d Station Wagon	$14,395	2,891 lbs.
T18	4d Station Wagon	$15,433	2,932 lbs.
Cherokee SE — Four-cyl — 4x4			
J17	2d Station Wagon	$15,910	3,058 lbs.
J18	4d Station Wagon	$16,944	3,102 lbs.
Cherokee Sport — Six-cyl — 4x2			
T17	2d Station Wagon	—	—
T18	4d Station Wagon	—	—
Cherokee Sport — Six-cyl — 4x4			
J17	2d Station Wagon	—	—
J18	4d Station Wagon	—	—
Cherokee Country — Six-cyl — 4x2			
T17	2d Station Wagon	—	—
T18	4d Station Wagon	—	—
Cherokee Country — Six-cyl — 4x4			
J17	2d Station Wagon	—	—
J18	4d Station Wagon	—	—
Grand Cherokee — Six-cyl — 4x2			
X28	4d Wagon SE	$23,638	3,569 lbs.
Grand Cherokee — Six-cyl — 4x4			
ZJ	4d Wagon SE	$25,575	3,674 lbs.
ZJ	4d Wagon Laredo	—	—
ZJ	4d Wagon Limited	—	—

NOTE 1: A total of 84,969 Wranglers of all models were built (model year extended into January 1996).

NOTE 2: A total of 122,880 Cherokees of all models were built (70 percent equipped with 4x4).

NOTE 3: A total of 263,335 Grand Cherokees of all models were built (85.8 percent equipped with 4x4).

Grand Cherokee Orvis still looks good today, and its level of luxury and comfort tops that of many of today's vehicles.

PRODUCTION/SALES- As reported in the industry trade paper the *Automotive News*, Jeep's U.S. retail sales for the calendar year were 426,628.

ENGINES

(STANDARD WRANGLER S & SE, CHEROKEE SE FOUR): Inline. Overhead valve. Cast-iron block. Bore & stroke: 3.88 x 3.19 in. Displacement: 150 cid (2.5 liters). Compression ratio: 9.2:1. Brake hp: 130 at 5250 rpm (123 hp in Wrangler). Throttle body fuel injection (TBI). VIN code P.

(STANDARD CHEROKEE SPORT & COUNTRY, GRAND CHEROKEE; OPTIONAL CHEROKEE SE, WRANGLER SAHARA SIX): Inline. Overhead valve. Cast-iron block. Bore & stroke: 3.88 x 3.41 in. Displacement: 242 cid (4.0-liter). Compression ratio: 9.2:1. Brake hp: 190 at 4750 rpm. Multi-port fuel injection (MFI). VIN code S.

(OPTIONAL GRAND CHEROKEE V-8): Overhead-valve. Cast-iron block. Bore & stroke: 3.91 x 3.31 in. Displacement: 318 cid (5.2 liter). Compression ratio: 9.2:1. Brake hp: 220 at 4800 rpm. Torque: 285 lbs.-ft. at 3600 rpm. Multi-port fuel injection (MFI). VIN code Y.

CHASSIS

(WRANGLER): Wheelbase: 93.5 in. Overall length: 153 in. Height (with hardtop): 69.3 in. Width: 66 in. Tread: front and rear, 58 in. Tires: P215/75R15 RWL.

(CHEROKEE): Wheelbase: 101 in. Overall length: 165.3 in. Width: 70.5 in. Height: 63.4 in. (4x2), 63.3 in. (4x4).

(GRAND CHEROKEE): Wheelbase: 105.9 in. Overall length: 176.7 in. Width: 69.2 in. Height: 64.9 in.

TECHNICAL

(WRANGLER): Five-speed manual transmission. Floor shift. Semi-floating rear axle. Standard drive ratio: 4.11:1. Power front disc/rear drum brakes. Command-Trac shift-on-the-fly part-time four-wheel drive.

(CHEROKEE): UniFrame construction. 5-speed manual transmission. Floor shift. Semi-floating rear axle. Power front disc/rear drum brakes. 4x4 models include Command-Trac shift-on-the-fly part-time four-wheel drive.

(GRAND CHEROKEE): UniFrame construction. Quadra-Coil four-wheel coil suspension. Four-speed automatic transmission with overdrive. Floor-mounted gearshift. Brakes: four-wheel disc with ABS.

OPTIONS

(WRANGLER): Three-speed automatic transmission. Hardtop. Tilt steering. Rear Trac-Lok differential. Air conditioning. Fog lamps. Power steering. Cruise control. Heavy-duty suspension. Heavy-duty cooling. Aluminum wheels. Conventional spare tire.

A new luxury Grand Cherokee Orvis Edition arrived in 1995.

The Country model was the top of the Cherokee line for 1995. It was available in a single four-door model.

The 1995 Grand Cherokee Limited.

(CHEROKEE): Power-Tech 4.0-liter inline six-cylinder engine (optional SE, standard on other Cherokees). Four-speed automatic transmission. AM/FM stereo. AM/FM cassette. Cruise control. Tilt steering wheel. Power door locks. Power windows. Power seats. Air conditioning. Rear window defroster. Roof rack. Selec-Trac full-time 4x4.

(GRAND CHEROKEE): 5.2-liter V-8 (4x4 only). Quadra-Trac. AM/FM cassette. AM/FM CD. Fog lamps. Power sunroof. Cruise control. Tilt steering wheel. Power door locks. Power windows. Power seats. Orvis edition package.

The great-looking 1995 Cherokee Sport.

The Grand Cherokee got some styling updates for 1996. The grille was larger, front and rear fascia were new, and the body cladding was revised.

Jeep claimed that for 1996 it offered "significant styling, capability, safety and security refinements" to its vehicles.

The 4.0-liter six-cylinder engine was redesigned this year with a new stiffer block, redesigned aluminum pistons, revised camshaft, and a new engine controller. The result was a smoother, quieter engine that now developed its peak torque of 225 lbs.-ft. at just 3000 rpm, down from 4000 on prior versions. Peak horsepower (190) now developed at 4600 rpms rather than 4750 rpms. The new six felt livelier and more responsive than before.

Grand Cherokee continued to lead the market with innovations other SUVs wouldn't have for years. Recognizing that Grand Cherokee buyers were interested mainly in premium models, Jeep dropped the base Grand Cherokee SE this year. Exterior styling received a freshening with new larger grille, new front and rear fascias, new body cladding, and nameplates. Integrated fascia-mounted fog lights were new, standard on Limited, and optional on Laredo. An all-new interior debuted this year and with it came dual front air bags, a significant upgrade from the former driver-only air bag of prior years. Laredo models now featured low back seats with adjustable head restraints and both Limited and Laredo got new seat fabrics. Limited models also got new memory seat, mirror, and radio settings standard, optional heated front seats, and an electrochromic outside rear view mirror. A wide-ratio transmission was offered with the 5.2-liter V-8, and both Selec-Trac and Quadra-Trac four-wheel-drive systems were improved. A new speed-sensitive variable-assist power steering system was standard on Limited models. Re-valved shock absorbers offered ride improvements. On Limited models, new 16-inch Goodyear Eagle LS all season performance radial tires were standard equipment. *Petersen's 4-Wheel & Off-Road* magazine named Grand Cherokee "4x4 of the Year."

The Cherokee got a new automatic transmission/brake pedal interlock, standard heavy-duty battery and alternator, and standard intermittent wipers. Five new exterior colors debuted. As before, Cherokee was available in SE, Sport and Country models. In August, the Toledo plant hosted a celebration to commemorate production of the 2 millionth Cherokee, and one of the guests attending was President Bill Clinton. By this time, Cherokees were being sold in more than 100 countries around the world, and were assembled in Thailand, Indonesia, Malaysia, Venezuela, Egypt, and China, as well as Toledo, Ohio. Export versions were available in left- or right-hand drive and could be ordered with a 2.5-liter turbo diesel engine.

The big shock this year was that there was no 1996 Wrangler in the line. The company was in the process of completely redesigning Wrangler, planned to introduce the new model as early as possible, and decided to skip the 1996 model year entirely. To make sure dealers would have enough product to sell, a longer-than-normal

Jeep dropped the base model for 1996, so the Laredo was the lowest-priced Grand Cherokee.

Grand Cherokee Laredo's instrument panel for 1996.

production run of 1995 Wranglers was scheduled to tide dealers over until the new Wranglers debuted in March of 1996. The build-out of 1995 Wrangler production was extended from July to December 1995.

It proved to be a phenomenal year for Jeep with 509,183 units sold in the U.S. —a new record that marked the first time Jeep retail sales topped the half million mark in a single year.

NOTABLE FOR 1996: There wasn't a 1996 Wrangler. However, the new-generation 1997 Wrangler was

introduced early in March 1996 (see 1997 Jeep).

I.D. DATA: The VIN has 17 characters. The first three symbols indicates the country of origin (1=USA, 2=Canada), manufacturer (J=Jeep/Eagle Division), and type (4=multipurpose). The fourth indicates the gross vehicle weight rating. The fifth indicates the model line (J=4x4 Cherokee, S=Grand Wagoneer, T=4x2 Cherokee, X=Grand Cherokee 4x2, Y=Wrangler, Grand Cherokee 4x4). The sixth indicates the series (1=standard/S, 2=SE, 3=Islander, 4=Sahara, 5=Grand/Laredo, 6=Sport/Renegade/SE, 7=Limited/Country, 8=Grand Wagoneer). The seventh indicates the body style (6=pickup, 7=2d wagon, 8=4d wagon, 9=open body). These last three symbols are the models indicated in detail below. The eighth indicates the engine. The ninth is a check digit. The 10th (a letter) indicates model year (1996=T). The 11th indicates the assembly plant (C=Jefferson, L and P=Toledo, Ohio). The remaining numbers indicate the sequential production number, starting with 000001, at each plant.

Model	Body Type	Price	Weight
Cherokee SE — Four-cyl — 4x2			
T17	2d Station Wagon	$15,145	2,905 lbs.
T18	4d Station Wagon	$16,183	2,955 lbs.
Cherokee SE — Four-cyl — 4x4			
J17	2d Station Wagon	$16,660	3,069 lbs.
J18	4d Station Wagon	$17,694	3,115 lbs.

Jeep enjoyed fabulous sales for 1996, selling more than half a million vehicles in the U.S., and many more in overseas markets.

Cherokee Sport — Six-cyl — 4x2

T17	2d Station Wagon	—	—
T18	4d Station Wagon	—	—

Cherokee Sport — Six-cyl — 4x4

J17	2d Station Wagon	—	—
J18	4d Station Wagon	—	—

Cherokee Country — Six-cyl — 4x2

T18	4d Station Wagon	—	—

Cherokee Country — Six-cyl — 4x4

J18	4d Station Wagon	—	—

Grand Cherokee — Six-cyl — 4x2

X28	4d Wagon Laredo	—	—
X28	4d Wagon Limited	—	—

Grand Cherokee — Six-cyl — 4x4

Z28	4d Wagon Laredo	—	—
Z28	4d Wagon Limited	—	—

NOTE 1: A total of 84,969 Wranglers of all models were built (extended 1995 model year).

NOTE 2: A total of 185,971 Cherokees of all models were built (75.1 percent equipped with 4x4).

NOTE 3: A total of 381,528 Grand Cherokees of all models were built (81.7 percent equipped with 4x4).

PRODUCTION/SALES: Jeep reported that its U.S. retail sales for the calendar year were 509,183.

ENGINES

(STANDARD CHEROKEE SE FOUR): Inline. Overhead valve. Cast-iron block. Bore & stroke: 3.88 x 3.19 in. Displacement: 150 cid (2.5 liters). Compression ratio: 9.2:1. Brake hp: 125 at 5250 rpm. Throttle body fuel injection (TBI). VIN code P.

(STANDARD CHEROKEE SPORT & COUNTRY, GRAND CHEROKEE; OPTIONAL CHEROKEE SE SIX). Inline. Overhead-valve. Six-cylinder. Cast-iron block. Bore & stroke: 3.88 x 3.41 in.. Displacement: 242 cid (4.0-liter). Compression ratio: 9.2:1. Brake hp: 190 at 4600 rpm. Multi-port fuel injection (MFI). VIN code S.

(OPTIONAL GRAND CHEROKEE V-8): V-block. Overhead-valve. Cast-iron block. Bore & stroke: 3.91 x 3.31 in. Displacement: 318 cid (5.2 liter). Compression ratio: 9.2:1. Brake hp: 220 at 4800 rpm. Torque: 300 lbs.-ft. at 3600 rpm. Multi-port fuel injection (MFI). VIN code Y.

CHASSIS

(CHEROKEE): Wheelbase: 101 in. Overall length: 165.3 in. Width: 70.5 in. Height: 63.4 in. (4x2), 63.3 in. (4x4).

(GRAND CHEROKEE): Wheelbase: 105.9 in. Overall length: 176.7 in. Width: 69.2 in. Height: 64.9 in.

TECHNICAL

(CHEROKEE): UniFrame construction. Five-speed manual transmission. Floor shift. Semi-floating rear axle. Power front disc/rear drum brakes. 4x4 models include Command-Trac shift-on-the-fly part-time four-wheel-drive.

(GRAND CHEROKEE): UniFrame construction. Quadra-Coil four-wheel coil suspension. Four-speed automatic transmission with overdrive. Floor-mounted gearshift. Brakes: four-wheel disc with ABS.

OPTIONS

(CHEROKEE): Power-Tech 4.0-liter inline six-cylinder engine (optional SE, standard other Cherokees). Four-speed automatic transmission. AM/FM stereo. Cassette or CD radio. Cruise control. Tilt steering wheel. Power door locks, windows, seats. Air conditioning. Rear window defroster. Luggage rack. Aluminum wheels. Selec-Trac full-time four-wheel drive.

(GRAND CHEROKEE): 5.2-liter V-8. Quadra-Trac. AM/FM CD. Fog lamps. Power sunroof. Orvis package.

The 1996 Grand Cherokee Limited had style, power and luxury.

The attractive interior of the 1996 Grand Cherokee Limited.

The 1997 Jeep Wrangler Sport. Jeep traditionalists especially liked the new Wrangler's round headlights.

With two of its three core products being substantially redesigned, this was destined to be one of the busiest years for new product in Jeep history.

The first new 1997 Jeep model to debut was the Wrangler, and it bowed in early 1996 (Jeep skipped the 1996 model year for Wrangler, going from the 1995 model directly to the 1997). Aside from its round headlights, the 1997 Wrangler looked remarkably similar to the previous models, but those looks were deceiving. It was, in fact, a giant step forward in design and engineering.

Perhaps the single biggest Wrangler improvement was the all-new Quadra Coil suspension, which placed coil springs at each wheel for the best on-road ride ever experienced in a small Jeep. The new suspension also improved Wrangler's off-road performance, with an amazing 7 additional inches of articulation over the previous leaf spring setup. In addition, the frame was strengthened to increase stiffness. Torsional stiffness was

increased 15 percent while bending stiffness was 30 percent greater. Jeep boasted that Wrangler offered "the best out-of-the-box off-highway capability of any of its competitors or predecessors."

Wrangler also got stronger bumpers and a redesigned hardtop that was 15 lbs. lighter for easier removal. The soft top was completely redesigned to minimize leaks and wind noise, and was said to require less than 1/3 the time of its predecessor to raise or lower. Wrangler's instrument panel had a new modern car-like design that featured a central stack for easier adaptability to right- and left-hand-drive models. For the first time, Wrangler featured an integrated heating, ventilating, and air-conditioning (HVAC) setup. The windshield wiper motor was relocated under the hood to reduce interior noise. Front seats were taller and wider

Dimensionally, the new Wrangler was a bit over 4 in. shorter in length than the 1995 model, although it had the same 93.4-in. wheelbase. Width was about 1/2 in.

greater, and the new Wrangler was a bit taller, too.

Of course, the thing most enthusiasts noticed first were the round headlights, and for good reason. Long-time Jeep aficionados had always rejected the rectangular headlights of the original Wrangler, and some had taken to wearing t-shirts with the slogan "Real Jeeps Have Round Headlights." They weren't all that happy with the old Wrangler's bent grille, either. For them the return of the traditional-style grille and headlights was a very welcome change.

There were some other changes. Park and turn signal lights were now located on the front fenders. Hood hinges and fasteners, though still exposed, were flush-mounted for a neater appearance. The trademark hood latches were redesigned for a cleaner appearance and improved operation.

This Wrangler was the first small Jeep designed with aerodynamics in mind. The base of the windshield was pulled 4 in. forward to improve airflow for reduced wind noise, while at the same time providing room for dual airbags—the first ever offered on Wrangler. The hood sloped down a bit, not enough to be controversial, but enough to reduce wind resistance significantly.

Three models were offered: SE, Sport and Sahara. As before, the base Wrangler SE came with the 2.5-liter four

cylinder, while the two upper models got the 4.0-liter six. Automatic transmission was available only with the Sport and Sahara.

The 2.5-liter was rated at 120 hp @ 5400 rpm and 140 lbs.-ft. of torque @ 3500 rpm. Improvements in camshaft profile and valve springs provided increased low-speed torque as well as smoother, quieter operation. The total investment in bringing the new Wrangler to market was $260 million. It seemed worth the effort: *Petersen's 4-Wheel & Off-Road* magazine picked the 1997 Wrangler to receive its "4x4 of the Year" award.

Midway through the model year a substantially refined XJ Cherokee was introduced. Although it retained the same basic design as the original 1984 model, for 1997 Cherokee received a complete freshening that improved it in many ways. After 13 years with little change, it was probably due.

The primary focus of the makeover was on a new interior, plus changes throughout the vehicle to reduce noise, vibration, and harshness. Front doors now featured one-piece glass, eliminating the small triangular glass panes to reduce wind noise. An entirely new instrument panel of modular design incorporated a new passenger-side airbag (the drivers side airbag had already been standard equipment). The modular dashboard was designed so that both right- and left-

The 1997 Sahara was the top of the Wrangler line.

Like Wrangler, Cherokee XJ got an all-new instrument panel with a "central stack" design in 1997.

Jeep Cherokee Country's interior was fancier and included wood-grain accents.

hand-drive versions could be produced with a minimum of fuss. Heating, ventilation, air-conditioning and radio controls were all placed in a center stack. The new HVAC system greatly improved airflow throughout the vehicle while reducing noise. A new center console incorporated rear seat heating vents, cup holders and new shift levers. New wingback seats with wide side bolsters, taken from Grand Cherokee, were standard equipment on Sport models, and optional on SE. An overhead console with trip computer was a new option.

On the exterior there was a new grille and headlight bezels, and new plastic end caps on the bumpers that blended into the side moldings. Under-bumper fog lamps were a new option. The overall look of the front end was softer and more rounded. At the rear, Cherokee's old plastic liftgate was replaced by a stamped-steel liftgate that allowed closer tolerances and was easier to close. The new liftgate also had a cleaner-looking design that greatly modernized Cherokee's appearance. A CHMSL was added just above the rear window. In addition,

overall build quality was improved by use of new or reconditioned stamping dies for all major body panels.

As before, three models were offered: SE, Sport and Country. SE and Sport were offered in two- or four-door models, while the Country came in a four-door style only. All could be had in either two-wheel-drive or four-wheel-drive models.

Meanwhile, the 1997 Grand Cherokee offered some new features. At announcement time, three Grand Cherokee models were offered: Laredo, Limited, and Orvis Edition. The Orvis Edition offered a new Light Driftwood color. The V-8 was now also available in a two-wheel-drive model. All Grand Cherokees benefited from improved floor carpeting appearance and fit, as well as an extended rear seat heating duct.

Later in the model year a sporty new Grand Cherokee TSI model was unveiled. The TSI included aggressive 16-in. wheels, Goodyear Eagle LS

Jeep Cherokee's styling was freshened up for 1997, and many improvements were introduced. The rear hatch was completely redesigned for better fit and easier use.

performance tires, and unique tape stripes. TSI interior trim included Rustic Bird's Eye Maple wood-grain trim and leather seats.

However, despite all the improvements to the Jeep lineup, retail sales fell to 472,872 units for the year. Other companies were introducing many new SUVs to the market, and competition was getting fierce.

NOTABLE FOR 1997: The all-new Wrangler TJ was introduced in March 1996, and came in three models: SE, Sport, and Sahara. The Cherokee was substantially improved this year. There was a new grille, new rear hatch, and an all-new interior. Inside was an all-new HVAC (heating/ventilation/air conditioning) system. Three models were offered: SE, Sport, and Country. Grand Cherokee got a new ABS system. Models were the Laredo, TSi, and Limited.

I.D. DATA: The VIN has 17 characters. The first three symbols indicate the country of origin (1=USA, 2=Canada), manufacturer (J=Jeep/Eagle Division), and type (4=multipurpose). The fourth indicates the gross vehicle weight rating. The fifth indicates the model line (J=4x4 Cherokee, S=Grand Wagoneer, T=4x2 Cherokee, X=Grand Cherokee 4x2, Y=Wrangler, Grand Cherokee 4x4). The sixth indicates the series (1=standard/S, 2=SE, 3=Islander, 4=Sahara, 5=Grand/Laredo, 6=Sport/Renegade/SE, 7=Limited/Country, 8=Grand Wagoneer). The seventh indicates the body style (6=pickup, 7=two-door wagon, 8=four-door wagon, 9=open body). These last three symbols are the models indicated in detail below. The eighth indicates the engine. The ninth is a check digit. The 10th (a letter) indicates model year (1997=V). The 11th indicates the assembly plant (C=Jefferson, L and P=Toledo, Ohio). The remaining numbers indicate the sequential production number, starting with 000001, at each plant.

Model	Body Type	Price	Weight
Wrangler TJ — 1/4-Ton — 4x4			
TJ	Wrangler SE	$13,995	3,093 lbs.
TJ	Wrangler Sport	—	3,229 lbs.
TJ	Wrangler Sahara	—	3,229 lbs.
Cherokee SE — Four-cyl — 4x2			
T27	2d Station Wagon	$15,300	2,947 lbs.
T28	4d Station Wagon	$16,340	2,993 lbs.
Cherokee SE — Four-cyl — 4x4			
J27	2d Station Wagon	$16,815	3,129 lbs.
J28	4d Station Wagon	$17,850	3,177 lbs.
Cherokee Sport — Six-cyl — 4x2			
T27	2d Station Wagon	—	3,150 lbs.
T28	4d Station Wagon	—	3,183 lbs.
Cherokee Sport — Six-cyl — 4x4			
J27	2d Station Wagon	—	3,312 lbs.
J28	4d Station Wagon	—	3,349 lbs.
Cherokee Country — Six-cyl — 4x2			
T28	4d Station Wagon	—	3,349 lbs.
Cherokee Country — Six-cyl — 4x4			
J28	4d Station Wagon	—	3,349 lbs.
Grand Cherokee — Six-cyl — 4x2			
ZJ	4d Wagon Laredo	$25,545	3,613 lbs.
ZJ	4d Wagon TSI	—	3,613 lbs.
ZJ	4d Wagon Limited	—	3,613 lbs.
ZJ	4d Wagon Orvis	—	3,613 lbs.
Grand Cherokee — Six-cyl — 4x4			
ZJ	4d Wagon Laredo	$27,515	3,790 lbs.
ZJ	4d Wagon TSI	—	3,790 lbs.
ZJ	4d Wagon Limited	—	3,790 lbs.
ZJ	4d Wagon Orvis	—	3,790 lbs.

PRODUCTION/SALES: Jeep reported that its U.S. retail sales for the calendar year were 472,872.

ENGINES

(STANDARD WRANGLER SE, CHEROKEE SE FOUR): Inline. Overhead valve. Cast-iron block. Bore & stroke: 3.88 x 3.19 in. Displacement: 150 cid (2.5 liters). Compression ratio: 9.2:1. Brake hp: 120 at 5400 rpm. (125 hp in Cherokee) Throttle body fuel injection (TBI). VIN Code P.

(STANDARD WRANGLER SPORT & SAHARA, CHEROKEE SPORT & COUNTRY, GRAND CHEROKEE — OPTIONAL CHEROKEE SE SIX): Inline. Overhead valve. Cast-iron block. Bore & stroke: 3.88 x 3.41 in. Displacement: 242 cid (4.0 liter). Compression ratio: 9.2:1. Brake hp: 190 at 4600 rpm (181 hp in Wrangler). Multi-port fuel injection (MFI).

(OPTIONAL GRAND CHEROKEE V-8): Overhead valve. Eight-cylinder. Cast-iron block. Bore & stroke: 3.91 x 3.31 in. Displacement: 318 cid (5.2 liter). Compression ratio: 9.2:1. Brake hp: 220 at 4800 rpm. Torque: 300 lbs.-ft. at 3600 rpm. Multi-port fuel injection (MFI). VIN Code Y.

CHASSIS

(WRANGLER): Wheelbase: 93.4 in. Overall length: 147.4 in. Height: 69.3 in. Width: 66.7 in. Tires: P215/75R15 OWL.

(CHEROKEE): Wheelbase: 101 in. Overall length: 165.3 in. Width: 70.5 in. Height: 63.4 in. (4x2), 63.3 in. (4x4).

(GRAND CHEROKEE): Wheelbase: 105.9 in. Overall length: 176.7 in. Width: 69.2 in. Height: 64.9 in.

TECHNICAL

(WRANGLER): Five-speed manual transmission. Floor shift. Semi-floating rear axle. Standard drive ratio: 4.11:1 Power front disc/rear drum brakes. Command-Trac shift-on-the-fly part-time four-wheel drive.

(CHEROKEE): UniFrame construction. Five-speed manual transmission. Floor shift. Semi-floating rear axle. Power front disc/rear drum brakes. 4x4 models included Command-Trac shift-on-the-fly part-time four-wheel drive.

(GRAND CHEROKEE): UniFrame construction.

The Grand Cherokee Orvis Edition for 1997.

Quadra-Coil four-wheel coil suspension. Four-speed automatic transmission with overdrive. Floor-mounted gearshift. Brakes: four-wheel disc with ABS.

OPTIONS

(WRANGLER): Automatic transmission. Air conditioning. Premium AM/FM stereo with cassette. Four-wheel ABS (Sport and Sahara). Aluminum wheels. Rear seat (SE). Hardtop.

(CHEROKEE): Power-Tech 4.0-liter inline six-cylinder engine (optional SE, standard all other Cherokees). Four-speed automatic transmission. AM/FM stereo. AM/FM CD. Cruise control. Tilt steering wheel. Sunroof. Power door locks, windows & seats. Air conditioning. Roof rack. Aluminum wheels. Selec-Trac full-time four-wheel drive.

(GRAND CHEROKEE): 5.2-liter V-8. Quadra-Trac. AM/FM CD. Power sunroof.

The Grand Cherokee 5.9 Limited was the fastest-accelerating SUV on the market, and the fastest Jeep ever. Note the unique grille and blackwall tires.

The 1998 new model announcement had some surprises this year. The most exciting news was a new Grand Cherokee model, the 5.9 Limited. Boasting a 5.9-liter (360-cid) V-8 that produced 245 hp and an amazing 335 lbs.-ft. of torque, Grand Cherokee 5.9 Limited set a new standard in high-performance SUVs. It was the fastest-accelerating SUV on the market and the fastest Jeep vehicle ever produced. Its 0 to 60-mph acceleration time of 7.3 seconds rivaled European high-performance machines, yet it retained all its legendary Jeep off-road performance capabilities. A new 46 RE transmission was included, along with a high-strength output shaft on the model 249 transfer case, electric cooling fan, and a high-output 150-amp alternator.

5.9 Limited models came standard with a Track-Lok rear axle and on-demand Quadra-Trac four-wheel-drive system. On the inside were leather-trimmed seats, door bolsters and armrests, leather-covered console armrest, and Rustic Bird's Eye Maple wood-grain accents on various interior pieces, including the instrument panel and door panels. The standard seats were 10-way power

adjustable, heated, and leather covered. Also included were steering wheel-mounted controls for the 180-watt, 10-speaker sound system. Additional standard features included a power sunroof and contoured black roof rack. New 16-in. Ultra Sparkle silver aluminum wheels were unique to the 5.9 Limited. A fine-mesh grille insert, louvered hood, and large chrome exhaust tip were unique, as were the 5.9 chrome badges on the side and rear of the vehicle.

Priced at $38,700, the 5.9 Limited was offered in three exterior colors: bright platinum, stone white, and deep slate. *Petersen's 4-Wheel & Off-Road* magazine gave Grand Cherokee 5.9 Limited its "4x4 of the Year" award.

In addition to the 5.9 Limited, the Grand Cherokee lineup included Laredo, TSi, and Limited models. The Orvis model was dropped. Wrangler HP VSB tires were new, along with airbags that deployed with less force, and a redesigned ignition key lock for improved security. The steering system offered improved response.

The 1998 Grand Cherokee Laredo was a very popular model.

The 1998 Cherokee Classic.

The 1998 Cherokee was available in two- and four-door models in both two- and four-wheel drive. This four-wheel-drive model is a Cherokee Sport.

The Cherokee model lineup was revised. In addition to the carryover SE and Sport models, a new Classic was added, and the Cherokee Country was replaced by a new Cherokee Limited. The Cherokee Classic was slotted in between the mid-range Sport and top-line Limited models. Monotone exterior paint and low-back seats with adjustable head restraints set the Classic apart from the Sport. Automatic transmission was standard on Classic and Limited models, and optional on Sport models. The SE offered automatic transmission only with two-wheel-drive models. Command-Trac part-time four-wheel drive was standard on SE, Sport, and Classic four-wheel-drive models, while Selec-Trac came standard on Cherokee Limited, and was optional on the others. The 4.0-liter six was standard on Sport, Classic, and Limited, and optional on SE, which got the 2.5-liter four as standard. Cherokees also got new airbags that deployed with less force. Each Cherokee model had its own distinct standard wheel. SEs got six-spoke styled steel wheels, Sports got full-face five-spoke styled steel wheels, Classics got Ecco cast aluminum five-spoke wheels painted Dark Quartz, and Limiteds got Luxury cast-aluminum wheels with Dark Silver accents.

Jeep Wranglers got improved off-road performance. A Dana 44 rear axle with a new 3.73:1 ratio replaced the former 3.55:1 ratio optional on 4.0-liter-equipped Wranglers. Steering response was also improved, and power steering was made standard equipment on all models. New Wrangler options included automatic speed control, Smart Key Immobilzer theft deterrent system, an easy-entry tilting driver's seat, and a sound system with cassette and CD players. The new reduced-force airbags were also included.

Jeep sales slipped a bit further this year, to 459,294, despite an overall improvement in the light-truck market. But a new Grand Cherokee was waiting in the wings and it was about to be unveiled. Jeep was going to end the decade with a bang

NOTABLE FOR 1998: An aluminum radiator was now fitted to all Cherokees. The Country model was dropped. The Cherokee Classic and Limited were new this year. Grand Cherokee offered a new 5.9 Limited model.

I.D. DATA: The VIN has 17 characters. The first three symbols indicate the country of origin (1=USA, 2=Canada), manufacturer (J=Jeep/Eagle Division), and type (4=multipurpose). The fourth indicates the gross vehicle weight rating. The fifth indicates the model line (J=4x4 Cherokee, S=Grand Wagoneer, T=4x2 Cherokee, X=Grand Cherokee 4x2, Y=Wrangler, Grand Cherokee 4x4). The sixth indicates the series (1=standard/S, 2=SE, 3=Islander, 4=Sahara, 5=Grand/Laredo, 6=Sport/Renegade/SE, 7=Limited/ Country, 8=Grand Wagoneer). The seventh indicates the body style (6=pickup, 7=two-door wagon, 8=four-door wagon, 9=open body). These last three symbols are the models indicated in detail below. The eighth indicates the engine. The ninth is a check digit. The 10th (a letter) indicates model year (1998=W). The 11th indicates the assembly plant (C=Jefferson, L and P=Toledo, Ohio). The remaining numbers indicate the sequential

Jerry Heasley photo

The 1998 Grand Cherokee 5.9 Limited.

production number starting with 000001 at each plant.

Model	Body Type	Price	Weight
Wrangler TJ — 4x4			
TJ	Wrangler SE	$14,615	3,045 lbs.
TJ	Wrangler Sport	—	3,257 lbs.
TJ	Wrangler Sahara	—	3,257 lbs.
Cherokee SE — Four-cyl — 4x2			
T27	2d Station Wagon	$15,965	2,979 lbs.
T28	4d Station Wagon	$17,005	3,032 lbs.
Cherokee SE — Four-cyl — 4x4			
J27	2d Station Wagon	$17,480	3,125 lbs.
J28	4d Station Wagon	$18,515	3,181 lbs.
Cherokee Sport — Six-cyl — 4x2			
T27	2d Station Wagon	—	3,150 lbs.
T28	4d Station Wagon	—	3,199 lbs.
Cherokee Sport — Six-cyl — 4x4			
J27	2d Station Wagon	—	3,307 lbs.
J28	4d Station Wagon	—	3,354 lbs.
Cherokee Classic — Six-cyl — 4x2			
T28	4d Station Wagon	—	3,199 lbs.
Cherokee Classic — Six-cyl — 4x4			
J28	4d Station Wagon	—	3,354 lbs.
Cherokee Limited — Six-cyl — 4x2			
T28	4d Station Wagon	—	3,349 lbs.
Cherokee Limited — Six-cyl — 4x4			
J28	4d Station Wagon	—	3,349 lbs.
Grand Cherokee — Six-cyl — 4x2			
ZJ	4d Wagon Laredo	$25,545	3,621 lbs.
ZJ	4d Wagon Limited	—	3,621 lbs.
Grand Cherokee — Six-cyl — 4x4			
ZJ	4d Wagon Laredo	$27,515	3,800 lbs.
ZJ	4d Wagon TSI	—	3,800 lbs.
ZJ	4d Wagon Limited	—	3,800 lbs.
Grand Cherokee — V-8 — 4x4			
ZJ	4d Wagon 5.9 Limited	—	4,218 lbs.

PRODUCTION/SALES: Jeep reported that its U.S. retail sales for calendar year 1998 were 459,294.

ENGINES

(STANDARD WRANGLER SE, CHEROKEE SE FOUR): Inline. Overhead valve. Cast-iron block. Bore & stroke: 3.88 x 3.19 in. Displacement: 150 cid (2.5 liters). Compression ratio: 9.2:1. Brake hp: 120 at 5400 rpm. (125 hp in Cherokee).

(STANDARD CHEROKEE SPORT, CLASSIC & LIMITED, GRAND CHEROKEE, WRANGLER SPORT & SAHARA): Inline. Overhead valve. Six-cylinder. Cast-iron block. Bore & stroke: 3.88 x 3.41. Displacement: 242 cid (4.0 liter). Compression ratio: 9.2:1. Brake hp: 190 at 4600 rpm (181 hp in Wranglers).

Grand Cherokee 5.9 Limited could outperform many so-called performance coupes!

Performance enthusiasts and luxury buyers could find what they wanted in the 5.9 Limited.

Multi-port fuel injection.

(OPTIONAL GRAND CHEROKEE V-8): Overhead valve. Cast-iron block. Bore & stroke: 3.91 x 3.31 in. Displacement: 318 cid (5.2 liter). Compression ratio: 9.2:1. Brake hp: 220 at 4800 rpm. Torque: 300 lbs.-ft. at 3600 rpm. Multi-port fuel injection.

(STANDARD GRAND CHEROKEE 5.9 LIMITED V-8): Overhead valve. Cast-iron block. Bore & stroke: 4.00 x 3.58 in. Displacement: 360 cid (5.9 liter). Compression ratio: 8.7:1. Brake hp: 245 at 4000 rpm. Torque: 345 lbs.-ft. at 3200 rpm. Multi-port fuel injection.

CHASSIS

(WRANGLER): Wheelbase: 93.4 in. Overall length: 147.4 in. Height: 69.3 in. Width: 66.7 in. Tires: P215/75R15 RWL.

(CHEROKEE): Wheelbase: 101 in. Overall length: 165.3 in. Width: 70.5 in. Height: 63.4 in. (4x2), 63.3 in. (4x4).

(GRAND CHEROKEE): Wheelbase: 105.9 in. Overall length: 176.7 in. Width: 69.2 in. Height: 64.9 in.

TECHNICAL

(WRANGLER): Five-speed manual transmission. Floor shift. Semi-floating rear axle. Standard axle ratio: 4.11:1.

Power front disc/rear drum brakes. Command-Trac shift-on-the-fly part-time four-wheel drive.

(CHEROKEE): UniFrame construction. Five-speed manual transmission. Floor shift. Semi-floating rear axle. Power front disc/rear drum brakes. 4x4 models include Command-Trac shift-on-the-fly part-time four-wheel drive.

(GRAND CHEROKEE): UniFrame construction. Quadra-Coil four-wheel coil suspension. Four-speed automatic transmission with overdrive. Floor shift. Brakes: four-wheel disc with ABS.

OPTIONS

(WRANGLER): Automatic transmission. Air conditioning. Premium AM/FM cassette. Four-wheel ABS (Sport and Sahara). Aluminum wheels. Rear seat (SE). Hardtop.

(CHEROKEE): Four-speed automatic transmission. AM/FM stereo. AM/FM cassette. Cruise control. Tilt steering wheel. Sunroof. Selec-Trac full-time four-wheel drive.

(GRAND CHEROKEE): 5.2-liter V-8. Quadra-Trac. Power sunroof.

In 1999, as before, the top of the Wrangler line was the Wrangler Sahara.

The biggest news for Jeep in 1999, product-wise, was an all-new Grand Cherokee. Chrysler management bragged that the new Jeep was the most changed vehicle in its history, claiming that the only parts carried over from the previous Grand Cherokee were 127 assorted screws, washers, and small fasteners. Chrysler didn't mince words when it came to describing its new Grand Cherokee. The firm called it "the most capable sport utility ever."

Essentially, every part of it had been redesigned and improved. The body was new, a rugged yet very stylish sport wagon. A V-shaped grille with Jeep's trademark seven slots was the centerpiece of the new front-end styling. New jewel-look headlights imparted an expensive look, while at the same time offering increased visibility. Extended body-color wheel arches reminded users that Grand Cherokee was still a serious off-roader. The new body structure was stiffer than before, for a quieter ride and less vibration. Only two Grand Cherokee models were offered for 1999: Laredo and Limited.

A new 4.7-liter V-8 replaced the former 5.2- and 5.9-liter V-8s. The new 4.7-liter offered 235 hp (15 more than the old V-8), faster acceleration, better fuel efficiency, and lower emissions. It even weighed 54 lbs. less. A new fully electronic automatic transmission debuted for the V-8, which utilized computer logic to automatically chose among a range of gear ratios to provide improved acceleration, shift smoothness, and quietness. Jeep called it a multi-speed transmission, though it was also referred to as a five-speed automatic. The V-8/automatic combination was rated at an outstanding 15 mpg city and 19 highway. Grand Cherokee also debuted the new Quadra-Drive four-wheel-drive system, in which the all-new Quadra-Trac II on-demand transfer case was mated to new Vari-Lok front and rear progressive axles. Quadra-Drive could transfer torque both front and rear as well as side to side, so that if only one wheel had traction the vehicle could still get through. One hundred percent of engine power could be directed to one wheel if necessary. Best of all, it worked automatically—so seamlessly that a driver might never feel it working.

The base 4.0-liter six-cylinder engine received improvements that boosted rated power to 195 hp and 230 lbs.-ft. of torque. Six-cylinder Grand Cherokees continued to offer the excellent four-speed automatic gearbox. A new 3.1-liter five-cylinder turbo-diesel engine debuted for international markets.

Grand Cherokee also got a new Quadra Coil suspension with refinements up front and all-new components in the rear. An all-new brake system with 12-in. brake rotors and dual piston front calipers for best-in-class braking ability, according to independent testing.

One major improvement was a spare tire stowed inside the vehicle, under the rear floor, a feature unique to Grand Cherokee among domestic SUVs.

Interiors were new and more luxurious than ever. Grand Cherokee Limited introduced an amazing improvement in air conditioning this year with its Infrared Dual Zone Climate Control System that continually measured surface temperatures of a range of interior areas, including both front seat passengers, and automatically adjusted the airflow and temperature to maintain the selected comfort level. Jeep bragged that if you had a fever, the air-conditioning would automatically adjust itself to keep you comfy.

Peterson's 4-Wheel & Off-Road magazine named Grand Cherokee "4x4 of the Year." The magazine *FOUR WHEELER* voted it "Four Wheeler of the Year." In addition, Grand Cherokee was named the "1999 North American Truck of the Year" by a panel of 48 influential automotive journalists.

Jeep Cherokee continued to offer four models for 1999. SE and Sport were available in either two- or four-door models, while Classic and Limited were offered in four-door models only. Cherokee Sport offered a freshened exterior appearance with body-color grille, headlight surrounds, front and rear bumpers, and rear license plate brow. Limited models offered optional heated seats with six-way power adjustment. All Cherokees got improved weather stripping around door windows to minimize wind noise and water intrusion. Chrysler's Sentry Key immobilizer was offered for the first time on Cherokee. The air-conditioning compressor included a shut-off strategy, automatically shutting down for a few seconds to improve low-speed performance when needed. Export Cherokees came only in four-wheel-drive models and offered a 113-hp 2.5-liter turbo diesel engine.

Jeep Wrangler's lineup for 1999 consisted of the SE, Sport, and Sahara models. New rotary controls for heating, ventilation, and air-conditioning were featured, plus new interior trim colors. A new Dark Tan color debuted for both hard and soft tops. There was an on/off switch for the front passenger air bag. Wrangler's frame was redesigned and now weighed 16 lbs. less.

Midway through the year it was announced that Chrysler Corporation was joining Daimler-Benz, builder of the Mercedes-Benz, in what was termed a "merger of equals." Jeep would have a new corporate parent—its fifth thus far.

In this final year of the decade, Jeep's sales network knocked the cover off the ball. For the calendar year, Jeep sold a total of 554,466 units in the U.S., a new record. Each of the three Jeep model series improved over the prior year, with Grand Cherokee leading the group with 300,031 sales. The company announced that it was looking for a plant to increase Grand Cherokee production. Plants in Detroit, Austria, Venezuela,

Jerry Heasley photo

The 1999 Wrangler Sports had a few minor changes. The Wranglers were also offered in SE and Sahara trim levels

Argentina, and Thailand could produce about 430,000 Grand Cherokees per year, but worldwide demand was running much higher than that. Jeep was on a roll.

NOTABLE FOR 1999: Grand Cherokee was all-new this year. A new 4.7-liter V-8 engine was coupled to an all-new four-wheel drive system, Quadra-Drive. With Quadra-Drive the transfer case could direct all of the engine's torque to one wheel. The Grand Cherokee came in Laredo and Limited models.

I.D. DATA: The VIN has 17 characters. The first three symbols indicate the country of origin (1=USA, 2=Canada), manufacturer (J=Jeep/Eagle Division), and type (4=multipurpose). The fourth indicates the gross vehicle weight rating. The fifth indicates the model line (J=4x4 Cherokee, S=Grand Wagoneer, T=4x2 Cherokee, X=Grand Cherokee 4x2, Y=Wrangler, Grand Cherokee 4x4). The sixth indicates the series (1=standard/S, 2=SE, 3=Islander, 4=Sahara, 5=Grand/Laredo, 6=Sport/Renegade/SE, 7=Limited 8=Grand Wagoneer). The seventh indicates the body style (6=pickup, 7=two-door wagon, 8=four-door wagon, 9=open body). These last three symbols are the models indicated in detail below. The eighth indicates the engine. The ninth is a check digit. The 10th (a letter) indicates model year (1999=X). The 11th indicates the assembly plant (C=Jefferson, L and P=Toledo, Ohio). The remaining numbers indicate the sequential production number starting with 000001 at each plant.

Model	Body Type	Price	Weight
Wrangler TJ — 4x4			
TJ	Wrangler SE	$14,805	3,060 lbs.
TJ	Wrangler Sport	—	3,216 lbs.
TJ	Wrangler Sahara	—	3,216 lbs.

Cherokee SE — Four-cyl — 4x2			
T27	2d Station Wagon	$16,405	3,017 lbs.
T28	4d Station Wagon	$17,445	3,067 lbs.
Cherokee SE — Four-cyl — 4x4			
J27	2d Station Wagon	$17,920	3,180 lbs.
J28	4d Station Wagon	$18,995	3,224 lbs.
Cherokee Sport — Six-cyl — 4x2			
T27	2d Station Wagon	—	3,154 lbs.
T28	4d Station Wagon	—	3,194 lbs.
Cherokee Sport — Six-cyl — 4x4			
J27	2d Station Wagon	—	3,337 lbs.
J28	4d Station Wagon	—	3,386 lbs.
Cherokee Classic — Six-cyl — 4x2			
T28	4d Station Wagon	—	3,194 lbs.
Cherokee Classic — Six-cyl — 4x4			
J28	4d Station Wagon	—	3,386 lbs.
Cherokee Limited — Six-cyl — 4x2			
T28	4d Station Wagon	—	3,386 lbs.
Cherokee Limited — Six-cyl — 4x4			
J28	4d Station Wagon	—	3,386 lbs.
Grand Cherokee — Six-cyl — 4x2			
X58	4d Wagon Laredo	$26,220	3,739 lbs.
X58	4d Wagon Limited	—	3,739 lbs.
Grand Cherokee — Six-cyl — 4x4			
Z58	4d Wagon Laredo	$28,190	3,916 lbs.
Z58	4d Wagon Limited	—	3,916 lbs.

PRODUCTION/SALES: For the final year of the decade, Jeep reported U.S. retail sales of 554,466 units.

ENGINES

(STANDARD WRANGLER SE & CHEROKEE SE FOUR): Inline. Overhead valve. Cast-iron block. Bore &

Jeep Cherokee Sport for 1999 was offered in both two- or four-wheel-drive models and with either two or four doors.

stroke: 3.88 x 3.19 in. Displacement: 150 cid (2.5 liters). Compression ratio: 9.2:1. Brake hp: 120 at 5400 rpm (125 hp in Cherokee). Throttle body fuel injection (TBI). VIN code P.

(STANDARD CHEROKEE SPORT, CLASSIC, & LIMITED; GRAND CHEROKEE — OPTIONAL WRANGLER SPORT & SAHARA SIX): Inline. Overhead-valve. Cast-iron block. Bore & stroke: 3.88 x 3.41 in. Displacement: 242 cid (4.0-liter). Compression ratio: 9.2:1. Brake hp: 190 at 4600 rpm (181 hp in Wrangler). Multi-port fuel injection (MFI).

(OPTIONAL GRAND CHEROKEE V-8): Overhead valve. Cast-iron block. Bore & stroke: 3.91 x 3.31 in. Displacement: 287 cid (4.7 liter). Compression ratio: 9.3:1. Brake hp: 235 at 4800 rpm. Torque: 295 lbs.-ft. at 3200 rpm. Multi-port fuel injection (MFI).

CHASSIS

(WRANGLER): Wheelbase: 93.4 in. Overall length: 147.4 in. Height: 69.3 in. Width: 66.7 in. Tires: P215/75R15 RWL.

(CHEROKEE): Wheelbase: 101 in. Overall length: 165.3 in. Width: 70.5 in. Height: 63.4 in. (4x2), 63.3 in. (4x4).

(GRAND CHEROKEE): Wheelbase: 105.9 in. Overall length: 181.5 in. Width: 72.3 in. Height: 69.4 in.

TECHNICAL

(WRANGLER): Five-speed manual transmission. Floor shift. Semi-floating rear axle. Standard drive ratio: 4.11:1. Power front disc/rear drum brakes. Command-Trac shift-on-the-fly part-time four-wheel drive.

(CHEROKEE): UniFrame construction. Five-speed manual transmission. Floor shift. Semi-floating rear axle. Power front disc/rear drum brakes. 4x4 models include Command-Trac shift-on-the-fly part-time four-wheel drive, except Limited, which includes Selec-Trac full-time four-wheel drive.

(GRAND CHEROKEE): UniFrame construction. Quadra-Coil four-wheel coil suspension. Four-speed automatic transmission with overdrive. Floor shift. Brakes: four-wheel disc with ABS.

OPTIONS

(WRANGLER): Three-speed automatic transmission. Air Conditioning. Tilt steering wheel. Cruise control. AM/FM stereo cassette. Four-wheel ABS (Sport and Sahara). Aluminum wheels. Rear seat (SE only). Hardtop.

(CHEROKEE): Four-speed automatic transmission. AM/FM stereo. AM/FM stereo Cassette. Cruise control. Tilt steering wheel. Power door locks. Power windows. Power seats. Air conditioning. Rear window defroster. Luggage rack. Aluminum wheels. Selec-Trac full-time four-wheel drive (standard Cherokee Limited).

(GRAND CHEROKEE): 5.2-liter V-8 (four-wheel-drive models only). Power sunroof. Quadra-Trac.

The 1999 Grand Cherokee also got a new 4.7-liter V-8 engine.

Grand Cherokee was redesigned for 1999. The 1999 is the one in the foreground.

JEEP VEHICLES IN THE NEW MILLENNIUM
2000-2003

When the decade of the 2000s opened (the so-called "New Millennium" though technically that didn't start until 2001), Jeep was once again involved in integrating itself into a new corporate parent. This time it was DaimlerChrysler, the German-owned firm created by the merger of Daimler-Benz and Chrysler. The new company's automotive products now included Mercedes-Benz, Plymouth, Dodge, Chrysler, and Jeep vehicles.

It was an easy decision to leave Jeep's engineering and product development teams pretty much as they had been, because despite M-B's undeniable skill in engineering automobiles, when it came to SUVs, it didn't have anywhere near the expertise the Jeep engineers possessed.

Jeep Cherokee Classic for 2000. Although the Cherokee XJ had been on the market for 17 years, it continued to be very popular. Cherokee was one of the most popular American vehicles in overseas markets, too.

There were only detail changes on the 2000 model Jeep vehicles. After all, in the period since 1997 every Jeep vehicle had been either completely redesigned or substantially upgraded. Jeep product development teams now were working on the next big step forward for Jeep vehicles.

Grand Cherokee, redesigned just one year earlier, returned for 2000 with an important new option: the Mopar Navigation System that used Global Positioning System satellite technology to guide drivers to their destinations. Navigation systems were showing up among other U.S. cars and, although early retail demand was less than expected, the public clearly was interested. Also new this year was Jeep's offering of the 4.7-liter V-8 engine on two-wheel-drive Grand Cherokee models.

Grand Cherokee's Quadra-Drive system got many compliments. *AutoWeek* magazine said "We were unable to find a situation that could confuse Grand Cherokee's Quadra-Drive four-wheel-drive system—on-road or off. The driver doesn't need to adjust switches or knobs, the system just does what it's supposed to do, as it did when we drove through a muddy puddle and could feel the various wheels pull or push as needed to get us through." As before, Grand Cherokee offered Laredo and Limited models.

Jeep Cherokee was offered in the same SE, Sport, Classic, and Limited models as before, but there were some refinements. Cherokee Limited now featured a very attractive bright grille, while Classic and Sport models continued to use a body-color grille, and the SE models had a black grille. Cherokee Limited models now included 16 x 7-in. Icon cast-aluminum Sparkle Silver wheels.

Wrangler continued to offer the same base SE, Sport, and Sahara. Wrangler Sahara now included as standard equipment the 16 x 7-in. Ultra Star cast-aluminum wheels. Optional on Sahara and Sport were new 15 x 8-in. Canyon cast-aluminum wheels, available with the 30-in. Tire and Wheel Group that also included heavy-duty suspension and 30 x 9.5-in. R15 Goodyear Wrangler GS-A OWL all-terrain tires, plus a full-size spare with a matching wheel.

For the year Jeep sold 495,434 vehicles in the U.S., down quite a bit from 1999. Still, when all was said and done, a half-million Jeeps at retail was nothing to sneeze at. It was a pretty decent year.

NOTABLE FOR 2000: There were only a handful of changes this year. Cherokee Limited got some exterior trim changes. Grand Cherokee got interior refinements.

I.D. DATA: VIN has 17 characters.

Model	Body Type	Price	Weight
Wrangler TJ — 4x4			
TJ	Wrangler SE	$14,995	3,060 lbs.
TJ	Wrangler Sport	—	3,216 lbs.
TJ	Wrangler Sahara	—	3,216 lbs.
Cherokee SE — Four-cyl — 4x2			
T27	2d Station Wagon	$17,215	3,014 lbs.
T28	4d Station Wagon	$18,255	3,067 lbs.
Cherokee SE — Four-cyl — 4x4			
J27	2d Station Wagon	$18,730	3,180 lbs.
J28	4d Station Wagon	$19,765	3,274 lbs.
Cherokee Sport — Six-cyl — 4x2			
T27	2d Station Wagon	—	3,154 lbs.
T28	4d Station Wagon	—	3,194 lbs.
Cherokee Sport — Six-cyl — 4x4			
J27	2d Station Wagon	—	3,313 lbs.
J28	4d Station Wagon	—	3,386 lbs.
Cherokee Classic — Six-cyl — 4x2			
T28	4d Station Wagon	—	3,194 lbs.
Cherokee Classic — Six-cyl — 4x4			
J28	4d Station Wagon	—	3,386 lbs.
Cherokee Limited — Six-cyl — 4x2			
J28	4d Station Wagon	—	3,194 lbs.
Cherokee Limited — Six-cyl — 4x4			
J28	4d Station Wagon	—	3,386 lbs.
Grand Cherokee — Six-cyl — 4x2			
X58	4d Wagon Laredo	—	3,773 lbs.
X58	4d Wagon Limited	—	3,773 lbs.
Grand Cherokee — Six-cyl — 4x4			
Z58	4d Wagon Laredo	—	3,955 lbs.
X58	4d Wagon Limited	—	3,955 lbs.

ENGINES

(STANDARD WRANGLER SE FOUR): Inline. Overhead valve. Cast-iron block. Bore & stroke 3.88 x 3.19 in. Displacement: 150 cid (2.5 liters). Compression ratio: 9.2:1. Brake hp: 120 at 5400 rpm.

(STANDARD CHEROKEE SE FOUR): Inline. Overhead valve. Cast-iron block. Bore & stroke 3.88 x 3.19 in. Displacement: 150 cid (2.5 liters). Compression ratio: 9.2:1 Brake hp: 125 at 5400 rpm.

(STANDARD WRANGLER SPORT & SAHARA SIX): Inline. Overhead valve. Cast-iron block. Bore & stroke 3.88 x 3.41 in. Displacement: 242 cid (4.0 liter). Compression ratio: 9.2:1. Brake hp: 181 at 4600 rpm. Multi-port fuel injection.

(STANDARD CHEROKEE SPORT, CLASSIC, & LIMITED SIX): Inline. Overhead-valve. Cast-iron block. Bore & stroke 3.88 x 3.41 in. Displacement: 242 cid (4.0 liter). Compression ratio: 9.2:1. Brake hp: 190 at 4600 rpm. Multi-port fuel injection.

(STANDARD GRAND CHEROKEE SIX): Inline. Overhead valve. Cast-iron block. Bore & stroke 3.88 x 3.41. Displacement: 242 cid (4.0 liter). Compression ratio: 9.2:1. Brake hp: 195 at 4600 rpm (181 hp in Wrangler). Multi-port fuel injection.

(OPTIONAL GRAND CHEROKEE V-8): V-block. Overhead valve. Cast-iron block. Bore & stroke 3.91 x 3.31 in. Displacement: 287 cid (4.7 liter). Compression ratio: 9.1:1. Brake hp: 235 at 4800 rpm. Torque: 295 lbs.-ft. at 3200 rpm. Multi-port fuel injection.

The Cherokee Limited was the plushest, most expensive 2000 Cherokee XJ.

The 2000 Grand Cherokee Limited.

CHASSIS

(WRANGLER): Wheelbase: 93.4 in. Overall length: 147.4 in. Height: 69.3 in. Width: 66.7 in. Tires: P215/75R15.

(CHEROKEE): Wheelbase: 101 in. Overall length: 165.3 in. Width: 70.5 in. Height: 63.4 in. (4x2), 63.3 in. (4x4).

(GRAND CHEROKEE): Wheelbase: 105.9 in. Overall length: 181.5 in. Width: 72.3 in. Height: 69.4 in.

TECHNICAL

(WRANGLER): Five-speed manual transmission. Semi-floating rear axle. Standard overall drive ratio: 4.11:1.

Power front disc/rear drum brakes. Command-Trac shift-on-the-fly part-time four-wheel drive.

(CHEROKEE): UniFrame construction. Five-speed manual transmission. Semi-floating rear axle. Power front disc/rear drum brakes. 4x4 models include Command-Trac shift-on-the-fly part-time four-wheel drive, except Limited, which has Selec-Trac full-time four-wheel drive.

(GRAND CHEROKEE): UniFrame construction. Quadra-Coil four-wheel coil suspension. Four-speed automatic transmission with overdrive. Floor-mounted gearshift. Brakes: four-wheel disc with ABS.

The 2000 Grand Cherokee Laredo offered an optional Mopar Navigation System.

As before, the top of the line in the 2000 Jeep Wrangler series was the Wrangler Sahara. This year, 16 x 7-in. Ultra Star cast-aluminum wheels were standard on Sahara.

OPTIONS

(WRANGLER): Three-speed automatic transmission. Air conditioning. Tilt steering wheel. Cruise control. AM/FM stereo cassette. Four-wheel ABS (Sport & Sahara). Hardtop.

(CHEROKEE): Four-speed automatic transmission. AM/FM stereo. AM/FM cassette/CD. Cruise control. Tilt steering wheel. Air conditioning. Rear window defroster. Roof rack. Aluminum wheels.

(GRAND CHEROKEE): Quadra-Trac. Power sunroof. 4.7-liter V-8. Multi-speed automatic transmission.

Wrangler Sport was the mid-range of the three-model Wrangler line for 2000.

The 2001 Cherokee Classic.

There were questions, as the new model year opened, as to whether or not Jeep was losing its edge. The U.S. operations of DaimlerChrysler (DCX) were suffering financial troubles that were dragging down the whole corporation.

As if in response to concerns about Jeep's future product plans, the company unveiled at that year's Detroit auto show an edgy new concept vehicle called the Jeep Willys. Jeep Willys combined traditional Jeep styling cues with new features such as molded plastic body panels and 22-in. wheels with gray-colored tires. Under the hood sat a 1.6-liter four-cylinder engine. The company didn't announce any plans to build it as a production vehicle. However, there was a new Jeep coming to replace the veteran Jeep Cherokee. The eagerly awaited vehicle would debut later in calendar year 2001 as a 2002 model.

In the meantime, the 2001 Jeep Cherokee, the last of its breed, debuted. There were changes in the model lineup. The SE and Classic models were dropped, leaving the more popular Sport and Limited as the sole offerings. Since the SE was gone, the four-cylinder engine was no longer offered, either. Both remaining Cherokees came with the 4.0-liter six-cylinder engine. Cherokee Sport offered a five-speed transmission as standard equipment, with the four-speed automatic optional, while Limiteds came only with the automatic transmission. Eight exterior colors were available. Both two- and four-wheel drive was offered, and as before, the Sport was offered in both two- and four-door variations.

Jeep Wrangler for 2001 changed little. As before, three models were available: SE, Sport, and Sahara. As in the previous year, SE came only with the 2.5-liter four, while Sport and Sahara models came only with the 4.0-liter six. Interiors featured two new consoles. The mini-console with two cup holders was standard on SE and Sport. A full-floor console with four cup holders, lockable storage, and a storage tray was standard on Sahara, optional on the others. The full-floor console included space for an integrated subwoofer. There was a new multifunction control lever on the steering column.

Jeep Grand Cherokee, flagship of the Jeep product line again offered the Laredo and Limited models. Two new wheels debuted this year. A 17 x 7 1/2-in. five-spoke Silverblade cast-aluminum with Sparkle Silver accents was standard on Limited models, and a 17 x 7 1/2-in. seven-spoke Silverblade cast-aluminum wheel with Silver accents was standard for Laredo models with the Special Appearance group. The Limited's body-color grille now included attractive bright accents around the openings. For the fifth time Grand Cherokee was named *4Wheel & Off-Road* magazine's "4x4 of the Year."

This year the company was celebrating the 60th anniversary of the first Jeep—the 1941 Willys MB military model. Three special anniversary models were offered in a choice of either Black or Silverstone Metallic paint. The 2001 "60th Anniversary Edition" Grand Cherokee included a unique two-tone interior trim, agate instrument panel, and door trim combined with Light Taupe leather-trimmed seats. Also included were unique chrome wheels and embroidered floor mats. The 60th Anniversary Cherokee included Ultra Star cast-aluminum wheels and embroidered floor mats. The Wrangler 60th Anniversary model got full metal doors, body-color wheel flares and rocker sills, Canyon 30-inch Tire and Wheel group, Fog Lamp and Tow Hook group, air conditioning, AM/FM stereo radio with CD player, five speakers and subwoofer, and embroidered floor mats. Grand Cherokee and Wrangler anniversary models came only in four-wheel-drive versions, while the Cherokee anniversary model could be had with either two- or four-wheel drive.

On Friday, June 22, 2001, America's last Jeep Cherokee rolled off the assembly line at Toledo, Ohio. The little sport utility wagon had proven the genius of AMC's design, with an estimated 2,707,645 units built since production began in mid-1983. Its replacement would have a new name and would be built in a brand-new factory not far from the old Toledo plant.

For the year, Jeep sold 455,417 units in the U.S., which was an 8% decline from the prior year. With a new Jeep debuting for 2002, DaimlerChrysler was hoping the sales slide would end.

NOTABLE FOR 2001: This was the 60th anniversary of Jeep. Special anniversary models were offered in Wrangler, Cherokee, and Grand Cherokee series. Jeep Wrangler Sport and Sahara got a more powerful version of the stand-by 4.0-liter six-cylinder engine. Jeep Cherokee's model lineup was trimmed to just Sport and Limited models. For its final year, Cherokee XJ was offered only with the 4.0-liter six.

I.D. DATA: The VIN has 17 characters. The first three symbols indicate the country of origin (1=USA, 2=Canada), manufacturer (J=Jeep/Eagle Division), and type (4=multipurpose).

Model	Body style	Price	Weight
Wrangler TJ — 4x4			
TJ	Wrangler SE	—	3,105 lbs.
TJ	Wrangler Sport	—	3,316 lbs.
TJ	Wrangler Sahara	—	3,316 lbs.
Cherokee Sport — Six-cyl — 4x2			
T27	2d Station Wagon	—	3,150 lbs.
T28	4d Station Wagon	—	3,190 lbs.
Cherokee Sport — Six-cyl — 4x4			
J27	2d Station Wagon	—	3,297 lbs.
J28	4d Station Wagon	—	3,355 lbs.
Cherokee Limited — Six-cyl — 4x2			
T28	4d Station Wagon	—	3,355 lbs.
Cherokee Limited — Six-cyl- 4x4			
J28	4d Station Wagon	—	3,355 lbs.
Grand Cherokee — Six-cyl — 4x2			
X58	4d Wagon Laredo	—	3,784 lbs.
X58	4d Wagon Limited	—	3,784 lbs.
Grand Cherokee — Six-cyl — 4x4			
Z58	4d Wagon Laredo	—	3,968 lbs.
X58	4d Wagon Limited	—	3,968 lbs.

For 2001, the Grand Cherokee was named *4Wheel & Off-Road* magazine's "4x4 of the Year."

The 2001 version of the Wrangler Sport.

ENGINES

(STANDARD WRANGLER SE FOUR): Overhead valve. Inline. Displacement: 2.5 liter (150 cid). Bore x stroke: 3.88 x 3.19 in. Sequential multi-point electronic fuel injection. Cast-iron block and head. Compression ratio 9.1:1 Brake hp: 120 @ 5400 rpm. Torque 140 lbs.-ft. @ 3500 rpm. .

(STANDARD CHEROKEE SPORT & LIMITED, WRANGLER SPORT & SAHARA SIX): Overhead valve. Inline. Displacement 4.0 liter (242 cid). Bore & stroke 3.88 x 3.41 in. Sequential multi-point fuel injection. Cast-iron block and head. Compression ratio 8.8:1. Brake hp: 190. Torque 235 lbs.-ft. @ 3200 rpm

(STANDARD GRAND CHEROKEE SIX): Inline. Overhead valve. Cast-iron block. Bore & stroke 3.88 x 3.41. Displacement: 4.0 liter (242 cid). Compression ratio: 9.2:1. Brake hp: 195 @ 4600 rpm. Sequential multi-point fuel injection.

(OPTIONAL GRAND CHEROKEE V-8): Overhead cam. 16-valve. Displacement: 4.8 liters (287 cid). Bore & stroke: 3.66 x 3.40 in. Sequential multi-point electronic fuel injection. Compression ratio 9.3:1. Brake hp: 235 @ 4800 rpm. Torque 295 lbs.-ft. @ 3200 rpm.

CHASSIS

(WRANGLER): Wheelbase: 93.4 in. Overall length: 147.4 in. Height: 69.3 in. Width: 66.7 in. Tires: P215/75R15.

(CHEROKEE): Wheelbase: 101 in. Overall length: 165.3 in. Width: 70.5 in. Height: 63.4 in. (4x2), 63.3 in. (4x4).

(GRAND CHEROKEE): Wheelbase: 105.9 in. Overall length: 181.5 in. Width: 72.3 in. Height: 69.4 in.

TECHNICAL

(WRANGLER): Five speed manual transmission. Semi-floating rear axle. Standard drive ratio: 4.11:1 Power front disc/rear drum brakes. Command-Trac shift-on-the-fly part-time four-wheel drive.

(CHEROKEE): UniFrame construction. Five-speed manual transmission. Semi-floating rear axle. Power front disc/rear drum brakes.

(GRAND CHEROKEE): UniFrame construction. Quadra-Coil four-wheel coil suspension. Four-speed automatic transmission with overdrive. Floor-mounted gearshift. Four-wheel disc brakes with ABS.

OPTIONS

(WRANGLER): Three-speed automatic transmission. Air conditioning. Tilt steering wheel. Four-wheel ABS (Sport and Sahara). Hardtop. Full console with lockable storage, dual cup holders, coin holder and storage tray. Dual Top group (hard and soft top in matching colors. Heavy-Duty Electrical group (117-amp alternator, 600-amp battery, fog lamp) and Tow Hook group (front fog lamps, two front tow hooks and one rear tow hook). Tire and Wheel group (30 x 9.5R15 Goodyear Wrangler GS-All-Terrain tires, high-pressure gas-charged monotube

The perennial off-road champ, Jeep Wrangler Sahara for 2001.

shock absorbers, 15 x 8-in. Canyon aluminum wheels [3.73 axle ratio only; includes conventional spare tire and matching wheel]). Tire and Wheel group (full face 225/75R15 Goodyear Wrangler GS-A outline white letter All-Terrain tires, full-size spare tire with matching wheel).

(CHEROKEE): AM/FM cassette/CD. Cruise control. Tilt steering wheel. Air conditioning. Roof rack. Trac-Lok rear differential. Deep tint glass.

(GRAND CHEROKEE): AM/FM/CD. Fog lamps. Power sunroof. Trailer Tow packages. Up-Country suspension. Matching full-size spare wheel and tire protection group. Cargo net. Front and rear floor mats. Retractable cargo compartment cover. Skid Plate group (front suspension, transfer case, and fuel tank skid plates). Smoker's group.

On 2001 Grand Cherokee Limited models, 17 x 7 1/2-in. five-spoke Silverblade cast-aluminum wheels with Sparkle Silver accents were standard equipment.

The 2002 Wrangler Sport.

This was a busy year for Jeep. The biggest news was the all-new Jeep Liberty, which replaced the trusty old XJ Cherokee.

At introduction time, Liberty was offered in two models, Sport and Limited. Both were built in Jeep's new 2 million-sq.-ft. Toledo North Assembly Plant (TNAP). Best practices learned from DCX's worldwide manufacturing operations resulted in the most dimensionally accurate Jeep vehicle ever produced.

Jeep Liberty was similar in size to the old Cherokee, but was new in just about every detail. The wheelbase was 104.3 in. and overall length was 174.4 in. The body, of course, was completely new—a four-door sport utility wagon with fairly conventional styling, save for a very unique front-end appearance. There, Jeep's traditional seven-slot grille was flanked by two round headlights, giving Liberty a look that set it apart from other small SUVs. Front-end styling was derived from the Jeepster concept of a few years earlier, while the roofline and side appearance were taken from the Jeep Icon concept vehicle.

The chassis was an advanced UniFrame structure that was the stiffest in Jeep history. Command-Trac part-time four-wheel drive was standard, with Selec-Trac full-time four-wheel drive optional. Two new engines debuted. Standard on Sport models was a 2.4-liter Power Tech inline four that produced 150 hp @ 5200 rpms. Standard on Limited and optional on Sport was a new 3.7-liter Power Tech V-6 engine that delivered 210 hp—more power from less displacement than the legendary 4.0 inline six. Jeep's multi-speed automatic transmission was standard on Limited models, optional on Sport, which came with a five-speed manual as standard equipment.

Liberty featured independent front suspension, the first four-wheel-drive Jeep to do so since Wagoneer offered it in the 1960s. Liberty's suspension included beefy control arms, deflected-disc shock absorbers, and concentric coil springs. The result was an outstanding off-roader that offered a full 8 in. of suspension travel, while at the same time providing an incredibly smooth on-road ride. Rack-and-pinion steering, a first for Jeep, supplied excellent steering feel and response. Front and rear stabilizer bars, mounted high so they wouldn't get hung up off road, helped contribute to Liberty's superb handling. A solid axle coil spring rear suspension was also included.

Jeep Liberty bristled with innovations. Instead of a conventional rear liftgate, Liberty came with a sideways-opening swing gate and a flip-up rear window. A 65/35 split-folding rear seat with adjustable head restraints was standard. Dual air bags were also standard, and side air bags were a new option.

Later in the model year a Liberty Renegade debuted, with standard V-6 engine, unique body-color wheel flares with bright fasteners, standard roof-mounted light bar, plus special badging.

Jeep Wrangler came in for some exciting changes this year. A new model was added to the lineup called the Wrangler X. It was slotted just above the base SE and included all the SE standard features, plus the 4.0-liter six, 3.07 axle ratio, Nomad cloth seats, P215/75 Goodyear Wrangler all-terrain tires and 15 x 7-in. full-face styled steel wheels. In addition, X models could be ordered with some options not offered on the SE, such as ABS, deep-tinted windows, and rear Trac-Lok differential. Wrangler X also offered a Wheel Plus group, which included AM/FM stereo radio with CD player, seven speakers, and the Ecco Wheel and Tire group. A new limited edition Wrangler also appeared this year. Called the Apex, it included Bright Silver Metallic paint,

a unique strobe decal on the hood, high-bolstered earth-tone Cognac Ultrahide seats, chromed full-face steel wheels with matching rear-mounted spare, seven-speaker AM/FM stereo with CD player, and a full-center console—all for an MSRP of $20,385.

Jeep Grand Cherokee for 2002 offered an additional engine choice. The high-output 4.7-liter V-8 produced 265 hp, which was 30 more than the carryover 4.7-liter. The H.O. 4.7's 325 lbs.-ft. torque rating was likewise 30 more than the standard 4.7-liter. The 4.0-liter Power-Tech six rated at 195 hp also returned, so Grand Cherokee buyers now had a choice of three engines. Grand Cherokee also offered three new models. The new top-of-the-line Grand Cherokee Overland featured standard equipment that included the high-output 4.7-liter V-8, rain-sensitive automatic windshield wipers, real Redwood Burl accents on the interior and steering wheel, and heated leather seats. A remote, 10-disc CD changer, side air bags, and power sunroof with sunshade were also included. The ever-popular Grand Cherokee Laredo and Limited models returned. Both featured the 4.0-liter as standard equipment, and the 235-hp 4.7-liter V-8. Limiteds offered the high-output 4.7 V-8 as well.

Two new "value" models were also offered. The first to arrive was called the Grand Cherokee Laredo Sport. It featured the 4.0-liter six, four-speed automatic transmission, Selec-Trac four-wheel-drive (two-wheeldrive was also available), remote keyless entry, 16-

For 2002, there was a new top-of-the-line model for Grand Cherokee, the Overland, which featured a 4.7-liter V-8 engine as standard equipment.

inch Timberline cast-aluminum wheels, heated power outside mirrors, fog lamps, leather-trimmed interior and steering wheel, six-way power seats, AM/FM/cassette/CD radio with steering wheel-mounted controls, lighted visor vanity mirrors, and a mini-overhead console with HomeLink Universal transceiver—all for an MSRP of $27,995! Next up was the 2002 Grand Cherokee Special Edition, which came with body-color front and rear fascias and cladding, a 10-disc CD changer, Infinity speakers, fog lamps, six-way power seats, 4.0-liter six, Selec-Trac four-wheel drive, and special badging, all for an MSRP of $30,790.

A new power adjustable pedal system that allowed drivers to adjust brake and accelerator pedals was available on all Grand Cherokees. A very sophisticated tire monitoring system used radio frequency technology to monitor air pressure in all tires, sounding a chime if pressure in any tire fell below parameters. The system would even report which tire needed service!

It was a great year for Jeep.

NOTABLE FOR 2002: A new Wrangler X model offered six-cylinder performance at a lower price. A new limited

The 2002 Jeep Liberty Sport was not short on room.

The Liberty tailgate opens sideways and has a hatchback-type rear window.

A Jeep owner always knows their vehicle is capable of handling the worst.

edition Wrangler Apex was also offered. The all-new Jeep Liberty debuted, along with new four-cylinder and V-6 engines. Grand Cherokee offered a Laredo Sport special value model.

I.D. DATA: The VIN has 17 characters.

Model	Body style	Price	Weight
Wrangler TJ — 4x4			
TJ	Wrangler SE	—	3,094 lbs.
TJ	Wrangler 'X'	—	3,294 lbs.
TJ	Wrangler Sport	—	3,294 lbs.
TJ	Wrangler Sahara	—	3,294 lbs.
Liberty — 4x2			
T28	4d Wagon Sport	—	3,507 lbs.
T28	4d Wagon Limited	—	3,850 lbs.
Liberty— 4x4			
T28	4d Wagon Sport	—	3,672 lbs.
T28	4d Wagon Limited	—	4,070 lbs.
Grand Cherokee — Six-cyl — 4x2			
X58	4d Wagon Laredo	—	3,784 lbs.
X58	4d Wagon Limited	—	3,784 lbs.
Grand Cherokee — Six-cyl — 4x4			
Z58	4d Wagon Laredo	—	3,968 lbs.
X58	4d Wagon Limited	—	3,968 lbs.

ENGINES

(STANDARD WRANGLER SE FOUR): Power Tech inline. Overhead valve. Bore & stroke: 3.88 x 3.19 in. Displacement: 2.5 liter (150 cid). Sequential multi-point

Liberty Limited's interior trim is among the most luxurious of any sport utility vehicle.

The Jeep Liberty compact SUV was new for 2002.

electronic fuel injection. Cast-iron block and head. Compression ratio 9.1:1. Output: 120 hp @ 5400 rpm. Torque: 140 lbs.-ft. @ 3500 rpm.

(STANDARD LIBERTY SPORT FOUR): Power Tech inline. Overhead valve. Bore & stroke: 3.44 x 3.98 in. Displacement: 2.4 liter (148.2 cid). Sequential multi-port electronic fuel injection. Compression ratio: 9.5:1. Output: 150 hp @ 5200 rpm. Torque: 165 lbs.-ft. @ 4000 rpm.

(STANDARD WRANGLER X, SPORT AND SAHARA SIX): Power Tech inline. Liquid-cooled. Bore & stroke: 3.88 x 3.41 in. Displacement 4.0 liter (242 cid). Sequential, multi-port electronic fuel injection. Cast-iron block and head Compression ratio: 8.8:1 Output: 190 break hp @ 4600 rpm. Torque: 235 lbs.-ft. @ 3200 rpm.

(STANDARD LIBERTY LIMITED — OPTIONAL LIBERTY SPORT V-6): Power Tech. Displacement: 3.7-liter. Output: 210 hp @ 5200 rpm. Torque: 235 lbs.-ft. @ 4000 rpm. Cast-iron block. Aluminum cylinder heads.

(STANDARD GRAND CHEROKEE SIX): Power Tech inline. Liquid-cooled. Bore & stroke: 3.88 & 3.41. Displacement 4.0 liter (242 cid). Sequential, multi-port electronic fuel injection. Cast-iron block and head.

Compression ratio 8.8:1 Output: 195 brake hp @ 4600 rpm. Torque: 230 lbs.-ft. @ 3000 rpm.

(OPTIONAL GRAND CHEROKEE V-8): Overhead-cam. Bore & stroke: 3.66 x 3.40 in. Displacement: 4.7 liter (287 cid). Sequential multi-port electronic fuel injection. Cast-iron block, aluminum cylinder heads. Compression ratio: 9.0:1 Output: 235 brake hp @ 4800 rpm. Torque: 295 lbs. ft. @ 3200 rpm.

(OPTIONAL: GRAND CHEROKEE V-8): High-output. Overhead-cam. Bore & stroke: 3.66 x 3.40. Displacement 4.7 liter (287 cid). Sequential multi-port electronic fuel injection. Cast-iron block, aluminum cylinder heads. Compression ratio: 9.7:1 Output: 265 brake hp @ 5200 rpm. Torque: 325 lbs.-ft. @ 3600 rpm.

CHASSIS

(WRANGLER): Wheelbase: 93.4 in. Overall length: 147.4 in. Height: 69.3 in. Width: 66.7 in. Tires: P215/75R15.

(LIBERTY) Wheelbase 104.3 in. Track, Front 60 in. Track, Rear 59.7 in. Overall Length,including spare 174.4 in.Overall Width 71.6 in.

(GRAND CHEROKEE): Wheelbase: 105.9 in. Overall length: 181.5 in. Width: 72.3 in. Height: 69.4 in.

Liberty replaced the Cherokee XJ. It provided more room and a smoother, quieter on-road experience.

The instrument panel on the 2002 Liberty Limited series.

TECHNICAL

(WRANGLER): Five-speed manual transmission. Semi-floating rear axle. Standard overall drive ratio: 4.11:1. Brakes: front disc with rear drum, power assisted. Command-Trac shift-on-the-fly part-time four-wheel drive.

(LIBERTY): UniFrame construction. Five-speed manual transmission. Semi-floating rear axle. Brakes: front disc with rear drum, power assisted.

(GRAND CHEROKEE): UniFrame construction. Quadra-Coil four-wheel coil suspension. Four-speed automatic transmission with overdrive (five-speed automatic w/V-8). Floor-mounted gearshift. Brakes: four-wheel disc with ABS.

OPTIONS

(WRANGLER): Three-speed automatic transmission. Air conditioning. Tilt steering wheel. Four-wheel ABS (X, Sport and Sahara). Alloy wheels. Hardtop. Dual Top group (hard and soft top in matching colors). Heavy-Duty Electrical group (117-amp alternator, 600-amp battery, fog lamp). Tow Hook group (front fog lamps, two front tow hooks, and one rear tow hook). Tire and Wheel group (30 x 9.5R15 Goodyear Wrangler GS-A All-Terrain tires, high-pressure gas-charged monotube shock absorbers, 15 x 8-in. Canyon aluminum wheels — 3.73:1 axle ratio only; includes conventional spare tire and matching wheel). Tire and Wheel group (full face 225/75R15 Goodyear Wrangler GS-A outline white letter All-Terrain tires, full-size spare tire with matching wheel).

(LIBERTY): AM/FM/CD. Cruise control. Tilt steering wheel. Sunroof. Power door locks. Power windows. Power seats. Air conditioning. Luggage rack. Off-Road group.

(GRAND CHEROKEE): Power sunroof. 4.7-liter V-8. 4.7-liter high-output V-8. Quadra-Drive full-time four-wheel drive. Trailer Tow group. Up-Country suspension.

Returning for 2003 was the Wrangler X, a value model powered by the potent Jeep 4.0-liter six-cylinder engine.

Technological advances and numerous refinements marked the 2003 Jeep product line.

Returning to the Jeep Wrangler lineup were the popular SE, X, Sport and Sahara models. The SE got a new standard four-cylinder engine this year. It was the same gutsy 2.4-liter also used in the Liberty. For Wrangler, the engine was rated at 147 hp @ 5200 rpm, and 165 lbs.-ft. of torque @ 4000 rpms, which was 22.5 percent more horsepower and 17.8 percent more torque than the old 2.5-liter four. Other Wranglers came with the 4.0-liter six. All Wranglers finally got a modern four-speed automatic transmission as an option with either the four- or six-cylinder engines, and it included a lock-up torque converter, automatic overdrive, and an off-road skid plate. The old three-speed automatic was no longer offered.

Standard equipment on Wrangler X now included an AM/FM stereo radio with cassette player and four speakers. As before, ABS was optionally available. SE models now offered optional 15 x 7-in. Ecco cast-aluminum wheels. Sahara models got an electrochromic rearview mirror with map lamps, plus temperature and compass display.

A new limited-production Wrangler, the Rubicon, debuted this year. Named after the famous off-road trail used by generations of Jeep engineers as the ultimate test of a vehicle's ability, the new Wrangler Rubicon was an off-roader's delight. Standard features included advanced design electronically controlled, air-actuated Tru-Lok locking differentials front and rear, heavy-duty Roc-Trac off-road transfer case with 4:1 low gear ratio, beefy front and rear Dana axles, and 31-in.-tall Goodyear MT/R off-road tires with Durawall triple-ply puncture resistant sidewalls. Body sills were protected by diamond-plate guards and, of course, underbody skid plates were also standard equipment. Wrangler Rubicon was without a doubt the most capable off-road production Jeep ever built. Four-wheel disc brakes were standard equipment on Rubicon and optional on Sport and Sahara.

Jeep Liberty returned for its second year with the same three models as before: Sport, Renegade, and Limited. New this year was standard four-wheel power disc brakes.

Grand Cherokee also offered the same three models as before. The Overland model continued as the top of the line, with Laredo as the entry-level Grand Cherokee, and the Limited model in between. The value-package Sport model wasn't offered.

NOTABLE FOR 2003: Wrangler SE got a more powerful four-cylinder engine this year. Wrangler Rubicon was a new heavy-duty model geared to off-road enthusiasts.

I.D. DATA: The VIN has 17 characters.

Model	Body Style	Price	Weight
Wrangler TJ — 4x4			
TJ	Wrangler SE	—	3,235 lbs.
TJ	Wrangler X	—	3,418 lbs.
TJ	Wrangler Sport	—	3,418 lbs.
TJ	Wrangler Rubicon	—	N/A
Liberty — 4x2			
T28	4d Wagon Sport	—	3,507 lbs.
T28	4d Wagon Renegade	—	3,666 lbs.
T28	4d Wagon Limited	—	3,666 lbs.
Liberty — 4x4			
T28	4d Wagon Sport	—	3,692 lbs.
T28	4d Wagon Renegade	—	3,857 lbs.
T28	4d Wagon Limited	—	3,857 lbs.

Model	Body Style	Price	Weight
Grand Cherokee — Six-cyl — 4x2			
X58	4d Wagon Laredo	—	3,784 lbs.
X58	4d Wagon Limited	—	3,784 lbs.
Grand Cherokee — Six-cyl — 4x4			
Z58	4d Wagon Laredo	—	3,989 lbs.
X58	4d Wagon Limited	—	3,989 lbs.
X58	4d Wagon Overland (V-8)	—	3,989 lbs.

ENGINES

(STANDARD WRANGLER SE & LIBERTY SPORT FOUR): Power Tech inline. Overhead valve. Bore x stroke: 3.44 x 3.98 in. Displacement: 2.4 liter (148.2 cid). Sequential multi-port electronic fuel injection. Compression ratio: 9.5:1. Output: 150 hp @ 5200 rpm (147 hp in Wrangler). Torque: 165 lbs.-ft. @ 4000 rpm.

(STANDARD WRANGLER X, SPORT AND SAHARA SIX): Power Tech inline. Liquid-cooled. Bore & stroke 3.88 x 3.41 in. Displacement: 4.0 liter (242 cid). Sequential multi-port electronic fuel injection. Cast-iron block and head. Compression ratio: 8.8:1 Output: 190 hp @ 4600 rpm. Torque: 235 lbs.-ft. @ 3200 rpm.

(STANDARD LIBERTY RENEGADE & LIMITED — OPTIONAL LIBERTY SPORT V-6): Power Tech. Displacement: 3.7 liter. Output: 210 hp @ 5200 rpm. Torque: 235 lbs.-ft. @ 4000 rpm. Cast-iron block, aluminum cylinder heads.

Wrangler Sport for 2003 continued to be extremely popular.

The Jeep Grand Cherokee Laredo offers a combination of style, power, and value that makes it one of the most capable four-wheel-drive vehicles in the world.

(STANDARD GRAND CHEROKEE SIX): Power Tech inline. Liquid-cooled. Bore & stroke 3.88 x 3.41 in. Displacement 4.0 liter (242 cid). Sequential, multi-port electronic fuel injection. Cast-iron block and head. Compression ratio 8.8:1. Output: 195 hp @ 4600 rpm. Torque: 230 lbs.-ft. @ 3000 rpm.

(OPTIONAL GRAND CHEROKEE V-8): Overhead cam. Bore & stroke: 3.66 x 3.40. Displacement: 4.7 liter (287 cid). Sequential multi-port electronic fuel injection. Cast-iron block, aluminum cylinder heads. Compression ratio: 9.0:1. Output: 235 brake hp @ 4800 rpm. Torque: 295 lbs.-ft. @ 3200 rpm.

The Wrangler line for 2003 was the broadest it had been in years, with base SE, X, Sport, Sahara, and the newest addition, the Wrangler Rubicon.

239

Powered by a standard 4.7-liter V-8, the 2003 Grand Cherokee Overland marked the very top of the Jeep line.

(STANDARD OVERLAND — OPTIONAL GRAND CHEROKEE V-8): Overhead cam. Bore & stroke 3.66 x 3.40. Displacement: 4.7 liter (287 cid). Sequential multi-port electronic fuel injection. Cast-iron block, aluminum cylinder heads. Compression ratio: 9.7:1. Output: 265 brake hp @ 5200 rpm. Torque: 325 lbs.ft. @ 3600 rpm.

CHASSIS

(WRANGLER): Wheelbase: 93.4 in. Overall length: 147.4 in. Height: 69.3 in. Width: 66.7 in. Tires: P215/75R15.

(LIBERTY): Wheelbase 104.3 in. Overall length (including spare): 174.4 in. Width: 71.6 in.

(GRAND CHEROKEE): Wheelbase: 105.9 in. Overall length: 181.5 in. Width: 72.3 in. Height: 69.4 in.

The historic Jeep Renegade name returned as a sporty 2003 model in the Liberty range of vehicles.

Jeep Liberty Sport for 2003 can be identified by its black wheel flares.

TECHNICAL

(WRANGLER): Five-speed manual transmission. Semi-floating rear axle. Standard axle ratio: 4.11:1. Brakes: power front disc/rear drum (four-wheel discs standard on Rubicon). Command-Trac shift-on-the-fly part-time four-wheel drive.

(LIBERTY): UniFrame construction. Five-speed manual transmission. Semi-floating rear axle. Brakes: front disc with rear drum, power assisted.

(GRAND CHEROKEE): UniFrame construction. Quadra-Coil four-wheel coil suspension. Four-speed automatic transmission with overdrive (five-speed automatic with V-8). Floor-mounted gearshift. Brakes: four-wheel disc with ABS.

OPTIONS

(WRANGLER): Four-speed automatic transmission. Air conditioning. Tilt steering wheel. Four-wheel ABS (X, Sport, and Sahara).

(LIBERTY): AM/FM/CD. Cruise control. Tilt steering wheel. Sunroof. Power door locks, power windows, power seats. Air conditioning. Luggage rack. Off-road group.

(GRAND CHEROKEE): Power sunroof. 4.7-liter V-8. 4.7-liter high-output V-8. Quadra-Drive full-time four-wheel drive. Trailer Tow group. Up-Country suspension (standard on Overland).

CONCEPT VEHICLES:
THE MOST SPECIAL JEEPS

Every Jeep, in a very real sense, is special, because it is a dual symbol. It is an emblem of American ingenuity and expertise, and it is its owner's personal statement.

But there are some Jeeps that are even more unique. These would include the limited production models of the 1960s and 1970s, and notable performance models like the Grand Cherokee 5.9 Limited. However, the most special Jeeps are the concept vehicles, the ones that people used to call "dream cars" or "cars of the future." Not only are the following concept vehicles some amazing pieces of machinery, they also help enthusiasts follow the history of the Jeep by providing us with a high-tech timeline of innovation.

Looking almost car-like is this station wagon concept.

The concept was for a sportier two-door Jeep wagon to compete with Bronco and Blazer.

In 1959, Jeep stylists created this specially trimmed concept called the Jeep Harlequin.

Designer Brooks Stevens proposed this futuristic-looking pickup.

The Jeep Sportif was a sporty version of the Jeep Dispatcher which could have been produced fairly easily but, unfortunately, it remained only a prototype.

The last concept developed under Kaiser Jeep stylists was the awesome XJ001, a proposed V-8-powered two-seat off-road sports car.

Jeep Cowboy was a proposed compact pickup truck that combined passenger car styling with utility. Unlike Chevy El Camino and Ford Ranchero, the Cowboy had a separate pickup bed.

The 1971 Jeep Cowboy concept was based on the AMC Hornet.

The 1977 Concept Jeep II was AMC's idea for a smaller, more fuel-efficient Jeep.

Topping Off The Jeep Mystique

How do you enhance the mystique of a Jeep Cherokee? By building the *convertible* Jeep Cherokee Freedom. This newest concept in four-wheel-drive truck ruggedness provides an unobstructed view of nature's sights—without losing sight of Jeep's reputation for rugged reliability. Make tracks for the great outdoors with the power of Jeep's 177 hp Power-Tech Six 4.0-litre engine, linked to the smoothness of a four-speed overdrive automatic transmission.

The Jeep Cherokee Freedom convertible was made for the fresh air enthusiast who wants to become part of the outdoors, to enjoy nature's sights and sounds up close. This is the truck that will take you to nature's heart—and get you back out. But it's not as

Take To The Wind

rough as it sounds, because this concept Cherokee offers such amenities as an ultrasoft interior that includes plush carpeting. And if Mother Nature

turns off the sunshine, modern technology is prepared—with a power-actuated soft top that slips smoothly into place to protect you from sudden showers. That's *Freedom.*

A sport bar and deck lid add touches of distinction to Freedom's

handsome appearance. There's plenty of room in the cargo compartment and space for even more gear when the rear seatback is folded down. The new Jeep Cherokee Freedom convertible is one more reason to believe that...
THERE'S ONLY ONE JEEP. ...

The 1990 Cherokee Freedom was a look at what a Cherokee convertible would be like. The prototype toured the auto show circuit for several years.

Beginning in 1989, Jeep and Renault worked together on a new small Jeep dubbed the JJ (for Junior Jeep), which they expected to offer in several countries around the world.

One of the last concepts to debut under American Motors leadership was the 1987 Thunderchief, a tricked-out version of the Jeep Comanche pickup. Styling cues included a bold grille design, larger wheel flares, side rocker panels with recessed step plates, and a unique roll bar/light bar.

Bigger

For nearly five decades Jeep has been at the forefront of four-wheel-drive technology and innovation. So it should come as no surprise that planning and development of rugged 4x4 Jeep vehicles to meet the needs of the '90s and beyond has been underway for some time.

The Jeep Concept I is an example of this advanced thinking. Built on a Cherokee underbody, the Jeep Concept I is longer and higher to provide increased interior room. The result is more comfort and more cargo room. The Jeep Concept I also features a longer wheelbase and a wider stance to help provide sure-footed movement over rocks and other rough terrain.

Bolder

The Jeep Concept I retains Cherokee's go-anywhere image while taking on a bold new modernistic appearance. A flush, clean front-end design gives this rugged sport utility the powerful, aggressive look that a vehicle of its capabilities deserves. A steeper raked windshield and flush side glass also contribute to the bold look of the Jeep Concept I while helping to eliminate wind noise. With just one look you realize that this is one tough performer.

Better

Innovations such as unique 17" cast aluminum wheels that carry custom-designed P295/55R17 Goodyear all-terrain tires mean the Jeep Concept I just has to be better. And it is. Designed to pick its way nimbly over obstacles and through mud, sand, or snow, the lower body of the Jeep Concept I is shielded from flying debris by a band of protective cladding that encircles the entire vehicle. Like so many of Jeep's other advanced engineering and design features, this cladding leaves the Jeep Concept I free to be itself—a rugged, versatile 4x4 of the future, destined to take on the challenges of tomorrow.

The 1989 Jeep Concept I was the forerunner of the Grand Cherokee. Note the flush door glass, without visible B pillars.

For 1992, Jeep came up with the small, car-like ECCO. The rear soft top provided
extra headroom for backseat passengers.

This unusual-looking
vehicle is a concept
called the Wagoneer
2000. It was unveiled
in 1993.

The 1997 Jeep Icon appeared
to be the design for a future
Wrangler or CJ-type Jeep.

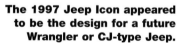

Also arriving in 1997 was the Jeep Dakar, a view of what a four-door Wrangler might look like.

Dakar generated a lot of publicity and many speculated it would become a production vehicle. Although that didn't happen, Dakar's roofline influenced the roof of the 2002 Jeep Liberty.

An artist's rendering of what the new Wrangler for 1997 would look like. The production model stayed true to this picture, which was drawn by a Jeep stylist.

The Jeepster name was resurrected on the 1998 Jeepster concept.

The Jeepster concept was a powerful two-passenger sports car, very similar to the earlier Jeep XJ-001 of 1970.

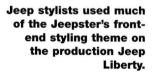

Jeep stylists used much of the Jeepster's front-end styling theme on the production Jeep Liberty.

A new concept for 1999 was this Jeep Commander.

Styling themes from the Jeep Commander may appear in future Jeep wagons.

Somewhat less exciting was the 1999 Jeep Journey, a concept vehicle not too far removed
from production. Jeep Journey had a unique mesh grille and headlight covers,
a custom brush guard, and a special roof top carrier.

Unveiled at the 2000 Detroit Auto Show, the Jeep Varsity looked both rugged and car-like,
yet was not a traditional wagon-style SUV. The Varsity was meant to appeal
to a new segment of the four-wheel-drive market.

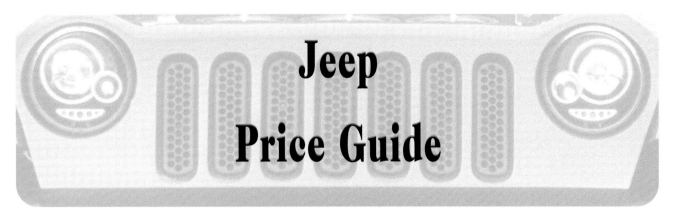

Jeep Price Guide

Vehicle Condition Scale

1: **Excellent:** Restored to current maximum professional standards of quality in every area, or perfect original with components operating and apearing as new. A 95-plus point show car that is not driven.

2: **Fine:** Well-restored or a combination of superior restoration and excellent original parts. Also, extremely well-maintained original vehicle showing minimal wear.

3. **Very Good:** Complete operable original or older restoration. Also, a very good amateur restoration, all presentable and serviceable inside and out. Plus, a combination of well-done restoration and good operable components or a partially restored car with all parts necessary to complete and/or valuable NOS parts.

4: **Good:** A driveable vehicle needing no or only minor work to be functional. Also, a deteriorated restoration or a very poor amateur restoration. All components may need restoration to be "excellent," but the car is mostly useable "as is."

5. **Restorable:** Needs complete restoration of body, chassis, and interior. May or may not be running, but isn't weathered, wrecked or stripped to the point of being useful only for parts.

6. **Parts car:** May or may not be running, but is weathered, wrecked, and/or stripped to the point of being useful primarily for parts.

WILLYS OVERLAND JEEP/TRUCKS (1945-1962)

	6	5	4	3	2	1
1945 Jeep Series, 4x4						
CJ-2 Jeep	800	2,350	3,950	7,900	13,800	19,700

NOTE: All Jeep prices in this catalog are for civilian models unless noted otherwise. Military Jeeps may sell for higher prices.

	6	5	4	3	2	1
1946 Jeep						
CJ-2 Jeep	800	2,350	3,950	7,900	13,800	19,700
Station Wagon	600	1,800	3,000	6,000	10,500	15,000
1947 Willys						
CJ-2 Jeep	800	2,350	3,950	7,900	13,800	19,700
Station Wagon	600	1,800	3,000	6,000	10,500	15,000
1947 Willys Jeep, 4x2						
Panel	700	2,150	3,550	7,100	12,500	17,800
1947 Willys Truck, 4x4						
PU	700	2,100	3,500	7,000	12,300	17,500
1948 Jeep Series, 4x4						
CJ-2 Jeep	750	2,250	3,750	7,500	13,100	18,700
1948 Willys Jeep, 4x2						
Jeepster (4-cyl)	700	2,150	3,600	7,200	12,600	18,000
Jeepster (6-cyl)	750	2,200	3,700	7,400	13,000	18,500
1948 Willys Jeep, 4x2						
PU	700	2,150	3,450	6,900	12,100	17,300
Panel	700	2,150	3,550	7,100	12,500	17,800
1949 Willys Jeepster						
Jeepster (4-cyl)	700	2,150	3,600	7,200	12,600	18,000
Jeepster (6-cyl)	750	2,200	3,700	7,400	13,000	18,500
1948 Willys Truck, 4x4						
PU	700	2,100	3,500	7,000	12,300	17,500
1949 Jeep Series, 4x4						
CJ-2 Jeep	750	2,250	3,750	7,500	13,100	18,700
CJ-3 Jeep	750	2,200	3,700	7,400	13,000	18,500

	6	5	4	3	2	1
1949 Willys Truck, 4x2						
PU	700	2,100	3,450	6,900	12,100	17,300
Panel	700	2,150	3,550	7,100	12,500	17,800
1949 Willys Truck, 4x4						
PU	700	2,100	3,500	7,000	12,300	17,500
1950 Jeep Series, 4x4						
CJ-3 Jeep	750	2,250	3,750	7,500	13,100	18,700
1950 Willys Truck, 4x2						
PU	700	2,100	3,500	7,000	12,300	17,500
Panel	700	2,150	3,550	7,100	12,500	17,800
1950 Jeep Truck, 4x4						
PU	700	2,100	3,500	7,000	12,300	17,500
Utl Wag	700	2,150	3,550	7,100	12,500	17,800
1950-51 Jeepster						
Jeepster (4-cyl)	700	2,150	3,600	7,200	12,600	18,000

Note: Add 10 percent for 6-cyl. models.

	6	5	4	3	2	1
1951 Jeep Series, 4x4						
Farm Jeep	750	2,200	3,650	7,300	12,800	18,300
CJ-3 Jeep	750	2,250	3,750	7,500	13,100	18,700
1951 Jeep Trucks, 4x2						
PU	700	2,100	3,450	6,900	12,100	17,300
Sed Dly	700	2,150	3,600	7,150	12,500	17,900
1951 Jeep Trucks, 4x4						
PU	700	2,100	3,500	7,000	12,300	17,500
Utl Wag	700	2,150	3,550	7,100	12,500	17,800
1952 Jeep Series, 4x4						
CJ-3 Open	750	2,250	3,750	7,500	13,100	18,700
1952 Jeep Trucks, 4x2						
Sed Dly	700	2,150	3,600	7,150	12,500	17,900
1952 Jeep Trucks, 4x4						
PU	700	2,100	3,500	7,050	12,300	17,600
Utl Wag	700	2,150	3,600	7,150	12,500	17,900

	6	5	4	3	2	1
1953 Jeep Series, 4x4						
CJ-3B Jeep	750	2,250	3,750	7,500	13,200	18,800
CJ-3B Farm Jeep	750	2,250	3,750	7,500	13,100	18,700
CJ-3A Jeep	750	2,250	3,750	7,500	13,100	18,700
1953 Jeep Trucks, 4x2						
Sed Dly	700	2,150	3,600	7,150	12,500	17,900
1953 Jeep Trucks, 4x4						
Sed Dly	700	2,100	3,450	6,900	12,100	17,300
PU	700	2,100	3,550	7,100	12,400	17,700
Utl Wag	700	2,050	3,400	6,800	11,900	17,000
1954 Jeep Series, 4x4						
Open Jeep	750	2,250	3,750	7,500	13,200	18,800
Farm Jeep	750	2,250	3,750	7,500	13,100	18,700
1954 Jeep Trucks, 4x2						
Sed Dly	700	2,150	3,600	7,150	12,500	17,900
1954 Jeep Trucks, 4x4						
PU	750	2,200	3,700	7,350	12,900	18,400
Sed Dly	750	2,200	3,700	7,350	12,900	18,400
Utl Wag	750	2,250	3,750	7,500	13,100	18,700
1955 Jeep Series, 4x4						
CJ-3B	750	2,250	3,750	7,500	13,100	18,700
CJ-5	750	2,250	3,750	7,500	13,100	18,700
1955 Jeep Trucks, 4x2						
Sed Dly	700	2,050	3,450	6,900	12,000	17,200
Utl Wag	700	2,100	3,500	7,000	12,300	17,500
1955 Jeep Trucks, 4x4						
Sed Dly	700	2,100	3,500	7,000	12,300	17,500
Utl Wag	700	2,150	3,550	7,100	12,500	17,800
1956 Jeep Series, 4x4						
CJ-3B	750	2,250	3,750	7,500	13,100	18,700
CJ-5	750	2,250	3,750	7,500	13,100	18,700
CJ-6	750	2,250	3,700	7,450	13,000	18,600
1956 Dispatcher Series, 4x2						
Open Jeep	700	2,100	3,450	6,900	12,100	17,300
Canvas Top	700	2,100	3,500	7,000	12,300	17,500
HT	700	2,100	3,550	7,100	12,400	17,700
1956 Jeep Trucks, 4x2						
Utl Wag	700	2,100	3,500	7,000	12,300	17,500
Sed Dly	700	2,050	3,450	6,900	12,000	17,200
1956 Jeep Trucks, 4x4						
Sed Dly	700	2,100	3,500	7,050	12,300	17,600
Sta Wag	700	2,150	3,550	7,100	12,500	17,800
PU	700	2,050	3,400	6,800	11,900	17,000
1957 Jeep Series, 4x4						
CJ-3B	750	2,250	3,750	7,500	13,100	18,700
CJ-5	750	2,250	3,750	7,500	13,100	18,700
CJ-6	750	2,250	3,700	7,450	13,000	18,600
1957 Dispatcher Series, 4x2						
Open Jeep	700	2,100	3,450	6,900	12,100	17,300
Soft Top	700	2,100	3,500	7,000	12,300	17,500
HT	700	2,100	3,550	7,100	12,400	17,700
1957 Jeep Trucks, 4x2						
Dly	700	2,050	3,450	6,900	12,000	17,200
Utl Wag	700	2,100	3,500	7,000	12,300	17,500
1957 Jeep Trucks, 4x4						
Dly	700	2,100	3,500	7,050	12,300	17,600
PU	700	2,050	3,400	6,800	11,900	17,000
Utl Wag	700	2,150	3,550	7,100	12,500	17,800
1957 Forward Control, 4x4						
1/2-Ton PU	650	2,000	3,300	6,600	11,600	16,500
3/4-Ton PU	700	2,050	3,400	6,800	11,900	17,000
1958 Jeep Series, 4x4						
CJ-3B	750	2,250	3,750	7,500	13,100	18,700
CJ-5	750	2,250	3,750	7,500	13,200	18,800
CJ-6	750	2,250	3,700	7,450	13,000	18,600
1958 Dispatcher Series, 4x2						
Open Jeep	700	2,100	3,450	6,900	12,100	17,300
Soft Top	700	2,100	3,500	7,000	12,300	17,500
HT	700	2,100	3,550	7,100	12,400	17,700
1958 Jeep Trucks, 4x2						
Dly	650	1,950	3,250	6,500	11,300	16,200
Utl Wag	650	1,950	3,250	6,500	11,400	16,300

	6	5	4	3	2	1
1958 Jeep Trucks, 4x4						
Dly	650	2,000	3,300	6,650	11,600	16,600
Utl Wag	650	2,000	3,350	6,700	11,700	16,700
NOTE: Add 3 percent for 6-cyl. trucks not available in Jeeps.						
1958 Forward Control, 4x4						
1/2-Ton PU	650	2,000	3,300	6,600	11,600	16,500
3/4-Ton PU	700	2,050	3,400	6,800	11,900	17,000
1959 Jeep Series, 4x4						
CJ-3	750	2,250	3,750	7,500	13,100	18,700
CJ-5	750	2,250	3,750	7,500	13,200	18,800
CJ-6	750	2,250	3,700	7,450	13,000	18,600
1959 Dispatcher Series, 4x2						
Soft Top	700	2,100	3,500	6,950	12,200	17,400
HT	700	2,150	3,550	7,100	12,500	17,800
Surrey	750	2,200	3,650	7,300	12,700	18,200
1959 Jeep Trucks, 4x2						
Utl Wag	650	1,950	3,300	6,550	11,500	16,400
Dly	650	1,950	3,250	6,500	11,400	16,300
1959 Jeep Trucks, 4x4						
Utl Dly	650	2,000	3,350	6,700	11,700	16,700
PU	650	1,900	3,200	6,400	11,200	16,000
Utl Wag	700	2,050	3,400	6,750	11,800	16,900
NOTE: Add 3 percent for 6-cyl. trucks not available for Jeeps. Add 5 percent for Maverick.						
1959 Forward Control, 4x4						
1/2-Ton PU	700	2,050	3,450	6,900	12,000	17,200
3/4-Ton PU	700	2,050	3,400	6,850	12,000	17,100
1960 Jeep Series, 4x4						
CJ-3	750	2,250	3,750	7,500	13,100	18,700
CJ-5	750	2,250	3,750	7,500	13,200	18,800
CJ-6	750	2,250	3,700	7,450	13,000	18,600
1960 Dispatcher Series, 4x2						
Soft Top	700	2,100	3,500	6,950	12,200	17,400
HT	700	2,150	3,550	7,100	12,500	17,800
Surrey	750	2,200	3,650	7,300	12,700	18,200
1960 Jeep Trucks, 4x2						
Economy Dly	650	1,900	3,150	6,300	11,000	15,700
Sta Wag	650	2,000	3,350	6,700	11,700	16,700
Utl Wag	650	1,950	3,300	6,550	11,500	16,400
Utl Dly	650	1,950	3,250	6,500	11,300	16,200
1960 Jeep Trucks, 4x4						
Utl Wag	650	2,000	3,350	6,700	11,700	16,700
Utl Dly	650	2,000	3,300	6,600	11,600	16,500
1960 Forward Control, 4x4						
1/2-Ton PU	650	1,950	3,300	6,550	11,500	16,400
3/4-Ton PU	650	2,000	3,300	6,650	11,600	16,600
NOTE: Add 3 percent for 6-cyl. trucks. Add 5 percent for custom two-tone trim.						
1961 Jeep Series, 4x4						
CJ-3	750	2,250	3,750	7,500	13,100	18,700
CJ-5	750	2,250	3,750	7,500	13,200	18,800
CJ-6	750	2,250	3,700	7,450	13,000	18,600
1961 Dispatcher Series, 4x2						
Jeep (Open)	700	2,100	3,500	7,000	12,300	17,500
Soft Top	700	2,100	3,500	7,050	12,300	17,600
HT	700	2,150	3,550	7,100	12,500	17,800
Surrey	750	2,200	3,650	7,300	12,700	18,200
1961 Jeep Trucks, 4x2						
Fleetvan	650	1,900	3,150	6,300	11,100	15,800
Economy Dly	650	1,900	3,150	6,300	11,000	15,700
Sta Wag	650	2,000	3,300	6,600	11,500	16,500
Utl Wag	650	1,950	3,250	6,500	11,300	16,200
Utl Dly	650	1,950	3,200	6,450	11,300	16,100
1961 Jeep Trucks, 4x4						
Utl Wag	650	2,000	3,300	6,600	11,600	16,500
Utl Dly	650	1,900	3,200	6,400	11,200	16,000
1-Ton PU	650	1,900	3,150	6,300	11,100	15,800
NOTE: Add 3 percent for 6-cyl. trucks.						
1961 Forward Control, 4x4						
1/2-Ton PU	650	1,900	3,200	6,400	11,200	16,000
3/4-Ton PU	650	1,950	3,250	6,500	11,300	16,200
1962 Jeep Series, 4x4						
CJ-3	750	2,250	3,750	7,500	13,100	18,700
CJ-5	750	2,250	3,750	7,500	13,200	18,800
CJ-6	750	2,250	3,700	7,450	13,000	18,600

	6	5	4	3	2	1
1962 Dispatcher Series, 4x2						
Basic Jeep	650	2,000	3,300	6,600	11,600	16,500
Jeep w/Soft Top	650	2,000	3,300	6,650	11,600	16,600
Jeep w/HT	650	2,000	3,350	6,700	11,700	16,700
Surrey	650	2,000	3,350	6,700	11,800	16,800
1962 Jeep Trucks, 4x2						
Fleetvan	600	1,800	2,950	5,900	10,400	14,800
Economy Dly	600	1,750	2,950	5,900	10,300	14,700
Sta Wag	600	1,850	3,100	6,200	10,900	15,500
Utl Wag	600	1,800	3,050	6,100	10,600	15,200
Utl Dly	600	1,800	3,000	6,050	10,600	15,100
1962 Jeep Trucks, 4x4						
Utl Wag	600	1,850	3,100	6,200	10,900	15,500
Utl Dly	600	1,800	3,000	6,000	10,500	15,000
1962 Forward Control, 4x4						
1/2-Ton PU	650	1,900	3,200	6,400	11,200	16,000
3/4-Ton PU	600	1,800	3,050	6,100	10,600	15,200
NOTE: Add 3 percent for 6-cyl. trucks.						

KAISER JEEP

1963 Jeep Universal, 4x4

	6	5	4	3	2	1
CJ-3B Jeep	700	2,050	3,400	6,800	11,900	17,000
CJ-5 Jeep	700	2,150	3,600	7,200	12,600	18,000
CJ-6 Jeep	700	2,100	3,500	7,000	12,300	17,500

1963 Dispatcher, 4x2

Jeep	600	1,750	2,900	5,850	10,200	14,600
HT	600	1,750	2,950	5,900	10,300	14,700
Soft Top	600	1,800	2,950	5,900	10,400	14,800

1963 "Jeep" Wagons and Trucks, 1/2-Ton

Sta Wag	550	1,700	2,800	5,600	9,800	14,000
Traveler	550	1,700	2,850	5,700	9,950	14,200
Utl (4x2)	450	1,400	2,300	4,600	8,050	11,500
Utl (4x4)	550	1,700	2,800	5,600	9,800	14,000
Panel (4x2)	450	1,350	2,250	4,500	7,850	11,200
Panel (4x4)	450	1,400	2,350	4,700	8,250	11,800

1963 "Jeep" Wagons and Truck, 1-Ton

PU (4WD)	450	1,300	2,150	4,300	7,550	10,800
NOTE: Add 3 percent for L-head 6-cyl. Add 4 percent for OHC 6-cyl.						

1963 Forward-Control, 4x4, 1/2-Ton

PU	450	1,350	2,250	4,500	7,850	11,200

1963 Forward-Control, 4x4, 3/4-Ton

PU	450	1,350	2,200	4,450	7,750	11,100

1963 Forward-Control, 1-Ton

PU	450	1,350	2,200	4,450	7,750	11,100
Stake	450	1,400	2,350	4,700	8,250	11,800
HD PU	450	1,350	2,250	4,500	7,850	11,200

1963 Wagoneer, 1/2-Ton

2d Wag	500	1,450	2,400	4,750	8,350	11,900
4d Wag	550	1,700	2,800	5,600	9,800	14,000
2d Cus Wag	550	1,700	2,800	5,600	9,800	14,000
4d Cus Wag	550	1,700	2,800	5,650	9,850	14,100

1963 Gladiator, 1/2-Ton, 120" wb

Thriftside PU	450	1,400	2,300	4,600	8,050	11,500
Townside PU	450	1,400	2,350	4,700	8,200	11,700
Panel Dly (108 wb)	350	1,100	1,850	3,700	6,500	9,300

1963 Gladiator, 1/2-Ton, 126" wb

Thriftside PU	450	1,350	2,250	4,500	7,900	11,300
Townside PU	450	1,400	2,300	4,600	8,050	11,500

1963 Gladiator, 3/4-Ton, 120" wb

Thriftside PU	450	1,350	2,200	4,450	7,750	11,100
Townside PU	450	1,350	2,250	4,500	7,900	11,300

1963 Gladiator, 1-Ton, 126" wb

NOTE: Add 5 percent for 4x4.

1964 Jeep Universal, 4x4

CJ-3B Jeep	650	1,900	3,200	6,400	11,200	16,000
CJ-5 Jeep	700	2,050	3,400	6,800	11,900	17,000
CJ-5A Tuxedo Park	700	2,100	3,500	7,000	12,300	17,500
CJ-6 Jeep	700	2,050	3,450	6,900	12,000	17,200
CJ-6A Jeep Park	700	2,100	3,500	6,950	12,200	17,400

1964 Dispatcher, 4x2

HT	600	1,750	2,950	5,900	10,300	14,700
Soft Top	600	1,800	2,950	5,900	10,400	14,800
Surrey	600	1,800	3,000	6,000	10,500	15,000

	6	5	4	3	2	1
1964 "Jeep" Wagons and Trucks, 1/2-Ton						
Sta Wag	450	1,400	2,300	4,600	8,050	11,500
Utl (4x2)	450	1,350	2,250	4,500	7,900	11,300
Utl (4x4)	450	1,400	2,350	4,700	8,250	11,800
Traveler (4x2)	450	1,400	2,350	4,700	8,200	11,700
Traveler (4x4)	550	1,700	2,850	5,700	9,950	14,200
Panel (4x2)	450	1,350	2,200	4,450	7,750	11,100
Panel (4x4)	450	1,400	2,300	4,650	8,100	11,600
1964 "Jeep" Wagons and Trucks, 1-Ton, 4x4						
PU	450	1,350	2,250	4,500	7,900	11,300
NOTE: Add 3 percent for L-head 6-cyl. Add 4 percent for OHC 6-cyl.						
1964 Forward-Control, 1/2-Ton, 4x4						
PU	450	1,300	2,150	4,300	7,500	10,700
1964 Forward-Control, 3/4-Ton, 4x4						
Stake	400	1,250	2,100	4,150	7,300	10,400
PU	400	1,250	2,100	4,250	7,400	10,600
HD PU	450	1,300	2,150	4,300	7,500	10,700
1964 Wagoneer, 1/2-Ton						
2d Wag	500	1,450	2,400	4,750	8,350	11,900
4d Wag	550	1,700	2,800	5,600	9,800	14,000
2d Cus Wag	550	1,700	2,800	5,600	9,800	14,000
4d Cus Wag	550	1,700	2,800	5,650	9,850	14,100
1964 Gladiator Pickup Truck, 1/2-Ton, 120" wb						
Thriftside PU	450	1,300	2,200	4,400	7,700	11,000
Townside PU	450	1,350	2,250	4,500	7,850	11,200
Panel Dly (108 wb)	450	1,350	2,250	4,500	7,900	11,300
1964 Gladiator Pickup Truck, 1/2-Ton, 126" wb						
Thriftside PU	450	1,300	2,150	4,300	7,550	10,800
Townside PU	450	1,300	2,200	4,400	7,700	11,000
1964 Gladiator Pickup Truck, 3/4-Ton, 120" wb						
Thriftside PU	400	1,250	2,100	4,250	7,400	10,600
Townside PU	450	1,300	2,150	4,300	7,550	10,800
1964 Gladiator Pickup Truck, 3/4-Ton, 126" wb						
Thriftside PU	400	1,250	2,100	4,200	7,350	10,500
Townside PU	450	1,300	2,150	4,300	7,500	10,700
1965 Jeep Universal, 4x4						
CJ-3B Jeep	650	1,900	3,200	6,400	11,200	16,000
CJ-5 Jeep	650	2,000	3,300	6,600	11,600	16,500
CJ-5A Tuxedo Park	700	2,050	3,400	6,800	11,900	17,000
CJ-6 Jeep	650	2,000	3,300	6,650	11,600	16,600
CJ-6A Tuxedo Park	650	2,000	3,350	6,700	11,800	16,800
1965 Dispatcher, 4x2						
DJ-5	450	1,400	2,300	4,600	8,050	11,500
DJ-6	450	1,400	2,300	4,650	8,100	11,600
1965 "Jeep" Wagons and Trucks, 1/2-Ton						
Sta Wag	450	1,400	2,300	4,600	8,050	11,500
Utl Wag (4x4)	450	1,400	2,350	4,700	8,250	11,800
Traveler (4x4)	550	1,700	2,850	5,700	9,950	14,200
Panel (4x2)	450	1,350	2,200	4,450	7,750	11,100
Panel (4x4)	450	1,400	2,300	4,650	8,100	11,600
1965 "Jeep" Wagons and Trucks, 1-Ton, 4x4						
PU	450	1,350	2,250	4,500	7,900	11,300
NOTE: Add 3 percent for L-Head 6-cyl. engine.						
1965 Forward-Control, 4x4, 1/2-Ton						
PU	400	1,250	2,100	4,200	7,350	10,500
1965 Forward-Control, 4x4, 3/4-Ton						
PU	450	1,300	2,150	4,300	7,500	10,700
1965 Wagoneer, 1/2-Ton						
2d Wag	500	1,450	2,400	4,750	8,350	11,900
4d Wag	550	1,700	2,800	5,600	9,800	14,000
2d Cus Wag	550	1,700	2,800	5,600	9,800	14,000
4d Cus Wag	550	1,700	2,800	5,650	9,850	14,100
1965 Gladiator Pickup Truck, 1/2-Ton, 120" wb						
Thriftside PU	450	1,300	2,200	4,400	7,700	11,000
Townside PU	450	1,350	2,250	4,500	7,850	11,200
Panel Dly (108 wb)	450	1,350	2,250	4,500	7,900	11,300
1965 Gladiator Pickup Truck, 1/2-Ton, 126" wb						
Thriftside PU	450	1,300	2,150	4,300	7,550	10,800
Townside PU	450	1,300	2,200	4,400	7,700	11,000
1965 Gladiator Pickup Truck, 3/4-Ton, 120" wb						
Thriftside PU	400	1,250	2,100	4,250	7,400	10,600
Townside PU	450	1,300	2,150	4,300	7,550	10,800

	6	5	4	3	2	1

1965 Gladiator Pickup Truck, 3/4-Ton, 126" wb
	6	5	4	3	2	1
Thriftside PU	400	1,250	2,100	4,200	7,350	10,500
Townside PU	450	1,300	2,150	4,300	7,500	10,700

1965 Gladiator Pickup Truck, 3/4-Ton, 120" wb
NOTE: Add 5 percent for 4x4. Add 5 percent for V-8. For "First Series" 1965 Gladiators, refer to 1964 prices.

1966 Jeep Universal, 4x4
	6	5	4	3	2	1
CJ-5 Jeep	650	2,000	3,300	6,600	11,600	16,500
CJ-5A Tuxedo Park	700	2,050	3,400	6,800	11,900	17,000
CJ-6 Jeep	650	2,000	3,300	6,650	11,600	16,600
CJ-6A Tuxedo Park	650	2,000	3,350	6,700	11,800	16,800

1966 Dispatcher, 4x2
	6	5	4	3	2	1
DJ-5	450	1,400	2,300	4,600	8,050	11,500
DJ-6	450	1,400	2,300	4,650	8,100	11,600

1966 Forward-Control, 4x4, 1/2-Ton
	6	5	4	3	2	1
PU	400	1,250	2,100	4,200	7,350	10,500

1966 Forward-Control, 4x4, 3/4-Ton
	6	5	4	3	2	1
PU	450	1,300	2,150	4,300	7,500	10,700

1966 Wagoneer, 1/2-Ton
	6	5	4	3	2	1
2d Wag	450	1,350	2,300	4,550	8,000	11,400
4d Wag	450	1,400	2,300	4,600	8,050	11,500
2d Cus Sta Wag	450	1,400	2,300	4,600	8,050	11,500
4d Cus Sta Wag	450	1,400	2,300	4,650	8,100	11,600
4d Super Wag	550	1,700	2,850	5,700	10,000	14,300

1966 Gladiator, 1/2-Ton, 120" wb
	6	5	4	3	2	1
Thriftside PU	450	1,350	2,250	4,500	7,850	11,200
Townside PU	450	1,400	2,300	4,600	8,050	11,500
Panel Dly (108 wb)	450	1,300	2,150	4,300	7,550	10,800

1966 Gladiator, 1/2-Ton, 126" wb
	6	5	4	3	2	1
Thriftside PU	450	1,300	2,150	4,300	7,550	10,800
Townside PU	450	1,300	2,200	4,400	7,700	11,000

1966 Gladiator, 3/4-Ton, 120" wb
	6	5	4	3	2	1
Thriftside PU	400	1,250	2,100	4,250	7,400	10,600
Townside PU	450	1,300	2,150	4,300	7,550	10,800

1966 Gladiator, 3/4-Ton, 126" wb
	6	5	4	3	2	1
Thriftside PU	400	1,250	2,100	4,200	7,350	10,500
Townside PU	450	1,300	2,150	4,300	7,500	10,700

NOTE: Add 5 percent for 4x4. Add 5 percent for V-8.

1967 Jeep Universal, 4x4
	6	5	4	3	2	1
CJ-5 Jeep	650	1,900	3,200	6,400	11,200	16,000
CJ-5A Jeep	650	2,000	3,300	6,600	11,600	16,500
CJ-6 Jeep	700	2,050	3,400	6,800	11,900	17,000
CJ-6A Jeep	700	2,100	3,500	7,000	12,300	17,500

1967 Dispatcher, 4x2
	6	5	4	3	2	1
DJ-5	450	1,400	2,300	4,600	8,050	11,500
DJ-6	450	1,400	2,350	4,700	8,200	11,700

1967 Jeepster Commando, 4x4
	6	5	4	3	2	1
Sta Wag	500	1,450	2,400	4,750	8,350	11,900
Roadster	650	1,900	3,200	6,400	11,200	16,000
PU	450	1,400	2,300	4,600	8,050	11,500

1967
	6	5	4	3	2	1
Conv	700	2,050	3,400	6,800	11,900	17,000

1967 Wagoneer
	6	5	4	3	2	1
2d Wag	450	1,350	2,300	4,550	8,000	11,400
4d Wag	450	1,400	2,300	4,600	8,050	11,500
2d Cus Sta Wag	450	1,400	2,300	4,600	8,050	11,500
4d Cus Sta Wag	450	1,400	2,300	4,650	8,100	11,600
4d Sup Wag	450	1,400	2,350	4,700	8,250	11,800

1967 Gladiator, 4x4, 1/2-Ton, 120" wb
	6	5	4	3	2	1
Thriftside PU	450	1,350	2,200	4,450	7,750	11,100
Townside PU	450	1,350	2,250	4,500	7,850	11,200
Panel Dly (108 wb)	450	1,300	2,150	4,300	7,550	10,800

1967 Gladiator, 3/4-Ton, 120" wb
	6	5	4	3	2	1
Thriftside PU	400	1,250	2,100	4,250	7,400	10,600
Townside PU	450	1,300	2,150	4,300	7,500	10,700

1967 Gladiator, 1/2-Ton, 126" wb
	6	5	4	3	2	1
Thriftside PU	450	1,300	2,150	4,300	7,550	10,800
Townside PU	450	1,300	2,200	4,350	7,650	10,900

1967 Gladiator, 3/4-Ton, 126" wb
	6	5	4	3	2	1
Thriftside PU	400	1,250	2,100	4,250	7,400	10,600
Townside PU	450	1,300	2,150	4,300	7,500	10,700

NOTE: Add 5 percent for V-8 (except Super V-8). Add 5 percent for 4x2 (Series 2500 only). Add 20 percent for V-6 engine. Add 5 percent for 4x4.

1968 Jeep Universal, 4x4
	6	5	4	3	2	1
CJ-5 Jeep	650	1,900	3,200	6,400	11,200	16,000
CJ-5A Jeep	650	2,000	3,300	6,600	11,600	16,500
CJ-6 Jeep	700	2,050	3,400	6,800	11,900	17,000
CJ-6A Jeep	700	2,100	3,500	7,000	12,300	17,500

1968 Dispatcher, 4x2
	6	5	4	3	2	1
DJ-5	450	1,350	2,250	4,500	7,850	11,200
DJ-6	450	1,350	2,250	4,500	7,900	11,300

NOTE: Add 20 percent for V-6 engine. Add 5 percent for diesel engine.

1968 Wagoneer, V-8, 4x4
	6	5	4	3	2	1
4d Sta Wag	450	1,400	2,350	4,700	8,200	11,700
4d Sta Wag Cus	450	1,400	2,350	4,700	8,250	11,800
4d Sta Wag Sup	500	1,450	2,400	4,750	8,350	11,900

1968 Commando, 4x4
	6	5	4	3	2	1
Conv	700	2,050	3,400	6,800	11,900	17,000
Sta Wag	500	1,450	2,400	4,750	8,350	11,900
Cpe-Rds	650	1,900	3,200	6,400	11,200	16,000
PU	450	1,400	2,300	4,600	8,050	11,500

NOTE: Add 4 percent for V-6 engine.

1968 Jeepster 4x4
	6	5	4	3	2	1
Conv	700	2,050	3,400	6,800	11,900	17,000

1969 Jeep
	6	5	4	3	2	1
CJ-5 Jeep	650	1,900	3,200	6,400	11,200	16,000
CJ-6 Jeep	650	2,000	3,300	6,600	11,600	16,500
DJ-5	450	1,400	2,300	4,600	8,050	11,500

1969 Commando, 4x4
	6	5	4	3	2	1
Conv	700	2,050	3,400	6,800	11,900	17,000
Sta Wag	450	1,300	2,200	4,350	7,650	10,900
Cpe-Rds	650	1,900	3,200	6,400	11,200	16,000
PU	400	1,250	2,100	4,200	7,350	10,500

1968 Jeepster 4x4
	6	5	4	3	2	1
Conv	700	2,050	3,400	6,800	11,900	17,000

1969 Wagoneer
	6	5	4	3	2	1
4d Wag	450	1,300	2,150	4,300	7,550	10,800
4d Cus Wag	450	1,300	2,200	4,350	7,650	10,900

1969 Gladiator, 1/2-Ton, 120" wb
	6	5	4	3	2	1
Thriftside PU	400	1,250	2,100	4,200	7,350	10,500
Townside PU	400	1,250	2,100	4,250	7,400	10,600

1969 Gladiator, 3/4-Ton, 120" wb
	6	5	4	3	2	1
Thriftside PU	350	1,050	1,800	3,550	6,250	8,900
Townside PU	400	1,200	2,000	4,000	7,000	10,000

1969 Gladiator, 1/2-Ton, 126" wb
	6	5	4	3	2	1
Townside	350	1,050	1,800	3,550	6,250	8,900

1969 Gladiator, 3/4-Ton, 126" wb
	6	5	4	3	2	1
Townside	350	1,050	1,750	3,500	6,100	8,700

NOTE: Add 4 percent for V-6 engine. Add 5 percent for V-8 engine. Add 10 percent for factory Camper Package.

AMC JEEP

1970-1973 Commando, 101" wb
	6	5	4	3	2	1
Sta Wag	300	950	1,600	3,150	5,550	7,900
Rds	400	1,150	1,950	3,900	6,800	9,700
Conv Commando	600	1,800	3,000	6,000	10,500	15,000

1970-1976 CJ-5, 1/4-Ton
	6	5	4	3	2	1
Jeep	600	1,800	3,000	6,000	10,500	15,000

1970-1976 CJ-6 1/2-Ton
	6	5	4	3	2	1
Jeep	600	1,750	2,900	5,800	10,200	14,500

1974-1976 CJ-7, 94" wb
	6	5	4	3	2	1
Jeep	600	1,750	2,900	5,800	10,200	14,500

1970-1973 DJ-5, 1/4-Ton, 81" wb
	6	5	4	3	2	1
Jeep	300	950	1,600	3,200	5,600	8,000

1970-1976 Wagoneer, V-8
	6	5	4	3	2	1
4d Cus Sta Wag	350	1,000	1,650	3,300	5,750	8,200

NOTE: Deduct 10 percent for 6-cyl.

1970-1976 J Series (2500)
	6	5	4	3	2	1
Thriftside PU	300	850	1,400	2,750	4,850	6,900
Townside PU	300	850	1,400	2,800	4,900	7,000

1970-1976 J Series (2600)
	6	5	4	3	2	1
Thriftside PU	250	800	1,350	2,700	4,700	6,700
Townside PU	250	800	1,350	2,700	4,750	6,800

	6	5	4	3	2	1
1970-1976 J Series 3/4-Ton						
Thriftside PU	250	750	1,250	2,500	4,350	6,200
Townside PU	250	750	1,250	2,500	4,400	6,300
1970-1976 J Series (3500) 1/2-Ton						
Townside PU	250	750	1,250	2,500	4,400	6,300
1970-1976 J Series (3600) 1/2-Ton						
Townside PU	250	750	1,250	2,500	4,350	6,200
1970-1976 J Series (3700) 3/4-Ton						
Townside PU	250	750	1,200	2,450	4,250	6,100
1977-1980 Wagoneer, V-8						
4d Sta Wag	300	950	1,600	3,250	5,650	8,100
1974-1980 Cherokee, 6-cyl.						
2d Sta Wag	300	950	1,550	3,100	5,450	7,800
2d "S" Sta Wag	300	950	1,600	3,150	5,550	7,900
4d Sta Wag	300	950	1,550	3,100	5,450	7,800
1977-1980 CJ-5, 1/4-Ton, 84" wb						
Jeep	550	1,700	2,850	5,700	9,950	14,200
1977-1980 CJ-7, 1/4-Ton, 94" wb						
Jeep	550	1,700	2,800	5,600	9,800	14,000
1977-1980 Series J-10, 1/2-Ton, 119" or 131" wb						
Townside PU, SWB	250	800	1,300	2,650	4,600	6,600
Townside PU, LWB	250	800	1,300	2,600	4,550	6,500
1977-1980 Series J-20, 3/4-Ton, 131" wb						
Townside PU	250	750	1,300	2,550	4,500	6,400
1981-1983 Wagoneer, 108.7" wb						
4d Sta Wag	300	950	1,600	3,200	5,600	8,000
4d Brgm Sta Wag	350	1,000	1,650	3,300	5,750	8,200
4d Ltd Sta Wag	350	1,000	1,700	3,350	5,900	8,400
1981-1983 Cherokee						
2d Sta Wag	300	850	1,400	2,750	4,850	6,900
2d Sta Wag, Wide Wheels	300	850	1,400	2,800	4,900	7,000
4d Sta Wag	300	850	1,400	2,850	4,950	7,100
1981-1983 Scrambler, 1/2-Ton, 104" wb						
PU	200	650	1,100	2,200	3,850	5,500
1981-1983 CJ-5, 1/4-Ton, 84" wb						
Jeep	250	700	1,200	2,400	4,200	6,000
1981-1983 CJ-7, 1/4-Ton, 94" wb						
Jeep	250	750	1,250	2,500	4,350	6,200
1981-1983 Series J-10, 1/2-Ton, 119" or 131" wb						
Townside PU, SWB	250	800	1,300	2,600	4,550	6,500
Townside PU, LWB	250	750	1,300	2,550	4,500	6,400
1981-1983 Series J-20, 3/4-Ton, 131" wb						
Townside PU	250	750	1,250	2,500	4,400	6,300
1983-1985 Wagoneer, 4-cyl.						
4d Sta Wag	350	1,100	1,850	3,700	6,450	9,200
4d Ltd Sta Wag	400	1,150	1,900	3,800	6,650	9,500
1983-1985 Wagoneer, 6-cyl.						
4d Sta Wag	400	1,150	1,900	3,750	6,600	9,400
4d Ltd Sta Wag	400	1,150	1,950	3,900	6,800	9,700
1983-1985 Grand Wagoneer, V-8						
4d Sta Wag	400	1,200	1,950	3,900	6,850	9,800
1983-1985 Cherokee, 4-cyl.						
2d Sta Wag	350	1,100	1,800	3,650	6,350	9,100
4d Sta Wag	350	1,100	1,800	3,600	6,300	9,000
1983-1985 Cherokee, 6-cyl.						
2d Sta Wag	350	1,100	1,850	3,700	6,500	9,300
4d Sta Wag	350	1,100	1,850	3,700	6,450	9,200
1983-1985 Scrambler, 1/2-Ton, 103.4" wb						
PU	250	750	1,300	2,550	4,500	6,400
1983-1985 CJ-7, 1/4-Ton, 93.4" wb						
Jeep	400	1,200	1,950	3,900	6,850	9,800
1983-1985 Series J-10, 1/2-Ton, 119" or 131" wb						
Townside PU	300	850	1,450	2,900	5,050	7,200
1983-1985 Series J-20, 3/4-Ton, 131" wb						
Townside PU	300	900	1,450	2,900	5,100	7,300
1986-1987 Wagoneer						
4d Sta Wag	400	1,250	2,100	4,200	7,350	10,500

	6	5	4	3	2	1
4d Ltd Sta Wag	450	1,300	2,150	4,300	7,550	10,800
4d Grand Sta Wag	450	1,400	2,300	4,600	8,050	11,500
1986-1987 Cherokee						
2d Sta Wag 4x2	350	1,100	1,800	3,600	6,300	9,000
4d Sta Wag 4x2	400	1,150	1,900	3,800	6,650	9,500
2d Sta Wag (4x4)	400	1,150	1,900	3,800	6,650	9,500
4d Sta Wag (4x4)	400	1,200	2,000	4,000	7,000	10,000

	6	5	4	3	2	1
1986-1987 Comanche, 120" wb						
PU	350	1,000	1,700	3,350	5,900	8,400
1986 CJ-7, 1/4-Ton, 93.5" wb						
Jeep	400	1,250	2,100	4,200	7,350	10,500
1986-1987 Series J-10, 1/2-Ton, 131" wb, 4x4						
Townside PU	350	1,100	1,800	3,600	6,300	9,000
1986-1987 Series J-20, 3/4-Ton, 131" wb, 4x4						
Townside PU	400	1,150	1,900	3,800	6,650	9,500
1987 Wrangler, 1/4-Ton, 93.4" wb						
Jeep 4x2	400	1,150	1,900	3,800	6,650	9,500

CHRYSLER JEEP
1988 Jeep Wagoneer
	6	5	4	3	2	1
4d Limited Sta Wag, 6-cyl.	500	1,450	2,400	4,800	8,400	12,000
4d Grand Wagoneer, V-8	550	1,600	2,700	5,400	9,450	13,500
1988 Jeep Cherokee, 6-cyl.						
2d Sta Wag 4x2	280	840	1,400	2,800	4,900	7,000
4d Sta Wag 4x2	300	900	1,500	3,000	5,250	7,500
2d Sta Wag 4x4	350	1,100	1,800	3,600	6,300	9,000
4d Sta Wag 4x4	400	1,150	1,900	3,800	6,650	9,500
2d Limited Sta Wag, 4x4	500	1,450	2,400	4,800	8,400	12,000
4d Limited Sta Wag, 4x4	550	1,600	2,700	5,400	9,450	13,500

NOTE: Deduct 7 percent for 4-cyl. models.

1988 Wrangler, 4x4, 93.5" wb						
Jeep	548	1,644	2,740	5,480	9,590	13,700
Jeep S	400	1,200	2,000	4,000	7,000	10,000
1988 Comanche, 113" or 120" wb						
PU (SBx)	352	1,056	1,760	3,520	6,160	8,800
PU (LBx)	368	1,104	1,840	3,680	6,440	9,200
1988 J10, 131" wb						
PU	520	1,560	2,600	5,200	9,100	13,000
1988 J20, 131" wb						
PU	540	1,620	2,700	5,400	9,450	13,500
1989 Jeep Wagoneer						
4d Sta Wag, V-6	640	1,920	3,200	6,400	11,200	16,000
4d Grand Wagoneer, V-8	600	1,800	3,000	6,000	10,500	15,000
1989 Jeep Cherokee, 4-cyl.						
2d Sta Wag 4x2	400	1,200	2,000	4,000	7,000	10,000
4d Sta Wag 4x2	408	1,224	2,040	4,080	7,140	10,200
2d Sta Wag 4x4	550	1,600	2,700	5,400	9,450	13,500
4d Sta Wag 4x4	550	1,650	2,700	5,450	9,500	13,600
1989 Jeep Cherokee, 6-cyl.						
2d Sta Wag 4x2	420	1,260	2,100	4,200	7,350	10,500
4d Sta Wag 4x2	424	1,272	2,120	4,240	7,420	10,600
2d Sta Wag 4x4	550	1,650	2,750	5,500	9,650	13,800
4d Sta Wag 4x4	550	1,700	2,800	5,600	9,800	14,000
2d Limited Sta Wag, 4x4	600	1,850	3,100	6,200	10,900	15,500
4d Limited Sta Wag, 4x4	650	1,900	3,150	6,300	11,000	15,700
1989 Jeep						
2d Wrangler, 4x4	550	1,600	2,700	5,400	9,450	13,500
2d Laredo Sta Wag 4x4	600	1,750	2,900	5,800	10,200	14,500
4d Laredo Sta Wag 4x4	600	1,750	2,950	5,900	10,300	14,700
1990 Wrangler, 6-cyl., 4x4						
Wrangler	548	1,644	2,740	5,480	9,590	13,700
Wrangler S	564	1,692	2,820	5,640	9,870	14,100
1990 Comanche, 6-cyl.						
PU	428	1,284	2,140	4,280	7,490	10,700
PU (LBx)	432	1,296	2,160	4,320	7,560	10,800
1990 Wagoneer, 6-cyl., 4x4						
4d Sta Wag	660	1,980	3,300	6,600	11,550	16,500
1990 Grand Wagoneer, V-8, 4x4						
4d Sta Wag	700	2,100	3,500	7,000	12,250	17,500

255

	6	5	4	3	2	1
1990 Cherokee, 4-cyl.						
4d Sta Wag 2x4	600	1,850	3,100	6,200	10,900	15,500
2d Sta Wag 2x4	600	1,800	3,000	6,000	10,500	15,000
4d Sta Wag 4x4	700	2,050	3,400	6,800	11,900	17,000
2d Sta Wag 4x4	650	2,000	3,300	6,600	11,600	16,500
1990 Cherokee, 6-cyl.						
4d Sta Wag 2x4	700	2,050	3,400	6,800	11,900	17,000
2d Sta Wag 2x4	650	2,000	3,300	6,600	11,600	16,500
4d Sta Wag 4x4	700	2,100	3,500	7,000	12,300	17,500
2d Sta Wag 4x4	700	2,050	3,400	6,800	11,900	17,000
4d Limited Sta Wag, 4x4	750	2,200	3,700	7,400	13,000	18,500
2d Limited Sta Wag, 4x4	700	2,150	3,600	7,200	12,600	18,000
1991 Wrangler Jeep						
2d Jeep	520	1,560	2,600	5,200	9,100	13,000
2d Sahara	560	1,680	2,800	5,600	9,800	14,000
2d Renegade	580	1,740	2,900	5,800	10,150	14,500
NOTE: Deduct 5 percent for 4-cyl.						
1991 Comanche						
2d PU	340	1,020	1,700	3,400	5,950	8,500
2d PU (LBx)	352	1,056	1,760	3,520	6,160	8,800
NOTE: Deduct 5 percent for 4-cyl.						
1991 Wagoneer, V-6, 4x4						
4d Limited Sta Wag	600	1,750	2,900	5,800	10,200	14,500
1991 Grand Wagoneer, V-8, 4x4						
4d Sta Wag	640	1,920	3,200	6,400	11,200	16,000
1991 Cherokee, 4-cyl.						
2d Sta Wag 4x2	320	960	1,600	3,200	5,600	8,000
4d Sta Wag 4x2	320	960	1,600	3,200	5,600	8,000
2d Sta Wag, 4x4	400	1,200	2,000	4,000	7,000	10,000
4d Sta Wag, 4x4	400	1,200	2,000	4,000	7,000	10,000
1991 Cherokee, 6-cyl.						
2d Sta Wag, 2x4	350	1,000	1,700	3,400	5,950	8,500
4d Sta Wag, 4x4	350	1,000	1,700	3,400	5,950	8,500
1991 Cherokee, 4x4						
2d Sta Wag	420	1,260	2,100	4,200	7,350	10,500
4d Sta Wag	420	1,260	2,100	4,200	7,350	10,500
4d Limited Sta Wag	600	1,800	3,000	6,000	10,500	15,000
4d Briarwood Sta Wag	600	1,850	3,100	6,200	10,900	15,500
1992 Wrangler, 4-cyl.						
Jeep S	520	1,560	2,600	5,200	9,100	13,000
Jeep	540	1,620	2,700	5,400	9,450	13,500
Jeep, 6-cyl.	600	1,800	3,000	6,000	10,500	15,000
1992 Cherokee, 4-cyl.						
2d SUV	260	780	1,300	2,600	4,550	6,500
4d SUV	280	840	1,400	2,800	4,900	7,000
2d SUV 4x4	350	1,000	1,700	3,400	5,950	8,500
4d SUV 4x4	350	1,100	1,800	3,600	6,300	9,000
NOTE: Add 10 percent for 6-cyl. Add 5 percent for Deluxe models.						
1992 Comanche, 6-cyl.						
2d PU (SBx)	360	1,080	1,800	3,600	6,300	9,000
2d PU (LBx)	380	1,140	1,900	3,800	6,650	9,500
NOTE: Add 5 percent for 4x4.						

	6	5	4	3	2	1
1993 Wrangler, 6-cyl.						
Jeep	540	1,620	2,700	5,400	9,450	13,500
1993 Cherokee, 6-cyl.						
2d SUV 4x2	272	816	1,360	2,720	4,760	6,800
4d SUV 4x2	276	828	1,380	2,760	4,830	6,900
2d SUV 4x4	350	1,050	1,750	3,500	6,150	8,800
4d SUV 4x4	350	1,050	1,800	3,550	6,250	8,900
1993 Grand Cherokee, V-8						
4d Sta Wag 4x4	600	1,800	3,000	6,000	10,500	15,000
4d Sta Wag 4x2 6-cyl.	550	1,600	2,700	5,400	9,450	13,500
1994 Wrangler 4x4						
2d Jeep S	400	1,200	2,000	4,000	7,000	10,000
2d Jeep Sahara	440	1,320	2,200	4,400	7,700	11,000
2d Jeep Renegade	460	1,380	2,300	4,600	8,050	11,500
1994 Cherokee, 6-cyl.						
2d Sta Wag	320	960	1,600	3,200	5,600	8,000
4d Sta Wag	332	996	1,660	3,320	5,810	8,300
2d Sta Wag 4x4	400	1,150	1,900	3,800	6,650	9,500
4d Sta Wag 4x4	400	1,200	1,950	3,900	6,850	9,800
1994 Grand Cherokee 4x4, V-8						
4d Sta Wag Laredo	560	1,680	2,800	5,600	9,800	14,000
4d Limited Sta Wag	600	1,800	3,000	6,000	10,500	15,000
1995 Wrangler 4x4						
2d Jeep S 4-cyl.	400	1,200	2,000	4,000	7,000	10,000
2d Jeep SE 6-cyl.	400	1,250	2,100	4,200	7,350	10,500
2d Jeep Sahara 6-cyl.	450	1,300	2,200	4,400	7,700	11,000
NOTE: Add 5 percent for Spt or Rio Grande trim package.						
1995 Cherokee, 4-cyl. & 6-cyl.						
2d Sta Wag	300	950	1,600	3,200	5,600	8,000
4d Sta Wag	350	1,000	1,650	3,300	5,800	8,300
2d Sta Wag 4x4	400	1,150	1,900	3,800	6,650	9,500
4d Sta Wag 4x4	400	1,200	1,950	3,900	6,850	9,800
1995 Grand Cherokee, 6-cyl. & V-8						
4d SE Sta Wag	400	1,200	2,000	4,000	7,000	10,000
4d SE Sta Wag 4x4	500	1,450	2,400	4,800	8,400	12,000
4d Laredo Sta Wag	500	1,450	2,400	4,800	8,400	12,000
4d Laredo Sta Wag 4x4	550	1,700	2,800	5,600	9,800	14,000
4d Limited Sta Wag	500	1,550	2,600	5,200	9,100	13,000
4d Limited Sta Wag 4x4	600	1,800	3,000	6,000	10,500	15,000
NOTE: Deduct 5 percent for 6-cyl.						
1996 Cherokee, 4-cyl. & 6-cyl.						
2d Sta Wag	300	950	1,600	3,200	5,600	8,000
4d Sta Wag	350	1,000	1,650	3,300	5,800	8,300
2d Sta Wag 4x4	400	1,150	1,900	3,800	6,650	9,500
4d Sta Wag 4x4	400	1,200	1,950	3,900	6,850	9,800
1996 Grand Cherokee, 6-cyl. & V-8						
4d Laredo Sta Wag	400	1,200	2,000	4,000	7,000	10,000
4d Laredo Sta Wag 4x4	500	1,450	2,400	4,800	8,400	12,000
4d Limited Sta Wag	500	1,550	2,600	5,200	9,100	13,000
4d Limited Sta Wag 4x4	600	1,800	3,000	6,000	10,500	15,000
NOTE: Deduct 5 percent for 6-cyl.						

About the Author

photo courtesy of Caitlin Foster

Pat Foster's name and reputation are familiar to Jeep enthusiasts around the world. His earlier work, *The Story of Jeep*, won the AACA's prestigious Thomas McKean Memorial Cup Award as the best book on automotive history for 1998. And his award-winning books, *American Motors, the Last Independent*, and *The Metropolitan Story*, are considered the standard texts for those brands. This newest volume, the eighth book book he has written, adds to a body of work that has made him one of America's best-known automotive book authors.

Foster has also written scores of articles for *Collectible Automobile*, *FORWARD*, *Automobile Quarterly*, *Special Interest Autos*, and others. Readers of *Old Cars Weekly* know him for his column "Foreign Favorites." He is also a member of Mensa, the society for people with high IQs.

Pat resides in Milford, Connecticut, a small city on Long Island Sound, with his wife, Diane, daughter Caitlin, and Samantha the cat.